A Sceptical Guide to Meaning and Rules

A Sceptical Guide to Meaning and Rules

Defending Kripke's Wittgenstein

Martin Kusch

McGill-Queen's University Press
Montreal & Kingston • Ithaca

© Martin Kusch, 2006

ISBN-13: 978-0-7735-3166-6   ISBN-10: 0-7735-3166-1   (hardcover)
ISBN-13: 978-0-7735-3167-3   ISBN-10: 0-7735-3167-X   (paperback)

Legal deposit third quarter 2006
Bibliothèque nationale du Québec

Published simultaneously outside North America
by Acumen Publishing Limited

McGill-Queen's University Press acknowledges the financial support of the Government
of Canada through the Book Publishing Development Program (BPIDP) for its activities.

Library and Archives Canada Cataloguing in Publication

A sceptical guide to meaning and rules : defending Kripke's Wittgenstein / Martin
Kusch.

Includes bibliographical references and index.
ISBN-13: 978-0-7735-3166-6   ISBN-10: 0-7735-3166-1 (bound)
ISBN-13: 978-0-7735-3167-3   ISBN-10: 0-7735-3167-X (pbk.)

1. Wittgenstein, Ludwig, 1889-1951. 2. Kripke, Saul A., 1940- Wittgenstein on
rules and private language. 3. Language and languages--Philosophy. 4. Meaning
(Philosophy). 5. Private language problem. I. Title.

B3376.W564K88 2006   192   C2006-902001-9

Designed and typeset by Kate Williams, Swansea.
Printed and bound by Cromwell Press, Trowbridge.

For Annabelle and Marietta

Contents

Acknowledgements

Although this is my first attempt to contribute to the discussion of Wittgenstein's philosophy, my interest in his work goes back more than twenty years, to my undergraduate days in Berlin and Finland. In 1981, Ernst Tugendhat (then at the Freie Universität Berlin) taught an introductory class on Wittgenstein's *Blue Book*; this was not only my very first philosophy class, but also a lasting and central influence. In subsequent years, I learnt much from the many Finnish Wittgenstein experts, among them Jaakko Hintikka, Heikki Kannisto, Juha Manninen, Thomas Wallgren and Georg Henrik von Wright.

Over the past fifteen years or so, much of my own work has straddled the boundary between philosophy and the sociology of knowledge. Wittgenstein's reflections on rules have been the topic of intense controversy in the latter field.[1] My own interest in "communitarian" interpretations of Wittgenstein on rule-following in general, and Kripke's version of such readings in particular, was origi-nally triggered by debates within the sociology of knowledge. I was David Bloor's colleague at the time when he wrote his important book *Wittgenstein, Rules and Institutions*, and the research reported here first started as an attempt to fill what I then perceived as one or two minor gaps in Bloor's argument. Although my project soon became more ambitious, and even though I no longer accept some of Bloor's central ideas, I continue to feel greatly indebted to his work and support.

For all the inspiration and encouragement I have received from the sociolo-gists of knowledge, this is nevertheless a philosophical book, written primarily for advanced students and teachers of philosophy. I defend Saul Kripke's controver-sial communitarian interpretation of Wittgenstein against the criticism of other philosophers, and I do so by means of philosophical arguments. The need for such philosophical treatment of the terrain was impressed on me by my under-graduate, MPhil and PhD students at the Department of History and Philosophy of Science here at the University of Cambridge. My greatest debt in this respect is to Anandi Hattiangadi, who was my PhD student between 1998 and 2001 and whose book-length criticism of Kripke's Wittgenstein will hopefully be available in print soon.

I produced a first draft of this essay at the *Wissenschaftskolleg zu Berlin* during the academic year 2001–2. A big *"Dankeschön"* is due to all the staff of this wonderful institution. Of my fellow fellows, I learnt most – at least with respect to the research reported here – from Cristina Bicchieri, Gottfried Boehm, Robert Boyd, John Breuilly, Raghavendra Gadagkar, Peter Galison, Richard Hauser, Sheila Jasanoff, Caroline Jones, Helmut Lachenmann, Keir Pearson, Edmund Wnuk-Lipinksi and Allan Young. I am particularly grateful to the *Wissenschaftskolleg* for funding a workshop on "Meaning and Normativity"; this allowed me to bring in Barbara Fultner, Hans-Johann Glock, Kathrin Glüer-Pagin, Anandi Hattiangadi, Jussi Haukioja, Matthias Kross, Alexander Miller, Peter Pagin and José Zalabardo. Their influence on this project is hard to exaggerate.

Alexander Miller deserves a separate paragraph. After the first two years of working on this project it dawned on me that I had bitten off a much bigger piece of philosophy than I might ever be able to chew and digest properly. I began to understand that, as Wittgenstein once put it, "these things are finer spun than crude hands have any inkling of".[2] I started to wonder whether I would ever be able to improve the flexibility of my "hands" to a degree that would allow me to convince at least some of the specialists. In this moment of crisis Miller's constructive input proved invaluable. Miller read the whole first draft of the manuscript and sent me a dozen pages (single-spaced, 11 point type!) of detailed comments. These comments ranged from pointers to important literature to proposals for improving my argument, from objections to specific claims to ideas for restructuring whole chapters. Receiving these comments from an established expert in the field was an enormous help. But most of all, Miller's positive assessment of the overall project gave me the courage to soldier on for another three years.

Almost equal in importance was Jim Edwards. Edwards read the penultimate version of the manuscript, a version that I had thought pretty close to being the final product. Edwards's critical but constructive comments convinced me that I still had more work to do. In particular his intervention led me to rewrite Chapter 5 almost from scratch; I shudder at the thought that without his intervention I would have published the previous version.

Back in my department in Cambridge, my greatest debt – aside from the aforementioned Anandi Hattiangadi – is to Lorenzo Bernasconi, Bill Grundy and, especially, Jeff Kochan. All three read the penultimate version of the manuscript and made numerous suggestions for linguistic and philosophical improvement. David Chart and Mark Sprevak had done the same for an earlier draft. Moreover, all five were frequent interlocutors on all matters relating to Kripke, Wittgenstein and meaning. I have also profited from discussing some ideas of the book with Peter Lipton. Many other Cambridge students, visitors and colleagues have contributed helpful comments: Alex Broadbent, Luis Campos, Anjan Chakravartty, Sungho Choi, Paul Dicken, Axel Gelfert, Sacha Golob, Jeremy Gray, Nick

Hopwood, Pedro Karczmarczyk, Jonas Larsson, Christina McLeish, Arash Pessian, Matthew Ratcliffe, Torben Rees, Simon Schaffer, Jim Secord, Benjamin Sun and, especially, Elie Zahar. I am also grateful to Tamara Hug for administrative support, and to Liba Taub for being a *Mensch*.

I have given talks drawn from the manuscript of this book in Basel, Berlin, Bielefeld, Cambridge, Hannover, Helsinki, Jyväskylä, Konstanz, London, Melbourne, Norwich and Vancouver. In addition to people already mentioned above, I wish to thank especially Tim Crane, Michael Esfeld, Paul Hoyningen-Huene, Esa Itkonen, Marja-Liisa Kakkuri-Knuuttila, Arto Laitinen, Mohan Matthen, Graham Priest, Rupert Read, Alan Richardson, Angus Ross, Barry Smith, Veli Verronen and Marcel Weber for their challenging and insightful objections and questions.

Juha Manninen – one of my former teachers – sent me many detailed and useful comments on the relationship between Kripke's Wittgenstein and "the real Wittgenstein". Paul Coates, Dagfinn Føllesdal, Eric Gampel, Jakob Hohwy, Stephen Mumford and Crispin Wright kindly answered various questions over email. Steven Gerrard at Acumen has been a very patient and always encouraging editor, and Kate Williams has been a wonderful copy-editor.

My greatest debt is, as ever, to my family. My wife Sarah has been the first hurdle for most ideas in this book. I shall always remember our long evening walks around Berlin and Potsdam, often talking (far too much!) about Kripke and Wittgenstein. Sarah's support has been crucial throughout. I dedicate this book to our baby daughters Annabelle and Marietta: although they care refreshingly little about rules, they have already developed a taste for (the corners of) Kripke's and Wittgenstein's books. Not to know what one is biting off seems to run in the family.

M. K.

Preface

This essay is an interpretation and defence of Saul Kripke's book *Wittgenstein on Rules and Private Language* (*WRPL*). To write about Kripke's Wittgenstein hardly needs a special justification; after all, over the past thirty years, more than five hundred authors have done likewise. However, the promise of an "interpretation" and a "defence" of Kripke's book is likely to raise more than just a few eyebrows: is not *Wittgenstein on Rules and Private Language* much too clear and punchy to need anything like "an interpretation"? And can one possibly defend a text that has been refuted dozens and dozens of times, both as an outline of a particular take on meaning and content, and as an interpretation of Wittgenstein? Let me address these two questions in turn.

Like many other readers I too believe that Kripke's book raises the traditional debate over meaning and content to a new and higher level of clarity and transparency. But as the debate over *Wittgenstein on Rules and Private Language* has brought to the surface, some of the apparent simplicity of Kripke's text is deceptive. For instance, it is not immediately clear whether the dialogical setting of the book is essential to the argument. Nor is it obvious who the interlocutors are: is Wittgenstein the sceptic, or is Wittgenstein the sceptic's critic? Is the proposed "sceptical solution" a form of reductivism or non-reductivism, factualism or non-factualism, scepticism or anti-scepticism? And how far does Kripke wish to push the parallels between Hume's and Wittgenstein's views? Of course, Kripke's critics have always made their choices regarding these options, but all too often they have not defended their choices in any detail. Here I hope to go further. My motivation is not just interpretational charity for its own sake; rather, I believe that my reading of the text gives Kripke's overall argument a new strength.

This brings me to my promise to *defend* Kripke's Wittgenstein. I suspect there is no other recent book in Anglophone philosophy that has attracted as much criticism and that has found so few friends. Although papers and book chapters on *Wittgenstein on Rules and Private Language* typically begin with the obligatory bow to Kripke's genius, they then equally typically go on to insist either that Kripke has made a simple mistake in his reasoning or that he has overlooked an important paragraph in Wittgenstein's *Philosophical Investigations*. I only know of one or two major steps in Kripke's overall argument that have not been challenged and rejected by at least one critic; more typically they have been attacked by at least a dozen authors. And among the critics one finds the very top of the philosophical profession, from Donald Davidson to John McDowell, from Jerry Fodor to Crispin Wright, from Paul Boghossian to Philip Pettit, from Simon Blackburn to Scott Soames, and from Paul Horwich to Christopher Peacocke, to mention just a few. Perhaps it is not surprising then that, at least in conversation, many colleagues have begun to treat Kripke's Wittgenstein in the very way in which Marx famously refused to treat Hegel: "*als toten Hund* [as a dead dog]".[1] As a historian and sociologist of philosophy, I understand: it is hard not to be impressed with, and overwhelmed by, the power of a twenty-five-year-old tradition of criticism. Even when one begins to harbour doubts about this or that particular attack on Kripke's Wittgenstein, one naturally assumes that the truly decisive refutations surely must all be there: they just "have to be" in the writings of some other critics. But are they really? As a philosopher myself, I cannot ignore that question. And having spent the past five years of my philosophical life reading, and thinking about, dozens and dozens of criticisms of *Wittgenstein on Rules and Private Language*, I have come to the conclusion that none of them are decisive. Many critiques are based on misunderstandings of Kripke's reasoning; many attacks can be blocked by refining and developing Kripke's position; and many alternative proposals turn out either to be unworkable or to be disguised variants of the view they are meant to replace. Needless to say, it is disconcerting to find oneself disagreeing with so many established and outstanding philosophers writing so near to, or even within, their area of specialization; but here I stand.

I should like to think that my essay is accessible not just to professional philosophers but also to advanced philosophy undergraduates and to academics in other, neighbouring fields, such as cognitive science, sociology or linguistics. Of course, it would make little sense to approach this book without at least some independent study of Kripke's book. The anthology of critical essays edited by Alexander Miller and Crispin Wright, *Rule-Following and Meaning*,[2] would make for a natural companion volume.

The expert reader will, of course, want some indication of the relative novelty and originality of the various chapters in this essay. Here is a brief preview for such readers. (Other readers could use the following paragraphs as a final summary after reading the book.) Chapter 1 outlines my interpretation of Kripke's Wittgenstein as a whole. Contrary to some other readers I pay close attention to the dialogical setting. In particular I seek to identify, in some detail, the "picture" of meaning and mental content that is attacked by the "sceptic". I call this picture "low-brow meaning determinism", and define it in terms of seven key assumptions. I reconstruct Chapter 2 of Kripke's book as a debate between the meaning sceptic and various "high-brow" versions of the picture. "High-brow meaning determinism" turns the initial picture into a more systematic, constructive, philosophical theory. Semantic reductive dispositionalism is one such high-brow version. I argue that the sceptic engages in an "immanent critique": he shows that all attempts to flesh out the "picture" of meaning determinism end up contradicting one or more of the picture's ingredients. But the sceptic also shows that the picture itself is incoherent. This leaves us with two main options: "reform" and "revolution". The way of reform is to improve meaning determinism by giving up one or two of its assumptions. The way of revolution is to replace the meaning-determinist picture altogether. Many critics of Kripke's Wittgenstein opt for reform. According to Kripke's interpretation, Wittgenstein himself rejects meaning determinism altogether, and replaces it with an alternative picture: "meaning scepticism". I show in some detail in what sense meaning scepticism is a "successor" to meaning determinism; each of the seven assumptions of meaning scepticism replaces one of the seven key ingredients of meaning determinism.

Chapter 2 discusses the role of normativity considerations in Kripke's argument against reductive semantic dispositionalism. I criticize Boghossian's interpretation of Kripke's alleged "normativity argument". I maintain that Boghossian's proposal not only leaves Kripke's Wittgenstein with a weak position but that it also fails to do justice to the text it purports to interpret. In rejecting Boghossian's interpretation I shield Kripke's view from the many critics (Fodor, Kathrin Glüer, Anandi Hattiangadi, Horwich, Peter Pagin) who have assumed that Boghossian's interpretation is correct. Subsequently I turn to a number of reformist recommendations (Paul Coates, Horwich, Ruth Millikan) on how to defend dispositionalism against arguments from normativity. I establish that none of these recommendations works. Finally I consider what *prima facie* seems to be a "revolutionary" alternative to Kripke's Wittgenstein. (A revolutionary alternative rejects meaning determinism without endorsing meaning scepticism.) This alternative chastises the role of normativity assumptions in both meaning determinism and meaning scepticism. I am referring, of course, to Davidson's philosophy of meaning and communication. The critical dialogue between Davidson and Kripke's Wittgenstein takes up almost half of Chapter 2. I argue that Davidson's own development has taken him ever closer to the position of Kripke's Wittgenstein, and that Davidson's criticism of *Wittgenstein on Rules and Private Language* is mistaken.

Chapter 3 homes in on the second prong of Kripke's argument against dispositionalism: the "extensional requirement". This is the demand that dispositional predicates must logically co-vary with meaning predicates. Many commentators feel that the extensional requirement can be met either within the confines of the original intuitive picture of meaning determinism or by relaxing some of the latter's demands. Of the various objections to, and elaborations of, "the second prong", I give most room to Fodor's criticism of Kripke's arguments against idealization and *ceteris paribus* laws, and to Boghossian's attempt to improve on Kripke's attack on dispositionalism. I argue that Fodor's criticism fails and that

Boghossian's proposal can be defended against Miller's intriguing objections. I also consider and reject – although somewhat more briefly – a number of specific counters to Kripke's use of the extensional requirement (Blackburn, Carl Ginet, J. Heil, Horwich, C. B. Martin, Soames).

Chapter 4 discusses other meaning-determinist proposals: the "algorithm response", the "simplicity response", "Platonism", and the "causal theory of reference". The first three were scrutinized and rejected already in Kripke's Wittgenstein, but several critics seek to improve on the versions considered there: Peacocke and Neil Tennant for the algorithm response, Wright for the simplicity response, and Jerrold J. Katz, Fred Feldman and José Zalabardo for Platonism. The Platonist answer to Kripke has been developed in a book-length study by Katz, and it demands a lengthier investigation. I suggest that none of these improvements can save meaning determinism. Finally, Maddy and McGinn have proposed enrolling Kripke's own causal theory of reference in the fight against Kripke's Wittgenstein's meaning scepticism. I am not convinced.

Chapter 5 discusses two radically different interpretations of the sceptical solution. According to the first, meaning scepticism proposes a non-factualist (projectivist or performative) reading of meaning attributions. According to the second interpretation, meaning scepticism advocates a minimal, deflationary form of factualism. I do not believe that a meaning scepticism based on a total non-factualism is tenable. Fortunately, the meaning scepticism in Kripke's Wittgenstein is not so committed. Here I side with Alex Byrne, David Davies and George Wilson. I go beyond them however by putting forward a new proposal on how to distinguish between the "inflationary factualism" of meaning determinism and the "deflationary factualism" of the sceptical solution. The central idea of my proposal is that meaning determinism and meaning scepticism put forward two radically different conceptions of terms such as "truth", "fact" and "proposition".

In Chapter 6 I investigate various issues relating to the private language argument as Kripke presents it. I point out that Kripke offers two different versions of how the argument is supposed to run: one version derives the impossibility of a private language from the social nature of assertability conditions; the other version infers the impossibility of a private language directly from the refutation of individualistic forms of meaning determinism. The second rendering is to be preferred, since convincing criticism has been levelled against the first (by Boghossian, Warren Goldfarb and Colin McGinn). I then turn to debates over whether a social isolate can follow rules. Here I respond to the many authors who have maintained – contrary to Kripke – that a Robinson Crusoe from birth could follow rules (G. P. Baker, Blackburn, Noam Chomsky, Michael Dummett, P. M. S. Hacker, McGinn, David Pears). In answering these authors I occasionally draw on previous defences of the "communitarian" view (David Bloor, Norman Malcolm, Norman Lillegard, Meredith Williams). In the final two sections I take up two further criticisms of Kripke's view of the community. Robert Brandom interprets the sceptical solution as an attempt to reduce normativity to "regularities of appraisals by the community as a whole". Brandom laments both the reduction and the "global privileging" of the community. Of course, Brandom's rendering fits neither with my interpretation nor with the actual text of *WRPL*. Baker and Hacker accuse Kripke of attributing to Wittgenstein a form of communal interpretationalism, that is, the view that the external relations between rules and their applications are established by the interpretations of the community. Against Baker and Hacker I show that the sceptical solution construes the relations between rules and applications as internal.

In Chapter 7 I engage with four authors (Boghossian, McDowell, Pettit, Wright) who have proposed different forms of semantic primitivism concerning meaning and content. All four regard their proposals as "straight" answers to the meaning-sceptical challenge posed in Kripke's Wittgenstein, and thus as defences of meaning determinism. The fact that I am turning to these authors only after my discussion of the sceptical solution already indicates my main line of response to at least three of them. I maintain that these philosophers misunderstand the nature of the sceptical solution and that their own proposals are much closer to meaning scepticism than to meaning determinism. The key to this realization lies in the distinction between two forms of semantic primitivism; one is meaning-determinist, one is meaning-sceptical.

Finally, in Chapter 8, I turn to defending Kripke's interpretation of Wittgenstein. I argue that Kripke's interpretation of the sections on rule-following in the *Philosophical Investigations* is, by and large, on target. I make my case by answering, point by point, the highly influential attack by Baker and Hacker in their book *Scepticism, Rules and Language*.[3]

As this summary shows, I take on a very large number of authors and arguments. And, as the (light) weight of this book gives away, I do so in a relatively short space. I am painfully aware of the fact that some of my responses and arguments are compressed, curt and sketchy. I do not wish to defend myself by pointing out that the same could be said of portions of Kripke's Wittgenstein or of many of the criticisms. I prefer to think that a relatively short and terse book has a greater chance of being read than a volume that is long and rambling.

Abbreviations

PI   Wittgenstein, *Philosophical Investigations* (2001).

SRL   Baker & Hacker, *Scepticism, Rules and Language* (1984).

WRPL Kripke, *Wittgenstein on Rules and Private Language* (1982).

ONE

Introduction

Introduction

This study is an interpretation and defence of Saul Kripke's essay *Wittgenstein on Rules and Private Language* (*WRPL*). Kripke's essay is, in turn, an interpretation and defence of one central theme in Ludwig Wittgenstein's principal work *Philosophical Investigations* (*PI*). Kripke insists that, in advocating Wittgenstein's views, he is not speaking for himself: "Primarily I can be read, except in a few obvious asides, as almost like an attorney presenting a major philosophical argument as it struck me" (*WRPL*: ix). Kripke is trying to make Wittgenstein's ideas as strong and convincing as possible, without however committing himself to their truth. This book is bolder – or more foolhardy: it seeks to show that the position Kripke attributes to Wittgenstein is the right one.

In this chapter I put forward my interpretation of *WRPL*. The categories I develop in the process will also be central for classifying different critical responses to Kripke's book. Not everything I develop here will be defended at length in later chapters. For instance, only in this chapter shall I comment on Kripke's suggestion concerning important resemblances between Berkeley, Hume and Wittgenstein, and only here shall I summarize and endorse Kripke's criticism of the "qualia theory" or the "use theory". I shall not deal further with the former topic since its more detailed discussion would take us too far afield. And I shall say no more on the latter, since at least this part of Kripke's book has not proved controversial. Finally, I shall confine my summary and interpretation to Chapters 2 and 3 of *WRPL*. The "Postscript: Wittgenstein and Other Minds" lies outside the focus of this study.

Ordinary talk of meaning and rules

In everyday life we occasionally say of other people and ourselves that they, or we, follow a rule, grasp a concept, or mean something by a given word or sign. Here are some examples of such talk taken from *WRPL*, several in their original formulation, others adapted so as to render them freestanding:

(a) Jones means addition by "+" (*WRPL*: 68).
(b) It is a fact that Jones means (or meant) addition by "+" (*WRPL*: 69).
(c) Jones's present use of the word "plus" does not accord with what he meant by "plus" in the past (*WRPL*: 79).
(d) Jones has grasped the concept of addition (*WRPL*: 107).
(e) Jones follows the rule for addition (*WRPL*: 69).
(f) Little Jones thinks she is following the rule for addition but she is just calling out numbers at random (*WRPL*: 88).
(g) Under the influence of LSD, Jones thinks he is following the rule for addition, when in fact he is calling out numbers at random (*WRPL*: 89).
(h) If Jones means addition by "+" then, if he remembers his past intention and wishes to conform to it, when he is asked "68 + 57 = ?", he will (or: must, ought to, should) answer "125" (*WRPL*: 89).
(i) When Jones follows the rule or formula "add 2" continuously, starting with "2, 4, 6, 8, ..." then all the subsequent steps of his counting are determined by the rule or formula. In a way, the future steps are, as it were, already present (*WRPL*: 70).

Examples (a), (b), (c) and (h) talk of Jones meaning something by a sign, (d) speaks of him possessing a concept, and (e), (f), (g) and (i) refer to him following a rule. There are obviously important differences between meanings, rules and concepts. As far as *WRPL* is concerned, however, these differences are less important than the commonalities: *WRPL* focuses on the question of what gives attributions (of meanings, rules and concepts) their significance. And it proceeds on the assumption that any solution that would emerge for one of the three cases would also solve the remaining two. I take this to be reason enough to simplify my terminology. I shall call all of (a) to (i) – and other sentences like them – "meaning sentences" (even when the attribution is of a rule or a concept). Some meaning sentences are "meaning attributions" (such as (a)) others are "meaning conditionals" (such as (h)). The cited meaning sentences concern a third person, speaking, as they do, about someone else's meaning or rule-following. This feature of (a) to (i) is not essential, however. For each given third-person meaning attribution and conditional, we can also formulate a first- or second-person equivalent; for instance, "I mean addition by '+'", or "You follow the rule for addition", or "If I mean addition by '+', then, when asked '68 + 57 = ?', I should (will, ought to) answer '125'". Not all of the meaning sentences (a) to (i) are equally natural or colloquial; for instance, meaning conditionals do not appear frequently in our everyday parlance. Nevertheless, they do surface occasionally, are easily understood, and they do not come across as overly technical or esoteric.

Common-sense philosophy: low-brow meaning determinism

WRPL is a critical study of philosophical analyses of meaning sentences. What is involved in such philosophical analyses? There is no generally agreed on answer to this question among *all* of the proposals considered in *WRPL*, except for the vague idea that a philosophical analysis should explain the significance of, make sense of or illuminate our meaning talk. But while there is no general agreement, there is at least a near consensus: *all but one* of the philosophical analyses under scrutiny in *WRPL* share the following view of what a philosophical analysis of meaning talk can and should do. A philosophical analysis of meaning talk should identify what makes meaning sentences true; it should identify the truth-conditions of meaning sentences, that is, it should identify the (types of) propositions that such sentences express. This is a highly plausible understanding of philosophical analysis of meaning talk; after all, to find the truth-conditions for different types of sentences or propositions – counterfactuals, moral claims, and so on – is an established and recognized method for clarifying the content of these sentences. The method is supported by the natural thought that "meaningful declarative sentences must purport to correspond to facts" (*WRPL*: 78–9).

Note finally that this type of analysis is usually seen as playing a *justificatory role*. Philosophical analysis is important because it is involved in separating meaningful utterances from mere gibberish. For the subject matter of meaning sentences this amounts to the notion that we are entitled to use these sentences if, and only if, we can show that they have determinate meanings. And we show that they have determinate meanings by identifying the propositions they express. This focus on propositions gives the justification an ontological or metaphysical flavour.

If this is what all but one of the proposals for philosophical analysis discussed in *WRPL* agree on, what then is the exception to the rule? This is best explained after I have given more details on the argument of *WRPL* as a whole. For present purposes it is sufficient to say this much: the exception denies that we can analyse the meaning of meaning sentences by identifying their truth-conditions; and it denies that the justification of types of sentences is a metaphysical endeavour. What gives meaning sentences their significance are not their truth-conditions, but rough and ready conditions concerning their proper use.

There is more to be said about philosophical analyses that focus on truth-conditions for explaining the significance of meaning sentences. Most of the analyses that fall into this group are based on the same intuitive picture of meanings and rules. I am not calling this picture "intuitive" because it is frequently produced

by native speakers. It takes some philosophical training to come up with this picture and to find it compelling. But its pervasiveness is not due to the influence of
a powerful authority; it is not, say, something we have all learnt from Plato, Descartes or Kant. Rather, the picture's pervasiveness is, as it were, due to its salience.
The intuitive picture seems to be the only sensible way to make sense of our meaning sentences. Indeed, it easily strikes philosophers as being without imaginable
alternative, and as forced on them by the very structure of meaning sentences
themselves. Perhaps we should say that the intuitive picture is the natural view for
the "common sense philosopher" as opposed to the "common sense man" (*WRPL*:
143). It is a view that fits with philosophical common sense, or with the view that
philosophers find natural to attribute to common sense.

Having belaboured the "intuitive" in "intuitive picture", it is worth saying more
about the concept of "picture", a term frequently used in both *PI* and *WRPL* (e.g.
WRPL: 50). "Picture" here contrasts with "theory". A picture of a phenomenon is
rough, vague, only in part explicitly formulated, metaphorical and amenable to
different ways of developing it and making it more precise. One and the same picture can therefore underlie different, indeed incompatible, theories. In the present
context, the claim is that philosophical common sense will naturally endorse and
rely on a rough picture of the kinds of facts that make meaning sentences true.

In order to facilitate putting together this rough picture, let us give it a name.
Going beyond Kripke's own text, I propose the name "low-brow meaning determinism". "Low-brow" here contrasts, of course, with "high-brow", and is meant to
remind us permanently of its picture-like status. The expression "meaning determinism" picks out one of the most central elements of the picture: the idea that
what someone means by a sign *determines* both how he *will* use it (if he wishes to
stick to his meaning), and how he *should* use it (if he wishes to speak correctly).
But much more is involved than is conveyed by the name. I shall introduce the
different ingredients of meaning determinism one by one, in each case presenting
key quotations from *WRPL* as my evidence. (This may seem pedantic at this stage,
but will prove useful in structuring the argument in the rest of the book.)

Meaning determinism – for the moment we can do without the "low-brow"
– holds that sentences of the form "person *x* means *Y* by sign '*z*'" (e.g. Jones means
addition by "+") are true if, and only if, *x* has a certain mental state. This mental
state *constitutes* *x*'s meaning *Y* by "*z*", or, put differently, this mental state is the
necessary and sufficient condition for *x*'s meaning *Y* by "*z*". Meaning determinism makes several assumptions about this mental state.

The first assumption is that *x* usually knows this mental state "immediately
and with fair certainty": "Do I not know, directly, and with a fair degree of certainty, that I mean plus?" (*WRPL*: 40); "each of us knows immediately and with
fair certainty that he means addition by 'plus'" (*WRPL*: 41; cf. 22). The knowledge
in question is introspective knowledge (*WRPL*: 51). For mnemonic purposes, I
shall give each core assumption of meaning determinism a name. The first such
assumption is "immediate knowledge".

4

The second assumption is "privacy". This is the idea that the meaning-constituting mental state is an intrinsic state of *x*: *x* could be in this state even if she had never had any contact with other human beings. Put differently, meaning and rule-following can be analysed and understood at the level of the individual:

> [A] single individual, considered by himself and in isolation, [can] … mean [… something]. (*WRPL*: 68–9)

> [We have] an intuitive feeling that no one else can affect what I mean by a given symbol. (*WRPL*: 69)

> [A] person following a given rule is to be analysed simply in terms of facts about the rule follower and the rule follower alone, without reference to his membership in a wider community. (*WRPL*: 109)

The third assumption of meaning determinism is "grasping". This introduces time and learning into the picture. We learn the meanings of words at one time, and then apply them at a later time. Grasping tells us how to think about the learning of meanings and rules. Put most simply, the thought is that to learn the meaning of a word is to grasp this meaning. Such acts of grasping are events that are potential causes of other events. If *x* has grasped the concept of addition, then – unless he decides to deviate from what he has grasped, and unless some other cause interferes – his subsequent answer to "68 + 57 = ?" is causally determined to be 125: "*if* I meant plus [i.e. if I grasped the addition function], then unless I wish to change my usage, I am … compelled to answer '125'" (*WRPL*: 11); "instructions I gave myself in the past compel (or justify) the answer '125' rather than '5'" (*WRPL*: 13). Call this "grasping as cause".

There are more aspects to grasping. Meaning determinism contains an analysis of what grasping a meaning consists in. To begin with, given privacy, we should not be surprised to be told that grasping a meaning can be a solitary act:

> [T]he grasping of a mathematical rule [is] the solitary achievement of each mathematician independent of any interaction with a wider community. (*WRPL*: 79–80)

> [O]thers may have taught me the concept of addition, but they acted only as heuristic aids to an achievement – the "grasping of the concept" of addition. (*WRPL*: 80)

> [I]n grasping a mathematical rule I have achieved something that depends only on my own inner state, and that is immune to Cartesian doubt about the entire external material world. (*WRPL*: 68)

The reason why acts of grasping can be private in this sense is that they consist of an individual's forming intentions, and thus giving herself instructions, concerning the future use of a sign ("grasping as intending"). Thus x's act of grasping Y is tantamount to x's forming intentions, or giving herself instructions, regarding a possibly infinite number of applications of "z" in the future. These intentions, and these instructions, of x are intentions to let her applications be governed by Y as a specific standard:

> This is the whole point of the notion that in learning to add I grasp a rule: my past intentions regarding addition determine a unique answer for indefinitely many new cases in the future. (*WRPL*: 7–8)

> Given my past intentions regarding the symbol "+" one and only one answer is dictated as the one appropriate to "68 + 57". (*WRPL*: 17–18)

> Granted that I mean addition by "+", then of course if I were to act in accordance with my intentions, I would respond, given any pair of numbers to be combined by "+", with their sum. (*WRPL*: 28)

> [I]nstructions I gave myself in the past compel (or justify) the answer "125" rather than "5". (*WRPL*: 13)

> [M]y actual computation procedure, following an algorithm that yields "125", [is] more justified by my past instructions than an alternative procedure that would have resulted in "5". (*WRPL*: 18)

To say that the act of grasping a meaning consists of forming intentions regarding future use captures two important elements of this act: what is being grasped (= the meaning) and what grasping results in (= having intentions regarding future use). A third element of the act of grasping concerns the "basis" of the act. According to meaning determinism this basis is inevitably *finite*: the set of examples that are used in teaching are always limited in number. We learnt to add on the basis of a finite number of instances of $m + n = p$; and we were taught the concept *cat* on the basis of a finite number of cats. Because the "learning set" is always and necessarily finite in this way, grasping a meaning or concept has the character of an *extrapolation*. Such extrapolations can of course go wrong. (A two-and-a-half-year-old child might well call all four-legged animals "dogs".) Let us call this assumption "grasping as extrapolating". In *WRPL* the phenomenon of grasping as extrapolating is mentioned in the following passage:

> when a teacher *introduces* such a word as "plus" to the learner, if he does not reduce it to more "basic", previously learned concepts, he introduces

it by a finite number of examples, plus the instructions: "Go on in the same way!" The last clause may indeed be regarded as vague, in the ordinary sense, though our grasp of the most precise concept depends on it. (*WRPL*: 82)

In other passages Kripke is more explicit about the links between finiteness of examples, grasping and rules, but in these other places he puts the whole phenomenon in a "private" perspective; that is, rather than focusing on the finite learning set *provided by a teacher*, he speaks of the rule-follower as giving *herself* a finite number of examples from which she then extrapolates:

By means of my external symbolic representation and my internal mental representation, I "grasp" the rule for addition. One point is crucial to my "grasp" of this rule. Although I myself have computed only finitely many sums in the past, the rule determines my answer for indefinitely many new sums that I have never previously considered. (*WRPL*: 7)

[I]n this new instance ["68 + 57 = ?"], I should apply the very same function or rule that I applied so many times in the past. But who is to say what function this was? In the past I gave myself only a finite number of examples instantiating this function. (*WRPL*: 8)

Closely related to grasping as extrapolating is "grasping as interpreting"; at least, it is closely related as long as we just focus on the idea that learning involves an *interpretation* of the learning set. But meaning determinism finds this idea of interpretation so compelling that it is willing to apply it not just to learning sets but to all contents of the mind. For the meaning determinist, to grasp a meaning – and thus to grasp how one is to apply a sign in a given situation – is always based on an interpretation, be it of a learning set, a set of instructions or intentions:

[N]o matter what is in my mind at a given time, I am free in the future to interpret it in different ways. (*WRPL*: 107)

[I]f "plus" is explained in terms of "counting", a non-standard interpretation of the latter will yield a non-standard interpretation of the former. (*WRPL*: 16)

How can I justify my present application of such a rule, when a sceptic could easily interpret it so as to yield any of an indefinite number of other results? (*WRPL*: 17)

Did I think explicitly of the Eiffel Tower when I first "grasped the concept of" a table, gave myself directions for what I meant by "table"?

> And even if I did think of the Tower, cannot any directions I gave myself mentioning it be reinterpreted compatibly with the sceptic's hypothesis? (*WRPL*: 19)

> [T]he sceptic argues, in essence, that I am free to give any new answer to an addition problem, since I can always interpret my previous intentions appropriately. (*WRPL*: 32)

> Can we conceive of a finite state which *could* not be interpreted in a quus-like way? (*WRPL*: 52)

Finally, meaning determinism uses the act of grasping also to explain why different speakers apply an expression in highly similar or identical ways. The reason why two persons x_1 and x_2 call the same animal "cat" is that they have grasped the same concept or meaning *cat* in the past: "grasping as explanation" – "we all respond as we do to '68 + 57' because we all grasp the concept of addition in the same way" (*WRPL*: 97).

The fourth assumption, "semantic normativity", is best understood as a covering term for five more specific ideas. First up is "non-blindness". Suppose that x has decided in the past to mean addition by the sign "+". Allow further that x gives the answer "125" in answer to "68 +57 = ?". As the meaning determinist sees it, in these circumstances x's response is not something x does "blindly", not "an unjustified leap in the dark", a "brute inclination", "an unjustified stab in the dark", an "unjustifiable impulse" or "a mere jack-in-the-box unjustified and arbitrary response" (*WRPL*: 10, 15, 17, 23). Non-blindness puts negatively what other components of semantic normativity put positively.

According to "guidance", x's meaning-constituting mental state guides and instructs x on how to apply "z"; that is, it tells x how he ought to apply "z" if he wishes to use "z" with the same meaning with which he used it before. In other words, the meaning-constituting mental state contains a standard of correct use. Here are some of the formulations of guidance in *WRPL*:

> Normally, when we consider a mathematical rule such as addition, we think of ourselves as *guided* in our application of it to each new instance. (*WRPL*: 17)

> [I]nner "ideas" or "meanings" guide our linguistic behaviour. (*WRPL*: 56)

> [T]here is something in my mind – the meaning I attach to the "plus" sign – that *instructs* me what I ought to do in all future cases. (*WRPL*: 22)

[T]he basic condition on [a candidate for a "fact" that determines what I mean] ... [:] it should *tell* me what I ought to do in each new instance. (*WRPL*: 24)

[I]n computing "68 + 57" as I do ... I follow directions ... (*WRPL*: 10)

"Justification" is the other side of guidance. Since the meaning-constituting mental state guides *x* in her use of "*z*", *x* can refer to this mental state in order to justify her use of "*z*":

[*I*]*f* I meant [addition by "+"], then unless I wish to change my usage, I am justified in answering (indeed compelled to answer) "125", not "5". (*WRPL*: 11)

An account of what fact it is (about my mental state) that constitutes my meaning plus ... must, in some sense, show how I am justified in giving the answer "125" to "68 + 57". (*WRPL*: 11)

On closer inspection, the meaning-constituting mental state not only justifies certain applications – in the sense that meaning addition justifies "125" in answer to "68 + 57 = ?" – it also justifies *the way* in which the answer is usually produced. Nearly always, we apply our words in an unhesitating and immediate fashion. And the meaning-constituting fact must be such as to justify this lack of hesitation. Kripke states this element of semantic normativity only once: "I immediately and unhesitatingly calculate '68 +57' as I do, and the meaning I assign to '+' is supposed to *justify* this procedure" (*WRPL*: 40). I shall call this element of semantic normativity: "justification of unhesitating application".

Finally, semantic normativity – in combination with grasping as cause – suggests a specific interpretation for meaning conditionals such as "If Jones means addition by '+', then (unless he is impeded or changes his mind) he ought to (must, should, will) give the answer '125' to '68 + 57 = ?'". According to this "left-to-right interpretation of meaning conditionals", the meaning conditional is true if, and only if, Jones has the appropriate meaning-constituting mental state: after all, this state guarantees (unless Jones changes his mind) both that he will in fact say "125" and that this is the correct answer. "If Jones means addition by '+', then if he is asked for '68 + 57', he will reply '125'. ... the conditional as stated makes it appear that some mental state obtains in Jones that guarantees his performance of particular additions such as '68 + 57'" (*WRPL*: 94–5).

Although the fifth key assumption of meaning determinism, "objectivity", is implicit in what has already been said above, it is useful to formulate it explicitly. The idea is that *x*'s meaning-constituting mental state contains and determines all future, potentially infinite, correct applications of "*z*". Sometimes meaning determinists despair of explaining what the relevant sense of "contains" or "determines" is; they then qualify these verbs with the adverbial phrase "in a queer way". Kripke writes:

> a state of "meaning addition by 'plus'" … [is] a finite object, contained in our finite minds. It does not consist in my explicitly thinking of each case of the addition table, nor even of my encoding each separate case in the brain: we lack the capacity for that. Yet ([*PI*:]§195) "in a *queer* way" each such case already is "in some sense present". (Before we hear Wittgenstein's sceptical argument, we surely suppose – unreflectively – that something like this is indeed the case. …).
>
> (*WRPL*: 52)

> [T]here is … [a] "superlative fact" (§192) about my mind that constitutes my meaning addition by "plus" and [that] determines in advance what I should do to accord with this meaning.   (*WRPL*: 65)

> See §195: "But I don't mean that what I do now (in grasping a sense) determines the future use causally and as a matter of experience, but that in a queer way, the use itself is in some sense present".
>
> (*WRPL*: 70, n.58)

> I think that I have learned the term "table" in such a way that it will apply to indefinitely many future items.   (*WRPL*: 19)

> The "directions" … that determine what I should do in each instance, [are] … somehow … "contained" in any candidate for the fact as to what I meant.   (*WRPL*: 11)

The sixth key ingredient of meaning determinism is "classical realism". Its core is the idea that "a declarative sentence gets its meaning by virtue of its *truth conditions*, by virtue of its correspondence to facts that must obtain if it is true" (*WRPL*: 72). The meaning determinist is committed to the ideas that meaning is given by (contribution to) truth-conditions, that truth is to be analysed according to the correspondence theory and that propositions play a central explanatory role in the philosophy of language and mind. This last claim emerges indirectly in a passage in which Kripke explains one of Wittgenstein's views: "We *call* something a proposition, and hence true or false, when in our language we apply the calculus of truth functions to it. That is, it is just a primitive part of our language game, not susceptible of deeper explanation, that truth functions are applied to certain sentences" (*WRPL*: 86). Wittgenstein is here said to contradict the meaning determinist, for the latter, pointing out that certain sentences express propositions, does explain why the calculus of truth-functions applies to these sentences. Finally, classical realism insists that the central assumptions of meaning determinism apply to the grasping of propositions. That

10

is to say, classical realism holds that a person x understands a declarative sentence s if, and only if, (i) x *grasps* the proposition p expressed by s, and (ii) x knows that s expresses p. Here the grasping is analysed as a mental state that is characterized by immediate knowledge, privacy, grasping, semantic normativity and so on.

The seventh and final assumption is "metaphysical justification". This takes us to the overall motivation of the meaning determinist. His overall goal is to justify our use of meaning sentences. He believes that our meaning sentences demand a philosophical licence and that his project can deliver the goods. For the meaning determinist the justification of our meaning sentences must come from ontological considerations; it is an exercise in metaphysics. This is clear from the very nature of the meaning-determinist proposal. After all, it is concerned with finding a (type of) proposition and fact that enables meaning sentences to be true or false, and hence meaningful. WRPL brings out this feature of meaning determinism quite late, and only by way of contrast with the very different form of justification offered by Wittgenstein: "our ordinary practice or belief is justified because – contrary appearances notwithstanding – it need not require the justification the sceptic has shown to be untenable" (*WRPL*: 66).

My reconstruction of low-brow meaning determinism can be summarized as follows:

"Person x means Y by sign 'z'" is true if, and only if, x has a certain mental state (MS) that *constitutes* x's meaning Y by "z". Furthermore:

(MD-1) Immediate knowledge: x usually knows MS "immediately and with fair certainty".

(MD-2) Privacy: MS is an intrinsic state of x.

(MD-3) Grasping:

(MD-3.1) Grasping as cause: x's act of grasping Y causes him – absent interference by other causes – to apply "z" in correct ways.

(MD-3.2) Grasping as intending: x's act of grasping Y is tantamount to x's forming intentions – or giving himself instructions – regarding a possibly infinite number of applications of "z" in the future.

(MD-3.3) Grasping as extrapolating: Since all learning sets are finite, grasping a meaning or concept has the character of an extrapolation.

(MD-3.4) Grasping as interpreting: Grasping a meaning or concept has the character of an interpretation.

(MD-3.5) Grasping as explanation: If x_1 and x_2 agree in all, or most, of their applications of "z", the best explanation is that they have grasped the same concept Y.

(MD-4) Semantic normativity:

(MD-4.1) Non-blindness: In applying "z" on the basis of Y, x is not acting blindly.

(MD-4.2) Guidance: MS guides x on how to apply "z".

(MD-4.3) Justification: x can justify his uses of "z" on the basis of MS.

(MD-4.4) Justification of unhesitating application: x can justify his unhesitating manner of applying "z" on the basis of MS.

(MD-4.5) Left-to-right interpretation of meaning conditionals: Meaning conditionals are to be read left to right.

(MD-5) Objectivity: x's MS contains and determines ("in a queer way") all future, potentially infinite, correct applications of "z".

(MD-6) Classical realism: What gives a declarative sentence (DS) its meaning is the proposition it expresses. Propositions have truth-conditions. DS is *true* if, and only if, the proposition it expresses corresponds to a fact. Propositions are grasped; and conditions MD-1 to MD-5, as well as MD-7, apply to the act of grasping.

(MD-7) Metaphysical justification: The justification of our meaning sentences must come from ontological considerations.

Other voices

The low-brow meaning determinism introduced in the previous section stands at the centre of *WRPL*. Chapter 2 of *WRPL* tests both this position and various attempts to give it theoretical precision. I shall call these later views "forms of *high-brow* meaning determinism". Chapter 3 of *WRPL* starts from the observation that both low-brow meaning determinism and these high-brow versions fail. Here failure is determined by the lack of success these views have in answering the so-called "sceptical challenge": in virtue of what can we say of Jones (or yourself) that he means (or you mean) addition rather than "quaddition" by "+"? Here quaddition is the function defined by:

$$\oplus = x + y, \text{ if } x, y < 57$$
$$= 5 \text{ otherwise} \qquad (WRPL: 9)$$

Chapter 3 then develops an alternative to all brands of meaning determinism, be they high-brow or low-brow. But let us not get ahead of ourselves. The natural next step in my reconstruction of *WRPL* is to introduce the other voices, that is, alternatives to low-brow meaning determinism.

I have followed Kripke in describing the low-brow meaning determinist as a common-sense *philosopher*, contrasting him with the common-sense *person*. The latter uses our ordinary and colloquial meaning sentences for attributing meaning to others and himself. He does so, however, without engaging in picture or theory building. And thus the person of common sense does not subscribe to any of the assumptions of meaning determinism. This is not to say that he might not be easily encouraged to develop meaning-determinist views. Be this as it may, at this point the important thing about the person of common sense is that his use of meaning sentences is *not* under attack in *WRPL*. *WRPL* is neither arguing that we need to change the ways in which we speak about meaning, nor suggesting that all meaning sentences are systematically false or in error. *WRPL* is testing and rejecting *philosophical theories* about meaning sentences, not these sentences themselves.

Another voice – or rather bundle of voices – is that of the philosophical theoretician. The most prominent group of these theoreticians *within WRPL* are the already mentioned high-brow meaning determinists. High-brow meaning determinists are, or at least intend to be, true to the low-brow version of meaning determinism. What sets them apart from the latter is that they seek to provide a systematic development and defence of the intuitive picture. Providing such system and defence can mean different things to different theoreticians, but it usually amounts to bringing low-brow meaning determinism in line with some general and fundamental philosophical commitments, such as reductivism or physicalism. Consider for instance "semantic reductive dispositionalism", the most important high-brow version of meaning determinism in *WRPL* and beyond. Semantic reductive dispositionalism attempts to tell us more about the mental state that constitutes someone's meaning something by a sign. It tells us that this mental state is reducible to dispositions to use that sign under certain conditions. In so doing, semantic reductive dispositionalism strives for an ontology in which "spooky" entities such as meaning find a proper place. These spooky entities turn out to be identical to entities that the physicalist finds acceptable.[1] In developing this position, the dispositionalist does not (usually) reject the broad low-brow meaning-determinist picture. And hence he would – by his own criteria – have failed in his endeavour if it turned out that his dispositionalist theory in fact contradicts the picture.

At the beginning of the previous paragraph I wrote that "the most prominent group" of philosophical theoreticians "*within WRPL*" are high-brow meaning determinists. I chose these words in order to signal that *outside WRPL* there are philosophical theoreticians who are not committed to remaining within the meaning-determinist picture. Here I am thinking of theories that – partly under the influence of *WRPL*, partly because of other philosophical commitments – seek to make do without *some* central elements of meaning determinism. Victims of such "reformist" theories have been privacy and semantic normativity, among others. Read through the perspective of *WRPL*, such theories are attempts at damage control. Since Chapter 2 of *WRPL* presents (to many) a successful argument against meaning determinism as it stands – that is against the conjunction of the seven assumptions – the natural first thought is to try to rescue it by dropping just one or two of the conjuncts. Kripke pays scant attention to these positions. The only proposal he considers is reductive dispositionalism *minus* privacy (*WRPL*: 111). Later in this book, we shall encounter other possibilities.

A further voice in *WRPL* is "the sceptic". The dialectic starts with the sceptic presenting a sceptical challenge to an interlocutor who has just confidently calculated that 68 plus 57 equals 125. The sceptic wants to know in virtue of what fact the interlocutor means addition rather than quaddition by "plus": in virtue of what fact the interlocutor has in the past grasped the addition rather than the quaddition function. One of the most important things to note about the sceptic in *WRPL* is that his scepticism is "constitutive" rather than "epistemological".[2] To appreciate the difference, consider the following two sceptical claims:

(a) There is a fact of the matter whether in the past you meant addition or quaddition by "+". But you cannot ever have a justification for your (possibly true!) belief that you did mean addition.
(b) There is *no* fact of the matter whether in the past you meant addition or quaddition by "+". And hence you cannot justify your claim that you did (mean addition by "+") by pointing to a fact about you.

Claim (a) formulates an epistemological, (b) a constitutive, or metaphysical, scepticism about meaning. That Kripke is concerned with the latter is clear throughout the whole argument. It is explicitly stated, too: the sceptic "questions whether there is any *fact* that I meant plus, not quus, that will answer his sceptical challenge" (*WRPL*: 11).

Two aspects of the sceptical challenge easily obscure its constitutive character. First, the sceptic presents the challenge in something of an epistemological guise. It is said (in the voice of the sceptic's interlocutor) that the "sceptic questions my certainty about my answer [i.e. '125' in answer to 68 + 57 = ?]" (*WRPL*: 8); or that the sceptic "questions whether I have any reason to be so confident that now I should answer '125' rather than '5'" (*WRPL*: 11). Secondly, it is important to remember that the sceptic's interlocutor(s) in Chapter 2 is (are) the meaning determinist(s). And even a quick perusal of the ingredients of that picture shows that some of its claims are epistemological. On the meaning-determinist picture, any putative fact of meaning must meet a number of epistemological constraints: it must be *knowable* "immediately and with fair certainty" (immediate knowledge); it must be able to *justify* use (semantic normativity as justification); and it must be able to *justify* unhesitating use (justification of unhesitating application).

Neither of these aspects of the sceptical challenge must be allowed to distract us from its constitutive character. As concerns epistemological constraints on possible facts of meaning, the crucial point is not to throw them out with the bathwater of a mistaken epistemological rendering of the sceptical challenge. Otherwise we will not be able to understand why certain forms of high-brow meaning determinism are found wanting in Chapter 2 of *WRPL*. Turning to the other potential source of misunderstanding, the epistemological guise, it is important to underline that this guise is really a *disguise*. This is obvious from the fact that the sceptic's interlocutor is granted God-like omniscience regarding his own past and present non-intentional mental states and physical behaviour:

> [I]t is clear that the sceptical challenge is not really an epistemological one. It purports to show that nothing in my mental history of past behaviour – not even what an omniscient God would know – could

establish whether I meant plus or quus. But then it appears to follow
that there was no *fact* about me that constituted my having meant plus
rather than quus.   (*WRPL*: 21)

If one cannot justify a self-attribution even under the assumption of omniscience
about oneself, then the logical conclusion must be that there is nothing, no fact,
to which such self-attribution corresponds.

To insist that the sceptical challenge in *WRPL* is constitutive and not epistemological is not, of course, to maintain that the dialogic setting itself is misleading
or distorting.[3] Although we can state the key issue of *WRPL* outside the dialogic
setting – that there are facts of the sort presupposed by meaning determinism
– there is still every reason to pay close attention to how Kripke frames the discussion. The use of different characters and voices provides important clues as to
how Kripke interprets Wittgenstein's position.[4]

This brings us to the most important voice, the voice that Kripke attributes to
Wittgenstein. The question of to what extent Kripke's Wittgenstein is Wittgenstein
himself is, of course, controversial. I shall address it in Chapter 8. At this stage it is
more to the point to address the question of whether Kripke's Wittgenstein should be
equated with the meaning sceptic (as he appears in *WRPL*). Unfortunately, Kripke's
text does not give an unambiguous answer. Equating the two voices is suggested by
the fact that Wittgenstein is said to have proposed a "sceptical solution" in response
to the failure of meaning determinism. It is natural to think that sceptical solutions are solutions brought forth by sceptics. And Kripke writes that Wittgenstein
"accepts his own sceptical argument and offers a 'sceptical solution' to overcome
the appearance of paradox" (*WRPL*: 68). He also speaks of "Wittgenstein's scepticism": "Wittgenstein's scepticism about the determination of future usage by the
past contents of my mind is analogous to Hume's scepticism about the determination of the future by the past (causally and inferentially)" (*WRPL*: 107–8). Passages
such as these make it sound as if the sceptical solution (of Chapter 3 of *WRPL*) is
part and parcel of Wittgenstein's own meaning scepticism. The sceptical solution is
then an attempt to explain that, and how, we can live with – *at least a mitigated form
of* – meaning scepticism.

In other places, Kripke intimates a looser relationship between the sceptic and
Wittgenstein:

Wittgenstein holds, with the sceptic, that there is no fact as to whether
I mean plus or quus. But if this is to be conceded to the sceptic, is this
not the end of the matter?   (*WRPL*: 71)

Wittgenstein's sceptical solution concedes to the sceptic that no
"truth conditions" or "corresponding facts" in the world exist that
make a statement like "Jones, like many of us, means addition by '+'"
true.   (*WRPL*: 86)

This suggests that Wittgenstein's sceptical solution is sceptical not because it is put forward by a sceptic but rather because it is put forward as a *response* to the sceptic. If one reads the sceptical solution through this perspective, then it really is a form of "diagnostic anti-scepticism". Let me explain. In the literature on epistemological scepticism, it is customary to distinguish between two forms of anti-scepticism: "direct" and "diagnostic".[5] The direct anti-sceptic accepts the terms of a sceptical challenge and seeks to answer it. For example, faced with dream-scepticism, the direct anti-sceptic tries to find a criterion that distinguishes dreaming from being awake. The diagnostic anti-sceptic rejects the terms of a sceptical challenge. He attempts to demonstrate that the sceptical challenge is based on inadmissable presuppositions. For instance, faced with dream-scepticism, the diagnostic anti-sceptic might challenge the idea that in order to know that I am standing here now, I must be able to rule out the possibility that I am currently dreaming. Now, in *WRPL* Kripke makes a distinction between "straight" and "sceptical" responses to the sceptical challenge of the meaning sceptic (*WRPL*: 66). Meaning-determinist responses all qualify as "straight", and only Wittgenstein's response (the response of the "sceptical solution") is called "sceptical". Meaning-determinist answers accept the sceptical challenge and its presuppositions; in particular they accept the presupposition that the significance of meaning sentences derives from their correspondence to facts (i.e. that their meaning is given by truth-conditions). Wittgenstein's reaction is different; he rejects that crucial presupposition. And in so doing, he develops a position against which the sceptical challenge is a blunt weapon. In light of this reconstruction, it seems natural to equate "straight" with "direct" and "sceptical" with "diagnostic" answers to (meaning) scepticism. And Wittgenstein turns out to be a diagnostic anti-sceptic.[6]

Which reading of the relationship between Wittgenstein and the meaning sceptic is to be preferred? The first interpretation has the advantage of familiarity, the second nicely brings Kripke's Wittgenstein in line with familiar anti-sceptical readings of *PI*.[7] Fortunately, we do not have to choose. Whichever perspective we pick, we can always translate it easily into the other. This is not to say that all forms of diagnostic anti-scepticism are forms of scepticism.[8] This much should be clear from the above example of dream-scepticism; there the sceptic and the diagnostic anti-sceptic hold very different, not translatable views. But in the present case, the two positions are closer together: it does not matter much whether we call the sceptical solution a form of "mitigated scepticism" or a version of "diagnostic anti-scepticism". In what follows, I shall usually equate Wittgenstein and the sceptic, thus giving more weight to the first perspective. However, my only reason for doing so is that this procedure facilitates the confrontation with the critics of *WRPL* (who invariably rely on this viewpoint).

I shall sketch my reconstruction of the sceptical solution later in this chapter. At this stage we need only note the following important feature. The sceptical solution is the one philosophical analysis of meaning sentences in *WRPL* that is not based on a study of truth-conditions for these sentences. It cannot do so since, as just quoted, it concedes the failure of the meaning-determinist project. And classical realism contains the idea that the meaning of a sentence it given by its truth-conditions.

The sceptical argument I: testing low-brow meaning determinism

I have now introduced the main voices or characters within *WRPL* and the debate surrounding it. The next stage is to explain their interaction. Here I shall focus only on their interaction *within* the book.

Chapter 2 of *WRPL* is a critical study of meaning determinism. The initial target is *low-brow* meaning determinism. The question is whether it has the resources to pick out a fact that makes it so that someone – Jones, say – means addition by "+". Two proposals are tried out and rejected. According to the first, the "use response", it is Jones's use of "+" that determines whether or not by "+" he meant and means addition or quaddition (*WRPL*: 8). This solution fails. Past use of "+" is necessarily finite and hence it cannot determine a unique function. (Kripke makes the simplifying assumption that Jones has not previously calculated with numbers larger than 57; needless to say in reality one would have to pick a much larger number.) Note here that in showing the use response to be untenable the sceptic is presenting an "immanent critique": he shows that the use response is unable to meet the meaning determinist's demands for justification and correct extrapolation.

The second response is the "algorithm response" (*WRPL*: 16–17). What makes "Jones means addition by '+'" true is that Jones is following, and has followed in the past, some algorithm for calculations with the sign "+". One such algorithmic procedure is the counting of marbles. Jones determines the result of 68 + 57 by forming two heaps of marbles, with 68 and 57 marbles respectively, by combining the two heaps into one, and by counting the overall number of marbles. This response fails as well. Trying to identify the mental state that constitutes Jones's meaning addition by "+", the meaning determinist invokes other of Jones's mental states; namely, the mental state that constitutes his possession of the concepts of *counting* and *heap*. And thus the real question – what makes it so that Jones has one concept or meaning rather than another – has not been answered. Again it is the meaning determinist's commitment to justification that blocks the response.

The sceptical argument II: against reductive semantic dispositionalism

It is at this point in the dialectic that high-brow meaning determinism enters the ring and takes over from its low-brow relative. Each version of high-brow meaning determinism tells us something more and new about meaning-constituting mental states. At the same time, high-brow meaning determinism seeks to preserve all the assumptions of low-brow meaning determinism. It is a *refinement* of low-brow meaning determinism. It follows that versions of high-brow meaning determinism can be evaluated by whether or not they remain truthful to their low-brow ancestry. And that is indeed how they are evaluated by the sceptic. In the case of every version of high-brow meaning determinism the sceptic shows that it violates at least one of the low-brow constraints.

The first proposal for a high-brow meaning determinism is the already mentioned "reductive semantic dispositionalism" (*WRPL*: 22–37). *WRPL* considers different forms of this proposal:

(D1) Simple past tense form: In the past, Jones meant addition by "+" since he then had the disposition to give sums in answer to queries of the form $m + n = ?$.

(D2) Simple present tense form: Jones now means addition by "+" since he now has the disposition to give sums in answer to queries of the form $m + n = ?$.

(D3) Sophisticated form: Jones now means addition by "+" since *ceteris paribus* he gives sums in answer to queries of the form $m + n = ?$. Here the *ceteris paribus* clause involves an idealization of Jones's abilities. It allows us to assume that Jones might have a brain much bigger than the one he in fact has.

(D4) Machine form: Jones now means addition by "+" since we can think of his mind/brain as containing a machine that (*ceteris paribus*) gives sums in answer to queries of the form $m + n = ?$.

The sceptic argues that none of these proposals succeeds. In order to be successful, they would have to meet two requirements: the extensional requirement and the intensional requirement.[9] According to the *extensional* requirement the dispositionalist has to find dispositional predicates (instances of "has the disposition to use sign 'z' under circumstances C") that logically co-vary with meaning predicates (instances of "means Y by 'z'"). This follows from the meaning-determinist assumption of objectivity. According to the *intensional* requirement the dispositionalist has to show that having the disposition to use "z" under conditions C *intuitively resembles* meaning Y by "z". This demand focuses in particular on the need to remain truthful to semantic normativity.

Simple forms of dispositionalism obviously fail the extensional requirement. I do not just have the disposition to call horses "horses"; I also have the disposition to make mistakes and call cows in the distance and on a foggy day "horses". Now, if my dispositions to use "horse" were to determine what I mean by "horse", then it would have to be said that by "horse" I mean *horses or cows in the distance on a foggy day*. Or consider the fact that the addition function is infinite. Low-brow meaning determinism allows us to say that I can have a mental state in which I mean an infinite function. Again, however, we run into difficulties when we try to reduce this mental state to dispositions (to give sums to various plus-queries). A finite mind might mean some infinite function, but it cannot harbour an infinite number of dispositions. Does it help to go for sophistication at this point, and endorse D3? The sceptic argues that it does not. Here the main issue is whether the dispositionalist is entitled to rely on an idealization of our abilities. The sceptic denies that he is so entitled: "How in the world can I tell what would happen if my brain were stuffed with extra brain matter, or if my life were prolonged by some magic elixir?" (*WRPL*: 27).

The intensional requirement centres around the idea that dispositionalism is unable to capture semantic normativity or, more precisely, non-blindness, guidance, justification and justification of unhesitating application. Consider:

- Non-blindness: On the meaning-determinist picture, if x applies "z" on the basis of his meaning Y by "z", then x is not acting blindly. But if x produces "z" as a manifestation of his disposition to produce "z" under circumstances C, he may well be acting blindly. There is nothing about dispositions as such that makes them non-blind.
- Guidance: If x produces "z" as a manifestation of his disposition to produce "z" under circumstances C, then he is not guided by the disposition. Compare: the sugar cube has the disposition to dissolve in water, but in manifesting this disposition on a given occasion the sugar cube is not guided by the disposition.
- Justification: If x produces "z" as a manifestation of his disposition to produce "z" under circumstances C, then x cannot invoke his disposition to justify his use of "z". Compare: I have the disposition to speed on empty motorways. This may explain my speeding on a given occasion, but no policemen in the world would accept this explanation as a justification.
- Justification of unhesitating application: If x produces "z" as a manifestation of his disposition to produce "z" under circumstances C, then x cannot invoke his disposition to justify the unhesitating way in which he uses "z". Dispositions do not justify anything – hence they do not justify the manner of using a given sign.

Needless to say, all of the sceptic's arguments against reductive semantic dispositionalism are controversial, and the debates over the extensional and the intensional requirements will preoccupy us at length later.

The sceptical argument III: against simplicity considerations

The second version of high-brow meaning determinism can be disposed of more quickly (*WRPL*: 37–40). Its advocate is not primarily motivated by physicalism

– as is the dispositionalist – but impressed by work in the philosophy of science. Philosophers of science have often been preoccupied with simplicity as a virtue of explanations and theories; the proposal under consideration transfers these concerns to meaning. The suggestion is that the meaning sentence "Jones means addition by '+'" is true if, and only if, "Jones means addition by '+'" is the simplest explanation of Jones's operating with the "+" sign.

The sceptic raises two objections. The first is that our philosopher of science has misunderstood the sceptical challenge. It is constitutive, not epistemological. Simplicity considerations can help us pick one of two hypotheses about unknown facts; but they cannot establish that there are facts (to be right or wrong about) in the first place. In order to be a refinement of low-brow meaning determinism, high-brow versions must tell us something new and compelling about the ontology of meaning-constituting mental states. The presently considered suggestion does not do this: it is only in the running as an epistemological proposal on how we might find out which meaning-constituting mental states we might have – assuming that we have any.

The second objection to simplicity considerations relies on the first ingredient of meaning determinism, immediate knowledge: if x means Y by "z", then x usually knows his meaning-constituting mental state "immediately and with fair certainty". The simplicity proposal cannot honour this condition. Accepting it commits us to the view that knowledge of meaning – even our own meaning-constituting mental states – is hypothetical and inferential rather than direct. And once our meaning-constituting mental states are known only hypothetically, then so too are the demands that our meaning makes on us, and the justifications it provides. Most importantly, we will no longer be able to justify the unhesitating manner in which we usually apply our words on the basis of our meanings. This unhesitating manner becomes unjustifiable once our knowledge of what we mean is merely based on conjectures. At this point the philosopher of science's failure to honour immediate knowledge results in the further failure to honour justification of unhesitating application.

The sceptical argument IV: against classical empiricism and the qualia theory

The semantic dispositionalism considered above tried to reduce mental states to something else. In contrast, step IV of the sceptical argument probes a form of high-brow meaning determinism that is non-reductive. It proposes that to be in one and the same type of meaning-constituting mental state is, first, to have one and the same type of qualitative "feel" or quale, and, secondly, to know of this quale directly on the basis of introspection (*WRPL*: 41–51). Thus the claim is not just that *every* *token* of a meaning-constituting mental state has some quale or other.

The theory in question is committed to something much stronger, namely, to a type–type identity of meaning-constituting mental states and mental states with certain qualia. Every mental state of meaning addition by "+" has the same type of unique qualitative feel; and so does the mental state of meaning any other function or property. At first sight this proposal might appear to answer the sceptical challenge. I can explain what constitutes my having the mental state of meaning addition rather than quaddition: what constitutes my meaning addition is simply that in considering 68 + 57 = ? I have an instance of the characteristic and unique quale for addition, and that I know directly of my having it.

Of course it takes little reflection to realize that this classical empiricist proposal is unsatisfactory. It fails for two reasons that roughly correspond to the distinction between extensional and intensional requirements in the criticism of dispositionalism. First, "qualia predicates" (instances of "has a mental state with quale q") do not co-vary with meaning predicates (instances of "means Y by 'z'"). Many states of meaning something by a word come with qualitative feels, but there is no systematic co-variation on the level of types. And hence the proposal fails to capture objectivity. Secondly, the proposal also fails to do justice to semantic normativity. This is most obvious in the case of guidance: on the meaning-deterministic picture, the mental state that constitutes Jones's meaning addition by "+" guides Jones on how to use "+", that is, guides him on how to answer plus-queries. It can do so – always on the meaning-determinist picture! – because it has intentional content; to mean addition by "+" is to intend *that* one use the "+" sign in certain specifiable ways. Unfortunately for the theory probed here, qualia do not have such content. And hence, on their own, they can provide neither guidance nor justification.

The sceptical argument V: against semantic primitivism

The qualia theory is a form of non-reductivism in so far as it does not identify types of mental states with types of dispositions to do non-intentional things. Yet in a weak sense the qualia theory might still be called reductive: it identifies one kind of mental state (meaning-constituting mental states) with another kind of mental state (mental states with particular and unique qualia). The next high-brow meaning-determinist proposal to be considered goes all the way towards non-reductivism. Meaning-constituting mental states are *primitive states*. The low-brow meaning-determinist picture cannot be amended or refined, if by such amendment or refinement we mean providing a further analysis of the ontology of meaning-constituting mental states. It is not that we lack the epistemic means to say more: the point is that there is nothing more to say. Meaning-constituting mental states are what they are and nothing else. They are not like dispositions, they are not identical to mental states with unique qualia, and therefore they are not known introspectively. It is important to see that "semantic primitivism" is more than just the low-brow meaning-determinist picture itself. The picture itself says nothing about the question of whether meaning-constituting mental states are primitive or not.

It will be of great significance in later chapters to remember that *WRPL* prefaces its criticism of this proposal with two noteworthy qualifications: that the proposal "may in a sense be irrefutable", and that "if it is taken in an appropriate way Wittgenstein may even accept it" (*WRPL*: 51). Nevertheless, the meaning sceptic labels this semantic primitivism "desperate" and "mysterious". One criticism focuses on the primitivist's admission that knowledge of meaning is not introspective; the meaning sceptic points out that this contradicts the assumption of immediate knowledge (*WRPL*: 51). According to the second line of criticism, there is a "logical difficulty" about the idea that there could be a state of meaning addition by "plus" at all. The problem is that such a state would be a finite state of a finite mind. And yet, in order to be the state of meaning addition by "plus", the state would have to determine the results for an infinite number of plus-queries. The advocate of semantic primitivism owes us an explanation of how any finite mental state could possibly have this capacity (*WRPL*: 52–3). Otherwise the meaning determinist fails to remain true to objectivity.

The sceptical argument VI: against Platonism

Platonism constitutes a different sort of semantic primitivism. With respect to the addition function the Platonist claims that it is primitive or objective in the sense of being fully mind-independent. The same goes for the objective senses *addition* or *plus*. As non-spatial and non-temporal objects, Platonist senses are not constrained by finitude. There is thus – *prima facie* – no problem with them determining an infinite number of cases. But how can Platonism help meaning determinism (*WRPL*: 53–4)? To do so, the Platonist senses must make contact with the mental states of human beings. The obvious proposal is this: the mental state that constitutes Jones's meaning addition by "+" is the mental state in and through which Jones grasps the objective sense *addition* and the objective mathematical entity *addition function*. Here, of course, all hinges on the analysis offered for this new type of grasping.

Little reflection is needed to see that Platonism does not solve the problems of meaning determinism. Like dispositionalism and the qualia theory, Platonism fails the extensional requirement. Mental states are finite, but the addition function is infinite. How then can a mental state grasp the latter? The Platonist thinks he is in a better position to answer this question since between mental states and the addition function he places the objective sense, which is thought of as having both a finite and an infinite side: it is finite – one sense – and yet determines an infinite number of truths. But the advance is dubious: if we do not understand how a mental state can grasp an infinity, then we do not understand how a finite mental state can grasp a finite objective entity that determines an infinity.

The sceptical paradox

The discussion of Platonism concludes *WRPL*'s criticism of high-brow forms of meaning determinism. Are there other forms not considered in *WRPL*? It seems that for Kripke the answer is that there are none. Otherwise he could not take the crucial step from claiming that the *considered forms* of meaning determinism fail to claiming that *all forms* fail. Many critics demur.

In the above, I have reconstructed the argument of Chapter 2 of *WRPL*. It is entitled "The Wittgensteinian Paradox". What is this paradox or, rather, what exactly is paradoxical for whom? The correct answer is that the paradox exists first and foremost for the meaning determinist. Consider his position in light of the above. For him, the meaning of the sentence type (α) "Person x means Y by sign 'z'" is given by truth-conditions. Central among these truth-conditions is a meaning-constituting mental state of x, a mental state that fits with the conditions of the low-brow meaning-determinist picture. Let us call this fact a "meaning-determining fact". Now, Chapter 2 has shown that there can be no such meaning-determining fact, neither on the basis of the low-brow picture, nor on the basis of high-brow theoretical refinements. There can be no such fact because the conditions imposed by meaning determinism do not form a coherent whole. For each proposal it was possible to show that it failed at least one of the conditions of meaning determinism itself. And now the meaning-determinist is in a quandary. He believes that (α) can be true only if there is a meaning-determining fact, and he believes, on the basis of the arguments given in Chapter 2, that there cannot be such a meaning-determining fact. He thus has to conclude that (α) is false, and false for all its instantiations. Alas, to conclude that (α) is false is to conclude that (β) "There can be no such thing as meaning anything by any word" (*WRPL*: 54). And this is obviously paradoxical: if (β) is true, then none of the words in (β) means anything, and hence (β) is meaningless. And meaningless sentences are not even in the running for being true or false. This is how things look to the meaning determinist.

Revisionists, reformers, revolutionaries

What about the other voices? What about Wittgenstein and (thus) the sceptic? Do they believe that "there can be no such thing as meaning anything by any word";

do they accept the sceptical paradox? Some interpreters answer in the affirmative but then go on to wonder how anyone could *both* accept the paradox and propose a novel answer for explaining the significance of meaning sentences.[10] The correct answer to these questions is not, however, an unqualified "yes"; it is a qualified "yes and no". Wittgenstein accepts the sceptical paradox as a natural consequence of meaning determinism. Accept the latter, and you have to accept the former. But Kripke's Wittgenstein does not view the sceptical paradox as the correct view of meaning *per se*; for him the sceptical paradox merely shows that the meaning determinist's way of handling meaning attributions and meaning conditionals is hopeless. This interpretation is obvious from the fact that Kripke – speaking for Wittgenstein – describes the sceptical paradox as "insane and intolerable", and as "incredible and self-defeating" (*WRPL*: 60, 71). Wittgenstein "does not wish to leave us with his problem, but to solve it" (*WRPL*: 60).

There are obviously alternatives to accepting meaning determinism (as formulated in *WRPL*) and (therewith) the sceptical paradox. These alternatives fall into the three categories of revision, reform and revolution. The revisionist aims to improve particular theoretical renderings of the meaning-determinist picture, without changing the picture itself in any way. This might, for instance, take the form of suggesting a more complex interplay of dispositions in order to protect dispositionalism from the normativity considerations. Reformers and revolutionaries go further and change key ingredients of the meaning-determinist picture. The contrast between reform and revolution is that between changing at most one or two of the elements of the meaning-determinist picture and abandoning almost all of them. The first path is that of reform, the second that of revolution. *WRPL* considers only one reformist proposal. This proposal is to keep all elements of meaning determinism except for privacy. Of course, this suggestion could be developed in more than one way: one can imagine different high-brow versions of meaning-determinism-*minus*-privacy. *WRPL* focuses on the attempt to develop reductive semantic dispositionalism in this reformist way. The result is "a social, or community-wide version of the dispositional theory" (*WRPL*: 111). It could be formulated as follows:

> A community *C* means addition by "+", if, and only if, *ceteris paribus* (nearly) all members of *C* have the disposition to give sums in answer to queries of the form $m + n = ?$.

WRPL does not criticize this position in detail; it simply comments that it is open to some of the criticisms levelled against individualistic forms of dispositionalism. Here too some critics have remained unconvinced.[11] Other commentators agree with Kripke that dispositionalism minus privacy fails but they fault him for giving insufficient attention to other reformist courses of action.

The sceptical solution I: from classical realism to assertability

The Wittgenstein of *WRPL* is a revolutionary by the standards of the previous section. This does not necessarily contradict Wittgenstein's oft-quoted remark that "philosophy ... leaves everything as it is" (*PI*: §124). After all, Kripke's Wittgenstein does not:

> wish to doubt or deny that when people speak of themselves and others as meaning something by their words, as following rules, they do so with perfect right. ... [Wittgenstein does] not even wish to deny the propriety of an ordinary use of the phrase "the fact that Jones meant addition by such-and-such a symbol", and indeed such expressions have perfectly ordinary uses.   (*WRPL*: 69)

In other words, the sceptical solution – or meaning scepticism – does not touch or concern the propriety of our ordinary meaning sentences. It "merely" takes issue with a certain picture that philosophers are prone to derive from, or to project onto, these sentences. Indeed, the sceptical solution is first and foremost a "diagnostic *dissolution*" of meaning determinism in all its forms. It seeks to free us from an intuitive picture that gives rise to endless philosophical problems. And it undertakes to replace this picture with reminders of the nature of our everyday practices. Taken in this way, there need be no clash either between Kripke's Wittgenstein's "revolution" and Wittgenstein's well-known "no theses" aphorism: "If one tried to advance *theses* in philosophy, it would never be possible to debate them, because everyone would agree to them" (*PI*: §128). The "theses" advanced as part of the sceptical solution are things we always already accept.

Be that as it may, here it is more important to reconstruct the train of thought that leads to the sceptical solution, or that motivates meaning scepticism. In order to be convincing, this reconstruction must be piecemeal: for each of the ingredients of meaning determinism, we need to learn whether, how and why it must be replaced with a successor concept. Such a successor must contain "all we can salvage of" these meaning-determinist notions (*WRPL*: 68).

First and foremost, meaning scepticism is based on the insight that there cannot be meaning-constituting mental states that fit with the meaning-determinist picture. Indeed, *WRPL* goes further: there can be no meaning-constituting mental states, period. That is to say, the meaning sceptic concedes to the meaning determinist that if mental states are meaning-constituting at all, then they have to be meaning-constituting in the way the meaning determinist assumes. Hence, no meaning-determining meaning-constituting mental states, no meaning-determining mental states.

Moreover, the meaning sceptic holds that having realized that *no mental fact* (i.e. no mental state) can act as the truth-maker for "x means Y by 'z'", we also have to accept that no classical-realist fact whatsoever can play this role. Consider what a theory would look like that got rid of mental facts but that nevertheless produced classical-realist facts as truth-makers for "x means Y by 'z'". The most obvious version of such theory would be a form of dispositionalism. The earlier considered form of reductive semantic dispositionalism had the following form:

> (I) "x means Y by 'z'" is made true by a meaning-constituting mental state (of an individual or group – x can be either); and this mental state is in turn reducible to dispositions (of the same individual or group) to produce "z" under conditions C.

Let us cut out the middleman, the mental state. That gives us:

> (II) "x means Y by 'z'" is made true by x's disposition to produce "z" under conditions C (again x may be either an individual or a group).

Clearly, if the first proposal fails, then so does the second. If (I) cannot meet the extensional requirement then neither can (II).

Once we accept that no classical-realist fact can make "x means Y by 'z'" true, we face a choice. Option one is to conclude that all meaning sentences are false. This leads to incoherence, as we already saw when following the meaning determinist's slide towards paradox. Start with the claim that

> (i) For all [x means Y by "z"]: [x means Y by "z"] is false.

If (i) is true then no person can ever mean anything, and hence no sentence ever has any meaning. But if no sentence ever has any meaning, no sentence is even in the running for being true or false. And hence (i) cannot be false.[12]

Since option one is incoherent, we had better try option two. Option two is to provide an alternative to meaning-determinist truth-conditional semantics. If meaning is not bestowed on a sentence by its truth-conditions (construed along the lines of classical realism), that is, if meaning is bestowed on a sentence by *some other* conditions, then the failure to produce a meaning-determinist truth-conditional analysis of meaning sentences does not precipitate the conclusion that all meaning sentences are meaningless. (Of course, going down this route is compatible with retaining a deflationary conception of truth-conditions, as we shall see in Chapter 5.)

Now, even before we go into any detail as to the nature of these alternative conditions ("a-conditions"), it must be emphasized that the a-conditions for a given meaning sentence s must not be necessary and sufficient for s to be meaningful. In other words, the sceptical solution had better not produce an analysis of the form:

> s means p if, and only if, a-conditions $a_1 \dots a_n$ are fulfilled.

For if a specific set of a-conditions were necessary and sufficient for s to be meaningful, we would have a specific (set of) classical-realist fact(s) that makes s meaningful. And we know already that no such fact is possible. Hence whatever the a-conditions turn out to be, they can, at best, take the form:

> It is often necessary and frequently sufficient for s to mean p that a-conditions $a_1 \ldots a_n$ are fulfilled.

WRPL identifies the new kind of meaning-conferring conditions as "assertability conditions" (*WRPL*: 73). These are rough and ready conditions for when it is appropriate, justifiable, permitted or obligatory to make assertions of a certain type. Here is an example from *WRPL*, and it gives the assertability conditions under which Jones is entitled to say "I mean addition by 'plus'":

> *Jones* is entitled, subject to correction by others, provisionally to say, "I mean addition by 'plus'", whenever he has the feeling of confidence – "now I can go on!" – that he can give "correct" responses in new cases; and he can give "correct" responses in new cases; and *he* is entitled, again provisionally and subject to correction by others, to judge a new response to be "correct" simply because it is the response he is inclined to give. (*WRPL*: 90)

Here "whenever" is not to be interpreted as "if and only if", but as "only if" at best; perhaps it would be clearer still to write "it is often necessary and frequently sufficient for Jones to be entitled ... to say ...". Kripke is not equally explicit about formulating assertability conditions for Smith's third-person assertion "Jones means addition by 'plus'", but it is not difficult to cull the elements from the text:

> It is often necessary and frequently sufficient for Smith to be entitled, subject to correction by others, provisionally to say, (#) "Jones means addition by 'plus'", when Smith "judges that Jones's answers to particular addition problems agree with those *he* is inclined to give", or, when they disagree, Smith "can interpret Jones as at least following the proper procedure". Here different kinds of errors have different weight. When Jones's answers differ even for small problems, then Smith is not (usually) entitled to assert (#). When Jones's answers differ in "bizarre" ways for larger problems – ways that cannot easily be put down to mistakes in calculation – then Smith is not (usually) entitled to assert (#). Past assertions of (#), assertions that were acceptable then, (usually) have some weight in assessing the assertability of (#) now, but they may be outweighed by the considerations mentioned here. (*WRPL*: 91)

The two examples give the assertability conditions for meaning attributions. This gives the impression that the new approach to meaning is domain-specific. This impression is misleading. As meaning scepticism has it, the significance or meaning of *all assertions* must be analysed in terms of assertability conditions. It is important to see that this move is forced on anyone who accepts the arguments against meaning determinism: classical realism does not survive for any declarative sentences, be they meaning sentences or not. Remember the conclusion the meaning determinist is forced to draw from his failed attempts to find a possible fact that would correspond to (#). The conclusion is that – given the meaning-determinist truth-conditional framework – Jones does not mean anything by "+"; there is no way in which Jones can latch on to the addition function and make it the referent for "+". Now consider the analogous case of a meaning attribution for a declarative sentence:

> (∗) By "The cat is on the mat", Jones means the (possible) fact that the cat is on the mat.

Since the lesson regarding individual words such as "plus" applies *mutatis mutandis* to whole sentences – after all, whole sentences consist of individual words – the meaning determinist is forced to draw the following conclusion: given his truth-conditional framework, and since it is impossible to find a possible fact that would correspond to (∗), Jones does not mean anything by "The cat is on the mat"; there is no way in which Jones can latch on to the possible fact that the cat is on the mat and make it the referent for "The cat is on the mat". There thus can be no correspondence between declarative sentences and facts; if the meaning of the former depends on our ability to somehow relate them to one another, then all declarative sentences are meaningless. Again the only way out is to shift to assertability conditions as conditions of meaning.

In one respect, however, the term "assertability conditions" is something of a misnomer. It suggests a privileged position for assertions, and leaves open how, say, questions or imperatives are to be analysed. In fact, the new framework concerns questions and imperatives as much as it concerns individual words. This is pointed out by *WRPL* itself. Indeed, Kripke emphasizes that for Wittgenstein – the assumed architect of the sceptical solution – the downgrading of the position of assertions in our overall picture of language is important:

> This in itself plays a central role in his repudiation of the classical realist picture. Since the indicative mood is not taken as in any sense primary or basic, it becomes more plausible that the linguistic role even of utterances in the indicative mood that superficially look like assertions need not be one of "stating facts". (*WRPL*: 73)

It would thus be better to speak of "appropriateness conditions". I shall, however, use Kripke's term throughout this book.

28

The sceptical solution II: From immediate knowledge to confidence

Classical realism is of course not the only ingredient of meaning determinism that has to go in order to preserve the significance our meaning sentences. We have already touched on the successor of immediate knowledge in the two examples for assertability conditions given above. Meaning determinism was wrong to assume that what makes "I mean addition by '+'" true is a meaning-constituting mental state of which I know "immediately and with fair certainty". Under the influence of the critical discussion of meaning determinism in Chapter 2 of *WRPL* we realize that there are no meaning-constituting mental states. Immediate knowledge imbued a correct insight with the mistaken ontology of meaning-constituting facts. The correct insight is captured by saying that we usually feel strongly confident both about how we apply our words, and about self-attributions of meaning. This confidence is not based on some special access to our mental life, or on some interpretation of our past performance; it is much more primitive. Someone who has undergone an extensive training in how to speak – a training in which the number of explicit corrections by teachers has decreased steadily over time – simply has developed this confidence in an unreflective manner.

The sceptical solution III: from privacy to intersubjectivity

Of course, confidence is one thing, knowledge another. What prevents us, within the sceptical solution, from moving from confidence to knowledge, is that our self-attributions are subject to corrections coming from others. This brings us to the rejection of privacy – and indeed to the "private language argument" as meaning scepticism sees it. Meaning determinism assumed that meaning-constituting mental states are intrinsic states of the individual who has them. If God created an atom-by-atom duplicate of me anywhere, then my duplicate would mean by his words exactly what I mean by mine. For instance, the duplicate could be situated in a world where he was living in total social isolation. *A fortiori*, any individual's meaning and rule-following can be analysed without bringing in a second or third person.

We have seen that meaning determinism fails: "having meaning-constituting mental states" cannot denote an *intrinsic property* (of Jones) since it cannot denote a *property* (of Jones) *at all*. Nothing can have the property in question. In rejecting meaning determinism, the sceptical solution also discards privacy and replaces it with intersubjectivity. Intersubjectivity has to be understood in the context of assertability. Rather than look for (possible) explanatory social facts to correspond to meaning attributions, we must appreciate that correction by, and comparison with, others, is essential to all meaning attributions, even to meaning attributions in the first person. The very possibility of meaningful meaning sentences hinges on this: since privacy *cum* classical realism ends in paradox, intersubjectivity *cum* assertability is the only option. And, of course, if intersubjectivity *cum* assertability is the only option then meaning and rule-following cannot be understood outside a social setting. This is the private language argument that Kripke sees as the upshot of Wittgenstein's reflections on rule-following. And it precedes what is more conventionally called "the private language argument" located in the sections following §243 of *PI*: the argument that there cannot be a language the words of which refer to its speaker's immediate, private sensations.

There are at least two objections that naturally arise at this point. One is directed against the argument of *WRPL* itself (as here reconstructed), the other more immediately directed against my reconstruction. The first objection is this. The last paragraph assumes that privacy is inseparable from classical realism, and that intersubjectivity is tied to assertability. This is too hasty. It begs the question against the combination of a deflated version of privacy and assertability.[13] I write "a deflated version of privacy" since the original privacy with its assumption of intrinsic meaning-constituting mental states cannot be a bedfellow to assertability. The deflated version of privacy is the simple view that meaning and rule-following can be understood without any reference to a social setting. This reformulation shields privacy from arguments against the possibility of meaning-constituting mental states. And the deflated privacy can then be given substance by combining it with "private" assertability conditions. These are assertability conditions that make no reference to others.

WRPL does not formulate this option very clearly, and hence it is not obvious what the intended reply is. But I take it that the main objection must be that once we put pressure on the proposal it either falls back on meaning-determinist notions, or else loses the idea, essential to our talk of meaning, that speakers and rule-followers can go wrong. The latter danger rears its head if the currently considered position ends up equating what the speaker is inclined to do with what it is right for him to do. Kripke makes this point by quoting *PI* (§202): "To think one is obeying a rule is not to obey a rule. Hence it is not possible to obey a rule 'privately'; otherwise thinking one was obeying a rule would be the same as obeying it" (*WRPL*: 89). There must remain a possibility for the private rule-follower or "meaner" to go wrong, for instance, by believing himself to be an adder when in fact he is not. In the intersubjective scenario the judgement "Jones is not following the rule for addition" is made by Smith on the basis of a comparison between the responses to plus-queries of Jones and Smith himself. How can the private rule-follower capture this duality of perspective? The natural solution is to replace intersubjectivity with intrasubjectivity. Unfortunately, in going down this route we end up having to return to meaning-determinist ideas. For what would it mean to say that a social isolate Jones judges himself to have misapplied one of his terms on a previous occasion? If it is to say more than that Jones had one inclination then, now another – losing again the difference between thinking one is obeying and obeying – then it can only amount to saying that Jones realizes now that his previous use was not in line with a still earlier *intention* to use his term one way rather than another. And with this talk of intention we are back at the beginning: what makes it so that Jones had the intention to mean *addition* rather than *quaddition*?

> As members of the community correct each other, might a given individual correct himself? ... Indeed, in the absence of Wittgenstein's sceptical paradox, it would appear that an individual remembers his own "intentions" and can use one memory of these intentions to correct another mistaken memory. In the presence of the paradox, any such "naive" ideas are meaningless. (*WRPL*: 112, n.88)

Two paragraphs earlier, I mentioned two objections to my way of presenting the argument against private language in *WRPL*. Here is the second. Is my reconstruction in line with how Kripke himself presents the argument? To put it in a nutshell, on my reconstruction the argument goes as follows:

[1] Meaning determinism is untenable.
[2] Privacy is a central part of meaning determinism.
[3] There are three alternatives to (the original) privacy:
    [a] deflated privacy (combined with assertability)
    [b] meaning-determinist intersubjectivity
    [c] intersubjectivity combined with assertability.
[4] Deflated privacy is untenable.
[5] Meaning-determinist intersubjectivity is untenable.
[6] Intersubjectivity combined with assertability is the correct view.
[7] Intersubjectivity must fit with assertability and assertability with intersubjectivity (since both have been established as correct.)
[8] Assertability conditions necessarily involve social settings.
[9] There cannot be a private linguist, a private rule-follower.

The objection insists on a different reconstruction:

[1] Classical realism is wrong.
[2] Assertability is correct.
[3] Our assertability conditions happen to make reference to social settings.
[4] There cannot be a private linguist.

In defence of the second reading, one might point to the following passages. Kripke writes that the "impossibility of private language emerges as a corollary of his [Wittgenstein's] solution to his own paradox" (*WRPL*: 68), and that the "argument against 'private' rules" is "consequent" on the sceptical solution. And he goes

31

on to urge that "[f]ollowing Wittgenstein's exhortation not to think but to look, we will not reason *a priori* about the role such statements [meaning attributions] *ought* to play; rather we will find out what circumstances *actually* license such assertions and what role this license *actually* plays" (*WRPL*: 86–7). These passages suggest that our meaning attributions can and should merely be described – we must not say which form they *must take*; all we can do is describe the form they *do in fact take*. In other words, contrary to my suggestion above, the sceptical solution cannot include a general argument as to why assertability conditions have to be social.

I remain unconvinced. My reconstruction does not "reason *a priori*" about the role of meaning attributions; it merely points out that whatever their role, their assertability conditions must involve other people (if not in how they are formulated, then at least in the way they are used). Nor does my reconstruction "reason *a priori*" about the circumstances that license meaning assertions; it merely points out that whatever these circumstances happen to be, they must involve an intersubjective comparison. I can even agree that the impossibility of private language emerges as a corollary of the sceptical solution. This is correct, provided one sees the shift from classical realism to assertability as the core of the sceptical solution, as Kripke tends to do.

There is a further reason for preferring my reconstruction. This is that on the second interpretation the whole argument against private language is open to a devastating objection: it is hard to see how we can derive an impossibility claim from a mere description of the assertability conditions of our language.[14] If the impossibility of private language depends only on potentially contingent features of our historically grown language and its assertability conditions – that is, that its assertability conditions are social – then there is no reason to believe that private languages are impossible in principle. After all, it is entirely possible that there might be languages in which other assertability conditions operate. Somehow I find it implausible that a modal logician of Kripke's standing could have overlooked this *non sequitur* from the actual to the impossible.

The sceptical solution IV: from semantic to intersubjective normativity

What happens to semantic normativity in the sceptical solution? The quick answer is that it is thrown out with the bathwater of meaning determinism. After all, there are no meaning-constituting mental states that can justify (future) use; no meaning-constituting mental states that can guide the (future) application of signs; and no meaning-constituting mental states that can justify the unhesitating way in which we operate with our words.

But normativity is not simply thrown out lock, stock and barrel; meaning determinism was not altogether wrong to capitalize on the evaluative, prescriptive and justificatory elements in our meaning talk. Rather, meaning determinism misidentified what we might call the "location" of the evaluation, prescription and justification of the use of signs. Meaning determinism tried to anchor these phenomena in the very same mental states that *cause* a speaker to use his words in certain ways. In other words, meaning-constituting mental states were supposed to determine future use both causally and normatively. Alas, there are no mental states such that they can determine actions in both of these two ways at once. This is one important way to read the outcome of the sceptical argument.

There are, of course, mental states that play the causal part. Training a child in the use of a word creates, in the child, inclinations and dispositions to use the word in certain ways and not in others. It also creates, in the child, inclinations and dispositions to declare certain uses of the word "correct" and certain other uses "incorrect". The training of the child, and her "catching on", are causes of her subsequent verbal behaviour. But all this does not take us out of the realm of causality, and it does not take us into the realm of normative talk where the distinction between "seems correct" and "is correct" is paramount.

Normative considerations enter through intersubjective comparisons and thus through assertability conditions for meaning attributions. This is easiest to appreciate in a language-teaching context (*WRPL*: 89–90). Teachers evaluate their pupils' linguistic performances as correct and incorrect, right and wrong. And they tell their pupils how they ought to, or must, use a word if they wish to use it correctly. (Usually this qualification plays a small role only: teachers demand that their pupils wish to speak correctly.) In this way, teachers – not meaning-constituting mental states – make the pupils' uses of their words "non-blind"; teachers – not meaning-constituting mental states – provide the pupils with guidance; and it is the teachers' advice and training – not meaning-constituting mental states – that pupils can draw on to justify the ways they apply their new terms. To use good old-fashioned Marxian jargon, in attributing the teachers' doing to a mental state, meaning determinism "reifies" a social process into an individual-psychological thing.

It is not just the pupils' linguistic behaviour that is subject to evaluation and justification. The teachers' interpretative doing in assessing whether their pupils mean, say, addition by "+", is itself usually non-blind, guided and justified. As a member of a linguistic community, the teacher has herself undergone training both in arithmetic and in how to determine whether a pupil ought to be classified as having mastered addition. The assertability conditions for meaning attributions such as "Jones means addition by '+'", or "Jones has mastered addition" include criteria such as:

> for small enough examples, the child must produce, almost all the time, the "right" answer. ... For larger computations, the child can make more mistakes than for "small" problems, but must get a certain number right and, when it is wrong, it must recognizably be "trying to follow" the proper procedure .... (*WRPL*: 89–90)

These rough and ready criteria guide the teacher in her assessment; they make her assessment non-blind and they allow the teacher to justify her meaning attributions. And they make it possible for others (other teachers, for example) to criticize a given teacher's assessments. Here too the guidance and justification does not come from meaning-determining mental states that determine in advance how these criteria ought to be used. The criteria exist as public, not as private, objects: they exist as objects that are produced by many community members in the appropriate circumstances, and as objects that are cited and invoked in the training of teachers.

I have focused on the case of the teacher, but what has been said here about the teacher–pupil relationship clearly holds, *mutatis mutandis*, much more generally. In attributing meaning to others, we all make use of rough and ready public assertability conditions; we all are guided by how others speak; and we all justify our uses of words with reference to how others, usually persons of some authority in linguistic matter, express themselves.

Before leaving intersubjective normativity, something has to be said about the fate of left-to-right interpretation of meaning conditionals. Take the meaning conditional "If Jones means addition by '+', then Jones will (must, ought to) reply '125'". (Of course, this ignores a host of qualifications that are needed in the antecedent.) Meaning determinists analyse meaning conditionals as follows. It is the mental state of meaning addition by "+" that makes it so that Jones will, and ought to, reply "125". Again, in moving from the antecedent to the consequent, the meaning determinist conflates causal and normative issues. Now, meaning conditionals are a central part of our everyday talk about meaning and thus meaning scepticism had better not reject them altogether. Reinterpretation is called for. Meaning conditionals must be understood in their contrapositive form, that is, read from right to left with both sides negated: "If Jones does *not* come out with '125' when asked about '68 + 57', we cannot assert that he means addition by '+'" (*WRPL*: 95).[15] In this form, they state (part of) an assertability condition for the meaning attribution "Jones means addition by '+'". And in this form they have an important role when we undertake to justify our meaning attributions. Their normativity is thereby twofold: they set a standard for the one who is being assessed, and they provide the assessor with a means of justifying her assessment.

The sceptical solution V: from metaphysical to functional justification

Recall that the meaning determinist engages in his project in order to make sense of meaning sentences. This project of making sense is ultimately a project of justification. The meaning determinist believes that our meaning sentences need a philosophical licence and that this licence is provided by his overall proposal. The sceptical argument has shown that this licence is unavailable. What happens to justification within meaning scepticism? Meaning scepticism insists that "our ordinary practice or belief is justified because – contrary appearances notwithstanding – it need not require the justification the sceptic has shown to be untenable" (*WRPL*: 66). And the sceptical solution goes on to offer an alternative form of justification.

This alternative is first introduced where Kripke presents Wittgenstein's overall alternative to (meaning-determinist) truth-conditional semantics:

> Wittgenstein replaces the question, "What must be the case for this sentence to be true?" by two others: first, "Under what conditions may this form of words be appropriately asserted (or denied)?"; second, given an answer to the first question, "What is the role, and the utility, in our lives of our practice of asserting (or denying) the form of words under these conditions?" (*WRPL*: 73)

The first new question is answered by identifying the assertability conditions for a given form of words. For present concerns, it is the second question that is more important. To answer it, for a given practice of asserting, is to show that the practice has a function in our social life, that is, that the practice is not idle: "granted that our language game permits a certain 'move' (assertion) under certain specifiable conditions, what is the role in our lives of such permission? Such a role must exist if this aspect of the language game is not to be idle" (*WRPL*: 75).

Before introducing the meaning sceptic's answer to this second question for the case of meaning attributions, it is important to underline the new sense of justification that is here introduced. For the meaning determinist the justification of our meaning sentences must come from ontological considerations. The justification of our meaning sentences is an exercise in metaphysics. For the meaning sceptic the justification of our meaning sentences must come from pragmatic, sociological or anthropological considerations. For him the justification of our meaning sentences is an exercise in (the philosophy of) the social sciences. The importance of this shift from meaning determinism to meaning scepticism can, of course, hardly be exaggerated.

The meaning sceptic's answer to the second question with respect to meaning sentences goes as follows. The practice of attributing meaning is useful because it allows us to signal to our interlocutors who is a reliable partner in various forms of interaction. By calling Jones "an adder", Smith might let his audience know that Jones can be relied on in business interactions, preparing tax declarations or counting the children in the schoolyard. More generally, by "attributing to others the mastery of certain concepts or rules" we show "that we expect them to behave as we do" (*WRPL*: 75). By the same token, we can also use meaning sentences to warn our audience of certain individuals: "Jones does not (yet) mean addition by '+'" can be reason enough not to leave a calculation in his incapable hands.

WRPL sometimes expresses these ideas in terms of "admitting someone into a community": "An individual who passes such tests [for being an adder] is admitted into the community as an adder; an individual who passes such tests in enough other cases is admitted as a normal speaker of the language and member of the community" (*WRPL*: 93). In another passage it is said that individuals who pass some "tests" are taken "provisionally into the community, as long as further deviant behaviour does not exclude them" (*WRPL*: 95).

How are we to interpret the view that is put forward in these passages? The standard answer in the secondary literature goes as follows. Kripke tells us two main things about utterances such as (#) "Jones means addition by '+'": first, they do not correspond to facts; and secondly, in uttering them we bring it about (or make it more likely) that Jones occupies a certain social status – the social status of being reliable in social interactions involving addition. Putting these two elements together, it seems obvious that meaning scepticism must be a form of non-factualism. A non-factualist about a certain class of declarative sentences denies that for any sentence *s* of this class we can infer "'*s*' is true" or "It is a fact that *s*" from *s*. Non-factualism is usually a form of projectivism. Forms of projectivism include emotivism,[16] quasi-realism,[17] and what we might call "performativism". For the emotivist and the quasi-realist (#) is similar in function to saying "Hooray to the way in which Jones operates with '+'". (The quasi-realist differs from the emotivist in that he seeks to explain how we can legitimately talk *as if* we were entitled to the assumption that there are meaning facts, even though we are not.[18]) The advocate of a performative reading of meaning attributions holds that in uttering (#) we change the social world: we make it so that Jones has now a certain social status as reliable partner in certain interactions (such as counting money).

Put in a nutshell, proponents of the non-factualist or projectivist reading reason as follows:

[1] The sceptic rejects classical realism.

Ergo: [2] The sceptic rejects truth-conditions and thus facts as providers of meaning for declarative sentences.

Ergo: [3] The sceptic commits to non-factualism (at least) with respect to meaning attributions.

Ergo – and since projectivism is the only alternative to non-factualism:

[4] The sceptic is committed to projectivism.

Ergo: [5] (#) must be analysed along projectivist lines.

I object to this argument. The sceptic does not reject all forms of truth-conditions, he merely rejects truth-conditions as construed by the meaning determinist. In other words, the sceptic opposes classical realism, but the rejection of classical realism leaves open the possibility that meaning attributions are descriptions of how things stand with a speaker or thinker. In other words, by ignoring the distinction between different conceptions of truth-conditions, the argument obscures the fact that projectivism and meaning-determinist factualism do not exhaust the theoretical options. According to the sceptical solution, meaning attributions are descriptions and they require a minimal conception of truth-conditions.

Taking this line is not, of course, to deny that utterances of (#) can serve the purpose of making it so that Jones receives the status of being a reliable adder. But taking this line allows us to say that utterances of (#) may well be reports (at the same time). After all, utterances of (#) report on Jones's reliability in matters to do with counting; and they may well report to a newcomer on the status that Jones has already achieved in the community (i.e. the status of being a reliable adder).

So, by means of utterances such as (#) we both (help to) confer social statuses and report on Jones's ability to add. The sceptical solution does not use the language of "(social) statuses", but it seems natural enough. Indeed, it even helps in making sense of a passage that takes us back to privacy: Kripke's discussion of Robinson Crusoe. Perhaps surprisingly, Kripke thinks that meaning scepticism is not obliged to insist that "Robinson Crusoe, isolated on an island, cannot be said to follow any rules, no matter what he does". Kripke continues:

> What does follow is that *if* we think of Crusoe as following rules, we are taking him into our community and applying our criteria for rule following to him. … Remember that Wittgenstein's theory is one of assertability conditions. Our community can assert of any individual that he follows a rule if he passes the tests for rule following applied to any member of the community. (*WRPL*: 110)

There is something *prima facie* implausible about this proposal. Of course we can only say of Crusoe that he follows rules if he fulfils our criteria for being a rule-follower. Who would have thought otherwise? But precisely because the thought is so pedestrian, it speaks *against* rather than in favour of intersubjectivity. Compare: we can only say of an animal that it is a frog if it fulfils our criteria for being a frog. Now, whether or not the animal fulfils our criteria of being a frog has nothing to do with whether or not we interact with it. And likewise, it seems, whether or not Crusoe fulfils our criteria for being a rule-follower is something that has nothing to do with whether or not we interact with him. But then, it seems, there is nothing to rule out a private rule-follower. Crusoe does not have to be part of our community – actually or virtually – for him to either be or not be a rule-follower (by our criteria).[19]

It is possible to answer this worry with the distinction between a social status and a natural category, a social kind (term) and a natural kind (term). Let us grant that something is correctly called "frog" if, and only if, it fulfils our criteria for being a frog. In the case of "frog", and other natural categories, such criteria all concern different features of the frog and its environment. But none concerns (except accidentally) our relationship with the frog. It is here that social statuses or social kind terms differ. Consider the social status of being a king. One of the central criteria for being (our) king is that some of us, some officials in our midst, have conferred this status on a particular individual. It is not enough for someone – say on Alpha Centauri – to fit ever so many of our criteria for kinghood; unless the status has *actually* been conferred, the person does not fit all of the criteria. Something similar holds in the case of Crusoe. It is not enough for a socially isolated Crusoe to fit many of our criteria for being a rule-follower. Unless the status has *actually* been conferred, unless Crusoe has been granted the status of being a rule-follower, unless Crusoe has been granted the status of being one of us, he cannot be thought of as a rule-follower at all.

The sceptical solution VI: from grasping to primitiveness

The meaning-determinist assumptions around grasping have already been undermined by what was said in previous sections. After all, grasping is inseparable from privacy and semantic normativity, assumptions that have been replaced with successor concepts. Moreover, some of the motivation for grasping has been captured in confidence: sometimes, at the conclusion of a learning process, we feel inclined and justified to say "now I have got it, now I can go on". But confidence does not help with some other ingredients of grasping, such as explanation, intending, or interpreting.

The meaning-sceptical alternative to these latter ideas is to see linguistic inclinations as "primitive". When we give the answer "125" to "68 + 57 = ?", we do so neither on the basis of an interpretation of previous linguistic intentions, nor on the basis of having grasped the concept of addition. Our inclination to give particular answers to particular addition problems is "to be regarded as primitive" (*WRPL*: 91). That is to say, we are entitled to say that Jones has grasped the concept of addition because he has passed our tests, among which, say, is that he answers "125" to "68 + 57 = ?". We cannot further explain Jones's inclinations regarding plus-queries by drawing on concepts such as meaning, intention, grasping or interpretation. To give up meaning determinism is to recognize that none of these concepts can be used to explain linguistic behaviour.

It is not just Jones's (or our) inclination to give particular answers to particular addition problems that is to be regarded as primitive. Equally primitive is his inclination to say "I have got it" when being taught how to apply a (for him) new word, and his inclination to self-ascribe meaning addition by "+". Here, too, the inclination is prior to, not dependent on, any interpretation of previous practice, previous intention or previous grasp of a concept.

Moreover, primitiveness is also important as a phenomenon of intersubjective normativity. Go back to the case where Smith tests whether it would be appropriate to assert that Jones means addition by "+". In doing so, Smith compares his primitive inclination to give particular answers to particular plus-queries with

Jones's primitive inclination. And no less primitive is Smith's inclination to judge that Jones is an adder. None of the three phenomena involved – Jones's giving his answers to plus-queries, Smith producing his own answers, and Smith comparing the two – are based on the interpretation of intentions or concepts. As Kripke puts it:

> In all this, Smith's inclinations are regarded as just as primitive as Jones's. In no way does Smith test directly whether Jones may have in his head some rule agreeing with the one in Smith's head. Rather the point is that if, in enough concrete cases, Jones's inclinations agree with Smith's, Smith will judge that Jones is indeed following the rule for addition. (*WRPL*: 91)

Finally, primitiveness also concerns agreement among ourselves. The practice of attributing meanings to others could not exist if we did not usually agree in our responses and inclinations. If Jones's and Smith's inclinations to answer plus-queries differed radically, then Jones could never arrive at meaning attributions for Smith. And so for all concepts. We would be reduced to a "babble of disagreement" (*WRPL*: 92), and would lack a common "form of life": "The set of responses in which we agree, and the way they interweave with our activities, is our *form of life*. Beings who agreed in consistently giving bizarre quus-like responses would share in another form of life" (*WRPL*: 97).

This "primitive agreement" in responses is the successor to grasping as explanation: we cannot explain agreement in inclinations on the basis of agreement in concepts or intentions. Just as an individual's inclinations are prior to his concepts, so the agreement in inclinations between individuals is prior to their agreement in concepts:

> We cannot say that we all respond as we do to "68 + 57" *because* we all grasp the concept of addition in the same way … There is no objective fact – that we all mean addition by "+", or even that a given individual does – that explains our agreement in particular cases. Rather our license to say of each other that we mean addition by "+" is part of a "language game" that sustains itself only because of the brute fact that we generally agree. (*WRPL*: 97)

The sceptical solution VII: from objectivity to finiteness

Meaning determinism is committed to (the) objectivity (of meaning). This is the idea that to mean addition by "+" is to have a meaning-constituting mental state that contains and determines ("in a queer way") an infinity of correct answers to plus-queries. Consider the consequences of this view for meaning attributions:

every attribution that someone means addition by "+" would inevitably be fundamentally underdetermined by the evidence. Alternative, sceptical, hypotheses would always be possible and legitimate. This underdetermination problem was exploited to the full by the meaning sceptic in Chapter 2 of *WRPL*.

How then does meaning scepticism deal with the infinity involved in attributing addition (and other mathematical functions) to someone? Given that the meaning sceptic has made so much of the finite character of mental states, is he not obliged to deny that we can ever attribute concepts involving infinities?

Here it is important to remember that throughout the whole argument of *WRPL* the legitimacy of our ordinary meaning sentences is never in doubt. Meaning determinism and meaning scepticism are alternative ways of making sense of our ordinary meaning sentences, but neither meaning determinism nor meaning scepticism seeks to reform the way we speak. It thus cannot be the position of meaning scepticism that we somehow go wrong in, say, attributing addition to one another. *WRPL* makes this point by contrasting meaning scepticism with "finitism" in mathematics. Finitists – noting that talk of infinities is based on "nothing more" than finite, "surveyable", proofs – insist on reforming mathematical language. All reference to infinities is to be dropped. For the meaning sceptic this move is illegitimate, precisely because it violates the stricture that the ordinary ways of speaking are not to be changed.

> Finitists … regard the infinitistic part of mathematics as meaningless. Such opinions are misguided: they are attempts to repudiate our ordinary language game. In this game we are allowed, for certain purposes, to assert statements about … mathematical functions under certain circumstances. Although the criteria for judging that such statements are legitimately introduced are indeed … finite, finite … statements cannot replace their role in our language as we use it.
>
> (*WRPL*: 107)

Statements such as "Jones means addition by '+'" have important functions in our language games of meaning attribution. We are inclined to produce these statements on the basis of a finite number of tests and comparisons with our own inclinations. This finiteness is not a regrettable shortcoming that would introduce uncertainty and underdetermination. To believe that it is a shortcoming is to contrast it with an ideal meaning determinism, which has proved untenable. At this point finiteness links up with primitiveness: finiteness is not "a problem" or "shortcoming" since our inclinations are always already broadly in agreement. As Wittgenstein put it in the *Investigations*: our "eyes … are shut" in similar ways (*PI*: §224).[20] This makes it unlikely, empirically unlikely, that our inclinations will deviate in the future. And it is this probability that makes it natural for us to always say more, in and with our meaning ascriptions, than is covered by our finite number of tests.

The sceptical solution: a summary

Here is a summary of the central ingredients of the sceptical solution or meaning scepticism[21]:

(MS-1) Confidence (successor to immediate knowledge): subject to the correction by others, we are entitled to ascribe meanings to ourselves.

(MS-2) Intersubjectivity (successor to privacy): attributions of meaning make sense only in a social setting. Assertability conditions essentially involve communities.

(MS-3) Primitiveness (successor to grasping): our inclinations to use our words, our feeling that we have "got it" and our first-person and third-person meaning attributions are all primitive. That is, they cannot be explained by the grasp of concepts, or interpretations of our past uses or past or present intentions.

(MS-4) Intersubjective normativity (successor to semantic normativity): there is no special form of normativity based on meaning-constituting mental states. We are guided by others; we justify our applications of terms, as well as our meaning attributions, on the basis of publicly available criteria.

(MS-5) Finiteness (successor to objectivity): the attribution of infinitary concepts to others is legitimate. But we attribute infinitary concepts on the basis of finite, surveyable, evidence. What makes this possible is that "our eyes are shut" in similar ways.

(MS-6) Assertability (successor to classical realism): the meaning of declarative sentences is given by rough and ready assertability conditions, not by (meaning-determinist) truth-conditions.

(MS-7) Functional justification (successor to metaphysical justification): our practices of meaning attribution are justified on the basis of social-functional considerations. To say that "Jones means addition by '+'" is not just a description; it is also to give Jones a certain social status.

Concepts and words, meanings and rules

Throughout the reconstruction of Chapters 2 and 3 of *WRPL* above I have not committed openly to stances with respect to two important interpretational issues. The time has come to address them. The first concerns the scope of Kripke's Wittgenstein's argument, the second the relationship between two of his key concepts.

It has sometimes been suggested that the scope of the sceptical argument is narrow in that it concerns only (word) meanings, but not concepts.[22] Here is what makes this thought initially plausible. The very formulation of the sceptical challenge – "How do you know that you mean addition rather than quaddition by '+'?" – is based on a distinction between the "meaning bearer" (+) and the meaning itself (addition or quaddition). This distinction is thus central to the sceptical argument. But in the case of concepts such a distinction cannot be made. A concept is the same as its content; there is no gap between bearer and content.

If this thought were correct then *WRPL* would not be a particularly interesting book. Consider what would happen if concepts were not affected by the argument. If concepts were not affected then they could be used to provide a straight answer to the sceptical challenge even with respect to word meaning. Roughly put, I could say: "I mean *addition* by '+' in a sentence such as '5 + 7 = 12' if in uttering this sentence I have the intention of producing in my audience the belief that *five added to 7 equals 12*". Here the italicized words are concepts in my thoughts.

Fortunately, the above train of thought is not correct.[23] The crucial mistake is to assume that there exists no distinction between content and bearer in the case of concepts. This is wrong. The well-known "language of thought hypothesis" does assume that thought takes place in a mental language and that this language involves *structured content bearers*.[24] The language of thought hypothesis is, of course, controversial. Fortunately, *WRPL* needs only a minimalist version of this idea. *WRPL* does not need the claim that the content bearers on the level of thought be structured. As long as there are representations at all, one can always ask in virtue of what they are representations of one content rather than some other content.

The second interpretational problem concerns the relationship between meaning and rule. *WRPL* treats the problem of rule-following ("What makes it so that Jones follows the rule for addition rather than the rule for quaddition?") and the problem of meaning ("What makes it so that Jones means addition rather than quaddition?") as closely related, or even as identical. Nevertheless, it has been claimed that, in *WRPL*, the connection between the concepts of meaning and content, on the one hand, and the concept of rule-following, on the other, remains obscure. Indeed, it has even been said that "'the rule-following consideration' is, strictly speaking, a misnomer for the discussion on offer".[25]

One way *not* to try to establish such a link between meaning, content and rule is this. What makes it so that an expression has "correctness conditions" is that people follow rules with respect to it. And to say that an expression has "correctness conditions" is to say that there are circumstances under which the expression is applied correctly and circumstances under which the expression is applied incorrectly. Evidently, to be meaningful an expression must have correctness conditions; and undoubtedly the sceptical argument is concerned with what makes it so that an expression has correctness conditions. Why then is it incorrect to say that an expression has "correctness conditions" if, and only if, people follow rules with respect to it? This answer is not hard to find. To follow a rule is itself an intentional action and thus to follow a rule involves concepts. And since, as we have seen, *WRPL* is concerned with both concepts and meanings, we have to explain not just how words acquire meaning – and thus correctness conditions – but also how concepts acquire content – and thus correctness conditions.[26]

Fortunately, I do not think that Kripke is making the unsuccessful suggestion just canvassed. In *WRPL* the concept of a rule does not figure as part of the analysis of the concepts of meaning or content. All three concepts are on a par as far as analysis and explanation are concerned. In each case the focus is on the question of what gives attributions (of rules, of meanings, of concepts) their significance. And the discussion is based on the belief that any solution that would emerge for one of the three cases would also (quickly) solve the remaining cases too. Read in this light, "rule-following considerations" is not a misnomer, although it does not cover the whole area of investigation.

The comparison with Berkeley and Hume

Kripke suggests that his reconstruction of Wittgenstein's position on meaning can be clarified and illuminated by comparing it with Hume's views on causation and Berkeley's discussion of objects. In all three cases we can identify something like the five-part structure of sceptical challenge, sceptical argument, sceptical conclusion, sceptical paradox and sceptical solution.

In Hume the sceptical challenge is to show that causal inference can be justified by a sound demonstration. The sceptical argument shows that all such attempts are bound to fail. Consider the causal inference:

(1) This is bread and thus it will nourish me.

Inference (1) is not itself a logical truth: no contradiction is involved in affirming the premise and denying the conclusion. Hence if we want a justification for (1) we must try to derive it from premises that we know to be true; this is what Hume means by providing a "demonstration" for causal inferences. It is clear that (1) cannot be derived from the two premises (2) and (3):

(2) This is bread.
(3) In the past, bread has nourished me.

Inference (1) does not follow from (2) and (3) since there is no logical necessity for the future to resemble the past. Nor does it help to add the further premise (4):

(4) Future experiences must resemble past experiences.

From (2), (3) and (4) we are entitled to infer (1): the argument is valid. But it is not sound: we do not know that (4) is true. Nor can we derive (4) from (5):

(5) Present experiences resemble past experiences.

The step from (5) to (4) is an instance of the very step that is at issue in (4): are we allowed to assume that the unobserved future will be like the observed past?

The sceptical conclusion is familiar: we cannot get a sound argument for (1). If the acceptability of causal inferences such as (1) depends on our being able to provide a sound demonstration for them, then these causal inferences are not acceptable. If our entitlement to speak of cause and effect depends on such demonstration then we end up with the sceptical paradox: we can never speak of causes and effects. This is paradoxical in so far as we would not know how to get by without causal talk.

Hume accepts the sceptical argument and the sceptical conclusion – he does not believe that there is a straight way out of the problem: there is no (type of) premise that the sceptic has overlooked, no (type of) premise that would allow us to demonstrate (1). Hume's own solution therefore is "sceptical", and he is the first to speak of a "Sceptical Solution of these Doubts".[27] A sceptical solution to a sceptical challenge consists of three elements. First, it accepts that – *under the original understanding of justification* – the sceptic wins. Hume thinks that the sceptical conclusion is inevitable as long as one assumes that a justification of causal inference must be based on a demonstration. Secondly, a sceptical solution holds that – on a different understanding of justification – we can defend the propriety of the practice in question. Hume does not think that we are wrong to engage in the practice of drawing causal inferences. Thirdly, and finally, a sceptical solution dismisses the original understanding of justification as a philosophers' chimera. To replace it by the "different understanding" is to champion common sense over philosophical speculation.

Hume's different understanding of justification is based on a reminder of our nature, of what kind of creature we are. Beings like us cannot help drawing causal inferences; this is a basic psychological fact about us. Our perception of the causal relation is nevertheless open to further analysis: such analysis reveals that contiguity in space and time, as well as a "necessary connexion" are central when we perceive a causal relation between two events. As is well known, the idea of such a "necessary connexion" is based on the experience of a "constant conjunction" between types of events. Instances of eating bread have always been followed by instances of feeling nourished. This constant conjunction "determines" my mind to expect the feeling of being nourished on having eaten bread. Moreover, this "determination of the mind" now becomes the psychological basis for my belief that there exists determination – causal necessitation – in the world outside me. The mind finds it hard to resist the temptation of projecting its own psychological determination onto the relation between the bread and the nourishing feeling itself.

Hume's sceptical solution thus involves an inversion of the relation between causal necessity and causal inference. The received view is to assume that causal necessity is out there in the world and that causal inferences are justified to just the extent to which they capture this necessity. On Hume's sceptical solution, it is our "custom" and "habit" to be disposed to draw causal inferences. And when drawing causal inferences we are prone to project the natural psychological determination of our own mind – the determination to expect certain events on the basis of certain other events – onto these events themselves. ("t'will appear in the end, that the necessary connexion depends upon the inference, instead of the inference's depending on the necessary connexion"[28]).

To this general parallel between Hume and Wittgenstein, Kripke adds three further observations. The first is that Wittgenstein's argument for the impossibility of a private language has a parallel in Hume's argument for the impossibility of "private causation":

> Only when the particular events a and b are thought of as subsumed under two respective event types, A and B, which are related by a generalization that *all* events of type A are followed by events of type B, can a be said to "cause" b. When the events a and b are considered by themselves alone, no causal notions are applicable. This Humean conclusion might be called: the impossibility of private causation.
> (*WRPL*: 67–8)

The second further parallel concerns the inversion of conditionals. Meaning scepticism reads meaning conditionals in their contrapositive form (right to left with both sides negated) and so do Humeans in the case of causal conditionals. Take the causal conditional: "If events of type A cause events of type B, and if an event e of type A occurs, then an event e' of type B must follow" (*WRPL*: 93–4). Humeans hesitate to read this conditional left to right since such reading encourages the view that e necessitates e'. Accordingly, Humeans interpret this conditional as an assertability condition concerning causal claims: "the conditional commits us, whenever we know that an event e of type A occurs and is not followed by an event of type B, to deny that there is a causal connection between the two event types. If we did make such a claim, we must now withdraw it" (*WRPL*: 94).

The third additional analogy exists between meaning scepticism's shift from grasping to primitiveness and Hume's inversion of the relation between causation and constant conjunction. Kripke's Wittgenstein holds that we "do not all say $12 + 7 = 19$ and the like because we all grasp the concept of addition; we say we all grasp the concept of addition because we all say $12 + 7 = 19$ and the like", and Hume insists that "[f]ire and heat are not constantly conjoined because fire causes heat; fire causes heat because they are constantly conjoined" (*WRPL*: 93–4). The same point can also be made by noting that both Hume and Kripke's Wittgenstein insist, respectively, that regularities or uniformities cannot be explained:

Naively, we may wish to explain the observed concomitance of fire and heat by a causal, heat-producing, "power" in the fire. The Humean alleges that any such use of causal powers to explain the regularity is meaningless. Rather we play a language game that allows us to attribute such a causal power to the fire as long as the regularity holds up. The regularity must be taken as a brute fact. So too for Wittgenstein: "What has to be accepted, the given, is ... *forms of life*".

(*WRPL*: 97–8)

Turning from Hume to Berkeley, the first thing to note is that Berkeley does not describe himself as a sceptic. Nevertheless, in his case too we can identify a similar overall argumentative structure. The sceptical challenge in Berkeley's case is to prove that there is anything beyond one's own ideas. The traditional metaphysician tries to meet this challenge by seeking to prove that our ideas are caused by mind-independent material objects. Berkeley's sceptical argument shows that these attempts all fail. For instance, Berkeley insists that we have no plausible account of how inert matter can cause events in our mind. And he argues that the following triad leads us into scepticism:

(a) The mind perceives only its own ideas.
(b) These ideas are produced in our mind by mind-independent external objects.
(c) These external objects cannot be perceived immediately.

Berkeley agrees with Locke on (a) but points out that (b) is a mere hypothesis and that it can be contrasted with other, equally good explanations. It follows that we have no satisfactory justification for our belief in anything beyond our own ideas. This is Berkeley's sceptical conclusion and paradox.

Berkeley accepts that his sceptical argument is sound. But he does not leave things here. Berkeley believes that we can get out of our philosophical difficulty by following his advice to "banish metaphysics ... and recall men to common sense".[29] We banish metaphysics when we give up speculating about matter and causal relations between matter and mind. Such metaphysics cannot justify our belief in a world beyond our ideas.

Berkeley's sceptical solution involves a different form of justification; rather than speculating about matter, Berkeley accepts the belief of "the vulgar" according to which real objects are precisely those objects that we immediately perceive. He then combines this common belief with two other ideas: that the mind perceives only its own ideas, and that only a mind can cause a mind to have ideas. These ideas then become the building blocks of his well-known brand of idealism. Berkeley does not deny that the last-mentioned two ideas are philosophical in origin. Perhaps he thought that they are nevertheless commonsensical enough not to fall under the charge of being "metaphysical".

Kripke gives more weight to the analogy between Hume and Wittgenstein than to the parallel between Berkeley and Wittgenstein. But he finds the latter comparison particularly illuminating when it comes to understanding how a sceptical solution relates to the ordinary talk and belief of the "vulgar" or the "common man". Berkeley denies that his rejection of matter and of mind-independent objects puts him at odds with common sense. When common-sense people speak of objects as being "external" or "material", they do not mean what the metaphysicians assume they must mean: they do not refer to the metaphysical absurdity of mind-independent entities. By "external" or "material objects" the common folks only mean something like "an idea produced in me independently of my will" (*WRPL*: 64). Kripke's Wittgenstein likewise holds that "the appearance that our ordinary concept of meaning demands such a fact [i.e. a meaning-constituting mental fact] is based on a philosophical misconstrual – albeit a natural one – of such ordinary expressions as 'he meant such-and-such', 'the steps are determined by the formula', and the like" (*WRPL*: 65–6). Kripke also sees the following passage from *PI* (§194) as clearly Berkeleyan in spirit: "When we do philosophy we are like savages, primitive people, who hear the expressions of civilized men, put a false interpretation on them, and then draw the queerest conclusions from it" (*WRPL*: 66).

Although Berkeley insists time and time again that common-sense people agree with his interpretation of their talk and beliefs, on some occasions at least he feels forced to backtrack. Kripke mentions a passage from the *Principles of Human Knowledge* where Berkeley admits denying a doctrine "strangely prevailing amongst men".[30] But Berkeley avoids contradicting himself; he goes on to explain that sometimes ordinary people – to their own detriment – let themselves be influenced by philosophical theory (*WRPL*: 70). On another occasion in the same work, a passage not noted in *WRPL*, Berkeley solves the same problem in a different way. Although it might *seem* that common sense believes objects of perception to exist independently of the mind, it cannot *really* do so. For Berkeley the concept of a mind-independent object is a *contradictio in adiecto*. And: "strictly speaking, to believe that which involves a contradiction, or has no meaning in it, is impossible".[31] It is also worth noting that Berkeley is sometimes satisfied to preserve ordinary people's talk rather than their beliefs: "we ought to think with the learned, and speak with the vulgar".[32] Thus when the vulgar speak of fire heating and water cooling we should interpret this talk in a way that acknowledges God as the ultimate source of all regularity in nature.

In Kripke's view, Berkeley's wavering and backtracking on this point is not due to sloppy thinking. Every proponent of a sceptical solution is faced with the following problem. He agrees with his "dogmatic" ("metaphysical" or "meaning-determinist") interlocutor that ordinary talk should not be changed; the sceptic and the dogmatic interlocutor disagree "merely" over the correct interpretation of ordinary talk. Unfortunately, the dogmatic interlocutor's philosophical interpretation of ordinary talk has been extremely influential. Indeed, so much so that this talk and that interpretation have become almost inseparable. Ordinary talk is "heard" by many of its (philosophical) users as expressing the dogmatic interpretation directly; it is as if it were not just an interpretation of that talk but its very meaning. The sceptical solution is, of course, the denial of the dogmatic interpretation. But how can this denial be stated? Given the way the dogmatic interpretation has become intertwined with ordinary talk, one tempting way would be to deny the ordinary talk and say: "meaning does not determine use", or "fire does not cause heat". Alas, in putting things this way the proposal of the sceptical solution would not leave ordinary talk unchanged. The only alternative is to emphasize the propriety of ordinary talk and restrict one's opposition to the talk's interpretation. This path too is not without problems, however. On the one hand, any affirmation of ordinary talk is easily "heard" as an affirmation of the dogmatic interpretation. On the other hand, stating the interpretation to be rejected is not easy. Take "fire burns the house". We might say it would be wrong to interpret this as "the external, mind-independent fire burns the external, mind-independent house", but this sentence too is alright, as long as it is not given the mistaken dogmatic interpretation.

Kripke suggests that these difficulties concerning the presentation of a sceptical solution explain, in part, why Wittgenstein wrote aphorisms and avoided "the form of definite theses". Wittgenstein has to shun definite theses on pain of "formulating his doctrines in a form that consists in apparent sceptical denials of our ordinary assertions" (*WRPL*: 69). Kripke feels slightly uneasy about this explanation. He worries that it contradicts Wittgenstein's "notorious and cryptic maxim" in §128 of the *Investigations*: "If one tried to advance *theses* in philosophy, it would never be possible to debate them, because everyone would agree to them" (*PI*: §128). Maybe so. But perhaps a different perspective is also possible, and indeed it would be in line with Berkeley's insistence on the proximity of his sceptical solution to common sense. Note that §128 is something like the conclusion of the two previous paragraphs:

> 126. Philosophy simply puts everything before us, and neither explains nor deduces anything. – Since everything lies open to view there is nothing to explain. For what is hidden, for example, is of no interest to us.
>
> One might also give the name "philosophy" to what is possible *before* all new discoveries and inventions.
>
> 127. The work of philosophy consists in assembling reminders for a particular purpose.

These passages suggest not that Wittgenstein was seeking to *avoid* advancing "definite theses" but that there *are no* definite theses for him to advance. The bulk of the work of a meaning-sceptical philosopher is negative or therapeutic: it is to remove confused philosophical ideas that obscure our view of our practices. Once these obstacles have been taken out, we see our practices as they are, and as not needing the confused ideas as their interpretation, explanation and justification. Of course, the sceptical solution itself also tells us things about our practices and talk. It has even been said above that it provides these practices and this talk with a new interpretation and justification. True enough. But we must not forget that this "new interpretation and justification" is fundamentally different from the interpretation and justification it replaces: it is based on anthropology and sociology (or theology, in Berkeley) rather than metaphysics, and it is exoteric rather than esoteric: one does not need to be a metaphysician (or trained philosopher) to identify our rough criteria for deciding whether a child means addition by "+", and one does not need to be a philosopher to recognize why we find it useful to identify people whose linguistic behaviour is erratic. The meaning-sceptical interpretation is something with which "everyone would agree". Or so Kripke's Wittgenstein might have thought.

Conclusion

I have tried above to make plausible a specific reconstruction of the overall argument in *WRPL*. Of course, my case in favour of this reconstruction is not yet complete. I hope to strengthen it in the remainder of this book. And I shall do so in the context of attempts to provide answers to all the major critics of *WRPL*. Chapter 2 will focus on debates over semantic normativity; Chapter 3 will concentrate on defences of reductive semantic dispositionalism: Chapter 4 will be concerned with new forms of Platonism and the algorithm response; Chapter 5 will revisit classical realism and factualism; Chapter 6 will shield intersubjectivity from its many detractors; Chapter 7 will turn to primitivist responses; and Chapter 8 will be a pleading for Kripke's interpretation of Wittgenstein.[33]

TWO

Normativitiy

Introduction

A good deal of the debate over Kripke's *Wittgenstein on Rules and Private Language* has concerned the role of normativity considerations in the sceptical argument and in the sceptical solution. Alas, there is little consensus among commentators on either the correct interpretation, or the truth, of these considerations in either context. Interpreters give different answers to the questions of how normativity considerations are supposed to tell against dispositionalism, and what kind of normativity survives the shift to the sceptical solution. And many critics insist that the normativity considerations of Kripke's Wittgenstein fail to convince under any of the proposed interpretations.

The discussion over *WRPL* has made salient a fundamental divide in contemporary philosophy of language and mind: the divide between "semantic normativists" and "semantic anti-normativists". Semantic normativists such as Crispin Wright regard it as "platitudinous to say … [that] … meaning is normative".[1] Semantic anti-normativists such as Akeel Bilgrami hold that "normativity is irrelevant to the meaning of words".[2] Almost all commentators assume that Kripke's Wittgenstein belongs among the semantic normativists. I shall argue that this classification is mistaken. Semantic normativity is a central part of meaning determinism. But far from endorsing semantic normativity, Kripke's Wittgenstein firmly rejects it.

The argument of this chapter develops in four stages. I shall start with a brief summary of the competing positions in the controversy over semantic normativity. This is meant to set the stage for my discussion of the disputes over *WRPL*. Then, in stage two, I shall present and criticize the most influential interpretation of the normativity considerations in *WRPL*. This interpretation was put forward by Paul Boghossian in 1989. I shall argue that Boghossian's proposal not only leaves Kripke's Wittgenstein with a deficient position but that it also fails to do justice to the text it purports to interpret. In the third stage, I shall discuss a number of revisionist and reformist recommendations for defending disposition-alism against normativity arguments. I shall seek to explain why none of these recommendations works. Finally, in stage four, I shall consider a revolutionary alternative to the sceptical solution. This position rejects semantic normativity as well as meaning determinism, but it refuses to endorse meaning scepticism. Of particular importance for our concerns is that this position criticizes the norma-tivity considerations in both the sceptical argument and the sceptical solution. I am referring of course to Donald Davidson's philosophy of meaning and com-munication. A critical dialogue between Davidson and Kripke's Wittgenstein will take up almost half of this chapter.

The normativity of meaning: between platitude and confusion

The contemporary controversy over the normativity of meaning is much broader than the debates surrounding *WRPL*. Leaving *WRPL* momentarily in the back-ground, it will be useful for what follows briefly to sample the wider dispute. As far as semantic normativists are concerned, suffice it here to cite five well-known statements of the position:

> [T]o learn the meaning of a word is to acquire an understanding that obliges us subsequently – if we have occasion to deploy the concept in question – to judge and speak in certain determinate ways, on pain of failure to obey the dictates of the meaning we have grasped …
> (John McDowell)[3]

> To mean something by a word, one must regard oneself as respon-sible to a norm. Wittgenstein himself extends his thoughts about rule-following from meaning to content-bearing states like wishes or expectations, and that suggests a generalization on these lines: our deal-ings with content must be understood in terms of the idea that mental activity is undertaken under the aspect of allegiance to norms.
> (John McDowell and Philip Pettit)[4]

> Meaning, it is again platitudinous to say, is normative: it is because statements have meaning that there is such a thing as correct, or incorrect, use of them. (Crispin Wright)[5]

> [A]ny speaker beyond the initial stages of mastering language must have some conception of what language he is speaking and hold him-self responsible to that. … a dictionary cannot help being treated as authoritative, just as a book of rules of games acquires an authority to

which its author may not have aspired. The reason is similar in both cases. Using language and playing a game are not like doing one's hair and taking a bath. One may do either of the last two things as one likes and still be doing it. But, if the game ceases to have rules, it ceases to be a game, and, if there cease to be right and wrong uses of a word, the word loses its meaning.   (Michael Dummett)[6]

The concept of meaning is a normative concept. … meanings determine [how words] ought to be used, how those who use concepts with those contents are committed thereby to apply them.
                                                (Robert Brandom)[7]

Semantic anti-normativists have produced a number of arguments in support of their position. These can be grouped into two main strategies. The first strategy is to insist that talk of semantic normativity is based on a misidentification. What the normativist sees as *semantic* normativity is really *some other form* of normativity.

Several semantic anti-normativists suggest that semantic normativists are misled by the frequency of normative-prescriptive language in teaching contexts.[8] Teachers frequently tell their students that they "ought" to speak in certain ways; for instance, that they "ought" to use the word "*Windpocken*" in German where in English they would use the word "chickenpox". As semantic anti-normativists see it, this use of "ought" does not rely on a special semantic or lexical form of normativity. The normativity in question is prudential only: the student is told how it would be wise to speak, provided she wants to be understood in German-speaking countries.

Uses of language are also subject to various pragmatic rules, for instance to rules that define speech acts and their constitutive commitments. But the existence of such rules does not tell in favour of semantic normativity either. The rules in question are, after all, *pragmatic*, not *semantic*. The semantic normativist does not have the option of denying the boundary between semantics and pragmatics. To do so would be to invoke or propose a highly controversial theory of meaning. And this does not square with the normativists' intention of invoking normativity as something like a "theory-independent 'litmus test'".[9]

According to semantic anti-normativists, their opponents also tend to conflate norms of semantics with norms of rationality.[10] The semantic normativist believes that "norms are built into – some would say they constitute – the concepts we apply. If we do not respect the norms … then we are not really applying these concepts". This thought is based on

a confusion between two quite different things – the norm-free concepts (meanings) we intentionally apply … and … the norm-laden intentions with which (or the actions in which) we apply them. … All intentional acts, in virtue of being intentional, bring the actor under the purview of norms in the sense that the actor is obliged (ought) to adopt the means she believes necessary (in the circumstances) to do what she intends to do. ... The same is true in applying concepts. If the act (of applying the concept) is intentional, it will come under the purview of norms, not because concepts or their application is a norm-governed activity, but because the act of applying them, *when it is intentional*, generates a set of norms associated with the actor's intentions and desires.[11]

One might sum up this criticism by saying that while the semantic anti-normativist accepts *general* rules of rational action, he rejects the "particularist" belief in *specific* semantic rules covering individual types of expressions.[12]

A closely related and highly influential line of argument is due to Donald Davidson. Successful communication does not presuppose shared semantic norms. I can come to understand what James Joyce meant by "Dyoublong" even though I do not have a semantic norm telling me how "Dyoublong" is to be used. Figuring out what someone else is trying to communicate to me does involve me in applying norms, but these norms are those of logic and rationality. In order to understand others I have to work on the assumption that the basic laws of logic and rationality apply to their language and linguistic behaviour. Otherwise I could not assume, for instance, that in using "Dyoublong" Joyce has the intention to convey something to his readers.[13]

Against Michael Dummett in particular, Davidson urges that in order for our words to have meaning, we need not feel obliged towards the norms of language:

> Suppose someone learns to talk as others do, but feels no obligation whatever to do so. ... [Suppose she said:] "I just do talk that way. I don't think I have an obligation to walk upright, it just comes naturally." If what she says is true would she not be speaking a language, or would she cease to be intelligible?[14]

Anti-normativists insist that this woman speaks a language and that semantic obligations are merely a non-essential extra, added on to the natural phenomenon of communicating:

> These [normative] pressures are social and they are very real. They do not, however ... have anything to do with meaning or communication. Using a word in a non-standard way out of ignorance may be a *faux pas* in the same way that using the wrong fork at a dinner party is, and it has as little to do with communication as using the wrong fork has to do with nourishing oneself, given that the word is understood and the fork works.[15]

In other words, linguistic justification and correction stand to the possibility of communication as dinner party etiquette stands to nourishing. It is a social extra imposed on a previously existing biological phenomenon.

A few paragraphs back I mentioned *two* important strategies employed by anti-normativists. The second strategy might be called the "missing rules strategy". Anti-normativists typically construe their opponents as believing that to speak a language, or to communicate, is to follow rules. Anti-normativists reject this idea. As they see it, rules are not essential to speaking a language or to communicating:

> Rules can be a help in learning a language, but their aid is available, if at all, only in the acquisition of a second language. Most language learning is accomplished without learning or knowing any rules at all. … We normally follow no procedure in speaking; nothing in the everyday use of language corresponds to taking the sum in adding.[16]

A different way of making the same point is to ask what form semantic rules might take. Are they, in John Searle's well-known terms, "regulative" or "constitutive" rules? Regulative rules have the form:

> In conditions *C* you ought to perform action *A*; or
> When in conditions *C* do *A*!

Constitutive rules have the canonical form:

> Doing *A* counts as *B* in context *C*.

In addition to this difference in form, Searle also gives a further criterion for drawing the distinction: "regulative rules regulate antecedently or independently existing forms of behaviour", whereas "constitutive rules … create or define new forms of behaviour".[17] Rules of etiquette are regulative rules; rules of games, such as chess or football, are examples of constitutive rules. Interpersonal relationships exist independently of rules of etiquette, but chess does not exist independently of the rules of the game.

It seems that the defender of the idea of semantic normativity must think of semantic rules as regulative rules: rules of meaning are supposed to tell us what we *ought to do*, how we *ought to speak*, in order for our words to have meaning. And only regulative rules, not constitutive rules, have this prescriptive character. Unfortunately for the semantic normativist, while the regulative reading seems natural and obvious, it also creates problems.[18] A first source of trouble is simply the existence of a long and important tradition in the philosophy of language that models rules of language on rules of games. Wittgenstein and Sellars are, of course, the outstanding figures in this tradition. And the rules of a game are constitutive. (Of course, Sellars and Wittgenstein may be wrong.) A second source of trouble is less straightforward but equally pressing. Above we saw – in the context of the first anti-normativist strategy – that the onus is on defenders of semantic normativity to show that the prescriptions governing the use of language are *semantic*, rather than prudential or pragmatic. In other words, the semantic normativist needs to show us that there is a distinctive form of normativity that deserves to be called "semantic". In order to meet this challenge, a semantic normativist might argue as follows. A norm of language is semantic if it owes its motivational force to nothing but the consideration that without this norm there would be neither language nor thought. Other forms of normativity have other, different, motivational bases; semantic normativity alone is based on what makes language and thought possible.[19] This line of argument sounds plausible at first, but only as long as we fail to see that it is based on a strange mix-up of regulative and constitutive rules. The argument seeks to motivate prescriptions, and hence *regulative* rules, by invoking their *constitutive* powers. After all, its bottom line is to say: follow the prescriptions or else there would be no meanings. And this will not do. A rule cannot be regulative and constitutive at the same time. A regulative rule legislates for an already existing domain of actions, whereas a constitutive rule *creates* such a domain.[20]

The normativist cannot escape this argument by suggesting that perhaps we can *derive* prescriptions (regulative rules) from constitutive rules. For such derived prescriptions would have to order us to do B in context C only by doing A, or prohibit us from doing B in context C in any other way than by doing A. Alas, these prescriptions would be futile: the order would command us to do something to which we have no alternative, and the prohibition would forbid the impossible.[21] The underlying difficulty here is that constitutive rules cannot be breached. Not doing A in context C does not break the rule; it simply is not doing something that counts as B.

The tension between regulative and constitutive elements also surfaces when we focus on semantic prescriptions for individual expressions. Assume the semantic normativist formulates a prescription and its motivation by saying "This [...] is how you ought to use the expression 'horse' in order for it to mean *horse*." Here the "[...]" is to be filled with a specification of a use. The *prima facie* problem with this suggestion is that it calls for an explanation of how falsehood is possible. If I mistakenly call a cow "horse" then I am clearly saying something false. But the semantic-normativist suggestion cannot account for this falsehood. If I do not follow the prescription of using "horse" only for horses then "horse" does not mean *horse*. And since it does not mean *horse*, I have not said something false.[22] In order to be a candidate for truth or falsity a sentence has to be meaningful.

WRPL and normativity: the received view

The "received view" of the role of normativity considerations in *WRPL* differs from the interpretation that I have sketched in my first chapter and restated briefly in the previous paragraph. It is therefore important that I investigate the received view in some detail. Its source is the perhaps single most influential discussion of *WRPL*: Boghossian's paper "The Rule-Following Considerations".

Boghossian's analysis of the normativity considerations in *WRPL* takes off on a negative note. He begins by criticizing Colin McGinn's view, according to which:

> the notion of normativeness Kripke wants captured is a transtemporal notion ... We have an account of this normativeness when we have two things: (a) an account of what it is to mean something at a given time and (b) an account of what it is to mean the *same* thing at different times – since (Kripkean) normativeness is a matter of meaning now what one meant earlier.[23]

It is easy to feel the initial plausibility of this suggestion. Does not the meaning determinist focus on the normative relationship between my grasping a meaning in the past and my applying an expression (with that meaning) in the present? And does not the sceptic want to know how a meaning grasped in the past can tell me what I am supposed to do now? Clearly "transtemporality" does make a prominent appearance in *WRPL*.

Nevertheless, Boghossian is right to point out that the aspect of "transtemporality" is not an essential aspect of the argument over normativity, and that the sceptical challenge is not to explain "what it is to mean the *same* thing at different times". The problem of normativity is the relationship between acts of meaning and application, regardless of whether these two are distributed over different times or not. Boghossian makes his case by pointing out that if transtemporality was the only issue then semantic reductive dispositionalism – the main target of the normativity considerations – would after all pass muster:

> since there are perfectly determinate facts about what dispositions are associated with a given expression at a given time – or, rather, since it is no part of Kripke's intent to deny that there are – it is always possible to ask whether an expression has the same or a different meaning on a dispositional theory, thus satisfying [the transtemporality] requirement.[24]

Having rejected the idea that the issue is transtemporality, Boghossian sets out his own view as to what Kripke means by semantic normativity. The passage is worth quoting at some length:

> Suppose the expression "green" means *green*. It follows immediately that the expression "green" applies *correctly* only to *these* things (the green ones) and not to *those* (the non-greens). The fact that the

expression means something implies, that is, a whole set of *norma-tive* truths about my behaviour with that expression: namely, that my use of it is correct in application to certain objects and not in appli-cation to others. ... The normativity of meaning turns out to be, in other words, simply a new name for the familiar fact that, regard-less of whether one thinks of meaning in truth-theoretic or assertion-theoretic terms, meaningful expressions possess conditions of *correct use*. ... Kripke's insight was to realize that ... it ought to be possible to read off from any alleged meaning-constituting property of a word, what is the correct use of that word.[25]

Later in the same paper Boghossian connects talk of correctness with talk about motivation and prescriptions: "To be told that 'horse' means *horse* implies that a speaker ought to be motivated to apply the expression only to horses".[26] A fur-ther influential formulation of his interpretation is given in another place: "Any proposed candidate for being the property in virtue of which an expression has meaning must be such as to ground the 'normativity' of meaning".[27] Boghossian thinks that his interpretation of the "normativity requirement" in *WRPL* allows us to see clearly how the argument against reductive semantic dispositionalism is supposed to run. Let us call Boghossian's reconstruction of the argument the "standard normativity argument":[28]

> Kripke seems to think that even if there were a suitably selected disposition that captured the extension of an expression accurately, the disposition could still not be identified with that fact of mean-ing, because it still remains true that the concept of a disposition is descriptive whereas the concept of meaning is not. In other words, according to Kripke, even if there were a dispositional predicate that logically co-varied with a meaning predicate, the one fact could still not be identified with the other, for they are facts of distinct sorts.[29]

Boghossian does not just offer a reconstruction of what he calls Kripke's "nor-mativity requirement", he also proposes an assessment of the role this requirement plays in the argument against reductive semantic dispositionalism. In order to understand his assessment we need to take note of the way in which Boghossian formulates the dispositionalist position.

I have any number of dispositions regarding my use of the word "horse". For instance, I have the disposition to use the word when I stand in front of a horse in clear daylight, with my eyes open, and after my two-year-old daughter has just asked me "What's that?" But I also have the disposition to use the word (in answer to my daughter's question) when I look at a cow, at least when the light-ing conditions are poor, there is fog about and I am not wearing my glasses. The dispositionalist believes that what I mean by "horse" can be read off my dispositions for using "horse". If *all* such dispositions were to qualify, then by "horse" I would mean (at least!) *horse or cow*. In order to avoid this unwanted result, the dispositionalist has to pick and choose from my dispositions for using "horse". He must pick out my dispositions to apply "horse" to horses and rule out my dispositions to apply "horse" to cows (among others things). Only the former, but not the latter, dispositions are meaning-constituting or meaning-determining "*M*-dispositions".[30] Here, "*M*" is the property that all meaning-constituting dispositions have in common. Of course, the question then becomes, "What property might *M* be?"[31]

With this terminology in place, I can now state Boghossian's assessment of the standard normativity argument. Boghossian is not convinced that it can be made to work. The reason for his pessimism is that it might be possible to specify *M* in a way that captures normativity:

> Perhaps the *M*-dispositions are those dispositions that a person would have when his cognitive mechanisms are in a certain state; and perhaps it can be non-question-beggingly certified that that state corresponds to a state of the *proper* functioning of those mechanisms. If so, it is conceivable that that would amount to a non-circular specification of how the person would *ideally* respond, as compared with how he actually responds; and, hence, that it would suffice for capturing the normative force of an ascription of meaning.
>
> There is clearly no way to settle the matter in advance of the consideration of particular dispositional proposals.[32]

Alas, Boghossian does not go on to consider such proposals in any detail. Boghossian's sceptical attitude towards the standard normativity argument can also be seen from the fact that it does little destructive work in his own criticism of two main forms of dispositionalism. These two main forms are: the "communitarian account", which says that "*M* is the *property of agreeing with the actual dispositions of the community*"; and the "optimal dispositions account", which says that *M* is the property of being in a "non-semantically, non-intentionally specifiable set of conditions" in which, say, all misidentifications and misjudgements are impossible.[33] As far as the optimality account is concerned, Boghossian is convinced that it cannot even meet the "extensional requirement" of finding dispositional predicates (instances of "has the disposition to use sign '*y*' under circumstances *C*") that logically co-vary with meaning predicates (instances of "means *X* by '*y*'"). And since the optimality account fails already at this first hurdle, not much is gained by checking how it does with respect to the normativity requirement.[34] With respect to the "communitarian account" Boghossian is "prepared to grant, for the sake of argument" that it can meet the "intensional requirement". That is to say, it is able to show that having the disposition to use "*y*" under conditions *C* *intuitively resembles* meaning *X* by "*y*".

Normativity considerations fall under the intensional requirement. Boghossian's reason for believing that the communitarian account passes by this criterion is that "non-collusive communal agreement on a judgement usually provide[s] one with some sort of reason for embracing the judgement".[35] However, if Boghossian is right, then this success with respect to normativity is cold comfort to the communitarian. For like the advocate of the "optimal dispositions account" so also the communitarian falls at the extensional fence. To summarize, in Boghossian's reconstruction of the criticism of dispositionalism, normativity considerations are neither useful nor decisive.

Problems with the received view

Boghossian is not alone in thinking that the normativity considerations of *WRPL* are not successful as an argument against dispositionalism. Taking Boghossian's interpretation as the correct view of *WRPL*, a number of critics have declared the normativity-based criticism of dispositionalism that Kripke formulates on Wittgenstein's behalf to be unsuccessful. Some of their reasons belong with the general anti-normativist arguments I have summarized above: the claim that the alleged semantic normativity is really some other form of normativity, and the suspicion that there are no rules that can give substance to the semantic normativist's proposal. I shall not rehearse these points again. At this stage it is more important to focus on criticisms that are closely geared to Boghossian's interpretation.

A first objection is that the standard normativity argument simply begs the question against the dispositionalist. Above I quoted Boghossian's demand that "any proposed candidate for being the property in virtue of which an expression has meaning must be such as to ground the 'normativity' of meaning". This does no damage to a dispositionalist who insists that such "grounding" has been delivered as soon as the extensional requirement has been met. In Jerry Fodor's words:

> requiring that normativity be grounded suggests that there is more to demand of a naturalized semantics than that it provide a reduction of such notions as, say, *extension*. But what could this "more" amount to? To apply a term to a thing in its extension *is* to apply the term correctly; once you've said what it is that makes the tables the extension of "table", there is surely no *further* question about why it's *correct* to apply "table" to a table. It thus seems that if you have a reductive theory of the semantic relations, there is no job of grounding normativity left to do.[36]

A second objection focuses on the gap that exists between saying "it is *correct* to apply 'horse' to horses", and claiming "'horse' *ought to be* applied only to horses". In Boghossian's reconstruction claims about correctness come first. We are told that facts about the extension of a term imply when and how it is correct to apply it. Knowledge about correctness conditions are then supposed to give rise to semantic prescriptions: beliefs or utterances about how the term ought to be applied. Boghossian does not tell us much about how we get from correctness conditions to prescriptions; the thought seems to be that once we know that doing *X* is correct we are motivated to regard doing *X* as obligatory. Critics have homed in on this transition from correctness to prescription.[37] They agree with Boghossian that facts about the extension of a term *t* provide us with a standard for sorting applications of *t* into those that are correct and those that are incorrect. But these critics deny that such a standard for sorting is normative-prescriptive:

> That something is used as a standard for ... sorting and classifying actions does not imply that this something is used as a normative [i.e. prescriptive] standard. A normative standard would be one that specifies which actions are good, and which actions should be carried out. ... [To get to semantic prescriptions] one would have to show that the speaker must take a prescriptive attitude towards the standard that merely sorts applications into correct and incorrect ones. It follows that even the concept of *linguistic mistake* is not necessarily a concept with prescriptive content.[38]

A third, closely related, objection alleges that the standard normativity argument is wrong about the relationship between meaning and truth. As just seen, Boghossian suggests that the normativist about meaning derives semantic prescriptions from facts about extensions. The fact that

> If you mean *horse* by "horse", then "horse" is true only of horses

is meant to somehow give rise to the semantic prescription

> If you mean *horse* by "horse", then you ought to apply "horse" only to horses.

This "derivation" will, of course, work only if speaking the truth is somehow obligatory. Or, put differently, the "derivation" would work only if truth were *intrinsically* valuable. Aiming for the truth would not then be conditional on aiming for something else. Unfortunately, it is hard to see how truth could be an intrinsic value in this sense.[39] Aiming for the truth seems always to be conditional on having other desires:

No doubt some people want their beliefs to be true regardless of any practical benefit. However, there are also people who do not care about "pure knowledge"; and it is not obvious that these people are deluded. In other words, if someone applies the word "dog" to a cat, he is certainly saying something false, and he is in a state that might well lead to effects that are bad for him – but whether, independently of these practical matters, he is doing something he should not do is not at all obvious.[40]

It is easy to see that a conditional obligation would not be good enough. A conditional obligation to speak the truth yields prescriptions of the following form: "If I wish to speak the truth, and if I mean *horse* by 'horse', then I should apply 'horse' to horses only". This conditional obligation does not show that there is anything specifically normative about meaning. This can be seen by formulating an analogous prescription regarding umbrellas. "If I wish to avoid getting wet, and if I use umbrellas for keeping myself dry, then I should take the umbrella when going out into the rain." Although the umbrellas figure in the normative sentence, they are not themselves normative.[41]

A fourth and final objection charges Boghossian with conflating two senses of correctness: correctness as *true application* and correctness as *use in accordance with the meaning of an expression*. The two senses can be brought out most easily by recalling a case made famous by Tyler Burge.[42] Take a patient who uses "arthritis" for any painful condition of the limbs or joints. This is not in keeping with our accepted and established meaning of "arthritis": the word refers only to painful conditions of the joints. Assume the patient tells his doctor that he has arthritis on the basis of his feeling pain in his limbs. In this scenario the patient both *misapplies* and *misuses* the term: he is saying something false and fails to use the term in accordance with its meaning. Misapplication and misuse can, however, come apart: if the patient were to tell his doctor that he has arthritis on the basis of his feeling pain in his limbs, then the patient would be saying something true while still failing to accord with the meaning of the term. Finally, consider again the original case (self-attribution of arthritis on the basis of pain in the limbs), but now from the perspective of the doctor who knows the correct meaning of "arthritis". If the doctor concludes that the patient has pain in the joints then the doctor is misapplying but not misusing the term.[43]

The two senses of correctness are not distinguished in Boghossian's reconstruction of the normativity considerations of *WRPL*. And it is because he fails to separate them that his reconstruction does not preserve the possibility of falsehood. There is no scope in Boghossian's reconstruction for the possibility of a false but meaningful utterance: if the utterance fails to be true then it fails to be meaningful.[44] It follows, of course, that if Boghossian's interpretation of *WRPL*'s account of normativity is correct, then that account is totally implausible.

The inadequacy of the received view as an interpretation

The objections summarized above were not directed at the received view as an *interpretation* of *WRPL*; they merely challenged the received view on systematic grounds, and under the assumption that it correctly reflect the gist of Kripke's Wittgenstein's argument. It seems to me undeniable that these objections are successful. Semantic normativity as reconstructed by Boghossian is not a defensible view. But we cannot leave things at that. For we will miss the true significance of this result for the argument of *WRPL* as a whole unless we reflect on how Boghossian's rendering of semantic normativity relates to Kripke's own text.

The first thing to note is that what Boghossian identifies as the thesis of the normativity of meaning – "simply a new name for the familiar fact that ... meaningful expressions possess conditions of *correct use*" and "to be told that 'horse' means *horse* implies that a speaker ought to be motivated to apply the expression only to horses" – is a very much *deflated version* of what is presented in *WRPL*. In Chapter 1 I tried to demonstrate in some detail that semantic normativity as part of meaning determinism is a much richer idea – and that it needs the richer idea to refute semantic reductive dispositionalism (see above, pp. 17–19). To repeat the main ingredients and the most telling quotations, semantic normativity is a covering term for five ideas:

- Non-blindness: applications of terms on the basis of what we mean are not "blind" and not due to "brute inclination" (*WRPL*: 10, 15, 17, 23).
- Guidance: "inner 'ideas' or 'meanings' guide our linguistic behaviour" (*WRPL*: 56); "there is something in my mind – the meaning I attach to the 'plus' sign – that *instructs* me what I ought to do in all future cases" (*WRPL*: 22).
- Justification: "an account of what fact it is (about my mental state) that constitutes my meaning plus ... must, in some sense, show how I am justified in giving the answer '125' to '68 + 57'" (*WRPL*: 11).
- Justification of unhesitating application: "I immediately and unhesitatingly calculate '68 + 57' as I do, and the meaning I assign to '+' is supposed to *justify* this procedure" (*WRPL*: 40).
- Left-to-right interpretation of meaning conditionals: "If Jones means addition by '+', then if he is asked for '68 + 57', he will reply '125'. ... the conditional as stated makes it appear that some mental state obtains in Jones that guarantees his performance of particular additions such as '68 + 57'" (*WRPL*: 94–5). Here instead of "will" we could also say "should".

It is also important to note that semantic normativity is closely intertwined with other elements of meaning determinism. In particular its links to immediate knowledge (we know our meaning-constituting mental states "immediately and with fair certainty") and to grasping as intending (my act of grasping a meaning X for sign "y" is tantamount to my forming intentions regarding a possibly infinite number of applications of "*y*" in the future) are well worth stressing. Semantic normativity's interconnection with immediate knowledge is clear from the fact that justification of unhesitating application relies on the immediacy of my knowledge of meaning. And grasping as intending is crucial for semantic normativity since it is intentions that – for the meaning determinist – constitute the normativity of meaning.

Let me clarify the last-mentioned point with a couple of quotations from *WRPL* itself. We are told that grasping a rule and forming intentions (regarding applications of the rule) are really the same thing: "This is the whole point of the notion that in learning to add I grasp a rule: my past intentions regarding addition determine a unique answer for indefinitely many new cases in the future" (*WRPL*: 7–8). Moreover, to form intentions regarding future applications is to give myself directions or instructions, or indeed, *prescriptions*: "Ordinarily, I suppose that, in computing '68 + 57' as I do, I do not simply make an unjustified leap in the dark. I follow directions I previously gave myself that uniquely determine that in this new instance I should say '125'" (*WRPL*: 10). To sum up, *my intentions and self-directed instructions or directions regarding future use oblige me to act in some ways and not in others*. If I have formed the intention to calculate in terms of addition, then I ought to say "125" to "68 + 57 = ?". My intentions "compel" me to say "125".

Boghossian has chosen to "filter out" from this involved and expansive picture just two elements: the element of correct use and the element of motivation. Unfortunately, he has done so without offering any justification. I am advocating that such filtering-out may not be the best strategy for making proper sense of the normativity argument in *WRPL*.[45] It seems to me that there are good reasons why *WRPL* is conducting its argument on the basis of the just-sketched richer and more involved conception. To begin with, Kripke's text seeks to be an interpretation of the sections on rule-following in *PI*. And Kripke rightly thinks that the position, or picture, under scrutiny is not the straightforward view that "meaningful expressions possess conditions of *correct use*", but a network of interconnected assumptions or intuitions. Kripke (and Wittgenstein!) do not see semantic normativity as an isolated, or isolatable, set of ideas. Talk of normativity in the context of meaning attributions is meaningful only against the background of broader and more comprehensive "pictures" of language and mind, the way both language and mind are embedded into the physical and social world, and the roles of truth and facts in meaning sentences. Accordingly the dialectic of Chapter 2 of *WRPL* shows us – if not always "tells us" – how semantic normativity is intertwined with the other ingredients of meaning determinism; and the exposition of Chapter 3 of *WRPL* shows us – if not always "tells us" – how intersubjective normativity is intertwined with the other elements of meaning scepticism.

Ultimately Kripke's Wittgenstein is not, of course, trying to defend semantic normativity. The whole point of the sceptical argument is to show that meaning determinism in all its forms is incoherent and beyond remedy, and that semantic normativity has to be thrown out with the rest. However, the sceptical argument is an "immanent critique": it does not bring to bear standards from outside meaning determinism. Instead it seeks to show that meaning determinism fails to live up to its own standards; there is no way to remain true to all of its assumptions at once.

In the light of these comments – and in the absence of any arguments by Boghossian or others to the contrary – it seems appropriate to focus the discussion of the normativity of meaning more closely on the actual text, the actual dialectic, of *WRPL*. If we do so, then the central questions must be these: assuming that one is already committed to the intuitive picture of meaning referred to as (low-brow) meaning determinism above, will one then be able to endorse reductive semantic dispositionalism? Will one have to acknowledge that semantic dispositions are unable to guide and justify? It seems obvious that the answer to the first question must be negative and the answer to the second question positive. At least this is so until one begins to tweak some ingredient of meaning determinism or some aspect of dispositionalism. We shall turn to such tweaking manoeuvres below.

Further criticisms of semantic normativity

I have stressed repeatedly that *WRPL* does not criticize semantic normativity in isolation from the rest of meaning determinism. The sceptic lays out the incoherence of meaning determinism as a whole, opts against piecemeal reforms, and then throws out semantic normativity with the rest of meaning determinism. Needless to say, we do not have to rest content with such *indirect* arguments. We can also try to come up with *direct* attacks on the claim that semantic normativity can be captured in terms of prescription-giving intentions. Three such arguments have been proposed. I have my doubts about the first two.

A first objection questions the idea according to which intentions to do *X* can constitute a prescription to do *X*. The relationship between intention and action is *internal* and *logical* rather than *external* and *prescriptive*. Intentional actions of a given type are criteria for the presence of the corresponding intentions, and intentions of a given type are criteria for the presence of the corresponding intentional actions. Hence we cannot generate semantic normativity from intentions to use expressions in certain ways.[46] Perhaps the meaning determinist need not accept this objection as decisive. Consider the distinction between action *explanation* on the one hand, and action *deliberation* or *justification* on the other.[47] It is true that when trying to explain why an action has occurred, we (often) choose our descriptions of intentions and actions in such a way that their relationship comes out as internal or logical. But the cases of deliberation and justification are different.[48] When I deliberate my future courses of action in light of my intentions, then I am deliberating what I *should do, ought to do* or *must do*, to carry out these intentions. And when justifying my own actions later, I give an account or a (rational) reconstruction of my deliberation process. In the debate between the sceptic and the meaning determinist, the latter is of course giving precisely such a justification-deliberation for his action of answering "125" to "68 + 57 = ?".

A related, second, objection[49] wonders whether it is at all possible for Jones to intend to mean addition by "+" and yet fail to reply "125" to "68 + 57". This would have to be possible if the intention to mean addition by "+" is meant to prescribe the answer "125" to "68 + 57". Here we must distinguish two scenarios, I and II. In scenario I, we exclude the possibility of mistakes in calculation (as Kripke does early on in Chapter 2 of *WRPL*). If we exclude mistakes in calculation, then surely Jones cannot fail to answer "125" to "68 + 57". And hence there is no conceptual space for a prescription to answer "125". In scenario II we allow for the possibility of mistakes in calculation. But even this does not help. For assume that Jones fails to answer "125" in reply to "68 + 57" because of a mistake in calculation. Then surely he has not failed to fulfil his intention to mean addition by "+". Indeed, for the mistake to be a mistake in calculation, the meaning determinist must mean addition by "+". Mistakes in calculation do not constitute violations of meaning-constituting intentions.

Once more the meaning determinist might have responses. Even in scenario I, there still remains room for Jones to fail in his attempt to fulfil his meaning-constituting intentions. To see this, it is important to note that more than one intention is in play and that mistakes in calculation ("arithmetical mistakes") are to be distinguished from misinterpretations of one's past intentions and actions. According to the meaning determinist, Jones's reasoning in defence of his answer of "125" to "68 + 57 = ?" must go as follows:

*Intention*₁   I intend to calculate on the basis of the correct interpretation of my past intentions (or uses) regarding "+".

*Belief*₁   This correct interpretation of my past intentions (or uses) regarding "+" is that I earlier meant addition by "+".

*Intention*₂   I now intend to calculate on the basis of addition.

*Belief*₂   When "+" denotes addition, 68 + 57 = 125.

Conclusion   I ought to say "125" in response to "68 + 57 = ?"

To exclude arithmetical mistakes is to grant infallibility to *Belief*₂ and thus to guarantee the fulfilment of *Intention*₂. But there remain *Intention*₁ and *Belief*₁. The meaning determinist insists that it is possible to have a false belief about the meaning facts of one's past and thus to fail in one's intention to act on the basis of the correct interpretation of these facts. Given then that *Intention*₁ can remain unfulfilled, there is room for a "should" or an "ought" in the *Conclusion*.

What if, as in scenario II, mistakes in calculation are part of the story? Is the meaning determinist right to insist that, if I make arithmetical mistakes, then "I have not acted in accordance with my intention" to mean addition by "+" (*WRPL*:

37)? To the proponent of the currently considered objection, this seems like a self-contradictory proposal. Consider:

(a) I can only miscalculate an addition task if throughout the calculation I mean addition by "+".
(b) To mean addition by "+" is to have and act on the intention to use "+" according to the addition function.
(c) If I miscalculate an addition task I do not act on the basis of the intention to use "+" according to the addition function.

If we accept (a)–(c) then we end up with the view that miscalculations are impossible.

The meaning determinist still has an answer. He must again insist that the relationship between intention and action is not always as tight as his opponent assumes. I do not necessarily cease to have the meaning-constituting intention to use "+" according to the addition function when I fail to act on this intention.

Finally, a third objection claims that in tying semantic prescriptions to intentions the meaning determinist has in fact reduced semantic normativity to some other form of normativity:

> If the act (of applying the concept) is intentional, it will come under the purview of norms, not because concepts or their application is a norm-governed activity, but because the act of applying them, *when it is intentional*, generates a set of norms associated with the actor's intentions and desires.[50]

This objection seems hard to rebut. In replacing semantic normativity with intersubjective normativity, *WRPL* acknowledges that this objection is on target.

Revisionists, reformers and revolutionaries

Let us take stock. I have been urging a new interpretation of *WRPL*. Kripke is not using a general idea of the normativity of meaning against dispositionalism. Rather, Kripke tries, on Wittgenstein's behalf, to show that high-brow forms of meaning determinism in general, and different versions of reductive semantic dispositionalism in particular, are unable to meet the constraints of the intuitive picture of low-brow meaning determinism. But this is not all. Ultimately Kripke seeks to show that no (possible) form of high-brow meaning determinism can meet these low-brow constraints. And the suggested consequence of this realization is that low-brow meaning determinism itself has to be given up and replaced by the sceptical solution.

How does the debate over normativity and *WRPL* fit with this new interpretation? To accept the new interpretation is to accept that much of the criticism of Kripke on normativity barks up the wrong tree; most participants in the debate have assumed a mistaken interpretation of *WRPL*. Fortunately, this does not make past contributions pointless; their central concerns can be assimilated into, and reorganized within, the new outlook. Authors who have provided arguments against the idea of semantic normativity can be resituated as allies of the sceptic; in attacking semantic normativity these authors can be read as giving us additional reasons to reject meaning determinism. Even authors who have taken the opposite stance are good news for a defence of the overall argument of *WRPL*. Authors who defend the intuitive plausibility of semantic normativity help us see why meaning determinism itself is common-sense philosophy, why it is itself intuitive. The authors prevent us from rejecting meaning determinism too quickly.

Of course at this point a new worry becomes pressing. It may seem that my assimilation of the normativity debate is too successful to be useful. If both semantic normativists and semantic anti-normativists confirm Kripke's position, does this not show that this position has become impossible to falsify? Heads Kripke wins, tails Kripke wins? I accept that it would be a disastrous outcome for my interpretation if it pointed towards a viewpoint that cannot be falsified at all. Luckily, this is not what my interpretation leads to. A whole spectrum of views would – if successful – show that the move towards the sceptical solution is not warranted. Some views within this spectrum are revisionist, some are reformist and some are revolutionary.

The move towards the sceptical solution would be blocked in a revisionist or reformist fashion if any of the following options were to work (assuming, for argument's sake, that they are able to meet the extensional requirement):

(a) Revision: We keep all elements of low-brow meaning determinism but improve on our conception of reductive semantic dispositionalism.
(b) Reform I: We keep *almost all* elements of low-brow meaning determinism and reductive semantic dispositionalism. But we replace privacy by intersubjectivity.
(c) Reform II: We keep *most* elements of low-brow meaning determinism and reductive semantic dispositionalism. But we replace semantic normativity with the weaker principle of "semantic correctness". A form of dispositionalism has met the criterion of semantic correctness if it has met the extensional requirement.
(d) Reform III: We keep *most* elements of low-brow meaning determinism and reductive semantic dispositionalism. But we bolster up the old semantic normativity by redefining it in terms of the biological concept of *proper function*.

So much for the revisionists and the reformers. Now for the revolutionary view that, if successful, would make the sceptical solution superfluous:

(e) We give up semantic normativity alongside most other ingredients of meaning determinism, low-brow or high-brow. But we do not join the meaning
sceptics. We show that the form of normativity at issue in the sceptical solution is no less flawed than is the form of normativity central to meaning
determinism. And thus we develop a conception of meaning that differs from
both meaning determinism and meaning scepticism.

In the remainder of this chapter I shall discuss these five positions in turn. I am
not claiming that these positions exhaust the spectrum. What I do believe, however, is that they constitute the most plausible and best-known options.

(a) Revision: increasing the number of dispositions

Paul Coates believes that dispositionalism can meet the constraints of semantic normativity provided only that we increase the number of dispositions.[51] The
needed additional dispositions are "second-order dispositions". Such dispositions
manifest themselves in the maintenance or change of first-order dispositions. For
instance, my clock radio has both a first-order disposition to indicate the correct time and the second-order disposition to maintain its first-order dispositions.
It does so by adjusting itself on the basis of radio signals. According to Coates,
second-order dispositions can be used to capture phenomena of commitment. For
instance, to be committed to fairness in treating one's students is to have the second-
order disposition to adjust one's (first-order) dispositions for treating each student
in certain ways. As Coates sees the sceptical challenge, the nub of the problem is a
commitment to consistency of use. What distinguishes rule-following from mere
rule-conforming is the presence of an intention to be consistent, that is, the presence of the intention to use the word in accordance with its extension. And precisely
this intention can be captured with talk of second-order dispositions:

> What is it that entitles us to move to a normative claim about how I
> *ought* to use a word? The answer consists in the fact that I committed
> myself to using the word consistently, and that this commitment was
> grounded in a robust second-order disposition to be consistent in my
> first-order dispositions to use the term; making this commitment is
> the best means open to me of satisfying my various goals. In order to
> achieve the various general goals I may be assumed to have, I *ought*
> now to be consistent in my use of language.[52]

There is reason to remain unconvinced. Let us be clear on the dialectic situation. If Coates's suggestion is to succeed then it has to show us why someone
who accepts low-brow meaning determinism would find his improvement on

the original dispositionalism convincing. The original dispositionalism fails the constraints of low-brow meaning determinism because it cannot meet semantic normativity. It fails because dispositions are entities of a sort that do not – in and of themselves – have normative consequences. Now, if one accepts this point for dispositions in general, it is hard to see how one would allow for exceptions in the case of second-order dispositions. Coates's suggestion therefore simply ignores the lesson already learnt.

There are further problems too. Consider what Coates could say in response to the sceptical challenge. Presumably his answer would be this: "What makes it so that I am an adder is that I have dispositions to give sums in response to plus-queries and that I have the second-order disposition to be consistent in my first-order dispositions and their manifestations." Would this reply defeat the sceptic? Surely not. The sceptic could retort as follows: "Alright, if you mean *addition* by 'plus' then you will be consistent in your dispositions to give sums, and if you mean *quaddition* by 'plus' then you will be consistent in your dispositions to give quums. But what makes it so that you mean *addition*?" In other words, invoking second-order dispositions does not solve the by now familiar problems of explaining why one's first-order dispositions to respond to plus-queries in certain ways must count as first-order dispositions *to add*.

There also is something circular about the proposal. How are we to understand the consistency of first-order dispositions? What is the yardstick of this consistency – if not the meaning? Is not Coates saying: "I mean *addition* by 'plus' because I have consistent dispositions to give sums in answer to plus-queries"? In this statement, "consistent" is merely an empty wheel unless it means "dispositions in accordance with the addition function". Here is a different way to make the same point. Take my first-order dispositions to apply "horse" to various animals. Undoubtedly, I have a whole range of second-order dispositions with respect to these first-order dispositions. For instance, I might have the second-order disposition to become dissatisfied with so coarse a category as "horse"; I might have the second-order disposition to improve my pronunciation of the word; or I might have the second-order disposition to switch into German or Finnish and say "*Pferd*" or "*hevonen*" instead. Each of these second-order dispositions sets the standard for a different kind of consistency. Of course, not one of these second-order dispositions is the one Coates has in mind. Alas, the only way to rule them out is to invoke the second-order disposition to maintain consistency regarding meaning. And this invocation renders the proposal circular.[53]

(b) Reform I: communal dispositionalism

I have touched on communal dispositionalism before, and shall return to it in the next chapter. Here I only wish to ponder whether going for communal

69

dispositions helps the reductive semantic dispositionalist (*qua* high-brow meaning determinist). The most elaborate proposal for such communal dispositionalism is Paul Horwich's "community-use theory". Horwich believes that communal dispositionalism is able to capture normativity. In his words, communal dispositionalism can capture the "normative implications" of meaning.[54] Such normative implications arise from the idea that "knowledge is valuable (both for its own sake and for its practical benefits)" and that therefore "we ought to strive for it": "there are certain propositions – namely, true ones – that we ought to believe. Moreover, given our language, we must express each of our beliefs in a particular way. Therefore, within a linguistic practice, certain sentences ought to be affirmed and others not".[55] Applied to Kripke's mathematical example, this position allows for the following reasoning:

> [O]ne ought (other things being equal) to assent to the truth. In particular, one ought to assent to the proposition that 68 + 57 = 125. Therefore, one ought to assent to any sentence that one understands to express that proposition. Now, given proficiency and participation in a linguistic practice in which the constituents of the sentence "68 + 57 = 125" are used in certain ways, one will understand that sentence to express the proposition that 68 + 57 = 125. Therefore, given participation in such a linguistic practice, one ought to assent to the sentence "68 + 57 = 125".[56]

Horwich's line of reasoning misses the point. He captures one normative aspect of meaning, namely the aspect that links meaning to truth and knowledge. But this is not the normativity at issue in the sceptical challenge of Chapter 2 of *WRPL*. The normativity at issue there has to do with intentions and the commitments that arise from the existence of these intentions. The intentions in question are intentions to use signs in some ways and not in other ways. They are not, as such, intentions to speak the truth or to form true beliefs.

Alan Millar has made the same point in terms of his aforementioned distinction between two senses of correctness: correctness as true application, and correctness as use in accordance with the meaning of an expression (see above, p. 61):

> If ... the normative claims we need to focus on are claims about how one ought to use words, then the particular ought-claims which need explaining are claims to the effect that one ought to use words in those ways which are in keeping with the relevant meaning and in *that* sense correct. If that is the issue then the considerations which Horwich adduces are irrelevant and could only seem relevant because of an equivocation over the notion of correctness.[57]

(c) Reform II: semantic correctness

A third reformist idea is to replace semantic normativity with something like "semantic correctness" and maintain that we have captured semantic correctness as soon as we have met the extensional requirement. This is the position that Fodor formulates in response to Boghossian's reconstruction of Kripke's normative considerations. Commenting on Boghossian's remark that "Any proposed candidate for being the property in virtue of which an expression has meaning must be such as to ground the 'normativity' of meaning …",[58] Fodor writes (as already seen above):

> requiring that normativity be grounded suggests that there is more to demand of a naturalized semantics than that it provide a reduction of such notions as, say, *extension*. But what could this "more" amount to? To apply a term to a thing in its extension *is* to apply the term correctly; once you've said what it is that makes the tables the extension of "table", there is surely no *further* question about why it's *correct* to apply "table" to a table. It thus seems that if you have a reductive theory of the semantic relations, there is no job of grounding normativity left to do.[59]

Such a position conflicts of course with the intuitive picture of low-brow meaning determinism: Fodor's proposal has nothing to say on such key ingredient of semantic normativity as guidance or justification. But since Fodor is not committed to being faithful to meaning determinism, any criticism on this score would be unfair. I therefore can see no other – neutral and fair – way of probing Fodor's dispositionalism than to check whether it meets the extensional requirement. This is a topic to which I shall return in Chapter 3.

(d) Reform III: normativity and biology

Ruth Millikan wants us to stop using the intuitive conception of semantic normativity as a constraint on reductive semantic dispositionalism. She proposes replacing the intuitive conception with a biological notion. Evolutionary biology gives us "the *normative* element that is involved when one means to follow a rule", it gives us "a *standard* from which … one's dispositions can diverge."[60]

The needed standard is a "purpose": one acts correctly if one meets one of one's purposes, incorrectly if one does not. Not all purposes are "expressed"; not all of our purposes are (immediately) accessible to us. Biological purposes usually are not so accessible. For instance, it is the purpose of my heart to pump blood around my body; it is not its purpose to make pounding noises in my ears. The reason why only the former activity qualifies is that hearts have pumped blood around

71

human bodies in the past, and that hearts have continued to proliferate precisely because of this pumping. Conforming to a rule can be an unexpressed biological purpose of a species. For instance, in order to intercept the female members of their species, male hoverflies conform to an intricate rule concerning their flight path and speed. The male hoverflies' conforming to this rule in part explains the existence and proliferation of hoverflies. The rule can therefore be regarded as the "biological norm" or "standard" for the male hoverflies.

The rules and purposes of hoverflies are probably all innate. But the members of other species learn in response to their environment. Rats, for instance, have the general innate rule not to eat anything that once made them sick. In a given individual rat this general rule may lead to the more specific, but equally unexpressed, rule of not eating soap. This latter rule is still a biological purpose of the animal since it is logically entailed by the general rule and a particular experience of falling ill after eating soap. Even a circus poodle that rides a bicycle is conforming to a biological purpose. General "dog rules" combined with the poodle's special environment have led it to develop unusual derived rules and purposes.

Turning to human purposes and rule-following, the first thing to note is that human beings are able to purposefully follow expressed rules. This sets them apart from other animals. At the same time, all purposeful following of expressed rules must ultimately be grounded in the purposeful following of unexpressed rules, on pain of an infinite regress of rule-following. Another key characteristic of human behaviour is its intentional character; we form intentions regarding our present and future behaviour. Such intentions are not mere epiphenomena of biology: they are derived biological purposes.

With this in place, we can see how Millikan wishes to answer the sceptic. While it is true that human behaviour can in principle be described in quaddition-like terms, biological purposes can be used as a constraint. For instance, consideration of biological purpose prevents us from thinking of the heart as essentially a noise-making device, or the eye-blink reflex as a device for pointing at one's navel. And thus there is also a fact of the matter as to whether I am an adder or a quadder:

> [W]hatever you mean to do when you encounter "plus", that content has been determined by your experiences coupled with evolutionary design. But, reasonably, whatever you mean by "plus" is the same as what other people mean who are endowed with the same general sort of cognitive equipment and have been exposed to the same sort of training in arithmetic. This meaning has been determined by the application of *Homo sapiens* rules of some kind to experience. … these considerations constitute, albeit in very rough and broad outline, the solution to the Kripke–Wittgenstein paradox.[61]

Like the meaning determinist, Millikan believes that reductive semantic dispositionalism has to meet some constraint having to do with the normativity of meaning. However, unlike the original meaning determinist of *WRPL*, Millikan lets her philosophical theory define what that constraint must be. In the original scenario of *WRPL*, semantic normativity was picture-dependent (i.e. part of low-brow meaning determinism), but not theory-dependent (i.e. not part of semantic dispositionalism). In Millikan's work the normativity of meaning is theory-dependent.

Millikan's proposal has consequences for meaning determinism that go beyond revising the conception of the normativity of meaning. In particular Millikan's version of normativity no longer passes the meaning determinist's criterion of immediate knowledge. Millikan's meaning-constituting facts are not known directly and with certainty. They are only known on the basis of hypotheses. It even seems to follow that only evolutionary biologists can ultimately tell us what we mean by our words. After all, according to Millikan's proposal, what we mean by our words is ultimately derived from our unexpressed biological purposes. And these purposes are studied and investigated by evolutionary biologists.

Putting the same point differently, Millikan assumes that the normativity of expressed intentions can ultimately be reduced to the normativity of unexpressed biological purposes. One difference between these two kinds of normativity is that the former is an "actor's category", whereas the latter is an "analyst's' category".[62] That is to say, the first but not the second is a form of normativity that is part and parcel of the self-understanding of every human rule-follower. That is a considerable deviation from the original meaning determinism. Perhaps it might even be judged that Millikan belongs in the category of "revolutionaries" rather than "reformers" (of course the borderline between these two groups has always been fuzzy).

Being judged a revolutionary might not worry Millikan. She thinks she has good reasons for deviating from the intuitive picture. Is this not what philosophical naturalism is often forced to do? But what should concern Millikan and us is the question of whether talk of biological functions is able to capture normativity. Here there is reason for doubt. Using normative language to describe proper functions seems inadequate. The norms and standards in question do not literally have a norm-authority, that is, someone who has introduced them and who sanctions deviation. How then are we to think of talk of biological norms? Is this talk not merely metaphorical? If so, then it is hard to accept that Millikan has given us a naturalization of meaning and normativity. After all, in order to understand the metaphorical sense of normativity we first have to understand the literal sense. And this literal sense presupposes an understanding of (expressed) intentions. To put the same worry in slightly different terms, one might wonder whether talk of functions does not presuppose a system of goals and values.[63] It is only because we value the heart's contribution to our, and other animals', survival that we speak of the heart's function of pumping blood. If we instead valued certain rhythms above all else, then we might well say that the heart's function was to produce its beats and sounds. The important point is that functions are aspects ascribed to entities by observers in light of their interests and values. And if that is true, the present attempt to ground explicit intentions in unexpressed biological purposes must fail.[64]

(e) An alternative revolution: "There is no such thing as a language …"

The positions discussed in the previous four sections all challenge *WRPL* by seeking to show that reductive semantic dispositionalism is, after all, able to meet a normativity constraint of sorts. In the remainder of this chapter I turn to a theory that challenges Kripke's Wittgenstein from the opposite direction. Like him, it dismisses meaning determinism and semantic normativity and, also like him, it replaces meaning determinism with a "revolutionary" alternative. However, rather than going along with the sceptical solution, the proposal in question casts aside what it construes as the conception of normativity involved in the sceptical solution. I am referring of course to the work of Donald Davidson.

To conclude this chapter with a critical dialogue between Davidson and Kripke's Wittgenstein is imperative for more than one reason. First, according to a widespread view, Kripke's Wittgenstein and Davidson mark opposite ends of the spectrum "semantic normativism versus semantic anti-normativism". Indeed, Davidson himself leaves no doubt that this is exactly how he himself perceives their relationship. Secondly, despite their alleged fundamental disagreements, Davidson and Kripke's Wittgenstein have been pilloried for putting forward rather similarly sounding and seemingly absurd claims about language: "There can be no such thing as meaning anything by any word" (*WRPL*: 55) and "there is no such thing as a language".[65] It seems worth investigating whether these statements indicate a degree of commonality that contradicts the received view. Thirdly, Kripke himself announces in a footnote that his Wittgenstein has no sympathies for Davidson's construal of meaning in terms of truth-conditions:

> Donald Davidson's influential and important theory of natural language has many features in common with the *Tractatus*, even if the underlying philosophy is different. … In particular, like the *Tractatus*, Davidson holds (i) that truth conditions are a key element in a theory of language; (ii) that the uncovering of a hidden deep structure of language is crucial to a proper theory of interpretation; (iii) that the form of the deep structure is constrained in advance by theoretical, quasi-logical considerations; (iv) that, in particular, the constraints show that the deep structure has a logical form close to that of a formal language of symbolic logic; (v) that, in particular, sentences are built up from "atoms" by logical operators; (vi) that, in particular, the deep structure of natural language is extensional in spite of the misleading appear-

ances of surface structure. All these ideas of the *Tractatus* are repudi-
ated in the *Investigations,* which is hostile to any attempt to analyse
language by uncovering a hidden deep structure.   (*WRPL*: 71–2)

Excursus: a précis of Davidson on meaning and communication

In order to answer the questions posed in the previous two paragraphs, we need
a sketch of Davidson's work. (Readers familiar with Davidson's philosophy should
jump ahead to the next section.) I begin with his work on formal theories of meaning.[66] The starting-point is the obvious idea that a systematic theory of meaning
should tell us, for each and every sentence of a given (object) language, what that
sentence means. The information concerning the meaning of the object-language
sentence should be given in a metalanguage. In other words, we want a systematic
theory of meaning for a given object language to provide us with some kind of
pairing between expressions in the object language and expressions in the metalanguage. In these pairings, it is the expression of the metalanguage that gives the
meaning of the expression of the object language.

What should the pairing look like? Let "*s*" be the name of a sentence in the
object language and *p* be the corresponding sentence in the metalanguage. Two
prima facie obvious candidates for the form of pairing then are:

    (a) *s* means *p*

and (b) *s* means that *p*.

Regrettably, neither will do. Candidate (a) makes "*p*" an expression that refers
to a meaning, and Davidson wants to avoid the ontology of meaning objects.
And (b) will not do since "it is reasonable to expect that in wrestling with the
logic of the apparently non-extensional 'means that' we will encounter problems
as hard as, or perhaps identical with, the problems our theory is out to solve".[67]
Davidson proposes replacing "means that'" with an extensional connective. The
obvious candidate is the biconditional "if, and only if", formally "$\leftrightarrow$". This would
give us:

    (c) $s \leftrightarrow p$.

Now (c) is on the right track, but not quite there yet. For *s* is the *name* of a sentence and *p* is a sentence. But a name and a sentence cannot be linked by "if, and
only if"; to say "Jones if, and only if, grass is green" is not false, it is meaningless.
So we need to turn the left-hand side of (c) into a sentence. This can be done by
applying a predicate. Let us use "*X*" as a stand-in for predicates. This gives us:

    (d) *s* is $X \leftrightarrow p$.

What predicate can take the place of X? This is like asking: which one-place predicate is such that applying it to the name of a sentence yields that sentence? Which one-place predicate can be used for purposes of disquotation, taking us from

(e) "Snow is white"

to   (f) Snow is white?

The answer is, of course, the "truth predicate". Writing T for "true" we thus get:

(g) s is $T \leftrightarrow p$.

Now (g) does not *state* that p is the meaning of s. It tells us what has to be the case for s to be true; p provides the *truth-conditions* for s. Nevertheless, Davidson believes (g) will do for our purposes. In *giving us* the truth-conditions for s, p offers us all we need for a theory of meaning.

Davidson wants a systematic, axiomatic, theory of meaning for a given language to generate, for each s, a "T-theorem" of the form (g). The most important element of Davidson's programme is contained in the realization that meaning-theorists are not the only people who want theorems of the form (g). Truth-theorists (for formal languages) want them too. Alfred Tarski's famous paper "The Concept of Truth in Formalized Languages",[68] formulates an adequacy condition for a definition of truth for a language. The condition is that an adequate theory of truth for a given language L must entail, for every sentence of L, a theorem of the form (h):

(h) s is $T_L \leftrightarrow p$.

where "s" is a "structural description" of the given sentence of L; "p" stands for a metalanguage expression that is synonymous with, or the translation of, s; and "T_L" stands for "true-in-L", the predicate to be captured. Tarski shows us how to construct formal axiomatic theories that deliver the goods. Davidson attempts to piggyback on the success of Tarski's methods. This cannot be done without some alterations, however. The main difference is that the *definienda* and *definientia* are different in the two cases. For Tarski's purposes of defining *true-in-L*, the *definientia* are s, p and the knowledge of when one expression is synonymous with, or a translation of, another expression. For Davidson, *true-in-L* belongs on the side of the *definientia*, and the *definiendum* is the knowledge of translation or synonymity between the expressions of the object and metalanguage. Davidson therefore needs to give us standards for determining how the sentences of one language should be mapped onto their translations in another language. Davidson of course does just that by giving us principles of interpretation for the scenario of "radical interpretation": the scenario where we face the speaker of a language unknown to us, and without the help of dictionaries or translators. We start by identifying which sentences our "interlocutor" holds true, and we assume that much of the time he is trying to express the same (true) beliefs that we would express in like circumstances. The methodology of radical interpretation is a *holistic* constraint: it is to be applied not just to single utterances but to all of the utterances that we can use for constructing our meaning theory for the speaker.

Davidson believes that using the methodology of radical interpretation allows interpreters to solve the tricky problem of "rogue T-theorems". A rogue T-theorem pairs a given *s* with a sentence *p* that, although it is true whenever *s* is true, intuitively fails to give *s*'s meaning. Consider:

(i)   "Schnee ist weiss" is true-in-German $\leftrightarrow$ grass is green.

Such theorems are prevented as long as the meaning theory is built on a sufficiently large sample of German utterances, and as long as the theory is constructed according to the right methodology. More complex "rogues", such as

(j)   "Schnee ist weiss" is true-in-German $\leftrightarrow$ snow is white and $1 + 1 = 2$

are ruled out by other considerations: we must think of our meaning-giving theory of truth as an "empirical theory" and of the theorems as:

> laws which state the truth conditions not only of actual utterances but also of unspoken sentences. Laws formulated as universally quantified biconditionals convey far more than identity of truth value. This consideration, and the constraints that follow from the logical relations among sentences should, when coupled with the usual pressure for simplicity, ensure that contrived, gerrymandered theories are weeded out.[69]

There is more to Davidson's philosophy of language than his Tarskian theory of truth-conditions. We get to some of his further views – developed in the 1980s and 1990s – by locating the theory of meaning within broader issues such as the definition of what a language is, or the determination of what makes communication possible. Davidson follows David Lewis[70] in thinking of languages as abstract structures: "A language may be viewed as a complex abstract object, defined by giving a finite list of expressions (words), rules for constructing meaningful concatenations of expressions (sentences), and a semantic interpretation of the meaningful expressions based on the semantic features of individual words."[71] For Davidson this viewpoint sits naturally with two other ideas: that "there must be an infinity of 'languages' no one ever has spoken or ever will speak",[72] and that we each speak our own language: "every speaker [has] ... his own quite unique way of speaking. ... Different speakers have different stocks of proper names, different vocabularies, and attach somewhat different meaning to words".[73] This claim brings all communication within the purview of the methodology of radical interpretation.

Davidson characterizes our daily radical interpretation with the concepts of "prior" and "passing" theory.[74] The prior theory consists simply of the interpreter's "expectations about what others in the community will mean by what they say".[75] When encountering a speaker, the interpreter adjusts his prior theory:

> to the evidence so far available to him: knowledge of the character, dress, role, sex, of the speaker, and whatever else has been gained by observing the speaker's behaviour, linguistic or otherwise. As the speaker speaks his piece the interpreter alters his theory, entering hypotheses about new names, altering the interpretation of familiar predicates, and revising past interpretations of particular utterances in the light of new evidence.[76]

The theory that results from such an alteration of a prior theory is the passing theory. Like the prior theory, the passing theory is a *theory* because it is systematic. Once you find out that I – whose English is not as good as I should like it to be – mean "to lend" when I say "to borrow", then you must give my "to borrow" all the powers that "to lend" has for you. And only a recursive theory can capture this.[77] Speaker and hearer usually have some expectations about the prior theories used by one another:

> For the hearer, the prior theory expresses how he is prepared in advance to interpret an utterance of the speaker, while the passing theory is how he *does* interpret the utterance. For the speaker, the prior theory is what he *believes* the interpreter's prior theory to be, while his passing theory is the theory he *intends* the interpreter to use.[78]

The important upshot of this train of thought is Davidson's attack on the idea that a shared language is a precondition for communication. Strictly speaking, no two people ever speak the same language, and hence all communication involves some level of radical interpretation. And by means of radical interpretation a speaker can in principle understand someone whose language has nothing in common with his own. Communication does not presuppose a prior agreement on the meanings of words; it merely demands that the agreement exists *after* the interpreter has done his work. And the latter work only presupposes that the interpreter is able to say in his language what the one to be interpreted says in hers.[79]

This is the point at which we can begin to understand Davidson's claim that "there is no such thing as a language".[80] The idea is that there is no such thing as a language if a language is thought of as something that must be shared between speaker and hearer in order for them to be able to communicate. Such shared language is neither necessary nor sufficient. It is not necessary for the reasons introduced in the previous paragraph. But it is also not sufficient. This claim goes back to the variety of information that an interpreter has to consider in order to succeed in his endeavour. It will not do for him to focus on just his knowledge of his prior theory; he must also take into account other, non-linguistic information: about character, dress, background and so on of the speaker. There is no special methodology for doing so:

> [W]e have abandoned not only the ordinary notion of a language, but we have erased the boundary between knowing a language and knowing our way around in the world generally. For there are no rules for arriving at passing theories, no rules in any strict sense, as opposed to rough maxims and methodological generalities. ... There is no more chance of regularising, or teaching, this process than there is of regularising or teaching the process of creating new theories to cope with new data in any field—for that is what this process involves.[81]

Davidson and meaning determinism

The above sketch of some key claims and issues in Davidson's philosophy of language will do for present purposes. I can now bring these claims and ideas into contact with *WRPL*. The natural first step here is to ask how Davidson stands with respect to meaning determinism. Davidson describes the conception of language he opposes as follows: "in learning a language, a person acquires the ability to operate in accord with a precise and specifiable set of syntactic and semantic rules; verbal communication depends on speaker and hearer sharing such an ability, and it requires no more than this".[82] Beginning with the second sub-sentence, the meaning determinism at issue in *WRPL* says of course little about the conditions of verbal communication. But it is easy enough to predict what meaning determinism would have to say. Grasping as explanation provides the crucial hint: a speaker and hearer are able to communicate if, and only if, they have grasped the same concept. Here then is the first important point where Davidson parts company from meaning determinism.

Grasping itself must also be suspect from a Davidsonian point of view. Applied to a language as a whole, grasping is the doctrine that to learn a language is to grasp once and for all a set of concepts or rules that subsequently determine, causally as well as normatively, how one must speak. Such a conception coheres badly with Davidson's emphasis on the context sensitivity of both language production and language interpretation. Davidson's speaker is not committed to being true to his prior grasping of a language; his only commitment is to being understood in the way he wishes to be understood by his current audience: "the speaker must intend the hearer to interpret his words in the way the speaker intends".[83] The same context-sensitivity might throw some doubts over Davidson's sympathies for objectivity as well.

Davidson's hostility to meaning determinism is strongest with respect to the twin principles of semantic normativity and privacy. As far as the former is concerned, enough has already been said in this chapter. Recall especially Davidson's insistence that someone who felt no linguistic obligations would not thereby be unintelligible:

> Suppose someone learns to talk as others do, but feels no obligation whatever to do so. ... [Suppose she said:] "I just do talk that way. I don't think I have an obligation to walk upright, it just comes naturally." If what she says is true would she not be speaking a language, or would she cease to be intelligible?[84]

Davidson offers two different considerations in criticism of privacy. First, he denies that a private linguist is able to establish a norm, and hence the distinction between the right and wrong uses of a language. Once a speaker directs himself to a hearer, however, such norms become conceivable and intelligible. The speaker gets things right if he is understood by the hearer in the way he wishes to be understood; he gets things wrong if he fails in this intention.[85]

Secondly, Davidson has an elaborate argument for the conclusion that the very possibility of thinking and learning presupposes "triangulation", that is, a triangle the corners of which are made up of (at least) two people and the world. For us to be able to think and speak about the world, we need to be able to perceive it. In order to analyse perception Davidson relies on a causal theory. Assume that perceiving my environment I say and believe "there is a stone". On Davidson's causal theory of perception, what the belief is about, and what the expression means, is determined by the cause of the belief. But what is the cause of my belief? The candidates range from the Big Bang, and the history of the universe, to my parents' falling in love, the stone itself and irritations on the surfaces of my eyes. As Davidson sees it, as long as I am on my own, there just is no way of deciding among these causes. Only the arrival of a second person can transform the situation. Imagine you join me and also form the same belief that there is a stone. And you hear me express my belief. For you to understand my utterance, and for you to come to believe that we believe the same thing, you have to identify the *common cause* of our beliefs. The requirement that the cause must be common rules out the irritations on the surfaces of my eyes. Moreover, not just any common cause will do: the Big Bang is a common cause but it is the cause of far too many things. The same is true even of my parents' falling in love. So you naturally opt for the *last common cause*. I do the same with you, and we communicate our reasoning to each other. We thereby enable each other to have determinate contents for our beliefs.[86]

In sum, of meaning determinism's various ingredients, Davidson clearly rejects privacy, grasping, semantic normativity and objectivity. Even though the evidence is less clear regarding some of the other elements, it is evident that Davidson's phi-losophy of language and communication is on the side of revolutionaries rather than reformers. After all, the four principles mentioned are, as it were, the heart of the meaning-determinist picture.

Critical dialogue I: Kripke's Wittgenstein as a critic of Davidson

Davidson and Kripke's Wittgenstein thus agree in their rejection of some very central ingredients of meaning determinism. But this is not to deny their differ-ences. In the next section, I shall discuss Davidson's criticism of the sceptical solu-tion. In the present section my focus will be on the question of what the meaning sceptic might dislike in Davidson's philosophy of language.

Above I quoted from a longish footnote in which Kripke presents Davidson's theory of meaning as having "many features in common with the *Tractatus*, even if the underlying philosophy is different". Kripke points out that Wittgenstein would repudiate a number of ideas that are central to Davidson's Tarski-inspired work; first and foremost the doctrine "that truth conditions are a key element in a theory of language" (*WRPL*: 71–2). That this is the main disagreement is clear also from the context in which the footnote appears. It is situated in connection with Kripke's exposition of why Wittgenstein casts aside "the classical realist pic-ture" and why Wittgenstein shifts from truth-conditions to assertability condi-tions (*WRPL*: 71–5).

It might seem obvious that Davidson's commitment to the idea that meaning is given by truth-conditions conflicts with meaning scepticism. Davidson seems to accept the very classical realism that the sceptic throws out as part and parcel of meaning determinism. The dialectical situation here is complicated since, as just seen, Davidson himself too dismisses most of meaning determinism. Has Dav-idson thus found a way of cleansing classical realism of its meaning-determinist background? If so then he will have developed a position that is not threatened by the sceptical argument of *WRPL*, a position that avoids the radical consequences of the sceptical solution. Now, it may well be the case that Davidson's position is not vulnerable to the arguments brought forth in Kripke's book. But this does not of course mean that it is above reproach. After all, there are weighty objections both to Davidson's equation of meaning with truth-conditions and to his opti-mism regarding the restraining of rogue T-theorems.[87]

It is also worth noting that Davidson himself has later become sceptical of some central aspects of his work on formal theories of truth-conditions. His work of the 1980s and 1990s, that is, his work on the most general conditions of com-munication, is in part a criticism of his own former self. This is so at least in so far as Davidson once used to believe that shared Tarski-style theories are a precondi-tion of successful communication. While the Davidson of the 1990s still regards such theories as useful for purposes of logical analysis, they are "neither necessary nor sufficient for understanding a speaker". And Davidson himself adds: "This is, after all, a Wittgensteinian point".[88]

Be this as it may, there is, in any case, a different perspective on the whole issue of the relationship between Davidson's formal theory of truth-conditions and the outlook of meaning scepticism. According to this different perspective the two positions do not conflict but are, at least to a significant extent, compatible.

To begin with, Davidson has insisted repeatedly that his formal theory of truth is merely a "model" for whatever enables us to produce and understand arbitrary utterances.[89] He has also remarked that "the implications of my approach to language for psychology are remote at best".[90] In other words, Davidson is not saying that interpreters *in fact* use theories of the sort he has developed. Davidson is not a realist about these theories. All he is saying is that his formal theory of truth-conditions is an effective and successful way of modelling some of our abilities in assigning meanings to old and new utterances.

Moreover, Davidson has emphasized that the Tarskian position on truth-conditions is unlike classical realism in important respects. Recall that the classical realist is committed to the correspondence theory of truth with its notion of facts as truth-makers, to propositions (realistically construed). Davidson rejects both. He insists that "no one knows how to individuate facts in a plausible way"[91] and that there is nothing to be gained by talking of propositions.[92] To say "that sentences or beliefs correspond to 'the facts'" remains "meaningful", but "this means no more than that they are true".[93] Davidson also speaks of "the dread idea that language and thought *represent* or mirror the world", and contends that given his outlook "there is no danger": "Tarskian semantics introduces no entities to correspond to sentences, and it is only by introducing such entities that one can make serious sense of language mirroring or corresponding to or representing features of the world."[94]

Finally, it is an open question whether the *true-in-L* in Davidson's meaning-giving theorems has much to do with a substantive understanding of truth.[95] At least until the late 1960s Davidson himself held the view that:

> the success of our venture depends not on the filling but on what it fills.
> The theory will have done its work if it provides, for every sentence *s*
> in the language under study, a matching sentence (to replace "*p*") that,
> in some way yet to be made clear, "gives the meaning" of *s*.[96]

In other words, it does not matter how thin a truth-predicate we put for X in (1):

(1) s is $X \leftrightarrow p$

As long as the truth-predicate allows us to construct an ideal machine that matches up, in the right way, sentences of the object language with sentences of the metalanguage, it does all it needs to do. Accordingly, Davidson has no difficulties with applying his truth-predicate to evaluative sentences such as "Bardot is good":

> [W]e ought not to boggle at "'Bardot is good' is true if and only if Bardot is good"; in a theory of truth, this consequence should follow with the rest ... What is special to evaluative words is simply not touched: the mystery is transferred from the word "good" in the object-language to its translation in the metalanguage.[97]

In his work from the 1970s onwards Davidson abandons this deflated understanding of truth and begins to treat truth as a key explanatory concept in theories of meaning. This shift is brought about by Davidson's work on the theory of radical interpretation. By 1990 he says that "it is our grasp of [the concept of truth] that permits us to make sense of the question whether a theory of truth for a language is correct".[98] That is to say, for Davidson the methodology of radical interpretation demands a substantive understanding of truth. This is not the place to discuss this position further, but two things are worth emphasizing. First, it is questionable whether Davidson is right in thinking that his methodology of radical interpretation really does presuppose a substantive notion of truth. John McDowell, among others, has challenged this position.[99] Secondly, if the Davidson of the 1960s and his critics are right, and if Davidson's theory of truth-conditions really can make do with no more than the deflated, theory-internal, conception of truth, then the tension between his theory of truth and the meaning sceptic's rejection of classical realism is greatly reduced.

What should we imagine Kripke's Wittgenstein to say about Davidson's argument against privacy? Here we need to distinguish two issues. The first issue is Davidson's argument that only by triangulating our perceptions with others and the world we are able to identify what our perceptions are about. The second issue is Davidson's idea that linguistic correctness and incorrectness are relative to the speaker's intentions to be understood in a certain way. I shall discuss the two issues in turn.

It should be noted first of all that a triangulation of sorts is also central to the sceptical solution. This is slightly obscured by the fact that Kripke's favoured example is mathematical. Since nothing of substance rides on this choice, let us focus on cases where people talk about chairs and other medium-size objects. In such cases we have a triangle: Jones, the speaker, who says things such as "Dies ist ein Stuhl"; Smith, the attributor, who says (or thinks) about the speaker "By 'Stuhl' he means *chair*"; and the chair that is perceived by both Jones and Smith. To understand meaning attributions we have to focus on the nature of situations in which an attributor ascribes meaning to someone whose responses he compares with his own. And the distinction between "correct" and "incorrect" is applicable to someone's responses to something only in so far as his responses can be related to, and compared with, another set of independent responses. In the most basic scenario, that second set is produced by a second person who thereby acts as yardstick and judge at one and the same time.

Kripke's Wittgenstein puts special emphasis on the fact that such triangulation usually is a "primitive" phenomenon. That is to say, the attributor–evaluator need not arrive at his conclusion – that someone else acts correctly or incorrectly – on the basis of an interpretation. To interpret something is to be aware of alternatives; but no such alternatives normally figure when we attribute meanings. This is important: unless our eyes are shut in similar ways, the problem of underdetermination of meaning attribution by verbal behaviour cannot be solved. The absence of interpretative hypotheses is thus crucial:

> *Smith* will judge Jones to mean addition by "plus" only if he judges that Jones's answers to particular addition problems agree with those *he* is inclined to give, or, if they occasionally disagree, he can interpret Jones as at least following the proper procedure. ... In all this, Smith's inclinations are regarded as just as primitive as Jones's. In no way does Smith test directly whether Jones may have in his head some rule agreeing with the one in Smith's head. Rather the point is that if, in enough concrete cases, Jones's inclinations agree with Smith's, Smith will judge that Jones is indeed following the rule for addition.
>
> (*WRPL*: 91)

In saying that the distinction between "seems right" and "is right" needs an intersubjective scenario, Kripke's Wittgenstein is not, of course, committed to the claim that the second person, the evaluator, inevitably gets things right. The point is more subtle: it is that the distinction between "seems right" and "is right" is applicable only when one evaluates the performances of another. Moreover, the claim that meaning attributors typically cannot but take their own responses as their yardstick should not be misunderstood as the idea that one's own responses are forever sacrosanct. It is part and parcel of our practices of meaning attribution that we treat our own responses as presumptively correct; but nothing prevents us from overriding this presumption.

Moreover, Kripke's Wittgenstein stresses that primitive responses on one level are compatible with flexible evaluations and interpretations on another level. That is to say, an evaluator-attributor might well conclude that she finds too many of her interlocutor's responses incorrect by her standards. In such a situation, the evaluator-attributor might decide to measure her interlocutor's responses against a different set of her own responses. That is to say, she might try a different meaning attribution: "Sometimes Smith, by substituting some alternative interpretation for Jones's word 'plus', will be able to bring Jones's responses in line with his own" (*WRPL*: 91).

Let us return to Davidson's triangulation. A superficial objection to it from a Wittgensteinian would be to chastise Davidson for his use of "interpretation".

Does not Wittgenstein insist that all interpretation comes to an end, and is not Kripke therefore right to emphasize the primitive – that is, *non-interpretative* – character of the "interpreter's" actions? Although this criticism of Davidson is sometimes made,[100] it overlooks that Davidson's understanding of "interpretation" is much wider than the Wittgensteinian ("we ought to restrict the term 'interpretation' to the substitution of one expression of the rule for another" [*PI* : §201]):

> Michael [Dummett] chides me for extending the usual use of the word "interpret" and its cognates to those ordinary situations in which we understand others without conscious effort or reflection ... I do not think we normally understand what others say by consciously reflecting on the question of what they mean, by appealing to some theory of interpretation, or by summoning up what we take to be the relevant evidence. We do it, much of the time, effortlessly, even automatically. We can do this because we have learned to talk pretty much as others do, and this explains why we generally understand without effort much that they say.[101]

While thus not being vulnerable on account of his use of "interpretation", Davidson's triangulation argument nevertheless conflicts with other meaning-sceptical tenets. There is something deeply reductive about the idea that we can individuate objects without the involvement of meaning, and on the basis of causation alone. A meaning scepticism (of the kind developed in Chapter 3 of *WRPL*) cannot accept this proposal. Indeed, the meaning sceptic will naturally feel inclined to search for arguments to the effect that object individuation on the basis of causality alone cannot succeed. Fortunately for the sceptic, such an argument already exists; it was developed by Dagfinn Føllesdal. Recall that the triangulation argument was built on a causal theory of perception. I know that I am perceiving a stone – rather than the Big Bang or surface irritations on my eyes – because the stone is the last common cause of both your and my perceptions. The argument presupposes that the candidates for common causes all lie on a single line, and that this line eventually splits into two: this is where your causes and my causes begin to differ. But why should we assume that for each of us there is just one line? Why not assume that there actually are tree-structures for each of us? In other words, why should we presuppose that there is just one unique last common cause? When you and I look towards a stone, the last common cause might be certain electromagnetic oscillations over there, the surface of the stone, various parts of this surface (that reflect light that reaches our eyes), the stone itself, or any one of a large number of further objects and events. It is obvious that causality alone cannot settle this question.[102]

Turning to Davidson's second consideration against privacy it might seem at first that the sceptic would have to take exception to the claim that what makes for correctness in communication is first and foremost the speaker's intention to be understood in a certain way by his audience. This position is forced on David-son since he has shown that shared linguistic norms – the traditional standard of correctness – are neither necessary nor sufficient for communication to succeed. The sceptical argument is of course an attack on the idea of one kind of inten-tion: to wit, that in answering "125" to "68 + 57 = ?" we are acting on the basis of a past (future-directed) intention to answer plus-queries on the basis of the addi-tion function. The sceptical argument shows that it is impossible to make sense of such intentions, at least within the meaning-determinist framework. Are not Davidson's intentions of a similar kind? The answer must be: "it depends". It all depends on how precisely Davidson's correctness-constituting intentions-to-be-understood-in-a-certain-way are construed. The meaning sceptic does not for-bid us to say things like: "I wanted to get my little daughter to stop pressing the remote control. So I said 'Stop pressing the remote control'. That was wrong. I should have known that she doesn't know the meaning of the words 'remote con-trol'". Such utterances are part of ordinary language; every parent has said them dozens of times. And such utterances are meaningful in so far as they have rough and ready assertability conditions. If "'Davidsonian intentions" are construed in this way then they are acceptable. They will be unacceptable only if they are ana-lysed along meaning-determinist lines. To analyse them in this inadmissible man-ner is to say that Jones means addition by "+" if he has a mental state of a certain kind: an intention to be understood by his audience as meaning addition by "+". And this mental state is such that the ten ingredients of the low-brow meaning-determinist picture all apply to it. There is no reason to think, and every reason to doubt, that Davidson is relying on such an analysis.

Critical dialogue II: Davidson as a critic of Kripke's Wittgenstein

In his paper "The Second Person", first published ten years after *WRPL*, Davidson levels a number of criticisms against Kripke's Wittgenstein. Most of these criti-cisms focus on the issue of normativity.

The first issue concerns an aspect of the exchange in the sceptical argument. Recall that Davidson individuates languages very finely: two languages differ pro-vided only that one of them diverges from the other over the presence of one extra personal name or one different meaning. Starting from this method of individu-ation, one might rephrase the original sceptical challenge – what makes it so that you mean addition rather than quaddition by "+"? – as: what makes it so that you speak one language rather than another, say English rather than Queng-lish (where Quenglish is like English except that it has a different function for "+")? The sceptic would, of course, contend here that however much data we have about a speaker we shall never have enough information to decide between the two hypotheses; maybe addition and the alternative function begin to differ only in numerical realms that human minds cannot reach. Davidson thinks that we should not worry about this possibility:

> There will ... be endless different languages which agree with all of a speaker's actual utterances, but differ with respect to unspoken sentences. ... So there will be endless languages consistent with all the actual utterances of a speaker none of which is "the" language he is speaking. ... This particular difficulty, though it may have troubled Wittgenstein, and certainly troubled Kripke, seems to me to have a relatively simple answer. The longer we interpret a speaker with apparent success as speaking a particular language the greater our legitimate confidence that the speaker is speaking that language, or one much like it.[103]

Secondly, Davidson believes that the sceptical solution is based on a mistaken view of normativity. As Davidson sees it, like the meaning determinist, the meaning sceptic also holds that "to speak a language is to follow rules". Davidson recognizes that meaning scepticism opposes the idea of an "inner mental act or process of 'grasping' or 'following' the rule". And he notes that "the criterion that decides what rule someone is following is just how she actually goes on, and the only test whether she has it right is whether she goes on as I (her interpreter) would". Davidson also puts the point in terms of meaning and language: "we judge that a speaker means what we would if we were to utter the same words. She speaks the same language we do if she goes on as we would".[104] Once the point is put in this way, we already know why Davidson has to oppose it. As seen previously, Davidson does not believe that to speak a language is to follow rules, and he rejects any suggestion that to speak correctly is to speak as others do. Here is a further quotation that illustrates his point well:

> If you and I were the only speakers in the world, and you spoke Sherpa while I spoke English, we could learn to understand one another, though there would be no "rules" that we jointly followed in our speech. What would matter, of course, is that we should each provide the other with something intelligible as a language. This is, as we saw, a condition speakers must intend to satisfy; but carrying out the intention, while it may require a degree of what the other perceives as consistency, does not involve following shared rules or conventions. ... So, while it may be true that speaking a language requires that there be an interpreter, it does not follow that more than one person must speak the same language. ... I conclude that Kripke's criterion for speaking a language cannot be right; speaking a language cannot depend on speaking as someone else does (or as many others do).[105]

Thirdly and finally, Davidson takes there to be a fundamental divide between philosophies of language that take idiolects as conceptually primary with respect to shared language, and philosophies of language that take a shared language as primary with respect to idiolects.[106] He counts Kripke's Wittgenstein among those who prioritize language over idiolects; and he regards his own work as an extended argument in favour of reversing this ranking.

Let us investigate the three objections in turn. According to the first we should not worry about the fact that a choice between hypotheses as to which language someone speaks – English or Quenglish, for example – is inevitably underdetermined by that person's speech behaviour. "The longer we interpret a speaker with apparent success, the greater our legitimate confidence". Is this a legitimate objection to the sceptical argument (i.e. the line of thought of Chapter 2 of *WRPL*)? I fail to see how it could be. To begin with, the sceptical argument is directed against meaning determinism; and it is the meaning determinist who believes that the speaker of a language knows *exactly* which language he is speaking. The meaning sceptic, however, is not at all committed to this view. Indeed, this very view is one of the victims of his attack. Moreover, note that Davidson's comment misses the mark also in an even more profound sense. The focus of the sceptical argument is on ontological or constitutive, not on epistemological questions. The question is not "How do you know which language you are speaking?"; it is "What makes it so that you speak one language rather than another?" In construing the question as being about evidence for alternative hypotheses, Davidson betrays his misunderstanding: that is, that the issue is epistemological.

The second objection is equally off target, but it will take more work to show this to be the case. To start us off, *WRPL* does not *equate* attributions of meanings with attributions of rules; it does not say that to attribute a meaning *is* to ascribe a rule. The data to be accounted for by both meaning determinist and meaning sceptic are attributions of meanings *and* attributions of rules (and concepts of course). Both protagonists hold that one and the same rough general account will cover both cases. But they do not believe that the one case somehow reduces to the other. It is easy to see why Davidson overshoots the mark here: the prominence of the mathematical example encourages equating meaning and rule. Davidson is right to say:

> Most language learning is accomplished without learning or knowing any rules at all. Wittgenstein does, of course, treat meaning something in much the same way he treats following some procedure, such as adding in arithmetic. But there is a clear distinction between the cases, which explains why we ordinarily use the word "rule" in one case and not in the other. In the case of adding, there is an explicit procedure for arriving at an answer; we can learn and describe the procedure, and it is appropriate to call the procedure or its description a rule. We normally follow no procedure in speaking; nothing in the everyday use of language corresponds to taking the sum in adding.[107]

That is all true, but then again, there is nothing that Kripke's Wittgenstein says that contradicts this view.

Moreover, it seems that Davidson's criticism itself falsely equates two very different ideas: that communication involves substantial agreement in primitive responses, and that communication involves prior agreement in rules and meanings. Davidson is right to locate the first idea in *WRPL* but he is wrong about the presence of the latter. Kripke's Wittgenstein explicitly rules out the notion that our responses agree because our concepts agree; indeed, he propounds the inverse (*WRPL*: 97). In emphasizing the need for agreement in responses rather than meanings, concepts and conventions, Kripke's Wittgenstein is close to Davidson's own position. Indeed such agreement is surely a precondition of radical interpretation as well: if the native did not respond to dogs and interpreters roughly the way we do, then we could not form the hypothesis that he is trying to tell us that the animal in front of us is a dog.

The crucial criterion for deciding whether Davidson's criticism is justified is what Kripke's Wittgenstein has to say on radical interpretation. Davidson's attack is on target, if, and only if, meaning scepticism rules out the possibility of radical interpretation. Assume that Kripke's Jones and Smith encounter each other in such a situation, Jones now being a tribesman speaking an unfamiliar language, a tribesman whom Smith encounters in the jungle, and without the benefits of dictionaries and interpreters (as normally understood!). Let Jungle-Jones make the noise "sulp" under different conditions and in different verbal contexts. Under what circumstances would Smith feel entitled to produce the meaning attribution "Jungle-Jones means *addition* by 'sulp'"? Obviously only under conditions in which Smith can somehow match Jungle-Jones's responses to his own. This might happen in circumstances where Jones utters "sulp" while performing various operations with pebbles, while rounding up cattle or while ordering his spears or axes. Being a member of our community, Smith will use our criteria, our assertability conditions for meaning attributions of "plus". The assertability conditions will be roughly similar to the assertability we considered in Chapter 1 for cases where a teacher attributes a command of addition to a child. There is no need for Jungle-Jones to share these assertability conditions. These conditions bind Smith and us, but they need not bind the one to be interpreted. That this is the natural way to read Kripke's Wittgenstein's position should be clear already from the original example. When a teacher attributes an understanding of "plus" (as referring to the addition function) to a child, the child usually will not be able to follow the teacher's rough and ready assertability conditions for such attributions.

But what about cases in our own culture? Does not the sceptical solution commit us to saying that Joyce's "Dyoublong" fails to mean anything since Joyce diverges from the way we speak? No it does not. Kripke writes: "If Jones consistently fails to give responses in agreement … with Smith's, Smith will judge that he does not mean addition by 'plus'. … Sometimes Smith, by substituting some alternative interpretation for Jones's word 'plus', will be able to bring Jones's responses in line with his own" (*WRPL*: 91). This passage makes clear that in order to speak meaningfully we need not speak as others do. It suffices that they have the resources to make sense of our words in their words.

But, one might wish to protest, does not Kripke's Wittgenstein insist that what gives words their significance is that they have assertability conditions? And are not these assertability conditions shared by a group? There is something in that protest. It is indeed the case that assertability conditions, rather than truth-conditions, give expressions their meaning. And it is true as well that assertability conditions are shared. And yet for all that, it does not seem contrary to the general position of the sceptical solution to allow for the possibility that assertability conditions can change and develop, or that new assertability conditions can be invented and spread through the community. This possibility sits naturally with the sceptical solution's "in-built" emphasis on contingency and circumstance: this emphasis is most evident in the idea that all assertability conditions identify only "roughly specifiable circumstances" and that assertability conditions are "not necessary and sufficient conditions" (*WRPL*: 78, 87). Precisely because they are rough and ready only, there is always scope for adjusting them to given circumstances.

If this comment is on target, then we can say the following. *WRPL* assumes that assertability conditions are usually shared. Whatever the differences in our idiolects – and these differences are often considerable – our idiolects do largely overlap. This is why we say in ordinary life that we speak English, German or Finnish, rather than "Davidsonese", "Kantese" or "Hintikkaian". Nevertheless, we do introduce new words: "Dyoublong", for example. In such cases, to get our interlocutors to understand what we mean is to stimulate them to modify existing, or invent new, assertability conditions. (Usually the new ones will be modelled on existing ones.) This is what Joyce does with "Dyoublong". We know that Joyce was associated with a city called "Dublin", and we recognize the expression "Do you belong?" We have rough assertability conditions for both. Joyce tries to get us to bring these assertability conditions together. He will succeed in his intention to the extent that we succeed in this endeavour.

In stressing this last point I have already made headway with respect to the dispute over conceptual priority between idiolects and "sociolect" (the shared language of a group). Kripke's Wittgenstein does not present an in-principle argument to the effect that the sociolect must be primary. If we wish to individuate languages as finely as Davidson proposes, then we are perfectly entitled to say that we all speak different languages: "Say what you choose, so long as it does not prevent you from seeing the facts" (*PI*: §79). And if we wish to focus on phenomena of radical interpretation, then it makes good sense to see idiolects as primary.

This does not mean that the meaning sceptic will applaud all aspects of Davidson's work on radical interpretation and the possibility of communication. Davidson's work on radical interpretation rests on idealizations – on a principled abstracting away from the human condition – that Kripke's Wittgenstein would be unwilling to contemplate. Davidson believes that it makes sense to ask "in a theoretical vein": "how many competent speakers of a language must there be if anyone can be said to speak or understand a language?"[108] To ask in this "theoretical vein" is to rely on an idealization: we ignore the fact that human beings grow up and live in communities; and we narrow our focus to the conceptual question of what are the minimal imaginable conditions of communication. Davidson's answer is that it takes no more than two to communicate. Elsewhere Davidson tells us that although it is "intolerable, perhaps humanly impossible" that there be a society in which each speaker has a "radically different language" there is still much to be learned from this scenario: the lesson of this scenario is that "each hearer would have to extemporise a mode of interpretation".[109] Here by "different languages" Davidson seems not to be thinking of languages that differ only in a personal name or two; if the envisaged scenario is to be "humanly impossible" it must mean languages that do not overlap at all.

Kripke's Wittgenstein's objections to idealization in the context of sophisticated dispositionalism would – *mutatis mutandis* – apply here too. We cannot claim that, *ceteris paribus*, we are disposed to give sums to plus-queries even in the realm of enormous numerals (i.e. numerals too large for creatures like us to even think). We are not permitted to make the *ceteris paribus* claim since to do so we must be able make sense of the idealization involved: "How in the world can I tell what would happen if my brain were stuffed with extra brain matter, or if my life were prolonged by some magic elixir?" (*WRPL*: 27). If that objection is on target – and I shall argue in Chapter 3 that it is – then it must also apply to Davidson's idealization in the present context. How in the world can we tell how we would communicate if we did not live, and had never lived, in our own, or indeed any, community? And how can we determine what life would be like if each one spoke a language that overlapped with the language of no one else?

Despite the many surprising affinities between Davidson and Kripke's Wittgenstein there remains a fundamental difference in orientation. It is this difference in orientation that ultimately generates the difference in attitudes towards idealization. Kripke's Wittgenstein takes as basic what one might call "the participant stance".[110] We can best understand the role of meaning attributions if we ask what role they play in our actual lives. Accordingly Kripke's Wittgenstein tries to learn from pedestrian phenomena such as buying apples from a grocer, or teaching a child to count. As participants in these practices we always already understand them. But we might need to be reminded of them in order to avoid falling prey to philosophical confusions that make the ordinary look mysterious. Davidson's stance is fundamentally different: the title "objective stance" seems appropriate. The paradigmatic Davidsonian interpreter is the jungle-linguist or the reader of James Joyce's enigmatic writings. Interpreter and interpreted do not meet as participants in a shared practice; they encounter each other as objects of an abstract, theoretical interest. It is not far from the abstractness of the interpreter's interest to the idea that the interpreter and the interpreted can themselves be abstracted away from the human condition.

Conclusion

In Chapter 1 I proposed a new interpretation of the normativity considerations in *WRPL*. According to this new interpretation it is important to distinguish between semantic and intersubjective normativity. Semantic normativity is a central assumption of meaning determinism; namely, the assumption that to mean something by a sign (to follow a rule, to possess a concept) is to have a mental state that guides and justifies one's application of the sign. Intersubjective normativity is a key idea of meaning scepticism: there is no special form of normativity based on meaning-constituting mental states; in our applications of terms we are guided by others; and we justify our uses of terms, as well as our meaning attributions, on the basis of publicly available criteria.

The sceptical argument is an "immanent critique" of meaning determinism; it seeks to show that meaning-deterministic theories of meaning fail by meaning determinism's very own standards. Ultimately therefore, meaning determinism must be given up in favour of the new picture of meaning scepticism. Semantic normativity does not survive into the new picture. This does not mean that all talk of "ought", "should", "correct" and "incorrect" concerning meaning is misplaced; but it does imply that there is no distinctively *semantic* form of normativity.

Semantic reductive dispositionalism is a theory intended to turn the picture of meaning determinism into a respectable naturalistic theory. In so doing, dispositionalism is meant to remain true to the elements of the original picture. Unfortunately, *WRPL* shows that dispositionalism fails in this respect: dispositionalism turns out to be unfaithful to semantic normativity. This failure constitutes a reason (for the meaning determinist herself) to reject dispositionalism.

In this chapter I have sought to further motivate my reading of the normativity considerations by confronting it with other interpretations and various criticisms of *WRPL*. The most important alternative interpretation was Boghossian's suggestion according to which the thesis of the normativity of meaning is (i) "simply a new name for the familiar fact that … meaningful expressions possess conditions of *correct use*", and (ii) the idea that "to be told that 'horse' means *horse* implies that a speaker ought to be motivated to apply the expressions to horses only". I have tried to show that Boghossian's deflated normativity requirement does not only fail to fit with Kripke's text, but that it is also unable to put much pressure on dispositionalism. The latter point is confirmed by Boghossian himself. And the same verdict has been reached by the many critics who – assuming that Boghossian's interpretation is correct – have pointed out that the normativity argument is question-begging, based on implausible claims concerning the link between meaning and truth-telling, or dependent on confusing different types of rules.

Up to this point, my arguments (in this chapter) were meant to show that – correctly interpreted – the normativity considerations of the sceptical argument do indeed tell against dispositionalism. But I could not leave things here. I also needed to consider what happens to the normativity considerations once we widen our perspective beyond the sceptical argument of *WRPL*, and allow various revisionists, reformers and revolutionaries regarding meaning determinism and semantic normativity to present their case. The second half of this chapter focused on these positions.

Revisionists change meaning-deterministic dispositionalism only marginally. They seek to escape the normativity considerations by increasing the number and types of dispositions in play. We saw that this proposal was not successful.

Reform of meaning-deterministic dispositionalism took the three forms of replacing: (i) privacy by intersubjectivity; (ii) semantic normativity by semantic correctness; or (iii) semantic normativity by the biological notion of proper function. I postponed the discussion of (ii) to Chapter 3, but established that (i) and (iii) were unconvincing.

Under the title "*Revolution*" I discussed Davidson's theory of meaning. Of particular interest were the questions of: (I) how Davidson's views compare with meaning determinism and meaning scepticism; and (II) whether Davidson's criticisms of *WRPL* in general, and its normativity considerations in particular, are decisive. Regarding (I), I maintained that there are important affinities between Davidson's philosophy and the meaning scepticism of *WRPL*. It is especially noteworthy that Davidson and the sceptic hold near-identical views on the normativity requirement: both reject semantic normativity, and both accept forms of intersubjective normativity. As concerns (II), I tried to show that Davidson's criticism of the role of normativity in *WRPL* is simply based on a mistaken interpretation of Kripke's book. *WRPL* does not *equate* attributions of meanings with attributions of rules; assertability conditions need not always and everywhere be shared; and *WRPL* does not present an in-principle argument to the effect that sociolects are primary with respect to idiolects.

If an even briefer summary is desirable, here are the three theses that I hope to have made plausible in this chapter:

(1) The normativity requirement tells against dispositionalism only if interpreted as semantic normativity. Deflated versions (such as Boghossian's) are inadequate to this task.
(2) Revision and reform of meaning-deterministic dispositionalism are unable to deflect the force of the normativity considerations.
(3) Davidson's attack on the normativity of meaning does not undermine the position of *WRPL*. Davidson's views on normativity are (in good part) shared by the sceptic.

THREE

Dispositions and extensions

Introduction

The argument of *WRPL* against reductive semantic dispositionalism can be reconstructed as having two prongs.[1] (In this chapter, "dispositionalism" always means "reductive semantic dispositionalism".) The first prong is the claim that dispositionalism fails the *intensional requirement*: it fails to show that having the disposition to use a sign "*y*" under conditions *C* intuitively resembles meaning *X* by "*y*". This criticism is tantamount to saying that dispositionalism is unable to do justice to semantic normativity. The second prong of the argument against dispositionalism is that it is unable to meet the *extensional requirement*: it does not succeed in identifying dispositional predicates that logically co-vary with meaning predicates. The need to meet this second requirement follows from the meaning-determinist commitment to objectivity.

I discussed the intensional requirement in Chapter 2, confirming and building on the negative assessment of *WRPL*. In this chapter I turn to the extensional requirement. Kripke's use of the extensional requirement as a weapon against dispositionalism has been discussed frequently in the literature, and with little sympathy. Almost all commentators feel that the extensional requirement can be met either within the confines of the original intuitive picture of meaning determinism or by relaxing some of the latter's demands. In discussing these positions, we need not distinguish sharply between original meaning determinists, reformers and revolutionaries. For the most part I shall allow that any element of meaning determinism can be relaxed or dropped, as long as the extensional requirement is still met.

Given the amount of discussion on the extensional requirement, we shall have to be selective. I cannot here reply to every single argument in the literature, and I shall have to be brisk with some of the ideas I consider. I have used two criteria of selection: influence and ingenuity. Usually, these two criteria have yielded the same verdict; the main exceptions are recent publications that have not yet had a chance to leave their mark on the field.

I begin with a summary of Kripke's case against the extensional requirement. Of the various objections to, and elaborations of, this case, I shall give most room to Fodor's criticism of Kripke's arguments against idealization and *ceteris paribus* laws, and to Boghossian's attempt to improve on Kripke's attack on dispositionalism. I shall also consider – although somewhat more briefly – defences of dispositionalism by Simon Blackburn, Carl Ginet, Paul Horwich, C. B. Martin and J. Heil, as well as Scott Soames.[2]

Simple and sophisticated dispositionalism

Kripke himself does not use the language of "extensional" and "intensional requirements" when discussing dispositionalism. It will prove useful in what follows to briefly introduce some of his own terms and conceptualizations.

Kripke distinguishes between "simple" and "sophisticated" dispositionalism. The simple version receives two formulations. According to its informal characterization, "to mean addition by '+' is to be disposed, when asked for any sum '$x + y$', to give the sum of x and y as the answer" (*WRPL*: 22). The more detailed, formal account is based on the following conventions: φ is a number-theoretic function; f a function symbol denoting φ; m, n and p are numbers; m, n and p are numerals denoting m, n and p, respectively; and the value for $\varphi(m, n)$ is p. Using these conventions, the dispositionalist can state his standpoint thus: "It is a fact about me that, when faced with the query '$f(m, n)$?', I am disposed to give the answer 'p'. And that I am disposed in this way shows that by the symbol '$f(\ldots, \ldots)$' I mean the function φ." Instantiating this formula in the obvious way for Kripke's central example, we get: "It is a fact about me that, when faced with the query '$68 + 57 = ?$', I am disposed to answer '125'. This shows that by the symbol '+' (or the expression 'plus') I mean the addition function."

Sophisticated dispositionalism differs from simple dispositionalism in one crucial respect. The sophisticated dispositionalist adds a *ceteris paribus* clause to the dispositionalist response. Sophistication thus takes the following form: "It is a fact about me that, when faced with the query '$f(m, n)$?', I am disposed, *ceteris paribus*, to give the answer 'p'. This shows that by the symbol '$f(\ldots, \ldots)$' I mean the function φ."

The finitude problem

According to *WRPL*, the first and main problem with dispositionalism is that it is unable to do justice to the normative aspects of meaning. Enough has been said about this issue in previous chapters. More important at this point is the "finitude problem". The addition function is infinite, but my dispositions to give sums in reply to plus-queries (of the form "$m + n = ?$") are finite. I have dispositions to respond with the sum for given plus-queries only as far as relatively small numbers are concerned. Let us call numbers that are too large for me to even consider "enormous numbers".[3] The addition function is defined for both non-enormous and enormous numbers. Nevertheless, my dispositions cover only the realm of non-enormous numbers. What then gives the dispositionalist the right to maintain that I mean the addition function by "plus" (*WRPL*: 26–7)?

At this point Kripke introduces sophisticated dispositionalism. I mean *addition* by "plus", the sophisticated dispositionalist insists, because *ceteris paribus* I would give sums even to plus-queries in the realm of enormous numbers. How are we to understand this *ceteris paribus* clause? Kripke offers this reconstruction:

> If my brain had been stuffed with sufficient extra matter to grasp large enough numbers, and if it were given enough capacity to perform such a large addition, and if my life (in a healthy state) were prolonged enough, then given an addition problem involving two large numbers, m and n, I would respond with their sum ...   (*WRPL*: 27)

Kripke rejects sophisticated dispositionalism as a solution to the problems with finitude. He gives two arguments. The first questions whether we have sufficient knowledge about the possible world in which my brain has the required size and age: "How in the world can I tell what would happen if my brain were stuffed with extra brain matter ... ? ... We have no idea what the results of such experiments would be" (*WRPL*: 27). I cannot claim to be an adder of enormous numbers, since I have no idea of how to find out what I would be like with a brain of the required size. According to the second argument, the dispositionalist cannot specify the required idealization without arguing in a circle. The dispositionalist must be able to explain why his dispositions regarding plus-queries are dispositions that track the addition function. Providing this explanation must include an account of how his dispositions are able to follow the addition function in the realm of enormous numbers. The dispositionalist replies to the latter challenge by idealizing his abilities: he is tracking the addition function in the realm of enormous numbers because – once appropriately idealized – he has dispositions to give sums in response to plus-queries even in this realm. But *how*, Kripke asks, do we have to idealize the calculator's current and real dispositions for the latter to be able to add enormous numbers? Surely we can imagine many different ways of idealizing his real dispositions (for the non-enormous numbers). And, most importantly, on some such idealization he turns out to be an adder in the realm of the enormous numbers, whereas on some other idealization he ends up tracking some other function. Which idealization is the right one? Which idealization gives us the right kind of dispositions? Here, it seems, the dispositionalist can do no better than come full circle by replying that the needed idealization is the one enabling me to add. And this is circular. His dispositions were meant to tell him what he means; but now it is the meaning that tells him how to idealize his dispositions (*WRPL*: 27–8).

The mistake problem

The third problem for dispositionalism, the "mistake problem", straddles the border between extensional and intensional requirements. It too has several strands. One such strand is introduced in a footnote (*WRPL*: 29) and points to a further dissimilarity between statements about what we mean and statements about what we are disposed to do. In claiming to mean *addition* by "plus", we do not take ourselves to be predicting our future linguistic behaviour. Alas, attributing dispositions to oneself does seem to involve such predictions. According to the dispositionalist, my existing (past, present and future) dispositions regarding plus-queries can be used to justify my claim that by "+" I mean *addition*. However, my dispositions can play this justificatory role only on the supposition that among them there is no – as yet unmanifested – disposition to go mad and deviate from the addition function in the future. If my dispositions regarding plus-queries determine what I mean by "+", then on what grounds do I exclude my "mad" disposition? To ignore it, as the dispositionalist is disposed to do, is tantamount to making the prediction that I shall be sane in the future.

The core of the mistake problem is the claim that dispositionalism is unable to distinguish between two clearly distinct scenarios: the scenario where I follow one rule correctly and the scenario where I follow another rule incorrectly. The difficulty is most evident in the context of dispositions to make systematic mistakes. In everyday life we allow for the possibility that someone means addition by "+" despite his making systematic mistakes in, say, "carrying". Such a person, let's call him Otto, would calculate 68 + 57 as:

$$
\begin{array}{r}
68 \\
+\ 57 \\
\hline
115
\end{array}
$$

A stranger to our arithmetical practices might interpret Otto's case differently. She might suggest that so far from being a faulty adder, Otto is in fact a successful "skadder". The extension of the "skaddition" function can be generated by adding without carrying. Needless to say, we have no difficulties telling whether someone is a faulty adder or a competent "skadder". Now consider the simple dispositionalist. He does not have a choice between calling Otto a skadder or an adder. Since Otto's dispositions regarding plus-queries show which function he means, the simple dispositionalist has no alternative to saying that Otto is a skadder. In equating "performance" and "competence", the dispositionalist has committed himself to this unacceptable answer (*WRPL*: 29–30).

Again the dispositionalist might be tempted to respond by going for sophistication. At this point, this would suggest insisting that *ceteris paribus* Otto means *addition* by "+". The *ceteris paribus* clause is meant to prevent Otto's systematic mistakes from turning him into a skadder. Unfortunately for the dispositionalist, sophistication again proves a futile hope. Difficulties surface the moment the dispositionalist attempts to give content to the idealization involved in the *ceteris paribus* provision. Kripke considers three alternatives. According to the first suggestion, competence is, by definition, the absence of dispositions to make mistakes. This is circular. In order to discard the right dispositions as dispositions to make mistakes, I must already know which function I mean (*WRPL*: 30). The second proposal says that competence is performance in the absence of fatigue, distraction, drunkenness, clutter and so on. This overlooks the fact that the mistakes in question are meant to be systematic. They are meant to occur even when the subject is well rested, not distracted, sober and so on (*WRPL*: 30–31). The third alternative is to go for a social account and translate "*Ceteris paribus*, Otto will reply with the sum" as "Otto will reply with the sum after Otto has been re-educated and corrected by other people". This too is unsatisfactory. It fails to account for the fact that even uneducable people can mean addition by "plus". What is worse, we are yet again trapped in circularity. How do the others know when to correct Otto? How do they know whether he is trying to add or seeking to skadd? It can hardly be on the basis of the function that Otto means! Nor can circularity be avoided by allowing Otto to decide for himself which randomly produced corrections he is going to heed. After all, a suggestible Otto might well change even his correct responses (*WRPL*: 32).

Communal dispositions

Kripke's scepticism concerning a *social* solution to the problems of dispositionalism is not confined to the mistake problem. Kripke thinks that dispositionalism fails regardless of whether we consider the dispositions of an individual or the dispositions of a whole group. It will not do to say: "By '+' we mean *addition* since we collectively – or most of us – are disposed to give sums in reply to plus-queries". Kripke believes, although he does not spell it out in detail, that such an idea "would be a social, or community-wide, version of the dispositional theory, and would be open to at least some of the same criticisms as the original form" (*WRPL*: 111).

The machine response

Kripke deems the above arguments decisive also against a *prima facie* different response to the sceptical challenge. According to this rejoinder, at least for some purposes, we can usefully think of ourselves as machines. And machines, it seems, can embody functions. Surely, the retort says, in the case of a computing machine (e.g. a pocket calculator) there is a fact of the matter as to which function the machine "embodies". And since this holds for machines, why not assume something similar in our own case? Can we not, for many intents and purposes, programme ourselves? Kripke reads the machine response as a version of dispositionalism: "the dispositionalist theory views the subject himself as a kind of machine, whose potential actions embody the function" (*WRPL*: 35). *WRPL* contains a longish discussion of this idea.

Imagine an engineer trying to fight the sceptic with technological means. She sets up a machine to give sums in response to plus-queries. When challenged by the sceptic to justify her own responses, she simply refers the sceptic to her machine. Whatever the machine produces is the correct answer because the machine has been set up so as to give sums. As the engineer sees it, her computing machine embodies the addition function. To block this technological escape, Kripke begins by pointing out that there is more than one way of identifying "the machine" in the given case. A first possibility is to think of a written version of the machine program as *the* machine. If our engineer opts for this suggestion, then she is immediately in trouble. For obviously a written program is no less open to multiple interpretations than is "+". Equally unsatisfactory is the idea of thinking of the machine program as an abstract (Platonic) object. This is unhelpful because it does not tell us which of an infinite number of possible abstract objects is instantiated in the mechanism of the machine (*WRPL*: 33).

This leaves the possibility of treating the physical object itself as the machine. Kripke advances three considerations regarding this proposal. First, the engineer needs to justify her way of interpreting the machine's output. And this calls for instructions. Alas, such instructions can again be variously interpreted. Secondly, the finitude problem can be brought to bear on the current case. No physically real machine can calculate more than a tiny segment of infinite functions such as addition or quaddition. And thus the observable behaviour of the machine underdetermines which function it is computing. Thirdly, and finally, the present case also allows for an application of the mistake problem. Our engineer needs to be able to tell us which of the physical changes undergone by a machine are part of its correct functioning and which are part of its deterioration and malfunctioning. A machine that answers "5" to all plus-queries with numbers higher than 57 might be a malfunctioning addition machine, but it might also be a well-functioning quaddition machine. The only way to answer this question is to refer to the program the designer of the machine had in mind. And this response returns us to the earlier difficulties of explaining how such program can avoid the sceptical challenge (*WRPL*: 36).

Idealization and *ceteris paribus* clauses

The time has come to face the critics. I begin with Fodor's attempt to defend dispositionalism. As will be recalled from Chapter 2, Fodor believes that dispositionalism need not worry about arguments from semantic normativity: to meet the extensional requirement is *eo ipso* to also meet the intensional requirement. And Fodor holds that Kripke has not given us reason for doubt that it can meet the extensional requirement.

Fodor agrees with Kripke that a simple dispositionalism is hopeless. But he maintains that a sophisticated version of the doctrine can pass muster. Kripke believes that it falls at the very first hurdle in that it makes illegitimate use of idealization. Fodor argues that if we fault dispositionalism for its use of idealization then we also must reject much of natural science. This is because, as Fodor maintains, natural science relies on idealization in pretty much the same way as does dispositionalism. In what follows, I shall argue that this claim is mistaken. I shall try to show that the use of idealization (and *ceteris paribus* clauses) in the sciences differs from the use of idealization (and *ceteris paribus* clauses) by dispositionalism.

To start us off, it may be useful to repeat the central passage from *WRPL* in which Kripke rejects the use of idealization:

> [H]ow should we flesh out the *ceteris paribus* clause? Perhaps as something like: if my brain had been stuffed with sufficient extra matter to grasp large enough numbers, and if it were given enough capacity to perform such large addition, and if my life (in a healthy state) were prolonged enough, then given an addition problem involving two large numbers, *m* and *n*, I would respond with their sum ... But how can we have any confidence of this? How in the world can I tell what would happen if my brain were stuffed with extra brain matter, or if my life were prolonged by some magic elixir? ... The outcome really is obviously indeterminate, failing further specifications of these magic mind-expanding processes; and even with such specifications, it is highly speculative. (*WRPL*: 27)

Fodor's reply to Kripke is relatively short and thus can be quoted in full:

> Apparently Kripke assumes that we can't have reason to accept that a generalization defined for idealized conditions is lawful unless we can specify the counterfactuals which would be true if the idealized conditions were to obtain. It is, however, hard to see why one should take this methodology seriously. For example: God only knows what would happen if molecules and containers actually met the conditions specified by the ideal gas laws (molecules are perfectly elastic;

containers are infinitely impermeable; etc.); ... But it's not required, in order that the ideal gas laws should be in scientific good repute, that we know anything like all of what would happen if there really were ideal gases. All that's required is that we know (e.g.) that if there were ideal gases, then, *ceteris paribus*, their volume would vary inversely with the pressure upon them. And *that* counterfactual *the theory itself tells us is true*. Similarly, if there are psychological laws that idealize to unbounded working memory, it is not required in order for *them* to be in scientific good repute that we know all of what would happen if working memory really were unbounded. All we need to know is that, if we did have unbounded memory, then, *ceteris paribus*, we would be able to compute the value of $m + n$ for arbitrary m and n.[4]

Fodor's line of thought mobilizes the authority of science against Kripke. Scientists seem happy to conceptualize dispositions with *ceteris paribus* clauses and idealizations; hence, Kripke's opposition to sophisticated semantic dispositionalism is out of touch with scientific thinking about dispositions.[5]

I now turn to showing that this quick dismissal of Kripke's criticism fails to reckon with the nature of idealization in science.[6] It is worth developing the example of the ideal gas law at slightly greater length. The law states the relationship between pressure (P), volume (V), temperature in degrees Kelvin (T), number of moles (n) and a constant (R) as follows:

$$PV = nRT$$

Fodor mentions two of the idealizations involved; others are that molecules have zero volume; that there are no attractive forces between gas molecules or between gas molecules and the sides of the container; and that heat is the only source of energy present in a gas.

If writers in the history and philosophy of science are to be believed, three features are important about laws such as the ideal gas law.[7] First, such laws are parts of systems of laws. For instance, the ideal gas law is part of the kinetic molecular theory of gases, further laws of which include Boyle's law ($PV = k$), Charles' law ($V \div T = k$), Avogadro's law ($V \div n = k$), and Gay-Lussac's law ($P \div T = k$). Secondly, although the idealizations involved in the ideal gas law are false in our world, we can experimentally approximate the values predicted by the law. We can, for instance, increase the permeability of the container, and we can lower the temperature (in order to decrease the volume). Thirdly, and most importantly, in scientific practice, idealization is typically followed by "de-idealization". That is to say, scientists seek to increase the predictive accuracy of their theories by removing idealizations. In the case of the ideal gas law for example, physicists have come to formulate corrections that make due allowance for the size of molecules and for their mutual attraction. Hence the volume occupied due to the finite size of the molecules (b) needs to be deducted from V, and the attraction of molecules on each other (a) needs to be added to P. These corrections lead to the van der Waals' equation:

$$(V - b)(P + a/V^2) = RT$$

If this thumbnail sketch of idealization in science is near the mark, how then should we think of the idealization involved in "If we did have unbounded memory, then, *ceteris paribus*, we would be able to compute the value of $m + n$ for arbitrary m and n"?[8] The answer seems obvious: Fodor's idealization differs in important respects from standard idealization in science.

To begin with, it is unclear to what body of theory "Fodor's law" is meant to belong. Is it part of mathematics or psychology? It is hard to tell. Which psychological theory makes use of such idealization? It is hard to think of any. And what other laws are there, laws that make use of the same idealization? None. But then, is not this idealization completely *ad hoc*? In response to these questions, Fodor had better not reply that we can *imagine* a body of theory to which his law belongs. Membership in a body of theory can be a constraint only if the body of theory in question is actual. After all, we can imagine all sorts of weird bodies of theory.

Moreover, it is dubious whether any experiments in calculation can be thought of as approximating the results predicted by this "law". To give this point its proper weight, remember that the enormous numbers really are *very* enormous indeed. Even the number of atoms in the universe to the order of the number of the atoms in the universe is still a fairly small number in comparison. And thus it is unwise to think of our actual calculating practices with non-enormous numbers as approximations of calculations in the realm of enormous numbers. Someone who sees an approximation here strikes me as someone who thinks that my leaping into the water from a one-metre-high diving platform approximates my "leaping" into the centre of the universe.

Finally, for much the same reason it is hard to imagine what a de-idealization of "Fodor's law" would look like. It could only mean returning us to what we already know about our performance in the realm of non-enormous numbers. I doubt very much that any scientist would be happy with a de-idealization that returns us to where we started.[9]

Maybe Fodor can recover by insisting that what is at issue is not so much idealization but the widespread use of *ceteris paribus* clauses in the special (non-fundamental-physical) sciences in general, and the cognitive sciences in particular.[10] Consider the following line of thought. All special sciences have to cope with the problem that there will always be circumstances that defeat their generalizations. The special sciences cope by attaching *ceteris paribus* clauses to their laws. Given that this is how the special sciences work, we are in no position to deny the dispositionalist the right to do likewise. Take for instance the reductive dispositionalist law "Whenever a human being has the disposition to token the thought 'Lo, a horse' then there is a horse in his or her vicinity". Obviously, there are many circumstances in which this law fails. Indeed, it is very unlikely that the dispositionalist can specify optimality conditions under which the law invariably would be true. Not to worry: all the dispositionalist needs to do is attach a *ceteris paribus* clause to his generalization, and he will be home and dry. This is, after all, what his colleagues in the cognitive sciences would do with most of their generalizations. After all, even well-established laws in psychology – say, the Müller–Lyer law – come with (implicit) *ceteris paribus* clauses.

What can be said in reply to this modified Fodorian position? Note first of all, that it is, of course, a matter of active debate in the philosophy of science whether the special sciences do have *ceteris paribus* laws at all and what role they play.[11] The very existence of this debate might be seen to weaken the force of the modified Fodorian position. But we need not resort to this abstract form of reply. A more direct response is available. We can grant the proposed analysis of *ceteris paribus* laws in the special sciences, and yet deny that it carries over to reductive-dispositionalist generalizations.

Compare the Müller–Lyer law ("*Ceteris paribus*, of two lines of equal length, one of which ends in 'arrows' (←———→), one of which ends in 'feathers' (>———<), human beings see the former as shorter than the latter") with the reductive dispositionalist's generalization cited above ("*Ceteris paribus*, when a human being has the disposition to token 'Lo, a horse', then there is a horse in her or his vicinity"). How are we to understand the *ceteris paribus* clause in the case of the Müller–Lyer law? In my view, the most persuasive analysis goes as follows.[12] *Ceteris paribus* laws are descriptions of experiments that sometimes fail. In the case of the Müller–Lyer law, this is an experiment in which subjects are asked to estimate the relative length of projected arrow- and feather-lines. Such experiment can fail for three reasons: (a) the experimenter might have made a mistake in setting up and conducting the experiment; (b) there might be random interference from the world; and (c) there might be identifiable groups of human subjects who judge the arrow-line to be longer than the feather-line. The *ceteris paribus* clause protects the law from (a) and (b). The reason in category (a) is obvious enough. The distinction between (b) and (c) is crucial although not equally obvious. Reason (b) covers cases where the failures of the experiment are few and far between, and where the failures can only be attributed to an irregular range of chance factors. Exactly why the experiment failed in these (b)-cases is not fully understood by the experimenter. And since the experimenter does not know the cause of the aberration, she is not able to reproduce the aberration in new circumstances, for instance, with new subjects. The *ceteris paribus* clause protects the law from such unusual failures. It does not shield it, however, from more systematic and reproducible failures (category (c) above). For example, it has sometimes been suggested that human beings growing up and living in round buildings do not judge the lengths of arrow and feather line as predicted by the Müller–Lyer law. If this turned out to be true, then the law would be refuted; the *ceteris paribus* clause would not provide a cover for this eventuality. The law would have to be revised by explicitly exempting people growing up in round buildings.

If this is the correct view of *ceteris paribus* laws in cognitive science, what are we to say about the dispositionalist's generalization "*Ceteris paribus*, when a human being has the disposition to token 'Lo, a horse', then there is a horse in her or his vicinity"? The first thing to note is that the dispositionalist's *ceteris paribus* law is not about an established experiment in cognitive science. Perhaps the dispositionalist can defend himself against this observation by suggesting that we might develop such an experiment.

Let us grant this assumption. We are still left with the question how to think about the three categories of experimental failure in the given case. We might allow that in the case of the dispositionalist law we also can speak of experimenters' mishandling of the experiment (category (a) above). Perhaps we might say that it constitutes a mishandling when I perform the experiment in the dark, or when I am unable to scan the environment for horses myself. We might also speak of inexplicable chance events that can defeat our generalization (category (b) above). This leaves category (c): systematic failures that force us to give up or refine the law. And here is where the dispositionalist law clearly differs from the Müller–Lyer law. In the case of the dispositionalist law there is an infinite number of possible constellations of beliefs, such that the presence of any of these constellations lead the subject to think 'Lo, a horse' even when no horse is present.[13] The subject might be confronted with cows but believe that horses in this region look more like cows than cows themselves; the subject might believe that all cows in his vicinity have been dressed up as horses; and so on. The important point about these possible failures is that they are infinite in number, systematic, explicable and open to replication: we know, or are able to work out, in given cases, what constellation of beliefs caused the subject to think 'Lo, a horse' when no horse was present. The *ceteris paribus* clause does not protect the dispositionalist law from these failures. The dispositionalist is left with a situation in which he knows that his law needs an infinite number of refinements before it stands a chance of being acceptable, even as a *ceteris paribus* law. And this makes his case different from that of other special scientists.

Here it might be objected that the above criticism relies on too rosy a picture of psychological and psychophysical laws. Many psychological and psychophysical laws can be systematically disrupted by beliefs and perhaps only a few psychological processes are "cognitively impenetrable", that is, immune to systematic modification by the subject's beliefs. Perhaps even the Müller–Lyer law is "cognitively penetrable". Ergo, if, say, we regard many psychophysical generalizations as laws, despite their cognitive penetrability, then we should do so also for the dispositionalist law. And hence the alleged gap between well-established laws in psychology and the dispositionalist law seems to disappear.

Fortunately, there is way to make the gap reappear.[14] It is natural to think of a *ceteris paribus* law as a description of a single force or disposition in a world where that force seldom if ever acts alone.[15] Moreover, it seems reasonable to maintain that we are often rightly confident about the nature and existence of the disposition even though we are unable to list every possible source of interference. And here our two kinds of laws (the psychological laws and the reductive dispositionalist laws) differ again. Psychologists feel confident that many of their laws – such as the Müller–Lyer law – do describe existing dispositions. But there is no reason to feel equally confident in the case of semantics, and for all the familiar reasons. For instance, why should we be at all confident that my disposition to add is identical with the disposition regarding plus-queries that I would have if my brain were the size of a universe?

Here is another way to make the same point. Surely psychological laws such as the Müller–Lyer law are true only in the case of human beings with roughly their current brain size and processing power. The Müller–Lyer law does not apply to human beings with brains the size of universes. In such extreme cases, psychologists would probably say that the disposition itself is lost. But this is a move the semantic dispositionalists cannot make. After all, they have to claim that the disposition remains unchanged no matter how enormous the numbers. And thus the gap between well-established psychological laws and the reductive dispositionalist laws remains unbridged.

Optimality conditions

Boghossian agrees with Kripke's conclusion, namely, that dispositionalism fails. However, since Boghossian accepts Fodor's defence of idealization and *ceteris paribus* clauses, he feels that we need a different and new argument against sophisticated dispositionalism.[16] Of course, if my defence of Kripke against Fodor is adequate, then the need for a new argument is not all that pressing. Be this as it may, Boghossian's line of thought is well worth investigating in its own right.

Boghossian focuses on mental expressions and their tokening "in the belief mode". He starts from the fact that we have many dispositions to token a given mental expression in this mode. For instance, I do not just have the disposition to token the mental expression "horse" (in the belief mode) in the presence of horses; I also have the disposition to make mistakes and token "horse" (in the belief mode) when I am in the vicinity of cows while it is dark or foggy outside, or I have had too much to drink. Now, if we were to let *all* of my dispositions to token "horse" (in the belief mode) determine the content of that concept, then we would end up with the wrong extension. We would then have to say that the meaning of my mental expression "horse" is (among other things): *horse, and cow on a foggy day, and cow in the dark, and cow when I have had too much to drink*, and so on. In order to avoid this problem, the dispositionalist has to distinguish between two kinds of dispositions regarding my tokening of "horse": dispositions that constitute the meaning of "horse", and dispositions that do not. How can we exclude the latter? The natural solution is to opt for "optimality conditions". These are conditions under which my tokening of "horse" (in the belief mode) inevitably co-varies with the presence of horses in my vicinity. Foggy or dark days, for example, do not count as optimal. If such optimality conditions can be specified then the dispositionalist has a way of saying which of my many dispositions regarding the tokening of "horse" are the meaning-constituting ones: those that operate under optimal conditions. Of course, in order to satisfy the reductive dispositionalist programme, such conditions need to be spelled out in non-semantic and non-intentional terms.

Boghossian seeks to give a general argument to the effect that the needed optimality conditions cannot be specified. His argument is based on the relatively uncontroversial premise of belief holism. He reminds us that the fixation of perceptual beliefs depends on both perceptual stimuli and background beliefs. The role of background beliefs is important since "just about any stimulus can cause just about any belief, given a suitably mediating set of background assumptions".[17] For instance, my belief "Lo, a horse" can be triggered by a bull, provided only that I believe, for example, that bulls and horses look alike; or that I am confronted with horses dressed up as bulls. The presence of all such error-producing beliefs is, of course, compatible with the claim that my mental expression "horse" means *horse* and has all and only horses as its extension.

Given the error-producing potential of background beliefs, what can the reductive dispositionalist do in order to specify the needed optimality conditions for *horse*? The answer is that he must find a way to specify and rule out all (complexes of) beliefs that lead me to misidentify non-horses as horses. Boghossian argues that this is a hopeless task:

> Since … there looks to be a potential infinity of such mediating background clusters of belief, a non-semantically, non-intentionally, specified optimality situation is a non-semantically, non-intentionally specified situation in which it is guaranteed that none of this potential infinity of background clusters of belief is present. But how is such a situation to be specified? What is needed is precisely what a dispositional theory was supposed to provide: namely, a set of naturalistic necessary and sufficient conditions for being a belief with a certain content. But, of course, if we had *that* we would already have a reductive theory of meaning – we would not need a dispositional theory![18]

Elsewhere, Boghossian puts the objection differently:

> The worry that needs allaying is that the specified [optimality] condition [C] is consistent with the presence of background beliefs that

would frustrate the covariation between symbol tokenings and their referents ... Putting this worry to rest requires showing that the situation's being C is enough to ensure the truth of the following open conjunction:

(∗)   ~Bel$_1$ & ~Bel$_2$ & ~Bel$_3$ & ...

where the ~Bel$_i$ stand for the various clusters of background beliefs which could potentially frustrate the connection between being a [horse] and the tokening of an expression which refers to it. Well, could C ever be recognised as sufficient for the truth of (∗)? ... The trouble is that proposition (∗) is not finitely stateable: there is no finite way to state what beliefs the [reductionist] must exclude before he may be assured of the desired concomitance of [horse] beliefs and [horses]. Literally any belief can frustrate the desired connection. So, there is no way to certify that C is sufficient for the truth of (∗), even granted a set of naturalistic necessary and sufficient conditions for meaning.[19]

Boghossian's argument has received surprisingly little critical attention in the literature. The exception is Alexander Miller, who has discussed Boghossian's attack on optimality conditions dispositionalism in several places. I shall focus on Miller's most recent, and most critical, contribution.[20] Here Miller attempts to establish that Boghossian's attack is not successful. I shall try to defend Boghossian against Miller.

Miller believes that Boghossian's argument is really three different objections rolled into one: the "circularity objection", the "open-endedness objection" and the "certification objection". In order to appreciate the point of the circularity objection, we only need to consider two beliefs, Bel$_1$ and Bel$_2$. Assume that it is part of the optimality conditions for Bel$_1$ that the presence of Bel$_2$ is excluded, and that it is part of the optimality conditions for Bel$_2$ that the presence of Bel$_1$ is excluded. Surely such scenarios are possible. But now the dispositionalist faces a problem: he must already have completed the task of specifying the non-intentional and non-semantic optimality conditions for Bel$_2$ in order to be able to begin specifying the non-intentional and non-semantic optimality conditions for Bel$_1$; and he must already have completed his task of specifying the non-intentional and non-semantic optimality conditions for Bel$_1$ in order to be able to begin specifying the non-intentional and non-semantic optimality conditions for Bel$_2$. According to the open-endedness objection it is hard to see how any non-semantically and non-intentionally specified optimality condition could possibly guarantee the absence of an open-ended set of items with propositional content. Finally, the certification objection is clearly stated in the second quotation above. The point is since optimality conditions are not "finitely stateable", we can never "certify" that we have actually captured them all.

Miller's strategy is to "divide and conquer". Having separated out three different objections, he proposes an answer to each of them separately. His answer to the circularity objection is that it can be met by David Lewis's technique for analysing theoretical terms.[21] Since this technique plays no role in my disagreement with Miller, I shall not go into its details here. His answers to the other two objections are more important in the present context. As concerns the open-endedness objection, Miller is taking a leaf out of Boghossian's own work. Consider Kripke's response to the suggestion – made by the advocate of semantic primitivism – that meaning-constituting mental states are *primitive states*. Kripke writes:

> Such a move may in a sense be irrefutable … But it seems desperate: it leaves the nature of this postulated primitive state – the primitive state of "meaning addition by 'plus'" – completely mysterious … Such a state would have to be a finite object, contained in our finite minds. … Can we conceive of a finite state which *could* not be interpreted in a quus-like way? How could that be? (*WRPL*: 51–2)

Boghossian rejects this reply as insufficient:

> Kripke's … objection to the anti-reductionist suggestion is that it is utterly mysterious how there could be a finite state, realized in a finite mind, that nevertheless contains information about the correct applicability of a sign in literally no end of distinct situations. But … this amounts merely to insisting that we find the idea of a contentful state problematic, without adducing any independent reason why we should. We *know* that mental states with general contents are states with infinitary normative characters; it is precisely with that observation that the entire discussion began. … What Kripke needs, if he is to pull off an argument from queerness, is some substantive argument, distinct from his anti-reductionist considerations, why we should not countenance such states. But this he does not provide.[22]

In an ironic twist, Miller uses a parallel argument in response to Boghossian's open-endedness argument:

> The *open-endedness objection* to the reductionist suggestion is that it is utterly mysterious how there could be a naturalistically specified condition that nevertheless guarantees the absence of literally no end of distinct content-bearing items. But, again, this amounts merely to insisting that we find the idea of a naturalistically specified necessary and sufficient condition for meaning something problematic, without adducing any independent reason why we should.[23]

Finally, Miller's reply to the certification objection begins by rejecting the idea that optimality conditions cannot be finitely stateable. We already know that an indefinite number of belief complexes might lead me to token "horse" when no horses are in my vicinity. Let Bel_1, Bel_2, Bel_3, … stand for such belief complexes. We know that an optimality condition C has to exclude them all; that is, it has to be sufficient for the truth of:

(∗) $\sim Bel_1$ & $\sim Bel_2$ & $\sim Bel_3$ & …

Boghossian's point is that (∗) is not finitely stateable. Miller agrees but then goes on to find a way around the problem. C does not have to be stated as (∗); it can be stated – finitely stated – as follows:

(#) For every belief, if that belief would lead a non-horse to cause me to token "horse", then I do not possess that belief.

Now (#) can be finitely stated and it entails (∗). But how can (#) itself be "certified", given that the quantifier "every" ranges over an indefinitely large set of beliefs? Miller's answer is that it cannot be certified if by certification we mean an *a priori* demonstration. Such *a priori* demonstration is not the only option, however. Just like it is an *a posteriori* truth that water is H_2O, it might equally be an *a posteriori* truth that in certain conditions I will not have any beliefs that lead me to token "horse" in the vicinity of a non-horse. Put differently, it is enough if the dispositionalist can show that the obtaining of C is nomologically sufficient for the truth of (#).[24]

The ingenuity of Miller's counter-criticisms notwithstanding, it seems hard not to continue feeling the force of Boghossian's argument. A first source of discomfort with Miller's position has to do with his strategy of "divide and conquer". It seems that Boghossian's argument is inadvertently weakened by pulling it apart into three strands. This seems particularly obvious with respect to Miller's separation of circularity from open-endedness. Lewis's technique for defining theoretical terms works well for a finite number of terms or – here – belief clusters, but when it is used in the context of an indefinite number of belief clusters then it reaches its limits. It then involves an inappropriate quantification into an open conjunction.[25] It also seems that Miller's replies to the *circularity* and the *certification objections* do not actually fit together well. The type of theory resulting from Lewis's formal technique is *a priori* rather than *a posteriori*.[26]

Moreover, I have difficulties with Miller's responses to the second and third objections. Miller thinks that Boghossian is right to believe that – in the absence of an argument to the contrary – we have no reason to doubt that "mental states with general contents are states with infinitary normative characters". But Miller thinks that Boghossian is wrong to believe that – in the absence of an argument to the contrary – we have reason to doubt that "there could be a naturalistically specified condition that nevertheless guarantees the absence of literally no end of distinct content-bearing items". I find it hard to see how these two beliefs work similarly with respect to the burden of proof. That mental states with general contents are states with infinitary normative characters is – although not in those words! – part and parcel of our intuitive common-sense understanding of the mind. Clearly Boghossian thinks that this belief is well entrenched in our overall web of beliefs, and that it thus needs no special argument in its defence. The burden of proof is therefore on someone who doubts the idea. It seems obvious, at least to me, that the idea that there could be a naturalistically specified condition that nevertheless guarantees the absence of literally no end of distinct content-bearing items is a very different matter. It certainly is not an idea that many of us will find intuitive or commonsensical; and it clearly is not part of our intuitive picture of the mind. Moreover, few of us have any grasp of how such a condition could be identified, specified and shown to be true. And thus the burden of proof now lies squarely with its advocates, not with the sceptics.

Miller's answer to the certification objection can, of course, also be used as an answer to the first (i.e. circularity) objection.[27] The point is that we can specify some optimality condition C that does not list the problematic belief clusters but where obtaining C would be nomologically sufficient for the covariance of my tokenings of "horse" with the presence of horses. Miller himself does not believe it likely that such an optimality condition C can be found. His point is rather that Boghossian has not provided us with a general argument against it; we therefore have not found reason to look carefully at specific proposals for such C. I agree with Miller that Boghossian has not given us a *demonstration* as to why the optimality condition C, that is, the natural laws ruling out the problematic belief clusters, could not be found. But I would still maintain that Boghossian has shown us, and rather convincingly so, just how improbable it is that we would ever come up with the goods.

Going somewhat beyond Boghossian, and linking the present discussion to themes in the last section, I offer the following subsidiary brief line of thought. My simple point is that I find it impossible to imagine what empirical programme of research could ever lead us to believe that we had captured all of the clusters in (∗) above. Note that literally every imaginable belief could under some, however rare, circumstances be a central part of one of the clusters that we need to exclude. Take "5 is a prime number". Combine this belief with the following further beliefs: "Farmer Jones gives each of his fields a number"; "Jones never puts horses on fields with prime numbers"; "I am standing in front of field number 5". This cluster of could cause me to think that the animal on field 5 is not a horse when in fact it is. And so on. Given that literally every imaginable belief could under some, however rare, circumstances, be a central part of one of the clusters of beliefs that we need to exclude, and given that conceptual development constantly enables us to believe new things, I fail to see how we could conceivably make real progress towards finding C.

The addition–subtraction strategy

A sizeable group of critics insist that the versions of dispositionalism considered by Kripke involve either too few or too many dispositions. Indeed, some critics make both complaints, arguing that, as Kripke sets up the dispositionalist position, it has too few dispositions of one kind and too many dispositions of another kind.[28]

Let us begin with commentators who think that Kripke assumes the need for too many dispositions.[29] Recall Kripke's finitude problem: whereas the addition function is infinite, the number of our dispositions is finite. The conclusion Kripke draws is that our meaning the addition function cannot be reduced to us having dispositions to give sums in answer to plus-queries. The present objection attacks the premise of this argument. It claims that Kripke's finitude problem can be solved by *reducing* the number of dispositions involved in addition. It is wrong to think – so the objection goes – that the dispositionalist must assume a separate disposition for each instance of the scheme $x + y = z$. We do not need an infinite number of dispositions in order to track an infinite function. All we need is a finite number of dispositions that can be manifested repeatedly as part of a recursive procedure. That is to say, we have one hundred dispositions to respond to $x + y = ?$ problems where x and y are different single digit numerals. For handling plus-queries involving numerals above nine we additionally have dispositions to manipulate them spatially. For instance, we have dispositions to write down the numerals below each other and align them in such ways that the addition task reduces to single-digit addition plus "carrying". In other words, our dispositions for single-digit addition operate without taking the context of the addition into account. For instance, the numeral "7" might occur in a simple single-digit addition task such as "7 + 1" or in the complex addition task

$$73,232,023,232,323,546,323,684,420,001,342,195,266,496$$
$$+ \ 12,400,000,000,000,248,001,992,343,555,219,424,546,298$$

The contexts of the "7" and "1" are different in the two cases, but our adding dispositions for single digit numerals "ignore" such differences. Our dispositions to add respond only to certain physical properties of the numerals, that is, to their shapes or to the associated sounds. In this respect, our arithmetical dispositions behave no differently from salt when allowed to manifest its disposition to dissolve in water. The salt too "ignores" much of the context – the colour of the water bucket for example.

In order to begin answering the objection, we need to recall that Chapter 2 of *WRPL* discusses and dismisses the idea according to which my meaning *addition* rather than *quaddition* by "+" is captured by my abiding by certain rules that determine a procedure for counting and (physically) manipulating heaps of objects. The sceptic dismisses this suggestion on the grounds that by "counting" I might really mean "quounting" – where "quounting" is counting or (physically) manipulating objects in accordance with the quaddition function. The procedure envisaged in the objection is not obviously vulnerable to the same reply. This is because in this case the procedure is not specified in terms of rules (or other intentional items). The procedure consists of, and operates with, exclusively non-intentional items: numerals, spaces and dispositions to respond to certain combinations of signs (say "68 + 57 = ") with other signs (e.g. "125"). We might put this point by saying that the present objection operates with a machine-like procedure.

Putting things in this way, however, immediately exposes the objection to a counter-attack. The problem with machines is that their inputs and outputs need to be interpreted. It is no good saying that our finite disposition machine crunches numerals in certain desirable ways; if we want an answer to the sceptical challenge we need an account of how we get from numerals to numbers. Maybe the output of my machine in answer to the string of signs "68" "+" "57" "=" is indeed the sign "125". But does that show that I (or the machine) mean addition by "+"? Obviously, it shows this only if it is correct to map the sign "68" onto the number sixty-eight, the sign "+" onto plus, the sign "57" onto the number fifty-seven, the sign "=" onto equals, and the sign "125" onto the number one-hundred-and-twenty-five. To assume that we are entitled to make these mappings is to presuppose that we have found an answer to the sceptical challenge. But if we had done that, then we would not need to invoke the disposition machine in the first place.

The objection is also unable to avoid the difficulties with idealizations and *ceteris paribus* clauses. The proponent of mechanical-procedure dispositionalism needs to tell us how it is possible for our procedure-defining dispositions to operate with enormous numbers. Even if we allow that we can add numbers on the basis of a small number of dispositions, we still need to explain how creatures like us can do so for numbers so enormous that we would need the lifespan of several universes to write them down. It will not help to reply by saying, "*Ceteris paribus*, my procedural dispositions specify a sum-answer for every possible plus-query". For at this point we can invoke the earlier worries about idealizations. We have no idea what we would do if we had infinite memory or a brain the size of the universe. And to insist on this point is not an expression of scepticism regarding standard procedures in physics or the special sciences.

Can we do better by increasing the number and kinds of dispositions? Consider first a line of argument due to Blackburn.[30] Blackburn advocates increasing the number and kinds of dispositions in order to overcome the mistake problem. Call "unchecked responses" those reactions to plus-queries that I am disposed to give quickly and without checking my response. Call "multiply-checked responses" those reactions to plus-queries that I am disposed to give on the basis of several recalculations. Blackburn's claim then is that multiply-checked responses allow for a straightforward dismissal of Kripke's mistake problem. The idea is that the dispositionalist can dismiss the problem by saying: "I mean *addition* rather than *skaddition* by '+' because, although my dispositions for unchecked responses to plus-queries match the skaddition function, my 'extended' dispositions for multiply-checked responses to plus-queries match the addition function".[31]

Blackburn's argument makes the questionable assumption that performing a calculation again and again will inevitably push me towards the right result. Alas, there is no inevitability here at all. It could well be the case that the reliability of the result *decreases* as I check my result repeatedly. And nothing rules out the possibility that I make systematic mistakes in checking my initial answers. Take the case of the neurotic student who takes a crucial exam in elementary arithmetic. His initial responses to plus-queries are correct, but given his neurotic tendencies, he makes more and more mistakes as he nervously rechecks his results. Surely, contrary to what Blackburn would have us think, the student qualifies as an adder. Note that an idealization of extended dispositions would not help the objection. Such idealization is again threatened by circularity. To know which of my many dispositions regarding plus-queries are dispositions to correct my initial reactions, I already need to know which function I mean. I cannot read off what I mean from the dispositions I have if I have to select the right dispositions on the basis of what I mean.[32]

A different proposal for increasing kinds of dispositions has been put forward by Ginet.[33] As Ginet has it, acts of rule-following involve two kinds of dispositions: dispositions of production and dispositions of recognition (my terms). Dispositions of production manifest themselves in acts of generating the values of the function that is targeted by the given rule. Dispositions of recognition manifest themselves in judgements according to which different manifestations of one and the same disposition of production are instances of "doing the same". Dispositions of recognition again fall into two different classes; this difference is important since it enables us to distinguish between "higher-level" and "brute-level" rule-following. In the case of higher-level rule-following, dispositions of recognition manifest themselves in judgements according to which the different manifestations of one and the same disposition of production are all instances of following the same *procedure*. In the case of brute-level rule-following the idea of a procedure is missing: here dispositions of recognition manifest themselves only in the thought that in different manifestations of the same disposition of production one is doing the same thing for the same reason on different occasions. Doing addition is higher level since a competent adder is able to identify a description of a procedure for finding sums. Identifying numerals with the shape "7" is brute-level, since we do not follow an explicit procedure for doing so. Nevertheless, on different occasions of identifying "7"s, we regard ourselves as doing the "same thing for the same reason".

Ginet holds that both kinds of rule-following can be evaluated as correct and incorrect. Brute-level dispositions are tied to "objective properties". A subject has a brute-level semantic disposition if she tracks an objective property. For instance, a subject has the disposition to mean *horse* by "horse" if her linguistic behaviour tracks "the property of being a horse". The objective property gives the criterion for determining whether or not the disposition is working correctly:

> The dispositionalist can characterize the reaction to which the subject is disposed as that of *recognizing the same property* in each case. The reaction is *correctly* so characterized only if the subject is disposed to have the appropriate reaction ... to every *possible* case where the property is in fact present.[34]

Higher-level dispositions are like trees rooted in brute-level dispositions. Descriptions of procedures for higher-level dispositions must "ultimately" consist of expressions that are applied like brute-level dispositions, that is, directly, and without using a further procedure.

According to Ginet, the machinery developed above gives us all we need to combat the sceptic. Since brute-level dispositions do not involve descriptions of procedures, no problem of alternative, quus-like descriptions can arise. Since brute-level dispositions track objective properties, there is an objective fact determining whether they are manifested correctly or incorrectly. And since higher-level dispositions are built up from brute-level dispositions, the objectivity of the latter transfers to the former:

> The unpacking of any particular higher level understanding can be represented by a downward branching tree. However many branches the tree has, they all eventually terminate in brute level understandings of terms, where, for any case in the domain of the application function, there is no difficulty about *S* having the capacity to consider it. For example, among the many brute level understandings at the base of my understanding the rule for adding two numbers ... would, perhaps, be the sets of dispositions to recognize marks as instances of the numerals "0" through "9", to recognize when two numeral marks are in vertical alignment, and the like.[35]

In assessing Ginet's proposal, it helps to imagine what he would reply to the sceptic. In order to justify his answer "125" in reply to "68 + 57 = ?", he would sketch a theory about himself. According to this theory some of his dispositions can be assessed as to how well they track physical, objective properties. The results of the manifestations of these dispositions are processed further in accordance with higher-level procedural dispositions. Other ingredients of the theory will be the objector's judgements concerning "doing the same thing" for both kinds of dispositions.

A first cause of unease here is the hypothetical status of this theory; it certainly does not square with the low-brow meaning-determinist's demand of immediate knowledge. Of course Ginet has the option of going for reform and rejecting this constraint. But Ginet decides explicitly against this option. At one point in his paper Ginet insists himself that our knowledge of our meaning-constituting dispositions is not hypothetical but direct.[36] However, it is hard to see how the above theory of what it means to mean *addition* by "plus" could possibly be direct or observational.

Moreover, Ginet seems much too generous in according the brute level a status beyond question and justification. It may be true that at this level I do not follow a procedure that can be explicitly formulated and written down. But this does not mean that this level is immune to sceptical challenges. Imagine you took yourself to be following the rule "Pick out shapes of the form 9". What is to stop the sceptic from asking what fact justifies you in calling a newly encountered sign a 9? Are not all of your previous identifications of 9-shapes compatible with the rule "Pick out shapes of the form 6?", when looked at from a different angle?

Finally, Ginet's objection is again based on the hope that we can escape sceptical challenges by focusing on non-intentional, machine-like performances. In the present case, such performances are manifestations of brute-level dispositions. The proposal considered here characterizes brute-level dispositions as little machines with clear and simple inputs and outputs. Unfortunately, Kripke's comments on machine dispositionalism bite here too. Interpretation has to come in at some point. Shifting from higher-level to brute-level rule-following avoids the problem of having multiple interpretations for the verbalization of the procedure. But any joy about this avoidance must be short-lived. This is because the sceptic can challenge us to explain why we settle on one interpretation of the outputs of the brute-level dispositions rather than another. And thus all the familiar sceptical problems of multiple interpretations are back.

Equivocation

Horwich and Soames argue that Kripke's main argument against dispositionalism is marred by an equivocation. They both locate this equivocation in the concept of "determination", even though they do not agree on the nature of the equivocation in question.

To begin with Horwich, consider what one might call Kripke's "central argument against dispositional theories of meaning"':

(1) Whatever constitutes the meaning of a predicate must determine its extension.
(2) The facts about how we are disposed to use a predicate do not determine its extension.
So: (3) The meaning of a predicate is not constituted by the facts about how we are disposed to use it.[37]

Horwich holds that the conclusion follows from the premises only if one equivocates on "determine". The two meanings of "determine" are justifiable in their respective premise, but given the difference, the conclusion is a *non sequitur*. The first premise uses "determine" in a weak sense: whenever two predicates differ in their meaning then they must also differ in their extension. Or, the other way around, "synonymous predicates must be co-extensional".[38] The second premise is true only if determination is understood in the sense of "possibility to read off". Dispositional facts would determine the extension of a predicate only if the extension could somehow be "read off" from these dispositions. One can acknowledge that the dispositionalist encounters insurmountable difficulties in meeting this challenge. Alas, this acknowledgement does not help Kripke's master argument; the equivocation has not been removed.[39]

Horwich's charge of equivocation can be deflected by offering a reading of "determination" that sits equally comfortably with both premises. Such a reading exists.[40] It can be formulated as follows. Given two meanings, x and y, that are not co-extensional, the fact that makes it so that "p" means x must rule out that "p" means y. For instance, given the two meanings, *addition* and *quaddition*, whatever makes it so that "+" means *addition* must rule out that "+" means *quaddition*. It is not difficult to see that this meaning of determination is at work in Kripke's text.

Kripke's overall argument then has the following content:

> (1') Whatever constitutes the meaning of a given predicate must distinguish this meaning from the meanings of other predicates with different extensions.
>
> (2') The facts about how we are disposed to use a predicate do not distinguish the meaning of a given predicate from the meanings of other predicates with different extensions.

So: (3') The meaning of a predicate is not constituted by the facts about how we are disposed to use it.

It is obvious that this captures one central thread of Kripke's text and that it fits all three major problems. The normativity problem accuses the dispositionalist of being unable to make sense of the idea that meaning justifies us in doing one thing rather than another thing. The finitude problem claims that dispositionalism is unable to distinguish meanings in realms where our dispositions run out. And the error problem insists that the dispositionalist cannot tease apart an erring adder from an error-free skadder.

According to Soames, the key equivocation in Kripke's argument is between "*a priori* determination" and "metaphysical determination". The general idea of Kripke's attack on dispositionalism is the insistence that non-intentional facts about my past dispositions are unable to *determine* my present intentional states. Some of Kripke's arguments suggest that the determination in question is meant as an "*a priori* determination" of the general form "P determines Q only if, given P, one can demonstrate Q without appealing to any other empirical facts".[41] Kripke is right to insist that dispositionalism fails by this criterion. It is hard to see how one could derive claims about meanings and propositional attitudes from statements concerning non-intentional facts: "Consequently, I am willing to grant that the sceptic might be right in maintaining that claims about what I mean are not *a priori* consequences of non-intentional truths".[42]

However, Soames insists, to grant that truths about meaning are not *a priori* consequences of truths about non-intentional facts is not to hand victory to the sceptic. This is because, in order to win, the dispositionalist need insist only on "metaphysical determination". Put differently, the dispositionalist need only maintain that intentional states are a necessary consequence of non-intentional facts.

Soames's discussion of metaphysical determination in Kripke turns on a specific argument in *WRPL* that I have not yet mentioned. Here it is. Consider the difference between a function that we mean to follow and a function to which we merely happen to conform. Assume that I give arbitrary numerical responses to queries of the form "How much is $m \star n$?" Let my answering take place in a fully deterministic universe, and under conditions where " $\star$ " means nothing to me.[43] Can we speak of my right or wrong responses here? Obviously not. Nor is this negative answer overturned if we imagine my having the firm intention to give the same answer for given m and n on different occasions. The introduction of this intention opens the door to one kind of normative claim: "Since you responded '3' to '$579 \star 13$' in the past, you have to give the same answer now". However, this response in not based on the meaning of $\star$; after all, consistency of intention is not the same thing as meaning. The case of $\star$ evidently contrasts with that of "+". In the latter case, we do not just *happen to* conform to a function, we *intend* to do so. Moreover, since we are dealing now with meaningful expressions, the language of "right" and "wrong" is applicable. As Kripke sees it, the difference between the cases of " $\star$ " and "+" brings out that dispositionalism cannot capture meaning. The dispositionalist does not have the resources to treat the two cases differently. And thus he turns out to fail to do justice to our intuitions (*WRPL*: 24).

Soames reads Kripke's discussion of the $\star$-example as an argument against metaphysical determination. Soames construes Kripke's remarks about this example as attempting to show my meaning something by a given sign cannot be the necessary consequence of my non-intentional dispositions to use that sign. More precisely: it is not the case that in every possible world w in which such non-intentional dispositional facts about my use of "+" obtain, I mean *addition* by "+".[44] Soames grants the point as such but constrains its scope: Kripke's point concerning necessary determination holds only as long as we think of the set of non-intentional facts in a very narrow manner. My meaning *addition* by "+" is not a necessary consequence of my non-intentional dispositions to use "+". But why not enlarge the set of non-intentional facts so as to include:

> (i) the internal physical states of my brain, (ii) my causal and historical relationships to things in my environment, (iii) my (non-intentionally characterized) interactions with other members of my linguistic community, (iv) their dispositions to verbal behaviour, and so on?[45]

Once we cast our net wide enough among the non-intentional facts, it becomes doubtful whether metaphysical determination or necessary consequence really fail. Consider facts (i)–(iv):

> Is there a possible world in which someone conforms to all those facts – precisely the facts that characterize me in the actual world – and yet that person does not mean anything by "+"? I think not. Given my conviction that in the past I did mean addition by "+", and given also my conviction that if there are intentional facts, then they don't float free of everything else, I am confident that there is no such world. Although I cannot identify the smallest set of non-intentional facts about me in the actual world on which meaning facts supervene, I am confident that they do supervene.[46]

I agree with Soames that Kripke's arguments are successful if *a priori* determination is at issue. But I disagree with him when it comes to metaphysical determination. It seems to me that Kripke's argument goes through for metaphysical determination as well. To see this, recall some basic distinctions regarding "supervenience". Supervenience is a relation between two kinds of properties, say X-properties and Y-properties. X-properties supervene on Y-properties if it is impossible for two situations to be identical in their Y-properties yet different in their X-properties. Supervenience can have different degrees of strength and scope. For present purposes, the distinction between "local" and "global" supervenience is of particular importance. The difference between these two forms of supervenience concerns the scope of "situation" in the above definition. We get "local" supervenience if we confine the situation to an individual; we obtain "global" supervenience if we enlarge the situation to a whole world. X-properties supervene *locally* on Y-properties if it is impossible for two *individuals* to be identical in their Y-properties and different in their X-properties. X-properties supervene *globally* on Y-properties if it is impossible for two *worlds* to be identical in their Y-properties and different in their X-properties. Obviously, local supervenience implies global supervenience but not *vice versa*. Local supervenience is the stronger requirement.[47]

Soames's discussion regarding necessary consequence can be summarized by saying that he agrees with Kripke as far as local supervenience is concerned, but disagrees with Kripke regarding global supervenience. Meaning facts do not supervene locally on my dispositions to use certain signs. Nevertheless, Soames thinks, they very probably supervene globally: it is impossible to imagine two possible worlds that are identical regarding all their non-intentional facts yet different in their intentional facts. Soames does not explicitly enlarge the set of relevant non-intentional facts so as to include a whole world. Ascribing this view to him seems justified, however, given the open-ended list he presents in the above quotation. The list contains not only the things of my own physical and social environment, but also the things of the physical and social environment of eve-ryone in my linguistic community.[48]

Let us assume then that Soames wishes to rescue dispositionalism by insisting that meaning facts supervene globally on non-intentional facts. Does this idea endanger Kripke's criticism of dispositionalism? I think not. Global superveni-ence is too weak a relation for it to help the dispositionalist. In fact, the sceptic can happily acquiesce in global supervenience; it does not force him to give up anything. Global supervenience does not enable the calculator to cite any (non-intentional) fact about what makes it so that she means *addition* by "+". Granted global supervenience, all she can point to is the history of the world as a whole: "I mean *addition* by '+'", she is able to reply, "because of the full history of the world up to now". Maybe so, but this is not much of a fact. It is odd to call the complete history of my world "a fact". It seems more appropriate to say that the history of the world is a set of facts. Putting this worry to one side, according to the proposal under consideration, every meaning attribution in our own world is justified by the very same fact, that is, the world: your meaning *nine* by "9", the Queen's mean-ing *country* by "country" and my meaning *coffee* by (the Finnish word) "kahvi". In every case, the relevant meaning-constituting non-intentional fact is the same. And to have one and the same fact justify all meaning attributions contradicts our intuitions about meaning.

Note also that the meaning sceptic can happily accept global supervenience, albeit in a vacuous form: two worlds that are identical in their non-intentional properties will, of course, not differ in their intentional properties if there are no such properties. This makes it obscure how demonstrating global supervenience in itself could make a case for intentional properties. All it could show is that *if* such intentional properties exist, then they will supervene in the way suggested.[49]

Realism about dispositions

One important tradition in the philosophical study of dispositions analyses statements attributing dispositions as counterfactual conditionals. To say that the glass is fragile is to say that (*ceteris paribus*) the glass would break if dropped or knocked. This analysis of disposition statements traditionally goes with the view that dispositional properties reduce to, or supervene on, categories prop-erties, and that our knowledge of dispositions and their categorical bases must be inferential rather than direct.[50] Kripke clearly holds the view that we are not directly aware of our dispositions; this view is central to the directness prob-lem. And Kripke's treatment of the error problem shows his commitment to the analysis of dispositions statements as counterfactual conditionals. Recall Jones, the skadder. If Jones were asked "How much is 68 + 57?", he would answer "115"; and if Jones were asked "How much is 769 + 2495?", he would answer "2154". The counterfactuals do not tell us whether Jones is an adder (who makes mistakes) or a skadder (who does not). And hence there is no fact of the matter whether Jones is a skadder or an adder. What is true here is true of Kripke's argument throughout: Kripke assumes that statement-attributing dispositions are best thought of as counterfactual conditionals. To attribute to Jones the disposition to give sums in answer to plus-queries is to claim that if Jones were faced with a query of the form $x + y = ?$, he would – *ceteris paribus* – come up with the sum of x and y.

A realist about dispositions rejects this traditional conception. Martin and Heil outline an alternative and apply it to combat Kripke's criticism of semantic dispositionalism. Their programme has four ingredients. First, dispositions are not reducible to, and do not supervene on, categorical properties. Rather, "every property has both a qualitative (or 'categorical') and a dispositional side or aspect ... [and] the dispositionality of an intrinsic property is as basic and irreducible as is its qualitative character".[51]

Secondly, disposition statements are not equivalent to counterfactual conditionals. Here is a well-known example suggested by Mark Johnstone. Imagine a chameleon sitting on a green baize in the dark. Assume the chameleon is red. Being red is the dispositional property of reflecting red light under ideal conditions. Let us try to capture this dispositional property with a counterfactual "the chameleon is red because under ideal conditions it will reflect red light". And this clearly is false. The moment we realize the ideal conditions, by turning on the light, the chameleon turns green. If the counterfactual analysis were on the mark then we would have to say that even when the chameleon was still in the dark, it was not red but green. And that conflicts with our intuitions about the case.[52]

Thirdly, since counterfactual analysis is unable to do justice to the intricacies of dispositions, we need a new conceptual tool for identifying dispositions. "Disposition lines" are that tool. Each disposition needs specific partners in order to manifest itself. Fragility has such partners in hard places. Solubility doubles up with various liquids. A disposition line is the imaginary line linking a disposition to its partners.[53] And fourthly, and finally, neurological systems often have direct – and not just inferential – access to their dispositions. This is because at least some of the dispositions of neurological systems have two kinds of manifestations: "typifying manifestations" and "cue manifestations". A typifying manifestation is the manifestation that defines the disposition: the typifying manifestation of my disposition to blush when faced with a difficult question from the audience is that I do indeed blush. The cue manifestation is some sort of *quale* telling me that I have the disposition in question. Such *quale* is an outcome of my "neurological system ... assess[ing] its capacity for a task without having to complete it or perhaps even begin it".[54]

With this rough outline of a realist conception of dispositions in place, we can turn to three objections: the mistake problem objection, the finitude problem objection and the normativity objection. (The last of the three should properly have been discussed in Chapter 2, but since it is closely connected to Martin's and Heil's other objection, it seemed best to save it for the present context.)

The mistake problem objection[55]

The mistake problem dissolves once we interpret dispositions in realist fashion. Take the following two scenarios. In scenario *A* Jones is an adder who makes systematic mistakes with carrying. In scenario *B* Jones is a skadder. A non-realist (counterfactual) theory of dispositions is unable to distinguish *A* from *B*. But a realist theory has no such difficulties. Whatever the counterfactuals might be, there is a fact of the matter whether Jones has the disposition to add or whether he has the disposition to skadd. In *A* Jones has in fact two dispositions that are relevant for our concerns: the disposition to add and the disposition to forget to carry. In *B* he has only one disposition: the disposition to skadd. The two scenarios are distinct and the realist about dispositions can tell us why they are distinct.

Reply: What is the difference between having the two dispositions of scenario *A* (i.e. the dispositions to add and to forget to carry) and having the one disposition of scenario *B* (i.e. the disposition to skadd)? Consider this mechanical analogue. Assume we have two machines. Machine *A* has all the circuitry of an adding machine, but, due to a loose wire, it is unable to carry. Machine *B* is a skadding machine in good working order. Machine *B* was produced by taking a working machine of type *A* and loosening the wire needed for carrying. What should we say about the relevant dispositions of *A* and *B*? Surely, to say that machine *A* has two dispositions whereas machine *B* has just one is to help oneself to information about the intentions of the designer of the two machines. And to make use of this information is clearly illegitimate under the rules of debate between the meaning sceptic and the semantic dispositionalist. Perhaps the realist replies by insisting that he needs no information about the intentions of the designers of *A* and *B*. It is enough that the causal history of *A* and *B* is different. In *A*'s history we start off with a functioning addition machine that deteriorates – via some physical or chemical process – into a faulty addition machine. In *B*'s case we start off with a functioning addition machine that is caused by human intervention to become a skaddition machine. Alas, this response will not save the realist-dispositionalist. We can easily imagine scenarios in which the two histories are identical except for the difference in intention of the designer. For instance, the physical modification of *B* might consist of just the physical or chemical processes undergone by *A*.[56]

The finitude problem objection[57]

Realism about dispositions solves Kripke's finitude problem. Kripke is wrong to say that my disposition to calculate plus-queries is finite. It is infinite. While it is true to say that I cannot add enormous numbers, it is false to say that the resulting limitation is a limitation of my dispositions to give sums in reply to plus-queries. What limitation there is in this case is due either to the lack of appropriate

121

disposition partners or due to the presence of blocking factors. In order to mani-fest itself in the realm of enormous numbers, my addition disposition depends for its typifying manifestation both on the right kind of brain and on the absence of blocking factors such as fatigue or disruption. How do we know then that we indeed have the disposition to add, even in the realm of enormous numbers? The answer lies with cue manifestations. They tell me that if my disposition to calcu-late with "+" was neither blocked nor short of partners, I would add in the realm of enormous numbers.

Reply: This objection seems to miss the point. First, to know what to count as a blocking factor or a disposition partner presupposes prior knowledge of which dispositions I have. The previous reply to the mistake problem objection showed that this was not a straightforward question of fact. Secondly, the introduction of cue manifestations is an altogether desperate and unconvincing move. One can-not simply posit a mental experience that tells me – albeit fallibly – which dispo-sitions I have. I cannot find such mental experiences in my mental life. Moreover, anyone wishing to defeat the sceptic by invoking qualia had better first address Kripke's argument against qualia as a straight solution. Put in a nutshell, Kripke reminds us that qualia can be interpreted in different ways. How do I know that some given mental experience is a cue manifestation of the disposition to add, and not a cue manifestation of the disposition to skadd, or quadd? The objectors do not address this question.

The normativity objection[58]

The realist theory of dispositions has the resources to capture semantic norma-tivity. Assume Jones intends to count by twos, starting from 0, and that after hav-ing reached "156" he continues with "157". Obviously, Jones is wrong; he *ought to* have continued "158". This "ought" can be cashed out in realist-dispositional terms in two steps. Step 1 is the idea that whereas "158" lies on the disposition line "associated with" the rule for adding twos, "157" does not. Step 2 is Jones's intention to stick to this rule. Such intention is itself "a complex dispositional state that includes cue manifestations".

Reply: If we already know that Jones *intends* to add twos then of course we have already captured the relevant phenomenon of normativity. After all, to *intend* to act in certain ways is *eo ipso* to *commit oneself* to act in these ways. What the dis-positionalist has to provide, however, is a way of making sense of such a commit-ment *without invoking an intention*. The normativity objection tries to do so by suggesting that an intention is itself a "complex dispositional state that includes cue manifestations". But the appeal to cue manifestations at this point is no bet-ter than it was in the previous objection. And to simply announce that having an intention is being in a complex dispositional state is no solution to the problem. The challenge is to *show that and how* we can reduce intentions and beliefs to non-intentional dispositions. Finally, a critical comment on the use of the term "disposition lines" seems in order. We know that addition is a function that maps the pairs <156, 2> and <2, 156> onto the number 158. The dispositionalist needs to tell us how our dispositions can possibly track such a function. The normativity objection responds to that challenge by saying that the pairs <156, 2> and <2, 156> are linked to the number 158 by means of a disposition line. Unfortunately, this answer is hopelessly metaphorical. And at no point are we told how we can cash in this metaphor.[59]

Communal dispositions

Almost all of Kripke's discussion of dispositionalism is concerned with an individualist version of the doctrine. Only late in *WRPL*, in something of an aside, do we learn that communal dispositionalism must walk the plank with the individualist version. This has not deterred Horwich from developing precisely such a position. We have already encountered Horwich's (unsuccessful) treatments of the normativity constraint and "determination". Here I shall enquire how his theory does concerning the finitude problem and the mistake problem. Horwich's communal-dispositionalist solution to the mistake problem is contained in the following passage:

> [O]ur normal ways of identifying mistakes (and conditions likely to produce mistakes) involve reference to *community* opinion: our criterion for "going wrong" is divergence from what is generally said. … Ordinarily, and subject to certain conditions, individuals are said to mean by a word whatever that word means in the linguistic community they belong to – even when their own usage is to some extent improper.[60]

Of course, the communal dispositionalist must make sure both that the mistake problem does not simply return on the level of the community; and that the community does not end up being infallible. This point has been pressed by Boghossian. Boghossian insists that individualistic and communitarian dispositionalism face the same structural problem. Both need to be able to separate meaning-constituting dispositions from error-producing dispositions regarding use:

> The community … is bound to exhibit precisely the same duality of dispositions that I do: it too will be disposed to call both horses and deceptively horsey looking cows on a dark night "horse". After all, if

I can be taken in by a deceptively horsey looking cow on dark nights, what is to prevent 17,000 people just like me from being taken in by the same, admittedly effective, impostor? The point is that many of the mistakes we make are *systematic*. ... The communitarian ... cannot call them *mistakes*, for they are the community's dispositions. He must insist, then, firm conviction to the contrary notwithstanding, that "horse" means not *horse* but, rather, *horse or cow*.[61]

Horwich disagrees. In his view, only an unsophisticated form of communal dispositionalism is committed to the infallibility of the community. Sophisticated communal dispositionalism works with a much richer inventory of dispositions than merely dispositions to give answers to plus-queries or dispositions to identify animals. The additional dispositions constitute a "practice of revising epistemological attitudes in specific ways in the light of new evidence, and of acknowledging that earlier claims were wrong".[62] The dispositions to correct and revise do not just concern the isolated judgements of individuals; they also concern judgements that are shared by the community as a whole.

This attempt to rescue communal dispositionalism should look familiar. It repeats – on the community level – a move that we found wanting in the case of the individual: the introduction of dispositions to correct, check and revise. We saw what was wrong with that suggestion above: our intuition says that the neurotic student might mean addition by "+", but he gets more and more of his sums wrong as he checks and rechecks his calculations. The same applies to the community. That a community means addition by "+" is not threatened by the fact that community members fail to spot the mistakes – perhaps even systematic mistakes – that are being made. Put differently, dispositions to correct, check and revise do not deliver a clear boundary around meaning-constituting dispositions. We do not get the right result by saying that a use disposition is meaning-constituting if, and only if, its manifestations survive a further act of checking. This does not work because manifesting a disposition several times does not necessarily increase its quality. Does the same move fare better when applied to communities rather than individuals? It is hard to see how it could. Repeated checking is compatible with making mistakes, regardless of whether the checking is done by an individual or a group. Moreover, our semantic intuitions clearly allow for the possibility that a community could mean *horse* by "horse" and yet make systematic mistakes not only in initial classifications of horses on dark nights, but also in repeated and communal acts of checking and rechecking. If that is correct, then "extended" communal dispositions (to recheck and correct) cannot deliver a borderline between those dispositions to use "horse" that are meaning-constituting and those that are not.

Finally, it should be obvious that communal dispositionalism does not give new tools for dealing with the finitude problem. If my dispositions run out before I reach the realm of enormous numbers, then so will the dispositions of my community. Perhaps mathematical cooperation can help us to reach at least some regions in the realm of enormous numbers; future generations might continue the calculations that we have begun. But of course even if all sentient beings in the universe collaborated in this way, time would still be too short. We still would only reach a minute subset of the integers.[63]

Conclusion

In Chapters 2 and 3 I have tried to vindicate and extend *WRPL*'s two-pronged attack on dispositionalism. Chapter 2 attempted to show that dispositionalism fails the *intensional* requirement, that is, the requirement of semantic normativity. Chapter 3 has argued that dispositionalism is also unable to meet the *extensional* requirement: it is unable to identify dispositional predicates that logically co-vary with meaning predicates. The need to meet this second requirement follows from the meaning determinist's commitment to objectivity.

As far as the extensional requirement is concerned, Kripke's master argument is that (sophisticated) dispositionalism makes illegitimate use of idealization and *ceteris paribus* clauses. If this charge were to be found wanting then Kripke's case against dispositionalism would collapse, at least in so far as this case relies on the extensional requirement. Given my overall aim of defending *WRPL*, it is thus of utmost importance that the master argument is protected from Fodor's highly influential criticism. As we saw above, Fodor argues that if we dismiss dispositionalism for its use of idealization then we also must reject much of natural science. Fodor insists that the idealizations involved for example in the ideal gas law are of a kind with the idealizations used in semantic-dispositionalist laws. I argued that this claim is false. The two cases are not alike. The legitimacy of idealization in the natural and cognitive sciences does not carry over to reductive-dispositionalist theories of meaning and content. And thus Kripke's master argument remains in force.

I regard Boghossian's *argument from optimality conditions* as an important supplement to Kripke's master argument. Boghossian shows that dispositionalism is unable to specify conditions under which my tokening of "horse" inevitably co-varies with the presence of horses in my vicinity. However, Boghossian's argument can do damage to dispositionalism only if Miller's criticism of the argument is answered. I tried to provide such answer above.

Under the title "The addition–subtraction strategy", I discussed three revisionist proposals regarding dispositionalism, initially proposed by Blackburn and Ginet. The first sought to make do with a finite number of dispositions (for doing addition); the second introduced meta-dispositions, that is, second-order dispositions that check the deliveries of first-order dispositions; and the third tried to anchor "brute-level" dispositions to "objective properties". All three ways of adding or subtracting dispositions turned out to be unworkable.

Horwich and Soames have claimed that *WRPL*'s central argument against dispositionalism is marred by *equivocations* concerning "determination". Horwich thinks that different notions of determination are in play in the sceptic's claims (i) that whatever constitutes the meaning of a predicate must determine its extension; and (ii) that the facts about how we are disposed to use a predicate do not determine its extension. Miller has proposed a reading for both (i) and (ii) according to which no equivocation is involved. Soames objects that Kripke's argument equivocates between *a priori* determination and metaphysical determination, and he suggests that metaphysical determination fails: it is impossible to imagine two possible worlds that are identical regarding all their non-intentional facts yet different in their intentional facts. My response was to grant this premise but to deny the conclusion: global supervenience is too weak a relation for it to help the dispositionalist.

I ended by reviewing and rejecting two further refinements of the sophisticated dispositionalism under attack in *WRPL*, one of them revisionist, one reformist. The revisionist proposal by Martin and Heil breaks the link between disposition statements and counterfactual conditionals. The reformist proposal by Horwich replaces the dispositions of a single individual with the dispositions of interacting individuals. I attempted to establish that neither of these refinements withstands critical scrutiny.

This chapter concludes my discussion of *WRPL*'s case against dispositionalism. If my analysis is correct then the case remains very strong – despite the various attempts by more than three dozen philosophers to deflect or refute Kripke's arguments.

FOUR

Other responses

Introduction

Chapters 2 and 3 showed that reductive semantic dispositionalism is not a sat-isfactory answer to the sceptical challenge. Alas, to show that dispositionalism is not up to the task is not yet to establish that high-brow meaning determinism fails. After all, dispositionalism is not the only high-brow meaning-determinist response to the sceptic. In this chapter I therefore discuss four other meaning-determinist proposals:

(i)   the simplicity response,
(ii)   the algorithm response,
(iii) the causalist response, and
(iv)   the Platonist response.

WRPL attacks versions of (i), (ii) and (iv). Critics of *WRPL* have sought to rebut these attacks either by finding fault with Kripke's specific arguments or by devel-oping new versions of the mentioned positions. I shall seek to advance the dis-cussion by demonstrating the insufficiency of both the fault-finding and the refinements.

By (iii), "causalist response", I mean an answer to the sceptical challenge based on Kripke's and Putnam's causal theory of reference. Interestingly enough, Kripke never brings up the causal theory in *WRPL*. Some commentators have lamented this fact and championed the causal theory as (part of) a successful meaning-determinist position. I remain unconvinced.

At the end of this chapter I shall have covered four of the seven high-brow meaning-determinist approaches distinguished in *WRPL*. The remaining three are the use response, the qualia response, and semantic primitivism. In Chapter 1, I outlined Kripke's Wittgenstein's criticism against all three. As far as the use and the qualia responses are concerned, there is nothing to add: to the best of my knowledge, no one has taken up their cause and defended them against the sceptic's attacks. Semantic primitivism is a different story: in many ways it equals dispositionalism in importance. And thus it deserves detailed and careful treatment. However, for reasons that will become apparent in due course, it is best to postpone this treatment until after a detailed consideration of the sceptical solution.

The simplicity response revisited

This topic can be dealt with quickly. Although the simplicity response itself has not found defenders, one important critic has taken issue with the way the response is dismissed in *WRPL*. Kripke writes:

> Let no one … suggest that the hypothesis that I meant plus is to be preferred as the *simplest* hypothesis. … The sceptic argues that there is no fact as to what I meant, whether plus or quus. Now simplicity considerations can help us decide between competing hypotheses, but they obviously can never tell us what the competing hypotheses are. If we do not understand what two hypotheses *state*, what does it mean to say that one is "more probable" because it is "simpler"? If the two competing hypotheses are not genuine hypotheses, not assertions of genuine matters of fact, no "simplicity" considerations will make them so.
>
> (*WRPL*: 38)

Wright argues that:

> this surely gets everything back to front. It is only *after* the sceptical argument has come to its conclusion that the sceptic is entitled to the supposition that there is indeed no such fact of the matter. In the course of the argument, *he* cannot assume as much without begging the question.[1]

In other words, Wright claims that during the sceptical argument there is no reason (yet) to assume that "Jones means addition by '+'" is meaningless (when construed along meaning-determinist lines). Hence for the proponent of the simplicity response it is not obvious that the two hypotheses under consideration – "Jones means addition by '+'" and "Jones means quaddition by '+'" – are without factual content.

Wright's objection is not decisive, however. As pointed out by Alexander Miller, the sceptic need not assume a non-factualism about meaning in order to raise his

128

objection against the simplicity response. It suffices for him to insist that, at this point in the dialectic, we do not yet have any acceptable proposal for what fact makes "Jones means addition by '+'" true. And since we have no such fact, we also cannot give content to the competing hypotheses. This gives the sceptic all he needs.[2]

The algorithm response revisited

Christopher Peacocke and Neil Tennant defend a high-brow version of the algorithm response. That is to say, whereas the original algorithm response used only the resources of meaning determinism as a picture, Peacocke and Tennant seek to embed the algorithm response in philosophical theories.

Peacocke's proposal can be put as follows. To mean addition by "+" is to find a number of transformations "primitively compelling". Here is an example of such transformation: if the sum of 5 and 6 is 11, then the sum of 5 and the successor of 6 is the successor of 11. Call this transformation "T". T is primitively compelling in so far as we do not find it compelling in virtue of something else we have learnt. We find transitions such as T primitively compelling because of their *form*. And this is true of us even when we (as children for example) are unable to make the general form explicit. Indeed, it often takes the work of theorists for the underlying general form to come fully to light. The general form underlying T is this: if the sum of two numbers, say x and y, is the number z, then the sum of x and the successor of y (y') will be the successor of z (z'). Obviously there are empirical circumstances under which we do not find transitions of this form compelling, but we do so under "normal conditions".[3] Indeed, someone is an adder if, under normal conditions, she find transitions of the given general form primitively compelling. The general "possession condition" for the concept *plus* (i.e. *addition*) is thus the following:

> *plus* is that concept C to possess which a thinker must find transitions of the form $m\ C\ k = n$ so $m\ C\ (k') = n'$ primitively compelling (where m, n, k are (senses of) canonical numerals), and find them compelling because they are of that form; and similarly for the principle $m\ C\ 0 = m$.[4]

The crucial feature of Peacocke's proposal is its emphasis on the primitive compellingness of *forms* of transition. Consider for instance Kripke's discussion of the question of whether by "count" we mean *counting* or *quounting*. Assume that we have never applied "count" to the union of sub-heaps either of which has 57 or more elements. Moreover, "to 'quount' a heap is to count it in the ordinary sense, unless the heap was formed as the union of two heaps, one of which has 57 or more items, in which case one must automatically give the answer '5'" (*WRPL*: 16). Kripke's sceptic insists that there is no telling whether we are counters or quounters. Peacocke disagrees. Counting and quounting involve different forms of transition from one number to the next, and we only find the counting transition primitively compelling. Kripke is wrong to focus on the idea that we have never dealt with unions of sub-heaps either of which has 57 or more elements. What is important is that in and through our dealings with these unions we have acquired a sense of what is compelling that extends beyond the limits of our past experiences.[5]

Peacocke's suggestion is intriguing but it does not seem to have the resources to fend off sceptical replies. To begin with, the sceptic does not deny that we find the answer "125" in reply to "68 + 57 = ?" compelling. Indeed, that we find the answer compelling is only to say that we are inclined to give it. And this is not in dispute. The sceptical challenge asks us to explain in virtue of what fact about us is it true to say that our inclination is justified. To answer "in virtue of us having the inclination" is not an admissible answer at this point; to give it is simply to admit that our inclination does not have a justification at all.

Of course, Peacocke is not proposing this obviously unsatisfactory response. But Peacocke's rebuttal too is ultimately unsuccessful. Consider, for instance, the invoking of "normal conditions". Peacocke insists that we find ($*$) "$m \, C \, k = n$ so $m \, C \, (k') = n'$" convincing only under "normal conditions". This has all the problems that we have already discussed in Chapter 3 in the context of dispositionalism. Think again of enormous numbers; do I really find ($*$) primitively compelling in the realm of enormous numbers? How would I know? And what kind of brain would I need for doing so? How do we know that it is ($*$) that I find primitively compelling and not:

> $m \, C \, k = n$ so $m \, C \, (k') = n'$ except when m or k are enormous, in which case $n = 5$?

And how do we know that we find "$m \, C \, 0 = m$" primitively compelling and not

> $m \, C \, 0 = m$ except when m is enormous in which case the sum is 5?

I shall not belabour these difficulties again. The point is that Peacocke's proposal does not contain a remedy against them.

Tennant believes that the sceptic is wrong to claim that our use of "+" is compatible with the *quaddition* hypothesis. Tennant directs his criticism at a footnote of *WRPL* that reads as follows:

> It might be urged that the quus function is ruled out as an interpretation of "+" because it fails to satisfy some of the laws I accept for "+" (for example, it is not associative; we could have defined it so as not

even to be commutative). One might even observe that, on the natural numbers, addition is the only function that satisfies certain laws that I accept – the "recursion equations" for +: (x) $(x + 0 = x)$ and (x) $(y)(x + y' = (x + y)')$ where the stroke or dash indicates the successor; these equations are sometimes called a "definition" of addition. The problem is that the other signs used in these laws (the universal quantifiers, the equality sign) have been applied in only a finite number of instances, and they can be given non-standard interpretations that will fit non-standard interpretations of "+". Thus for example "(x)" might mean for every $x < h$, where h is some upper bound to the instances where universal instantiation has hitherto been applied, and similarly for equality.

In any event the objection is somewhat overly sophisticated. Many of us who are not mathematicians use the "+" sign perfectly well in ignorance of any explicitly formulated laws of the type cited. Yet surely we use "+" with the usual determinate meaning nonetheless. What justifies us applying the function as we do?   (*WRPL*: 16–17, n.12)

As Tennant sees it, the sceptic overlooks (at least) three ways in which our use of "+" is constrained. Tennant formulated these ways as three problems for the sceptic.

- *Problem 1*: The sceptical hypothesis conflicts with our intuition that the universal quantifier must have a uniform interpretation. We cannot uniformly interpret every occurrence of "(x)" in mathematics as $(x < h)$. For instance, in some mathematical laws universal quantifiers range over *terms* for numbers rather than over the numbers themselves. And whereas it makes sense to say that a number is smaller than 57, it does not make sense to say so of a term for a number.
- *Problem 2*: Addition (with natural numbers) displays the following pattern. Any given number n is the sum of $n + 1$ ordered pairs of numbers: there are two such pairs for the number 1, three such pairs for the number 2, four for the number 3, and so on:

$0 + 1 = 1$	$0 + 2 = 2$	$0 + 3 = 3$	$0 + 4 = 4$	$0 + 5 = 5$
$1 + 0 = 1$	$1 + 1 = 2$	$1 + 2 = 3$	$1 + 3 = 4$	$1 + 4 = 5$
	$2 + 0 = 2$	$2 + 1 = 3$	$2 + 2 = 4$	$2 + 3 = 5$
		$3 + 0 = 3$	$3 + 1 = 4$	$3 + 2 = 5$
			$4 + 0 = 4$	$4 + 1 = 5$
				$5 + 0 = 5$

This theorem can be given a formal rendering.[6] But the important point is that we all accept this result. For instance, we all accept that there are exactly six addition sums with 5 as the total. If we were quadders, we most certainly would not be happy with this claim. The fact that we are shows that the sceptical hypothesis about us is untenable.

- *Problem 3*: Our use of numerals is constrained by the following scheme: "For every natural number n, there are n F's if and only if the number of F's $= n$."[7] For instance, the following is true of the number two: whenever there are *two* entities instantiating the same property F, then the number of entities instantiating F equals two. The "n" and "two" in a different font are not numerals but numbers. The meaning of two here is captured by the following logical formula (I use "$\exists(x)$" for the existential quantifier):[8]

$$(\exists x)\,(\exists y)\,(Fx \ \& \ Fy \ \& \ {\sim}x = y \ \& \ (w)\,(Fw \to (w = x \lor w = y)))$$

In this formula, no numeral appears, even though the twofold occurrence of the existential quantifier "shows something about the two-ness of F".[9] The same sorts of formula can of course also be constructed for 57 and 68. Assume we have 57 things that are F and 68 things that are G. There are then 125 things that are either F or G. This sum is captured by the following formula:

$$(\exists x_1)\,(\exists x_2)\,\ldots\,(\exists x_{125})\,(Fx_1 \lor Gx_1) \ \& \ (Fx_2 \lor Gx_2) \ \& \ \ldots \ \& \ (Fx_{125} \lor Gx_{125})$$
$$\& \ (y)\,((Fy \lor Gy) \to (y = x_1 \lor y = x_1 \lor \ldots \lor y = x_{125}))$$

Again, this formula "says nothing about the number 125 (the sum of 68 and 57); rather it shows the 125-ness of $(F$ or $G)$".[10] The quadder arrives, of course, at a different formula. For him the formula for $F + G$ has only five existential quantifiers. "Yet he will have to maintain that it follows logically from the two formulae saying, respectively, 'There are exactly 68 F's' and 'There are exactly 57 G's', along with the premises 'Nothing is both F and G'." And this forces the sceptic into "very difficult logical gerrymander indeed".[11]

Here are sceptical solutions to Tennant's three problems. Concerning problem 1 it must be acknowledged that – given our normal understanding of "uniformity" – the sceptical reinterpretation of quantifiers is not uniform. But maybe we are wrong about our past intentions regarding the use of "uniformity". Maybe by "uniform" we really mean *quuniform*, where *quuniformity* is compatible with different interpretations for different occurrences of the universal quantifier. Regarding problem 2 we only need to note that the meta-mathematical result is no independent touchstone. Once more, the sceptical challenge asks us in virtue of what fact we mean addition rather than quaddition by "+". What is Tennant's response? Is it this: the fact that makes it so that we mean addition is that we can be brought to accept the meta-mathematical result? It would be strange if this was Tennant's proposal. To give this answer would be to claim that before the meta-mathematical result was known no one could really believe himself to be an adder. To this difficulty we can add another. The meta-mathematical result can, of course, itself be reinterpreted in familiar ways. For instance, the sceptic might ask how we know that by "addition sums" we did not mean "addition sums in which neither summand is bigger than 57". The sceptic might also propose that by the expression "for every n" we really meant "for every n except 5". Similar difficulties bedevil problem 3. The move from arithmetic to logic is not of much help here, after all, in logic too we rely on the meaning of words and thus on the description of procedures. The sceptic can grant that the two logical formulas with 57 and 68 existential quantifiers respectively do not contain numerals but *show something* about the "fifty-seven-ness" and the "sixty-eight-ness" of the two sets. And yet, anyone who seeks to decide whether the union of these two sets has 57 or 68 elements will still have to count – or quount. And thus we are back in familiar sceptical territory.

The causalist response

It would be ironic if the causal theory of reference succeeded where all other responses to the sceptical challenge have failed: on the one hand, Kripke is one of the two chief authors of this theory; and, on the other hand, Kripke never brings up the theory in *WRPL*. One obvious reason why he does not mention the theory in *WRPL* has to do with the central example of the book: the causal theory of reference is not a strong contender in the philosophy of mathematics. Nor does anyone advocate it for prepositions, or for logical terms such as quantifiers and connectives. All this is bad news for the causal theory of reference as a solution to the sceptical challenge. The latter is perfectly general: the meaning of all expressions is at issue. For all that, it would still be intriguing if the causal theory worked as an answer to the sceptic at least for the expressions for which it was primarily designed: names and natural kind terms. Indeed, this is what Colin McGinn and Penelope Maddy propose.

Before going to answer their specific objections, it is worth while noting in general why the causal theory of reference does not seem promising as a reply to the sceptic. The point is simple. The causal theory of reference anchors the reference of names and kind terms in acts of "baptizing" or "reference fixing". The name "Nutty" refers to my daughters' hamster because my wife and I decided to call him so. In the baptizing situation we were in perceptual contact with the hamster. We were both causally affected by him. And so were the thoughts that lead to the dubbing event. My wife pointed at him, and uttered the words "Let's call him Nutty". I agreed. That is the basic story. Now if this were all there is to it, we would indeed have a promising idea against the sceptic. But of course it is not all there is to it. We already saw the limitations of a purely causal theory of perception in Chapter 2, when discussing Davidson. In the context of the causal theory of reference the objection to a simple causal theory comes under the title of the "qua-problem".[12] It is not enough for the baptizer to be causally affected; he must be able to individuate the relevant cause if he is to baptize one thing rather than another. For instance, in the baptizing situation my wife and I were in perceptual contact not with the hamster as a whole, but only with an undetached part of him (his face, as he was sticking his head out of his little house). Does this mean that by "Nutty" we really mean the *face of* our daughters' *hamster*? Obviously not. And the reason why not is that during the baptizing situation my wife and I had meaningful mental states that made it so that "Nutty" could only refer to the hamster as a whole. We were thinking of the cause of our perceptual experience under a certain general category.

Similar issues arise for baptizing natural kinds.[13] The baptizer is in perceptual contact with an individual in the jungle; the individual causes the baptizer to have certain mental states; and these mental states form part of the overall set of mental states that result in the dubbing "This is a tiger". Again we face a difficulty. The problem is that the sample individual is a member of many natural kinds: "*Panthera tigris*", "Panthernae", "Carnivora", "Mammalia", "Chordata" and "Animalia". So which of these is the baptizer picking out? Again there is no hope of handling this problem unless we allow mental states of the baptizer to play a role in the story. He has to think of the sample under certain descriptions.

The causal theory of reference looks promising at first because a purely causal contact with the referent seems to avoid the difficulties with intentional states, the states the sceptic homes in on. But it quickly turns out that the causal theory of reference cannot get off the ground unless intentional states are reintroduced. And once such intentional states are part of the story, the sceptic can run his usual arguments. With this in mind, we can turn to McGinn and Maddy.

McGinn insists that the name "Saul Kripke" refers to Saul Kripke for the following reason. The man in question was baptized "Saul Kripke" some time in the past, and the link between him and this name has been passed on through the years until it has reached us. Our uses of tokens of "Saul Kripke" are correct if we use them to refer to the person who was baptized in this way, and it is incorrect if we use them to refer to anyone else (ignoring the possibility that there are more people with this name). What could the sceptic reply? As McGinn sees it, the sceptic could do no better than invoke a sceptical hypothesis of the following kind: "Kripke" really refers to *Kripnam*, where Kripnam is either Kripke if encountered before 2006 or Hilary Putnam if encountered after 2006. On this hypothesis "Kripke" should be applied to Putnam from 2006 onwards, and to Kripke before 2006. Does this save the sceptical position? McGinn thinks that it does not. The reference of the name "Kripke" is fixed by the baptizing of that very man. Putnam played no role in that baptizing, neither as baptizer nor as baptized. And hence "Kripke" could not mean *Kripnam*.[14]

There is an easy rebuttal to McGinn's thought. Imagine that the original baptizer said, or thought (of the man we call "Kripke"): "I hereby baptize you 'Kripke'". The next question then is obvious. What makes it so that in saying, or thinking this, the baptizer did not mean the following: "I hereby baptize you (the man we call 'Kripke') 'Kripke'; but you shall have this name only until 2006 after which the name 'Kripke' is to be transferred to the individual who previously was called 'Putnam'"? Obviously, we cannot retort that such a baptizer would be deviating from the normal practice of keeping the personal names of individuals fixed. This is because the sceptic can wonder whether by "individual" we do not perhaps mean *quindividual* where a quindividual is an entity that is spread over time-slices of two people. He might also wonder whether by "fixed" we do not perhaps mean *quixed* where quixing again allows for the schizophrenic naming practice.

Maddy recognizes the difficulties with finding the right kind of causal connection between baptizer and sample. In order to overcome these problems she combines the causal theory of reference with neuroscience and scientific realism. Consider the act of baptizing. In calling a given lump of matter "gold", the baptizer might be naming its shape, its colour or its material. How could we ever know? This is often called the "qua-problem". The answer, Maddy suggests, lies with neurology. Depending on whether he is focusing on shapes, colours or materials, the brain of the baptizer will be in different states. The perception of shapes, colours and materials is linked to different cell assemblies in the brain. And thus there will be a fact of the matter as to whether the baptizer "meant" the sample for his baptismal act to be the metal, the colour or the material. Lest Maddy's idea is misunderstood, it is important to stress that her idea is not to define natural kinds on the basis of cell assemblies. When the baptizer gives the name "gold" to a lump of material, one specific cell assembly of his brain is stimulated. But we cannot define the extension of the term "gold" as whatever stimulates that same cell assembly. First, there are "pieces of gold that are too small, too large, too far away, or too tarnished" to stimulate the cell assembly in question. Secondly, our neural machinery can malfunction. And thirdly, the currently considered proposal is unable to capture the normativity of meaning: "a purely causal account can only tell us how the baptist goes on to use the word, not why his baptismal act justifies him in so using it".[15] Maddy insists that we can avoid all these difficulties by denying that it is up to the baptizer to determine what belongs to the same kind as his sample:

> the world determines that. His cell assembly only functions to pick out that determinate sample, so it need not be universally applicable or infallible. This is why, presented with another member of his sample's natural kind, the baptist should call it "gold" even if the various causal mechanisms fail and he does not.[16]

Maddy acknowledges that the sceptic has the retort of denying that the world is pre-packaged into natural kinds. But to give this reply, Maddy holds, would be to shift the debate into a different realm. There are no knock-down arguments against (scientific) realism about natural kinds and thus the realist is entitled to rely on her worldview in replying to the sceptic.[17]

At first sight it seems as if Maddy is able to solve the qua-problem in a way that avoids descriptions and other intentional items. In her theory, the work of fixing the level and scope at which the baptizing occurs is done by non-intentional items such as the stimulation of cell assemblies in the brain. Maddy tells us that different cell assemblies are stimulated when the baptizer focuses on shapes, colours and materials respectively; presumably the same is true when the baptizer (in our tiger example) focuses on phylum, class, order, family or subfamily. Unfortunately, Maddy does not tell us how these brain events relate to mental states. One option would be for Maddy to believe that our mental states of thinking about a certain description or level of classification can be reduced to events in the brain. That would be a bold and provocative suggestion; but it would also need a lot of argument in its defence. Moreover, it would be strange if Maddy held this view for only those intentional states that are involved in fixing the level of classification in the context of the causal theory of reference. If the reduction of intentional states to brain states works here, then it surely works everywhere. Suppose then that Maddy wishes to advocate the reductive thesis across the board. She would then be committed to saying, among other things, that Jones means addition by "+" provided only that his brain is in a certain state. Putting things in this way takes us full circle back into the domain of the sceptical challenge and the sceptical argument. Let quaddition be a function that diverges from addition only in the realm of enormous numbers. It follows that if we say that Jones means addition rather than quaddition by "+" we are talking about what his brain states *would be* if his brain were large enough to calculate with enormous numbers. And this returns us to by now familiar difficulties with idealization and *ceteris paribus* laws.

But maybe Maddy does not wish to go down the road of reduction. Perhaps she would prefer to be an eliminativist about intentional states. This would be an extreme view; it would amount to an error theory with respect to all of our intentional talk. And we have already seen that this view cannot even be coherently stated.[18] I conclude therefore that Maddy's proposal for improving the causal theory of reference fails. Kripke was right not to discuss the causal theory of reference in *WRPL*: it is unworkable as an answer to the sceptical argument.

The Platonist response revisited I: Katz's new Platonism

Kripke is brief in rejecting Platonism as a solution to the sceptical challenge. Applied to the central example of the sceptical argument, Platonism holds that the addition function has a "non-mental ... independent, 'objective', existence", and that the addition function "contains all its instances, such as the triple (68, 57, 125)" (*WRPL*: 53). According to Frege's version of Platonism, we need to distinguish four elements in order to understand an individual's usage of the "+"-sign:

"(a) the addition function, an 'objective' mathematical entity; (b) the addition sign '+', a linguistic entity; (c) the 'sense' of this sign, an 'objective' abstract entity like the function; [and] (d) an idea in the individual's mind associated with the sign". The idea is a private mental entity; the addition function and the sense are abstract objects. They are the same for all individuals who "grasp" them. Individuals grasp abstract objects in and through their ideas of these objects. Finally, the sense "*determines* the addition function as the *referent* of the '+' sign" (*WRPL*: 54). As Kripke sees it, the Achilles heel of Platonism is the relationship of grasping:

> [U]ltimately the sceptical problem cannot be evaded, and it arises precisely in the question how the existence in my mind of any mental entity or idea can *constitute* "grasping" any particular sense rather than another. The idea in my mind is a finite object: can it not be interpreted as determining a quus function, rather than a plus function? Of course there may be another idea in my mind, which is supposed to constitute its act of *assigning* a particular interpretation to the first idea; but then the problem obviously arises again at this new level. (A rule for interpreting a rule again.) And so on.   (*WRPL*: 54)

Platonism has not been a fashionable viewpoint during the past twenty years, and thus defences of Platonism against the sceptic's attack have been few and far between.[19] Of these texts, Jerrold J. Katz's book of 1990, *The Metaphysics of Meaning*, is undoubtedly the most important. Katz's discussion of the sceptical challenge is part of a book-length attack on naturalism in twentieth-century analytic philosophy, and a wholesale attempt to rehabilitate Platonism in linguistic theory. It continues and deepens Katz's earlier study *Language and Other Abstract Objects*.[20] I shall outline Katz's general position and his attempt to reply to the sceptical challenge. I shall maintain that despite his argumentative sophistication, Katz's defence of Platonism is unsuccessful.

Katz's position is complex and intricate and it takes some care to set it out clearly. The central concepts of Katz's theory are "meanings" or "senses". These are mind-independent, abstract objects, outside space and time. Senses have properties and relations. Two senses can, for example, be synonymous, antonymous or similar. Senses "determine" "type-extensions". For instance, the sense *table* determines the set of all tables as its "type-extension". Senses are correlated with "expression types". Or differently, for every expression type there is one sense to which it is linked by "grammatical principles". For example, the sense *table* is correlated with the expression type "table". (I use a different typeface for expression types and the normal typeface for expression tokens.) Syntactically simply expressions can have a complex structure of sense. "Woman", for instance, is syntactically simple, but its sense structure is *female human being*. The sum of all correlations between senses and expression types is the "domain of language" or the "grammatical structure". Each such correlation is a "grammatical fact".

An expression type can be instantiated by "expression tokens"; my saying "table" at 1.34pm on 2 May 2005, and your saying "table" at 2.30am on 21 December 2001 are two tokens of the same expression type "table". Expression tokens occur in "utterances". The realm of expression tokens and utterances is the realm of "use". The grammatical structure – the correlations of senses with expression types – constitutes the "norm" for correct utterances. An utterance is grammatically correct if it "corresponds" to the grammatical facts.

Katz's Platonism differs from Frege's mainly in how it construes the relationship between sense and reference. For Frege, sense "determines" reference: the sense of an expression contains the information needed for fixing the reference for the expression. As Katz sees it, sense merely "mediates" reference. That is to say, the meaning of an utterance can deviate from the meaning of its expression type. For example, if the speaker uses the register of irony, the meaning of his utterance "John is a really clever chap" is *John is not very smart*. Such ironic speech is an instance of "non-literal" speech. Sense determines reference only in the case of literal speech. In literal speech the meaning of an utterance can be identified with the meaning of the linguistic type of which the utterance is a token. Non-literal speech is not just governed by grammatical principles; the shift in sense typical of non-literal speech is governed by "pragmatic principles". Katz's new theory of sense seeks to make sense independent of reference. This is done by defining sense as "that aspect of the grammatical structure of an expression in virtue of which it has properties and relations like synonymy, antonymy, meaningfulness, meaninglessness, and redundancy". This definition makes no mention of a link between sense and reference and thus makes "sense independent of reference and purely internal to the language".[21]

Finally, we need to bring the speaker or thinker into the picture. The speaker "grasps" the sense via an "idea" of the sense. By grasping the sense, the speaker "targets" the sense's extension. And the speaker "intends" to speak either literally or non-literally. This intention fixes which sense is to be grasped and linked to his utterance. In *The Metaphysics of Meaning*,[22] Katz does not go into any detail as to how we are able to grasp senses. He refers his readers to the theory suggested in *Language and Other Abstract Objects*. There we get the following proposal. What enables us to grasp senses – as abstract Platonic objects – is our possession of three innate features. First, we have a Chomsky-style innate language acquisition device. This innate language acquisition device enables us to identify linguistic rules in the linguistic data presented to us. Secondly, we have the innate notion of the relation "*knowledge-of*". Possessing this notion provides us with the possibility of treating our identification of linguistic rules as *knowledge of* something, namely, as knowledge of the grammatical structure of language. And thirdly, in addition to the innate concept of "knowledge-of", we also have the innate idea of "abstract object". All three innate features are used by the faculty of "intuition". Intuition uses the innate notions of *knowledge-of* and *abstract object* in order to "de-psychologize" the output of our innate language acquisition device. In this process, internally represented mental objects are turned into concepts of abstract objects. In this way we have "intuitive apprehension" of senses. And the outlined proposal shows, so Katz claims, how we can know of abstract objects without standing in causal relations to them.

The above thumbnail sketch of Katz's general position suffices as background for understanding his attempt to reply to Kripke's anti-Platonist arguments.[23] Katz takes it upon himself to show both what fact it is about a speaker that constitutes his meaning addition rather than quaddition by "+", and what justifies the speaker in answering "125" to "68 + 57". Much of Katz's discussion is not, however, conducted in terms of Kripke's central addition/quaddition example. Instead Katz refers to another example that Kripke introduces as follows:

> I think that I have learned the term "table" in such a way that it will apply to indefinitely many future items. So I can apply the term to a new situation, say when I enter the Eiffel Tower for the first time and see a table at the base. Can I answer a sceptic who supposes that by "table" in the past I meant *tabair*, where a "tabair" is anything that is a table not found at the base of the Eiffel Tower, or a chair found there? Did I think explicitly of the Eiffel Tower when I first "grasped the concept of" a table, gave myself directions for what I meant by "table"? And even if I did think of the Tower, cannot any directions I gave myself mentioning it be reinterpreted compatibly with the sceptic's hypothesis? (*WRPL*: 19)

Let us assimilate the situation as much as possible to the addition/quaddition case and clarify it by distinguishing more sharply between object and metalanguage. Assume that I – a native speaker of German – have just entered the base of the Eiffel Tower and have been asked by a fellow German to identify a table in front of me. I reply with "Das ist ein Tisch". Enter the sceptic. He asks me how I know that in the past by "Tisch" I meant *table* and not *tabair*. If in the past I meant *table* by "Tisch", then my current answer is metalinguistically correct. But if I meant *tabair* by "Tisch" then I should not call this table at the base of the Eiffel Tower "Tisch". Which fact about me makes it so that in the past I meant *table* and not *tabair*, and what justifies me in calling the object in question "Tisch"?

Katz reconstructs the distinction between the *table*-hypothesis and the *tabair*-hypothesis as follows. If the first is true, then by "Tisch" I mean:

(C) a piece of furniture consisting of a flat surface, to serve as the locus of activities in the use of the artefact, and supports for holding the surface in a position for it to function as a locus for those activities.

If, however, the *tabair*-hypothesis is on target, then by "Tisch" I mean:

(C′) something that is a table not found at the base of the Eiffel Tower, or a chair found there.[24]

Katz suggests that the searched-for fact is a "mixed grammatical/psychological fact".[25] Take the grammatical side first. Here we have the grammatical fact that in the German language the expression type "Tisch" is correlated with the sense *table*. This sense is complex, and contains as its elements features such as: *is a piece of furniture*; *has a flat surface*; *serves as a locus of activities*; and *has supports for holding the surface in a position for it to function as a locus of activities*. The expression type "Tisch" is not correlated with the sense *tabair*. As far as the psychological side is concerned, the needed facts are that I now intend, and earlier intended, to speak German; that I now intend my utterance to be literal rather than ironic or metaphorical; and that I grasp the sense "table" via an appropriate idea of it. In Katz's own words (with the minor adjustment of using the German term): "[W]e can say that the speaker's literal use of 'Tisch' means *table*, rather than, say, *tabair*, in virtue of the fact that 'Tisch' means (C) in German, not (C′), and that the speaker has the communicative intention to use the utterance of 'Tisch' literally …".[26]

Turning from the fact to the justification, Katz offers the following account of how I can justify my answer "Tisch" in the situation given above. Again this justification comes in two steps, corresponding to the grammatical and the psychological side of the meaning-determining fact. In order to support the claim that "Tisch" in German means *table* (or C) rather than *tabair* (or C′), it suffices to look at the sense of German expressions in which "Tisch" appears. For instance, the compositional meaning of such expressions as "Spieltisch" (gaming table), "Zeichentisch" (drawing table), "Operationstisch" (operating table) and so on, "in each case involves the sense of the modifier's specifying the activities for which the surface serves as the locus". Furthermore, "guter Tisch" (good table) refers to a table whose surface serves well for whatever activity happens to be appropriate for a table of this type. Or, "Nothing designed to serve as a seat and serving solely and exclusively as a seat is properly called 'Tisch'".[27] And finally, we can argue indirectly that "the information it [i.e. (C′)] contains over and above that in (C) unnecessarily complicates the definition of 'Tisch' since that information is not required to account for any sense property or relation of expressions in which 'Tisch' occurs".[28] As far as the psychological and evidential side of my justification is concerned, it suffices for me to do two things. On the one hand, I honestly report that I have the intention to apply the token "Tisch" literally. And, on the other hand, I supply evidence for the truth of my belief that the object referred to falls into the extension of *table*. As Katz sees it, "these justifications seem to do the trick".[29]

To secure his argument, Katz also considers some further elements of Kripke's original argument as well as possible replies to his proposals. To begin with, he rejects as irrelevant Kripke's question "Did I think explicitly of the Eiffel Tower when I first 'grasped the concept of' a table, gave myself directions for what I meant by 'table'?" The question can safely be answered in the negative since I need not have considered objects at the base of the Eiffel Tower in order to be able to intend to mean *table* by "Tisch". That chairs do not fall into the type-extension of "Tisch" is not a question of my intentions and considerations; the relation between *table* "and its type-extension is an objective relation between an abstract concept and a collection that contains tables but not the Eiffel Tower".[30]

Katz also addresses the objection and concern that support for the *table*-hypothesis might be re-interpretable as support for the *tabair*-hypothesis. This worry can be developed into two different directions. The first direction is to renew the doubt that "Tisch" means *table* in German. We have already learnt above what kind of evidence is needed for rebutting such doubts. The second direction, however, introduces a new idea. The question is "How can I legitimately assert that the sense I grasped in forming the communicative intention to use a token of the type 'Tisch' literally is the sense *table*?"[31] Here Katz turns to Kripke's main point of contention: the question of how an idea – that is, a finite mental object – can pick out one unique infinite function or collection of objects. How can a finite object "project to" an infinite sequence? Katz's answer is predictable. What enables the mind to do so is its ability to grasp a sense. A sense is both infinite and finite at the same time: it determines an infinite series while itself being a finite object:

> [T]he projection argument of Kripke's sceptic will not work. ... Intensionalist Platonism introduces a new element. In addition to *infinite extensions* like $(58, 67, 125)$, $(2, 2, 4)$, ... and *open extensions* like the tables, there are also their *finite intensions*, i.e., senses such as the concept of m and n (i.e., the notion of taking the nth successor of m) and the concept (C). On the intentionalist position, there are inner graspings of senses over and above inner graspings of proper parts of extensions. ... Moreover, ... senses are finite entities.[32]

Katz's claim that "senses are finite entities" has been challenged by Boghossian.[33] Boghossian and Katz agree that it is hard to see how a finite idea can latch on to an infinite extension. But Katz thinks the problem is overcome once we replace the infinite extension with a finite intension. Boghossian denies this. For Boghossian it is every bit as hard to understand how a finite idea can latch on to a finite intension – that determines an infinite extension – as it is to understand how a finite idea can latch on to an infinite extension directly. In his words, "it is as hard to explain how a finite mind might grasp an infinite object – such as the addition table – directly, as it is to explain how it might grasp something that uniquely determines such an infinite object".[34] For that reason Boghossian maintains, "senses are in every relevant respect themselves infinitary objects".[35] In his reply to Boghossian, Katz rejects this line of thought. He claims that the mind need not grasp extensions at all. Rather than "grasping" extensions by "grasping" intensions, the mind merely "targets" or "fixes" extensions. And the latter can be done by grasping the intensions. Ultimately, what entitles us to regard all senses as finite is that "they are finite combinations of finitely many finite component senses". All senses are either simple or built up from a finite number of simple components.[36]

The Platonist response revisited II: sceptical objections

Katz's theory is one of the most elaborate forms of Platonism currently around, and there is much one can learn about the strengths and appeals of this classical position from his two intriguing books. Moreover, Katz is right in taking on Wittgenstein's and Kripke's challenges, and in developing his own position in constant debate with them.[37] No Platonist proposal in the philosophy of language can even begin to seem convincing unless it explains how these challenges can be deflected. But for all that, I do not believe that Katz has found a convincing reply to the sceptical argument. The following objections seem to me to be decisive.

First objection: two kinds of finitude

Let us first take Katz's attempt to circumvent the problem of finitude. The sceptic made much of the idea that mental states are finite whereas the extensions of arithmetical terms such as "addition" are infinite. And the sceptic is unconvinced by the move to solve the problem by introducing an intermediary. For him [a] is as miraculous as is [b]:

> [a] *finite* mental state GRASPS *infinite* extension
> [b] *finite* mental state GRASPS *finite* sense, WHICH DETERMINES *infinite* extension

Katz's reply is to say that all senses are "finite combinations of finitely many finite component senses". In other words, he reads the challenge as asking him to explain how a sense can be finite. But this is not the sceptic's (and Boghossian's) problem. Their problem is to understand how the mind can grasp something that can yield verdicts in an infinite number of cases. Consider an analogy. Take a wall built from bricks. There are two ways in which we might look on the wall as finite. On the one hand, it might be finite in so far as it consists of a finite number of bricks stuck together in a finite number of distinct ways. On the other hand, the wall might also be regarded as finite because it encloses a finite number of blades of grass. Assume someone wondered how a wall can enclose an infinite number of blades of grass. Surely it would not be a satisfactory answer to reply by explaining how a wall is built out of a finite number of bricks. The puzzle is how one would have to build and structure walls for them to be able to capture an infinity of some kind. Explaining the structure and material of the wall, on its own, does not do the trick. The same applies, of course, to senses. The puzzle is how the mental grasp of a sense can enable us to track, or fix on, infinite extensions. To learn that senses are constructed out of a finite number of other senses is not to arrive at a solution to this puzzle.

Second objection: grasping abstract objects

Katz is to be complimented for taking on the ultimate challenge for any Platonist proposal: to explain how creatures in space and time, such as ourselves, can come to have knowledge about entities outside space and time, such as senses or numbers. Katz's solution is the innateness of a language acquisition device, the notion of *knowledge-of*, and the idea of *abstract object*. The innate notion and the innate idea enable us to de-psychologize the linguistic rules identified by the language acquisition device.

It is hard to see how this helps with the problem at hand. Katz gives us a theory that explains – or rather "seeks to explain" – how creatures like us might come to believe that they have knowledge of abstract objects. But he does not give us a theory of how creatures like us manage to have true beliefs about these abstract objects. Consider another analogy. Suppose someone defended his belief in witchcraft by appeal to innate mental capacities. He points out that we have an innate module of social cognition that disposes us to ostracize outsiders; that we have an innate notion of *knowledge-of*, and that we have an innate notion of *witch*. The innate notion and the innate idea enable us to de-psychologize the outputs of our innate module, and to take witches to be real. Few of us would be persuaded. We would point out that whatever our modules and innate notions and ideas suggest to us, there are no witches. None of the described mechanisms and notions make it so that we are judging truly when judging someone to be a witch. The same applies of course to the case of abstract objects. Mechanisms for explaining our predisposition to form beliefs need not be mechanisms for explaining our predisposition to form *true* beliefs. With respect to abstract objects, Katz has given us the former, not the latter.

Note, furthermore, that if Katz's theory were true, it would be hard to understand why so many of us are opposed to the assumption of abstract objects outside space and time, and thus outside the causal nexus. If all of us have the innate concepts and ideas, then we should all end up finding Katz's – or Frege's or Gödel's – form of Platonism irresistible. Unfortunately for Katz, most of us do not. The least he owes us is an account for why so many of us are able to form beliefs in opposition to our innate predispositions.

Third objection: the multiple interpretability of the mental state

The key difficulty for all meaning-determinist accounts discussed in the sceptical argument is to prevent meaning-constituting mental states from being multiply interpretable. It is hard to see how Katz's proposal makes any progress regarding this difficulty. Recall that Katz's speaker must form the intentions – now and in the past – to speak German and to aim for a literal meaning. Forming such intentions involves concepts. And thus the intentions are open to sceptical challenges. Assume the German speaker formed his intention concerning the language by thinking "Ich spreche Deutsch". What can he reply to the challenge that by "Deutsch" in the past he meant *Sherman* rather than *German*, where *Sherman* is just like *German* except that "Tisch" in *Sherman* means *tabair* rather than *table*? Or assume that the German speaker formed his intentions concerning literalness of speech by thinking "Ich spreche wörtlich". What can he reply to the challenge that by "wörtlich" in the past he meant *quiteral* rather than *literal*, where *quiteral* is just like *literal* except that using "Tisch" quiterally it to use it with the meaning *tabair* rather than *table*?

Fourth objection: knowledge of a language

Note also that Katz changes the terms of the sceptical argument. The sceptical argument is conducted as a critical study of meaning determinism. According to meaning determinism the speaker is assumed to have direct knowledge of the meaning of the expressions in his language (his idiolect) since he has himself set up the rules according to which the expressions are to be used. Katz's scenario is different. He is concerned with a situation in which a speaker is challenged to defend his knowledge of, and commitment to, a natural language, such as German or English. This move makes it more natural to speak of our knowledge of language as hypothetical. Katz's way of setting up the problem suggests that the meaning determinist might answer the sceptic by marshalling evidence about correlations between the meanings and the expressions in the natural language in question. Katz chooses English as his example; I have chosen German in order to establish a clearer separation of object and metalanguage. Adjusting for this difference, Katz's evidence against the tabair-hypothesis is that expressions such as "Schreibtisch", "Essenstisch" and "Zeichentisch" all contain implicit references to a surface of activity; that "Einige Tische sind Tische" (Some tables are tables) is analytic, whereas "Einige Tische sind Stühle" (Some tables are chairs) is not; that "Tisch" and (C) are synonymous, whereas "Tisch" and (C′) are not; and that "a Tisch that is a piece of furniture" is redundant whereas "a Tisch that is not found at the base of the Eiffel Tower or a chair found there" is not.

We have already seen that even if the sceptic granted that things are this way in German, he could still wonder what fact makes it so that the speaker is committed to German rather than Sherman, the variant of German in which "Tisch" means *tabair*. If "Tisch" were to mean *tabair* it would still be true that "Schreibtisch", "Essenstisch" and "Zeichentisch" all contain implicit references to a surface of activity. The fact that a surface supported by legs and found at the base of the Eiffel Tower does not fall into the extension of "Tisch" does not change this situation. "Einige Tische sind Tische" would still be analytic, and "Einige Tische sind Stühle" might well fail to be analytic. After all, a table found at the base of the Eiffel Tower is rightly called "Tisch" but for all we know it might not be rightly called "Stuhl". If that is the case, then "Einige Tische sind Stühle" is neither analytic nor true.[38]

More importantly, Katz's way of rewriting the sceptical argument loses track of an important aspect of the dialectic: namely, that at issue is the application of an expression in a new situation, a situation in which it has not previously been used. The problem is that no amount of knowledge of how a given language has been used in the past determines how it *should be* used in the future. Even if the Germans up to now have called "Tisch" all and only those things that fulfil (C), it might well be possible that, on encountering a table at the base of the Eiffel Tower, they decide not to call it "Tisch". Katz is helping himself to the distinction between a community going on in the same way as before, and the community developing a new way. But to assume this distinction as unproblematic is to beg the question against the sceptical argument.[39]

At issue it thus not just the question of whether the sceptic's interlocutor knows to which language – German or Sherman – he has committed himself in the past; at issue is also the question of how any facts about the past can constitute an obligation for the future. Even if the meaning determinist had succeeded in committing himself to German in the past, he still would not have escaped the Sherman option for good. The problem is to decide what the German language requires us to do in a newly encountered case. Call "German$_1$" that continuation of past German that involves calling the table at the base of the Eiffel Tower "Tisch", and call "German$_2$" that continuation of past German that involves not calling the table at the base of the Eiffel Tower "Tisch". Which fact about past German makes it so that German$_1$ is the correct continuation of past German and not German$_2$? Asking this question is of course tantamount to reintroducing the dilemma of choosing between German and Sherman, only now in a form that takes into account Kripke's temporal version of the problem.

Such problems are invisible to Katz. His Platonism has no space for the intuitive and common-sense idea that languages change. For him linguistic change only occurs on the level of our knowledge of languages; as abstract objects these languages themselves do not change at all. Nothing in Katz's response to the sceptic gives us a good reason to adopt this picture.

The Platonist response revisited III: Platonism without intermediaries?

For Platonists such as Frege or Katz, we "grasp" abstract objects like senses in and through mental states. Kripke emphasizes that it is these mental states that cause difficulties for the Platonist. This is because all the standard problems of reinterpretability recur with respect to these mental states. How do I know that my mental state grasps the sense *addition* and not the sense *quaddition*? Under what interpretation does it grasp the one sense rather than the other sense? And so on.

Perhaps the Platonist can regroup and return to the oldest form of Platonism. Fred Feldman has suggested as much.[40] They propose to get rid of the intermediate mental state. In other words, a subject's grasp of an abstract object is an unmediated relation between that subject and the abstract object. Feldman explains the position as follows. Consider what happened when you taught me the use of a new colour word, say "sepia". You showed me different samples of the colour. As the Platonist sees it, in and through this process of instruction I noticed a universal: the property of being *sepia*. I grasped this property. And subsequently my grasp of this property enabled me to use "sepia" correctly. This is so because the property *sepia* came to serve me as "the sense, meaning or intension of the word, 'sepia'". The property became the sense of the word for me since "I resolved to use the word with this property as sense. Hence, I was committed to using 'sepia' in such a way that it expresses *sepia*".[41] Feldman acknowledges that the sceptic might come back and wonder whether I really grasped *sepia* and not some Goodman-esque alternative. Maybe I grasped *seplue* rather than *sepia*: something is seplue if it is sepia until tomorrow and blue thereafter. But Feldman is not worried. He believes the problem can be solved "in familiar ways" by showing more samples. And "in the long run, considerations of simplicity will favour the hypothesis that I mean *sepia* by 'sepia'". Moreover, "if God had been watching, he would have seen that it was *sepia* I was grasping, not … some other queer property".[42]

I am not convinced. First of all, note that Feldman is still working with an intermediate mental state, that is, the resolution to use "sepia" with *sepia* as its sense. And this resolution has all the familiar problems. When I say to myself "I shall use 'sepia' with *sepia* as its sense", how do I know that the second "sepia" refers to *sepia* and not to *seplue*? Moreover, Feldman's reply to the sceptic's appeal to Goodmanesque predicates is unsatisfactory. On the one hand, further samples will not help decide whether I grasped *sepia* or *seplue*. On the other hand, the bland reference to simplicity considerations is a non-starter. It is central to our common-sense notion of meaning that we know what we mean directly and not on the basis of judgements about the relative simplicity of elaborate hypotheses concerning abstract objects. And, finally, Feldman's reference to God is not of much help. The problem is that although we can *say* or *write* that God would know which universal I had grasped, we cannot really understand what that means. Since we have not been given an analysis of what would constitute grasping a universal, we also have no idea how God would be able to tell which universal we have grasped. Of course, ultimately the Platonist may dig in his heels and refuse to be moved by objections on this score. He might simply insist that we do grasp universals in unmediated ways and that this is all that can be said. With that position one cannot argue further. But there is no particular reason to accept it either.[43]

Conclusion

In this chapter I have discussed four meaning-determinist responses to the sceptical challenge: the simplicity response, the algorithm response, the causalist response, and the Platonist response. Wright's objection to Kripke's rejection of the simplicity response turned out to be misplaced. The sceptic is entitled to the observation that it is at least unclear whether the addition hypothesis is simpler than the quaddition hypothesis.

Peacocke's and Tennant's refinements of the algorithm response were unsuccessful. Peacock's "primitively compelling" transformations fell prey to the by now familiar problems with idealization and *ceteris paribus* clauses. Tennant tries to block sceptical reinterpretations of algorithms by introducing yet more algorithms. Alas, if one algorithm allows for reinterpretations, so do many.

McGinn's and Maddy's attempt to turn Kripke against Kripke – the causal theory of reference against the sceptical challenge – is intriguing but unconvincing. On the one hand, no one expects the causal theory to work for mathematics, connectives and quantifiers. On the other hand, the causal theory is unable to answer the sceptic also because of the qua-problem.

Finally, Katz's new Platonism is an impressive and complex theoretical edifice, but in the end it succumbs to the simple problem already identified by Kripke in *WRPL*: at some point even the Platonist has to invoke mental states of "grasping". And with respect to these mental states the usual sceptical problems apply with full force.

Leaving aside semantic primitivism, I have now completed the first half of my overall project: the updating of the sceptic's criticism of low- and high-brow versions of meaning determinism. All of the investigated versions of meaning determinism fail; and no other plausible versions have been proposed. (And semantic primitivism will later turn out to be a form of meaning scepticism.) The natural next step is to turn to the second half of my project: an interpretation and defence of the sceptical solution.

Factualism and non-factualism

Introduction

In this and the following two chapters I turn to the main controversies regarding the sceptical solution. In this chapter I discuss the issue of whether the sceptical solution features a credible successor to classical realism; in Chapter 6 I show that the private language argument *as rendered by WRPL* is defensible; and in Chapter 7 I ask how the sceptical solution relates to semantic primitivism.

The first topic is naturally subdivided into three questions. First, does the sceptical solution propose a factualist or a non-factualist reading of meaning attributions? Secondly, assuming – as the majority view among critics has it – that the sceptical solution offers a non-factualist account of meaning attributions, is the resulting position defensible on systematic grounds? Thirdly, assuming – as only very few interpreters have done – that the sceptical solution is factualist, how does this factualism differ from the factualism that is part and parcel of meaning determinism in general and semantic realism in particular? To anticipate briefly, I shall defend the views that the sceptical solution is factualist in a minimalist sense; that non-factualism about meaning attributions is incoherent; and that whereas meaning-determinist factualism is inflationary, meaning-sceptical factualism is deflationary.

Non-factualism in the sceptical solution

A non-factualist about a certain class of declarative sentences denies that they are "truth-apt" or "fact-apt":[1] he denies that for any sentence *s* of this class we can infer "*s* is true" or "It is a fact that *s*" from *s*. Non-factualism is usually a form of projectivism. Its basic idea is well captured in the following quote:

We project an attitude or habit or other commitment which is not descriptive onto the world, when we speak and think as though there were a property of things which our sayings describe, which we can reason about, know about, be wrong about, and so on. Projecting is what Hume referred to when he talks of "gilding and staining all natural objects with the colours borrowed from internal sentiment", or of the mind "spreading itself on the world".[2]

Forms of projectivism include emotivism,[3] quasi-realism[4] and what we might call "performativism". For the emotivist and the quasi-realist

(∗) "Jones means addition by '+'"

is similar in function to saying "Hooray to the way in which Jones operates with '+'". (The quasi-realist differs from the emotivist in that he seeks to explain how we can legitimately talk *as if* we were entitled to the assumption that there are meaning facts, even though we are not.[5]) The advocate of a performative reading of meaning attributions holds that in uttering (∗) we change the social world: we make it so that Jones has now a certain social status as reliable partner in certain interactions (such as counting money).

Is the sceptical solution committed to a non-factual analysis of meaning attributions? Most commentators and critics have given a positive answer to this question.[6] And it is not difficult to see how they have reached this view. First of all, according to *WRPL*, Wittgenstein holds that no facts correspond to meaning attributions:

Recall Wittgenstein's sceptical conclusion: no facts, no truth conditions, correspond to statements such as "Jones means addition by '+'."
(*WRPL*: 77)

Wittgenstein's sceptical solution concedes to the sceptic that no "truth conditions" or "corresponding facts" in the world exist that make a statement like "Jones, like many of us, means addition by '+'" true.
(*WRPL*: 86)

Secondly, the sceptical solution rejects classical realism, that is, the view that "a declarative sentence gets its meaning by virtue of its *truth conditions*, by virtue of its correspondence to facts that must obtain if it is true" (*WRPL*: 72):

So stated, the *Tractatus* picture of the meaning of declarative sentences may seem not only natural but even tautological. Nonetheless, as Dummett says, "the *Investigations* contains implicitly a rejection of the classical (realist) Frege-*Tractatus* view that the general form of explanation of meaning is a statement of the truth conditions".[7]
(*WRPL*: 72–3)

149

> If Wittgenstein is right, we cannot begin to solve [the sceptical paradox] if we remain in the grip of the natural presupposition that meaningful declarative sentences must purport to correspond to facts …
>
> (*WRPL*: 79)

Thirdly, Kripke points out that the sceptical paradox involves a general attack on the idea that mental representations can correspond to facts:

> [T]he paradox of the second part of the *Investigations* constitutes a powerful critique of any idea that "mental representations" uniquely correspond to "facts", since it alleges that the components of such "mental representations" do not have interpretations that can be "read off" from them in a unique manner. So *a fortiori* there is no such unique interpretation of the mental "sentences" containing them as "depicting" one "fact" or another. (*WRPL*: 85)

Fourthly, Wittgenstein is said to deny a necessary link between the indicative mood and assertions or fact-stating:

> Since the indicative mood is not taken as in any sense primary or basic, it becomes more plausible that the linguistic role even of utterances in the indicative mood that superficially look like assertions need not be one of "stating facts". (*WRPL*: 73)

Fifthly, Kripke insists that for Wittgenstein meaning attributions play an important role in our social life. By means of meaning attributions we signal that individuals can be either trusted or must be distrusted in certain forms of interaction. And such signalling has consequences; it plays a role in taking individuals into our community, or in excluding them from it:

> An individual who passes such tests [i.e. tests concerning addition] is admitted into the community as an adder; an individual who passes such tests in enough other cases is admitted as a normal speaker of the language and member of the community. (*WRPL*: 92)

> When we pronounce that a child has mastered the rule of addition, we mean that we can entrust him to react as we do in interactions such as that … between the grocer and the customer. … When the community denies of someone that he is following certain rules, it excludes him from various transactions such as the one between the grocer and the customer. It indicates that it cannot rely on his behaviour in such transactions. (*WRPL*: 93)

> [*I*]*f* we think of Crusoe as following rules, we are taking him into our
> community ...   (*WRPL*: 110)

Sixthly, and finally, a projectivist interpretation of meaning attributions can also point to the parallels between Hume and Wittgenstein (*WRPL*: 62–3, 66–7). Kripke claims that both Hume and Wittgenstein develop sceptical solutions: Hume for causation, Wittgenstein for meaning. And in Hume's case the sceptical solution is projectivist; when perceiving a constant conjunction between types of events, we cannot help *projecting* the idea of a necessary connection on to that conjunction.

In the light of these (and other) passages, a projectivist reading seems hard to resist. Meaning attributions must be given a non-factualist reading; meaning is not given by truth-conditions; sentences in the indicative mood need not be fact-stating but can have other functions; and the function of meaning attributions is to signal approval for individuals' membership in our community.[8]

Boghossian's argument against local projectivism

Call "local projectivism" the view that meaning attributions must be given a non-factualist reading. Call "global projectivism" the position according to which every statement – meaning attribution or not – must be understood along projectivist lines. Wright's 1984 review of *WRPL* formulated two questions that have become the central questions about projectivism: does local projectivism about meaning attributions lead to global projectivism; and what, if anything, is wrong with local or global forms of projectivism?[9] The most important answers to these questions come from Boghossian and Wright himself.[10]

Boghossian has suggested that *local* projectivism is incoherent since it is simultaneously committed to two different views of truth. Since (as ever) Boghossian's argument is sophisticated and complex, it is best to lay it out pedantically in six steps.

1. Every theorist of truth has to make up her mind concerning the question of whether truth is "robust" or "deflationary". If we think of truth as "robust" we think of the predicate "true" as standing for "some sort of language-independent property". If we adopt a "deflationary" view of truth we deny that "true" stands for a language-independent property and insist that its meaning is exhausted by certain syntactic–semantic operations it allows for.[11] Boghossian insists that we have to choose between these two options:

   > Whether truth is robust or deflationary constitutes the biggest decision a theorist of truth must make. But decide he must. ... a concurrent commitment to *both* a robust and a deflationary concept of truth would

be merely to pun on the word "truth". We should not confuse the fact that it is now an open question whether truth is robust or deflationary for the claim that it can be both.[11]

2. Let us say – as we have already done above – that a sentence is "truth-apt" if, and only if, it is apt for "semantic ascent"; that is, a sentence *s* is truth-apt if, and only if, we are permitted to infer "'*s*' is true" from *s*. Obviously we do not want to count just any sentence as truth-apt; questions and commands clearly do not qualify. Which conditions shall we adopt? And what should determine the answer? Boghossian submits that the two conceptions of truth – robust and deflationary – each come with their own requirements concerning "truth-aptness": "Any proposed requirement on candidacy for truth must be grounded in the preferred account of the nature of truth".[13] A deflationary theory of truth makes minimal (deflationary) demands on a sentence being truth-apt: it is enough for a sentence to be truth-apt that it be meaningful, declarative and "disciplined" by norms of correct use. A robust theory of truth will expect more of a sentence before it considers it a candidate for robust truth. For instance, a correspondence theorist might demand that the sentence contain the right kind of referring expressions, or that it be reducible to the theorist's favourite scientific language – usually the language of physics.

3. Projectivism about meaning is committed to a robust notion of truth as a property. Here is why. Meaning attributions clearly are significant, declarative and "disciplined" sentences. Hence any advocate of deflationism about truth must regard meaning attributions as truth-apt. Not so the projectivist, however. It follows that he must be thinking of conditions of truth-aptness beyond the deflationary conditions. And the only conditions beyond deflationary conditions are robust conditions. Finally, being committed to robust conditions for truth-aptness is tantamount to being committed to a robust notion of truth.

4. Steps 1–3 have shown that the projectivist is committed to speak of truth-aptness and truth-condition in the robust sense. Thus, whenever he grants or denies truth-conditions, he grants or denies robust truth-conditions or robust truth-aptness. His commitment to robustness goes even further: it is not just that the projectivist grants or denies robust truth-conditions; his own judgements according to which sentences have robust truth-conditions (or not) have themselves robust truth-conditions. Put differently, if some sentences are robustly truth-apt, then the judgement that they are so truth-apt must itself be robustly truth-apt. Or, if one is committed to truth as an independent property, then the question of whether some sentence is a candidate for such truth cannot be up to us: it must likewise be a question of truth as an independent property.

5. Unfortunately, a different line of reasoning shows that local projectivism is committed also to the precise opposite of what step 4 has established. What defines local projectivism is the claim that meaning attributions – and hence

meaning itself – are not factual matters; that there is no fact of the matter as to what a given sentence means. But once this is accepted, robust truth, that is, truth as a property, is no longer an option. As emphasized by Wright: "If the truth value of [a sentence] S is determined by its meaning and the state of the world in relevant respects, then non-factuality in one of the determinants can be expected to induce non-factuality in the outcome".[14] In other words, if the meaning of S is not factual, then neither is the truth of S. And to deny that truth is factual is to reject the notion that truth is an independent property.

6. Local projectivism about meaning and content is thus simultaneously committed to contradictory assumptions: that truth is robust and an independent property (step 4) and that truth is not robust and not an independent property (step 5).[15] Hence local projectivism is an unstable position.

I now turn from the exposition of Boghossian's argument to its critical evaluation.[16] It seems that it can be challenged at a number of points. First, step 1, according to which a truth theorist *must* choose between robust and deflationary truth, is unconvincing. Although it is implausible to operate with the two conceptions of truth simultaneously for the same discourse, there is nothing to be said against the practice of advocating different notions of truth in different domains.[17] And once the non-factualist is given this option, the first step of the argument collapses.

Step 2 does not fare any better. It is not correct to assume that deflationism about truth and deflationism about truth-aptness must go hand in hand. One can deny that truth is an independent property while insisting that more is needed for truth-aptness than fulfilling the criteria of being significant, declarative and disciplined by norms. Perhaps one can even argue that deflationism about truth-aptness is never an option.[18] For instance, one might argue as follows:

I A state of mind is a belief if, and only if, it stands in the right kind of relation to information, rationality and action.

II A sentence is truth-apt if, and only if, it can be used to give the content of a belief (ignoring problems with excessively long sentences, contradictions, etc.).

III If it must be possible to use a truth-apt sentence for the purpose of giving the content of a belief, then a truth-apt sentence must meet the requirement of *I*; that is, its content must stand in the right kind of relation to information, rationality and action.

IV If the truth-aptness of a sentence is determined by the condition of standing in the right kind of relation to information, rationality and action, then truth-aptness is subject to a stronger requirement than that imposed by deflationary truth-aptness. It is not enough for a truth-apt sentence to be meaningful, declarative and "disciplined" by norms of correct use.

Ergo: V Deflationism about truth-aptness is never an option.[19]

A third counter-argument to Boghossian's attempted refutation of local projectivism could be based on the distinction between "promiscuous" and "non-promiscuous" forms of deflationism: the promiscuous deflationist applies the disquotational scheme to any sentence that fulfils the mentioned minimal conditions. The non-promiscuous deflationist demands more of truth-aptness. For instance, he might decide that counting a sentence as eligible for truth is a compliment that she only wishes to pay to certain sentences: "attributions of truth conditionality are compliments paid to those indicatives a speaker regards as explanatorily ineliminable".[20] In the same way one might also challenge step 5, that is, the claim that judgements about factuality of a sentence must themselves be factual. There is nothing contradictory about assuming that sentences such as "S has truth-conditions", "S is factual" or "S is descriptive" are expressions of a stance or commitment "about the proper role of S in the inferential/explanatory game".[21]

Wright's argument against local and global projectivism

Boghossian's argument against local projectivism is inconclusive at best. But Wright has shown that we can do better. The trick is to demonstrate, first, that local projectivism leads to global projectivism and, secondly, that global projectivism is incoherent. Wright has presented two lines of argument to this effect. The first is (relatively) quick and consists of three ideas:

- Idea I establishes that local projectivism leads to global projectivism:

    (*Idea I*) If the truth value of [a sentence] *s* is determined by its meaning and the state of the world in relevant respects, then non-factuality in one of the determinants can be expected to induce non-factuality in the outcome. (A rough parallel: If among the determinants of whether it is worthwhile going to see a certain exhibition is how well presented the leading exhibits are, then, if questions of good presentation are not considered to be entirely factual, neither is the matter of whether it is worth while going to see the exhibition.) A projectivist view of meaning is thus, it appears, going to enjoin a projectivist view of what it is for a statement to be true.[22]

- *Idea II* supplements *Idea I*. It points out that if "'p' is true" is projectivist, then "p" must be too: after all, it is impossible that the right and left sides of the disquotational scheme ("p" is true if and only if p) could fall on different sides of the projectivist-factualist divide.[23]
- Finally, *Idea III* is that global projectivism is an incoherent view. When we first reflect on the thesis of global projectivism we surely regard it as a statement

that is either *descriptively* correct or *descriptively* incorrect about meaning. In other words, the thesis of global projectivism purports to state a discovery about meaning. But if global projectivism is correct, then it cannot state such a discovery. The problem is that the thesis of global projectivism must apply to itself. If every statement is projective then so is the statement that every statement is projective. And thus it turns out that the thesis of global projectivism cannot state a discovery about meaning; it merely expresses an attitude towards meaning.[24]

This is the quick argument. I regard it as entirely convincing. Nevertheless, Wright has also presented a much more complex proof of the incoherence of projectivism (local and global). The structure of the proof mimics the "quick argument". The first part establishes once more that local projectivism leads to global projectivism. This part of the proof was first put forward by Boghossian.[25] The second part, developed by Wright, goes on to show that global projectivism is incoherent. Here the incoherence takes the precise form of global projectivism, implying that local projectivism (and hence global projectivism) is false.[26] I have found it helpful to reconstruct the proof in formal-logical terms.[27] I shall explain every step of the proof in some detail so as to help readers unfamiliar with the techniques used.

To be a projectivist about semantic discourse is to deny that declarative sentences of semantic discourse have truth-conditions. Thus, for example, "Jones means addition by '+'" or "'Katze' means *cat*" do not have truth-conditions. Formally:

(i) $(s)\,(p)\,(\varphi)\,(\sim\!\Delta\,(\Delta\,(s, p), \varphi))$

Explanation[28]
1. Small letters of the Roman alphabet are sentential variables, small letters of the Greek alphabet are propositional variables. "$(x)(\dots x \dots)$" is the universal quantifier, to be read as "for all x: x ...". "$\sim$" is the sign for negation. "$\Delta(\dots, \dots)$" is a two-place predicate in which the first argument stands for a sentence, and the second argument stands for either a sentence or a proposition. When the second argument is a proposition, "$\Delta(\dots, \dots)$" says that the second argument is the truth-condition of the first argument; when the second argument is a sentence, "$\Delta(\dots, \dots)$" says that the second argument expresses a proposition that is the truth-condition of the first argument. "$\Delta(\dots, \dots)$" is always a sentence, regardless of whether the second argument stands for a sentence or a proposition.
2. An instance of "$\Delta(\dots, \dots)$" can itself be substituted for the first argument. The embedded "$\Delta(\dots, \dots)$" is then mentioned, not used, and its second argument is a sentence.
3. Formula (i) says that for all sentences s and p and for all propositions φ: it is not the case that the sentence "s has the truth-condition expressed by p" has a truth-condition φ.

4. Strictly speaking, local projectivism says that sentences of the form "*s* means φ" do not have truth-conditions. I here assume that to claim that "*s* means φ" is tantamount to claming that Δ(*s*, *p*).

   (ii)   (φ) (~Δ (Δ (*s*, *p*), φ))

Explanation
Here we use the principle of universal (quantifier) elimination. It says, roughly, that if a sentence of the form "(*x*)(... *x* ...)" is true, then we can replace it with a ground term (a terms with no variables). Here we use this step to get rid of the first two universal quantifiers in (i).

   (iii)   ~T (Δ (*s*, *p*))

Explanation
1. "T(*x*)" says that sentence *x* is true. "~T(*x*)" says that sentence *x* is not true.
2. Formula (iii) follows from (ii) on the grounds that if a sentence does not have truth-conditions then it cannot be true. Formally, the principle used is:

   $$T(x) \rightarrow (\exists\varphi) (\Delta (x, \varphi))$$

   where "→" stands for "implication", and "(∃φ)" is the existential quantifier ("there is a proposition φ such that ...")
3. Formula (iii) says that it is not true that *s* has the truth-condition expressed by *p*.

   (iv)   ~ Δ (*s*, *p*)

Explanation
From (iii) *via* the principle ~T(*x*) → ~*x*.

   (v)   (*s*)(*p*) ~ Δ (*s*, *p*)

Explanation
1. From (iv) by universal (quantifier) introduction: since we have proved ~ Δ(*s*, *p*) for "anonymous" sentences *s* and *p*, we are entitled to assume that ~ Δ(*s*, *p*) holds for all *p* and all *s*.
2. Formula (v) says that no sentence has truth-conditions. This is one way to capture global projectivism. The argument shows that global projectivism follows from local projectivism as far as sentences are concerned.

Global projectivism follows from local projectivism also if we consider propositions. The starting-point is once again (iii):

   (iii)   ~T (Δ (*s*, *p*))

156

(vi) $(p) \sim T (\Delta (s, p))$

Explanation
From (iii) by universal quantifier introduction.

(vii) $(\varphi) \sim T (\Delta (s, \varphi))$

Explanation
In order to get from (vi) to (vii), we need the intuitively plausible principle:

$$(p) \sim T (\Delta (s, p)) \leftrightarrow (\varphi) \sim T (\Delta (s, \varphi))$$

(viii) $\sim T (\Delta (s, \varphi))$

Explanation
From (vii) by universal quantifier elimination.

(ix) $\sim \Delta (s, \varphi)$

Explanation
From (viii) via the principle: $T(x) \leftrightarrow I$.

(x) $(s) (\varphi) \sim \Delta (s, \varphi)$

Explanation
 1. From (ix) via universal quantifier introduction.
 2. At this point we have established once more that local projectivism leads to global projectivism; but here we have shown this also for propositions.

The remaining steps establish that global projectivism contradicts local projectivism:

(xi) $a = $ "$(s) (p) (\varphi) (\sim\Delta (\Delta (s, p), \varphi))$"

Explanation
This is just a labour-saving move. We simply stipulate that a stands for (i), the thesis of local projectivism.

(xii) $(\varphi) (\sim\Delta (a, \varphi))$

Explanation
Substituting a for s in (x), using the principle: $(s)H(s) \rightarrow H(a)$.

(xiii) $\sim T(a)$

Explanation
From (xii) by universal quantifier elimination, and the principle explained under
(iii)(2).

(xiv) $\sim a$

(xv) $\sim (s)\,(p)\,(\varphi)\,(\sim\!\Delta\,(\Delta\,(s,p),\varphi))$

Explanation
With (xv) we have derived the negation of (i), the thesis of local projectivism.
Hence our overall result is this: if local projectivism is true, then global projectivism is true. And if global projectivism is true, then local projectivism is false. This
is not a good result for either local or global projectivism![29] (Of course, whether
or not one finds all this compelling depends on how comfortable one is with the
idea of variables that have wffs of the system in their range.)

Two forms of factualism I: Byrne

Given the problems of the projectivism canvassed above, there is good reason to
review the evidence for and against the non-factualist rendering of meaning attributions in Chapter 3 of *WRPL*. Fortunately, over the past ten years, three authors
– Alex Byrne, David Davies and George Wilson – have assembled an impressive
case against the projectivist reading.[30]
    The most intriguing observation of Byrne's paper concerns the following pas-
sage in *WRPL*:

> Do we not call assertions like ["Jones, like many of us, means addition
> by '+'"] "true" or "false"? Can we not with propriety precede such asser-
> tions with "It is a fact that" or "It is not a fact that"? Wittgenstein's way
> with such objections is short. Like many others, Wittgenstein accepts
> the "redundancy" theory of truth: to affirm that a statement is true (or
> presumably, to precede it with "*It* is a fact that …") is simply to affirm
> the statement itself, and to say that it is not true is to deny it: ("p" is true
> = p) … We *call* something a proposition, and hence true or false, when
> in our language we apply the calculus of truth functions to it.
>
> (*WRPL*: 86)

Byrne points out that this paragraph puts forward not only a deflationism about
truth but also a deflationism about "truth-aptness". As will be recalled, a sentence
s is truth-apt if we are willing to infer "'S' is true" from S. A deflationary account
of truth-aptness makes minimal demands on such an S; a robust theory expects

more (e.g. that the relevant S passes muster by the standards of physicalism). Kripke tells us that we can "with propriety" precede meaning attributions with "It is true that" and "It is a fact that". There are no special demands on meaning attributions over and above – presumably – their being meaningful and disciplined by norms of correct use.

What makes Byrne's interpretative point intriguing is that we now have an argument against a non-factualist reading of the sceptical solution. Non-factualism regarding meaning attributions is incompatible with deflationism about truth- and fact-aptness. By deflationist standards, if meaning attributions are significant and declarative in form then they also are truth-apt. The sceptical solution clearly regards them as significant and declarative in form – hence it cannot claim that meaning attributions are not apt for semantic ascent.

In order to further defend a factualist reading of the sceptical solution, Byrne also draws attention to two other ideas in *WRPL*. The first is Wittgenstein's supposed response to the suggestion that meaning addition by "+" is a "primitive state". Kripke tells us that "such a move may in a sense be irrefutable, and if it is taken in an appropriate way Wittgenstein may even accept it" (*WRPL*: 51). Byrne points out that if Kripke's Wittgenstein were a non-factualist then there could be no such appropriate way *at all*.[31]

The second idea highlighted by Byrne is the distinction between fact and "superlative fact" (as §192 of *PI* put it).[32] Kripke writes that Wittgenstein's "solution to his own sceptical problem begins by agreeing with the sceptics that there is no 'superlative fact' … about my mind that constitutes my meaning addition by 'plus' and determines in advance what I should do to accord with this meaning" (*WRPL*: 65). Perhaps even more telling is a slightly later passage:

> We do not wish to doubt or deny that when people speak of themselves and others as meaning something by their words, as following rules, they do so with perfect right. We do not even wish to deny the propriety of an ordinary use of the phrase "the fact that Jones meant addition by such-and-such a symbol", and indeed such expressions do have perfectly ordinary uses. We merely wish to deny the existence of the "superlative fact" that philosophers misleadingly attach to such ordinary forms of words, not the propriety of the forms of words themselves. (*WRPL*: 69)

Such passages can be taken to indicate that when Kripke's Wittgenstein rejects factualism for meaning attributions (and assertions) he has in mind a very specific doctrine. Rejection of this doctrine – with its superlative meaning facts – does not involve a rejection of meaning facts *tout court*. Unfortunately, Byrne does not go very far in spelling out the difference between the brand of factualism to be rejected and the brand of factualism to be preserved.

Two forms of factualism II: Wilson

George Wilson's treatment of factualism is more detailed than Byrne's, and based on an overall interpretation of Kripke's book. As Wilson sees it, the meaning sceptic of *WRPL* is a local non-factualist (about meaning attributions) since he infers (3) from (1) and (2):

(1) *No* sentence has classical realist truth-conditions.[33]
(2) Sentences of the form "*x* means *Y* by '*z*'" do not have classical realist truth-conditions.[34]
(3) There are no facts about *x* that assertions of the form "*x* means *Y* by '*z*'", even when they are correct by ordinary criteria, *describe truly*.[35]

According to Wilson, we need to distinguish sharply between the meaning sceptic and Kripke's Wittgenstein. The meaning sceptic and his interlocutor share a commitment to "Classical Realism". A terminological comment is called for. For Wilson "Classical Realism" is the overall position under attack in *WRPL*. His Classical Realism thus plays the same role as my "meaning determinism". In my usage "classical realism" refers to just one ingredient of meaning determinism. In order to mark the difference, I shall continue to use lower case letters for my classical realism, and capitalize Wilson's Classical Realism. The meaning sceptic believes that (1) is forced on us by the realization that the sceptical challenge cannot be answered on classical-realist grounds. And the sceptic then goes on to infer (2) and (3) from (1). However, Wilson goes on, Kripke's Wittgenstein is not committed to Classical Realism. And hence he can read the sceptical argument differently: not as establishing (1), but as constituting a *reductio* of Classical Realism. And thus Kripke's Wittgenstein's position differs from both classical-realist factualism and sceptical non-factualism. Whether this is a plausible take on *WRPL* depends, of course, on how Classical Realism is defined.

Classical Realism is a specific conception of what it is to mean something by a term. According to this conception, if Jones means addition by "+", then Jones must have the intention to let his use of "+" be governed by the addition function. It is because Jones has this intention that he means what he does; his intention to let the addition function as his standard *constitutes* his meaning addition by "+": "the existence of [Jones's] conceptually prior intention *explains* constitutively how the meaningfulness of '+' arises for [him] and that *determines* what [he] means by that term".[36] Moreover, in order for Jones to be able to let the addition function govern his use of "+", he must be able to *single out* the addition function from all other possible standards. In order to get a firmer grasp on such "singling out", Wilson drops the mathematical example, and focuses on descriptive terms. Consider an open-ended domain of objects *D*, each exemplifying a range of determinate properties (independently of our beliefs and our language). Let "*t*" be a descriptive term for Jones. The classical realist insists that for "t" to be meaningful for Jones he must have a standard for the correct application of "t" to elements in D. The obvious standard in the case of a descriptive term must involve a set of properties, P_1-P_n. Jones must have adopted the "semantic rule that 't' is to be applied to a D-item o just in case o has precisely *these* properties. Varying the formulation, S is to have the meaning constituting intention, concerning P_1-P_n, that 't' applies to o iff o exemplifies those conditions".[37] The singling out of a standard for terms will be different depending on whether the terms in question are primitive or not. The singling out of non-primitive terms may involve other terms. But the singling out of primitive terms may not. The classical realist insists that "if 't' is primitive for [Jones], then ... the properties P_1-P_n must be *non-linguistically* 'singled out' for s as the *de re* subject of her meaning-constituting intentions".[38]

The basic theses of Classical Realism (CR) and its main implication – the demand for a "grounding" (G) or singling out – can be summed up as follows:

CR: If [person] x means something by a term "t", then there is a set of properties, P_1-P_n, that have been established by x as the meaning-constituting standard of correctness for her application of "t".[39]

G: If there is a set of properties, P_1-P_n, that have established by x as the meaning-constituting standard of correctness for her application of "t", then there must be facts about x that fix P_1-P_n as the standard x has adopted.[40]

The sceptical argument shows that Classical Realism is mistaken. It does so by targeting G. The sceptic demonstrates, case-by-case, that we cannot make sense of the idea of singling out a set of properties or a function in a non-linguistic way. For instance, one kind of classical realist tells us that his dispositions to give sums in answer to plus-queries shows that he has singled out the addition function as his standard for calculating with "+". The sceptic retorts by convincing us that these dispositions are compatible with many different functions. The outcome of the sceptical argument is the "basic sceptical conclusion" (BSC):

BSC: There are *no* facts about x that fix any set of properties as the standard of correctness for x's use of "t".[41]

The most radical claim of *WRPL* of course is not BSC, but the radical sceptical conclusion (RSC):

RSC: No one ever means anything by any term.[42]

How does RSC relate to BSC? Wilson's answers is that here we have to distinguish carefully between two positions: the position of the meaning sceptic, and the position of Kripke's Wittgenstein. Wilson sees the meaning sceptic as fully committed to Classical Realism and thus the grounding condition. And since the sceptic is so committed, he has to reason as follows:

> Classical Realism
> Grounding
> Basic sceptical conclusion
> *Ergo*: Radical sceptical conclusion

But this is not the way in which Kripke's Wittgenstein reasons. Kripke's Wittgenstein is opposed to Classical Realism and he rejects the radical sceptical solution. After all, does not Kripke write: "Of course [Wittgenstein] does not wish to leave us with his problem, but to solve it: the sceptical conclusion is insane and intolerable" (*WRPL*: 60)? Accordingly, Kripke's Wittgenstein endorses the "contrapositive argument" or *reduction*:[43]

> Classical Realism   (Assumption)
> Grounding
> Basic sceptical conclusion
> Radical sceptical conclusion
> ~ Radical sceptical conclusion   (New premise)
> ~ Classical Realism   (*Reductio*)

Having identified Classical Realism as Kripke's Wittgenstein's target, Wilson is able to distinguish clearly between three positions:

(i)   a form of factualism that Kripke's Wittgenstein rejects: this is Classical Realism and it denies (1), (2) and (3) above;
(ii) a form of sceptical non-factualism that Kripke's Wittgenstein finds unacceptable: it too is based on Classical Realism; it holds all of (1) to (3);
(iii) a form of minimal factualism that Kripke's Wittgenstein allows for: it rejects Classical Realism, accepts (1) and (2), but denies (3).

Wilson does not tell us much about (iii). His main point is that Kripke's Wittgenstein leaves room for it: that the rejection of factualism in *WRPL* concerns a highly specific version of the general position. An additional reason why it is natural to attribute the minimal position to Wittgenstein is that it naturally fits with his remarks on the family resemblance between concepts. According to the family-resemblance doctrine the term "game" does not have classical-realist satisfaction conditions. But from this it does not follow that utterances such as "John is playing a game" do not describe facts. *Mutatis mutandis*, Kripke's Wittgenstein should be taken to allow that meaning attributions describe facts, and this despite his contention that they do not have classical-realist truth-conditions.[44]

Wilson's interpretation has much to recommend itself. He establishes convincingly that Kripke's Wittgenstein leaves the "logical space" for a minimal form of factualism. And Wilson provides us with the wherewithal for blocking a projectivist reading of the text. For instance, whenever Kripke's Wittgenstein denies that there are meaning facts, Wilson recommends that we gloss him as having classical-realist meaning facts in mind. It is easy to develop this strategy further. We can insist that Kripke never actually attributes to Wittgenstein the view according to which utterances in the indicative mood do not (normally) state facts. Kripke writes that for Wittgenstein "the linguistic role even of utterances in the indicative mood that superficially look like assertions need not be one of 'stating facts'" (*WRPL*: 73). Note the "need not be". One might add that it does not contradict a factualist reading of meaning-attributions that by means of the latter we take individuals into the community. An utterance can be both factual *and* do something. And finally, it is far from compelling that the parallel with Hume supports a projectivist rendering of meaning attributions. Kripke never says that the parallel between Wittgenstein and Hume extends as far as a common commitment to projectivism.

Superficially it might seem that Wilson and I have very different views of the dialectic of *WRPL*: am I not seeing Wittgenstein and meaning sceptic as bedfellows whereas Wilson stresses the common assumptions of classical realist and sceptic? Fortunately, not much substance hinges on this difference. For both Wilson and me, Kripke's Wittgenstein turns out to be a diagnostic anti-sceptic – and that is really what matters.

Nevertheless, Wilson's reconstruction of the different versions of factualism and Classical Realism is not fully satisfactory. One weakness is that Wilson has too narrow a conception of the position under attack in *WRPL*. As I have tried to show in previous chapters, the targeted position is more complex and intricate than Wilson allows for. In his reconstruction there is no mention of, or allusion to, many of the meaning-determinist assumptions that I distinguished in Chapter 1, and used for reconstructing the dialectic and immanent critique of the sceptical argument. The same applies *mutatis mutandis* to Wilson's take on the sceptical solution.

I am also doubtful that Wilson is right to suggest that the targeted position is centrally concerned to explain how we non-linguistically single out properties for primitive terms. I cannot find this emphasis on the non-linguistic in the sceptical argument; I do not think that this condition is central in the argument. The sceptic challenges the meaning determinist to explain how we could have singled out any standard at all – but there is no suggestion that the singling out must have been non-linguistic.

Two final critical comments point ahead to the next two sections. On the one hand, one might complain that Wilson's reconstruction does not result in a sufficient precise formulation of classical-realist and minimal-factualist truth-conditions. On the other hand, it seems that Wilson fails to pick up on some key minimal-factualist passages in Chapter 3 of *WRPL*. The first comment naturally leads over to Soames's attempt to make Wilson's two forms of factualism more precise. The second comment will be expanded in the final section.

Two forms of factualism III: Soames

Soames distinguishes between two truth-conditional conceptions of meaning.[45] The first is a minimal form. In Soames's view it is "virtually undeniable".[46] If the sceptical solution is factualist at all, then it must accept the minimal truth-conditional conception of meaning. Soames formulates it for both declarative sentences and predicates, and thus for both propositions and properties; for our purposes it suffices to focus on sentences and propositions.

> *A minimal truth-conditional conception for declarative sentences (MTC)*
> (i) A normal declarative sentence is meaningful iff it expresses a proposition; it is true iff the proposition it expresses is true. The proposition that *P* is true iff *P*; hence if a sentence *s* expresses the proposition that *P*, then *s* is true iff *P*.
> (ii) A speaker understands a sentence *s* that expresses the proposition that *P* iff the speaker knows that *s* expresses the proposition that *P*; and hence knows that *s* is true iff *P*.[47]

If this is the minimal position of Kripke's Wittgenstein, what then is the non-minimal view of the classical realist? Soames has a number of proposals here; for our purposes it is most interesting to study his attempt to make sense of Wilson's reconstruction. Soames picks up on Wilson's suggestions that (for the classical realist) to mean addition by "+" I have to single out a certain function as governing my use of "+", and that in singling out this function, I establish a standard for my subsequent use of "+". Soames reads these remarks as submitting that to advocate a classical-realist conception of meaning as truth-conditions is to champion an *explanatory* project concerning meaning:

> [M]y meaning addition by "+" is *explained* by my having the relevant intentions about the addition function; I mean addition by "+" *because* I have independently singled out the addition function and decided to use "+" to stand for it. In general the idea seems to be that in order to *bring it about* that I mean something by a word, I must first pick out a property and form the right sort of intention.[48]

Building on this idea, Soames formulates an explanatory version of the truth-conditional conception of meaning (ETC). ETC "incorporate[s] everything included in the minimal truth-conditional conception given above, plus the following claims":[49]

> *The explanatory version of the truth-conditional conception of meaning for sentences (ETC)*
>
> (i) A speaker x who understands a sentence s, which expresses the proposition that P, does so *because* x knows that s expresses the proposition that P, and hence is true iff P. x's knowledge of these facts *explains*, and is *prior* to, x's understanding of s.
>
> (ii) If a sentence s, as used by a speaker x, means that P, then s has this meaning for x *because* x has the intention that s is to express the proposition that P, and hence to be true iff P. In general, a sentence that expresses a proposition is meaningful *because* speakers have a system of intentions the content of which assigns that proposition to the sentence. These intentions *explain*, and are *prior* to, the fact that the sentence means what it does.[50]

Soames also recommends that Wilson's formulation of Classical Realism be strengthened into the following explanatory claim:

> CR_E: If x means something by a (general) term φ, then x does so *because* there is a set of properties $P_1 - P_n$, of which x has a *prior* grasp, and x has the intention (has adopted the linguistic commitment) that φ is to apply to an object o iff o has the properties $P_1 - P_n$.[51]

What does all of this come down to in more simple terms? Soames eventually gives this answer:

> The key claim made by this conception [i.e. ETC] is that one kind of intentional fact – namely, semantic beliefs and intentions relating sentences and expressions to propositions, properties, and objects – is prior to, and part of the explanation of, another kind of intentional fact – namely, understanding sentences and expressions, and meaning something by them.[52]

Having formulated ETC with exemplary clarity and precision, Soames turns to its assessment. He is happy to acknowledge that – unlike a denial of MTC – a rejection of ETC is not obviously absurd. Indeed, Soames himself believes that ETC fails for many of our concepts. But he does not accept that ETC fails for all sentences, expressions and speakers; ETC works for an important range of expressions, among them Kripke's prime example, "+" or "plus". It follows that either Wilson's interpretation of *WRPL* is right, but the argument of *WRPL* is defective, or that Wilson's rendering of the sceptical argument and its conclusion is not satisfactory.

All this needs spelling out in more detail. Soames's reason for rejecting ETC *as a general account* is as follows. Think of how you came to have "Pluto" as a name in your idiolect. You heard and began to understand sentences about Pluto, for instance,

(a) "Pluto is a distant planet".

In other words, you developed a linguistic competence regarding sentences about Pluto. And in so doing, you came to conform to the ways in which your parents, friends and teachers talk and think about Pluto. Having developed this linguistic competence, you eventually learnt to have beliefs about the term "Pluto" and sentences involving it. For instance, you now have beliefs such as

(b) "'Pluto' refers (in English) to Pluto".
(c) "'Pluto is a distant planet' is true (in English) if, and only if, Pluto is a distant planet".
(d) "'Pluto is a distant planet' means (in English) that Pluto is a distant planet".

Call (b), (c) and (d) "semantic beliefs", and (a) a "non-semantic sentence". Now, if ETC were true, then (b), (c) and (d) would have to be *prior to*, and *explanatory of*, your non-semantic beliefs about Pluto (such as (a)). Soames finds this implausible. It is simply not the case that I understand "Pluto is a distant planet" because I believe that "'Pluto' refers (in English) to Pluto".[53] Thus, in the case of "Pluto" – as well as many other names and theoretical terms – ETC is false.

So far, so good for the sceptic (*qua* critic of ETC). Alas, if Soames is to be believed, ETC cannot be cast aside altogether. There are many expressions in our language for which ETC is exactly right. And to make matters worse, Kripke's paradigm, "+" or "plus", is one of those expressions. Recall, Soames proposes, how you came to mean addition by "+". Presumably the following happened. You first grasped the addition function in the form of a rule. Whatever that rule might have been in your primary school, for present purposes we might as well assume – counterfactually – that the rule was the standard number theoretic characterization (+):

(+) For all natural numbers x and y, $x + 0 = x$ & $x + y' = (x + y)'$

Having grasped this rule, you then formed the intention to associate the sign "+" or the word "plus" with it. In this case then your semantic belief – "'+' denotes the addition function" – explains why you form beliefs such as "2 + 2 = 4" or "68 + 57 = 125". Here Soames does not accept the objection according to which grasping (+) presupposes a prior grasp of other signs, such as "=" or " ' " (the successor symbol). Of course it does. We may even have to concede that the successor symbol does not yield to the ETC treatment. But whichever way I came to understand " ' ", the fact remains that my understanding of "+" fits with ETC.[54] And thus Soames concludes that for "+" ETC is correct.[55]

There are then, according to Soames, terms for which ETC is adequate and terms for which it fails. And this in itself constitutes an argument against Wilson's rendering of the sceptical solution. Kripke tells us that *no* sentence has truth-conditions according to the model of Classical Realism, and Wilson (in Soames's reconstruction) translates this as the claim that *no* sentence has truth-conditions on ETC. And this latter claim, Soames holds, has now turned out to be wrong. Soames's conclusion is that "either … the sceptical solution fails in an utterly obvious way to establish what it sets out to achieve, or … its real target is not the explanatory truth-conditional conception of meaning … but something else".[56] Soames deems the second option more likely. He points out that *WRPL* simply does not marshal the sort of argument that would be needed to show the incorrectness of ETC. Kripke's Wittgenstein never seeks to establish that semantic beliefs (i.e. one kind of intentional fact) are not prior to the understanding of sentences and expressions (i.e. another kind of intentional fact). Much of *WRPL* focuses on the question of whether semantic beliefs (*qua* intentional facts) can be reduced to dispositions and other non-intentional facts. And this issue has nothing to do with ETC.[57]

Turning from summary to assessment, I find Soames's distinction between the two truth-conditional conceptions of meaning an important advance over Wilson's slightly hand-waving opposition between Classical Realism and the denial of sceptical non-factualism. Furthermore, I agree that MTC is something that the sceptical solution had better accept, although as we shall see below, Kripke's Wittgenstein accepts it only under a certain deflationary (or meaning-sceptical) interpretation. Soames's contention that ETC cannot quite be the position targeted in *WRPL* also seems compelling. Soames is right to say that Kripke's sceptic does not offer the kinds of arguments that could undermine ETC.

I am less convinced by three of Soames's other claims. First of all, consider once more Soames's reflections on how we came to mean addition by "+". We are supposed to accept that this happened in and through our *grasping* of the addition function in form of a rule, and in and through our *forming an intention* to associate the sign "+" with that function. This suggestion is very odd. How can Soames – in an attempt to rebut the sceptic – help himself to these italicized concepts when it is precisely these very concepts that the sceptical attack has rendered problematic? Surely Soames has to earn the right to use these concepts; and surely he can earn this right only by telling us how these terms are to be understood. If they are to be understood in meaning-determinist ways, then of course all questions have been begged in the most dramatic way. But if they are to be understood in some other way then Soames needs to tell us what that way is.

Secondly, I am unsure whether it is correct to say that ETC and CR_E really do capture Wilson's Classical Realism. Note that Wilson does not just suggest that Classical Realism is the programme of explaining intentional acts of rule-, meaning-, or concept-application in terms of intentional acts of singling out properties and functions and associating them with signs. Wilson adds to this that Classical Realism is committed to providing an explanation of how such singling out of properties and functions is possible. And these explanations may well go beyond the realm of intentional acts; they may well invoke non-intentional events to which the intentional acts can be reduced.

Thirdly, and finally, it seems to me that we can advance further than Wilson or Soames by paying close attention to what *WRPL* tells us about truth, propositions and "the classical (realist) Frege–*Tractatus* view that the general form of explanation of meaning is a statement of the truth conditions" (*WRPL*: 73).[58]

Two forms of factualism IV: inflationary and deflationary

Having criticized existing proposals for understanding the factualisms in play in *WRPL*, it is time for me to put forward my own suggestion. In one important respect my task is much easier than that of either Soames or Wilson: since I have already characterized meaning determinism (as the position under attack in *WRPL*) in some detail in previous chapters, I need not here develop a general interpretation of Kripke's book as a whole. Instead I only need to explain how classical realism fits into meaning determinism. As we shall say, one way to summarize my suggestion would be to say that classical realism simply is meaning determinism applied to truth, facts and propositions. Something similar holds for my interpretation of the factualism of the sceptical solution: whatever factualism survives the sceptical argument, it must be a minimal factualism that fits in with meaning scepticism and assertability.

In most general terms, my suggestion is that both meaning determinist and meaning sceptic can accept the wording of Soames's MTC, but that they interpret key concepts of MTC in very different ways. The meaning determinist gives a "realist" (or "inflationist", or "substantive") reading to "facts", "propositions" and "truth", whereas the meaning sceptic renders the same terms in a minimalist, "deflationist", manner. Whereas the meaning determinist interprets MTC as a general truth-conditional conception of meaning with metaphysical foundations, the meaning-sceptic sees in MTC no more than a number of trivial platitudes that have no implications for either metaphysics or the theory of meaning.

Kripke first introduces "the classical (realist) view" in the form in which it can be found in Wittgenstein's *Tractatus*:

> To each sentence there corresponds a (possible) fact. If such a fact obtains, the sentence is true; if not, false. For atomic sentences, the relation between a sentence and the fact it alleges is one of a simple correspondence or isomorphism. The sentence contains names, cor-

responding to objects. An atomic sentence is itself a fact, putting the names in a certain relation; and it says that (there is a corresponding fact that) the corresponding objects are in the same relation. Other sentences are (finite or infinite) truth-functions of these.   (*WRPL*: 71)

It is clear, however, that classical realism refers to a much broader spectrum of views about meaning. Kripke formulates the general idea as follows:

[A] declarative sentence gets its meaning by virtue of its *truth conditions*, by virtue of its correspondence to facts that must obtain if it is true. For example, "the cat is on the mat" is understood by those speakers who realize that it is true if and only if a certain cat is on a certain mat; it is false otherwise. The presence of the cat on the mat is a fact or condition-in-the-world that would make the sentence true (express a truth) if it obtained.   (*WRPL*: 72)

Kripke even goes on to say that "so stated, the *Tractatus* picture of the meaning of declarative sentences may seem not only natural but even tautological" (*WRPL*: 72–3).

It seems natural to add propositions to the general idea of classical realism. First, propositions are often thought to be the truth-conditions of declarative sentences; secondly, propositions figure centrally in philosophical theories that the later Wittgenstein attacked and rejected; and thirdly, Kripke himself discusses propositions as part of classical realism later in the book. Having introduced Wittgenstein's redundancy theory of truth, Kripke goes on to present an objection to it *in the voice of* the meaning determinist classical realist:

[O]ne might object: (a) that only utterances of certain forms are called "true" or "false" – questions, for example, are not – and these are so called precisely because they purport to state facts; (b) that precisely the sentences that "state facts" can occur as components of truth-functional compounds and their meaning in such compounds is hard to explain in terms of assertability conditions alone.   (*WRPL*: 86)

As the continuation of the passage makes clear, Kripke takes the meaning determinist to use propositions *for explanatory purposes*. This is obvious from the fact that Kripke lets his Wittgenstein deny that propositions have such a function:

We *call* something a proposition, and hence true or false, when in our language we apply the calculus of truth functions to it. That is, it is just a primitive part of our language game, not susceptible of deeper explanation, that truth functions are applied to certain sentences.
                                                                       (*WRPL*: 86)

The *classical realist* is thus a realist about truth, facts and propositions. Going slightly beyond the wording of *WRPL*, and factoring in the familiar outlines of a realist conception of propositions,[59] we can summarize classical realism in the following theses:

(CR-1)   The meaning of a declarative sentence is given by its truth-conditions.

(CR-2)   A declarative sentence is true if, and only if, the proposition it expresses corresponds to a fact. Propositions are the primary truth-bearers; sentences are true in so far as they express true propositions.

(CR-3)   It is possible to individuate facts *qua* truth-makers. Facts are objective entities in the world, independent, for the most part, of thought.

(CR-4)   The fact that a declarative sentence expresses a proposition *explains* why the sentence is true or false, and why the calculus of truth-functions applies to it.

(CR-5)   Propositions have – or are – truth-conditions. The proposition expressed by a sentence is the sentence's truth-conditional, cognitive or informational, content.

(CR-6)   Propositions are abstract entities; they exist necessarily and independently of minds and languages.

(CR-7)   A person x understands a declarative sentence s if, and only if, (i) x *grasps* the proposition p expressed by s, and (ii) x knows that s expresses p.

This "picture" of classical realism can of course be developed in different ways: for instance, one might take propositions to be unstructured or structured entities, and one might debate what form such structure must take. And one can imagine – and indeed identify in the existing literature – various ways of "reforming" this picture. Here I shall not try to distinguish between all these options. At this point it is more important to emphasize that this classical-realist picture is to be read through the general assumptions of meaning determinism. To make this link as transparent and strong as possible, I can do no better than go through the ingredients of meaning determinism one by one:

(MD-1)   Immediate knowledge: It is very much part and parcel of the traditional realist view of propositions that we usually know immediately and with fair certainty which propositions we have grasped.[60]

(MD-2)   Privacy: The mental state through which Jones grasps a proposition is an intrinsic state of Jones.

(MD-3)   Grasping:

(MD-3.1) Grasping as cause: Jones's act of grasping that sentence *s* expresses proposition *p* causes Jones – absent interference from other causes – to use *s* only when it is true that *p*.

(MD-3.2) Grasping as intending: Jones's act of grasping of the fact that *s* expresses *p* is tantamount to Jones's forming intentions – or giving himself instructions – regarding a possible infinite number of uses of *s* in the future.

(MD-3.3) Grasping as extrapolating: Since all learning sets are finite, grasping a proposition has the character of an extrapolation.

(MD-3.4) Grasping as interpreting: Grasping a proposition has the character of an interpretation.

(MD-3.5) Grasping as explanation: If Jones and Smith agree in all, or most, of their uses of *s*, the best explanation is that they have grasped the same proposition *p*.

(MD-4) Semantic normativity:

(MD-4.1) Non-blindness: In applying *s* on the basis of *p*, Jones is not acting blindly.

(MD-4.2) Guidance: Jones grasp of *p* guides *x* on how to apply *s*.

(MD-4.3) Justification: Jones can justify his uses of *s* on the basis of his grasp of *p*.

(MD-4.4) Justification of unhesitating application: Jones can justify his unhesitating manner of applying *s* on the basis of his grasp of *p*.

(MD-4.5) Left-to-right interpretation of meaning conditionals: Meaning conditionals are to be read left to right.

(MD-5) Objectivity: Jones's act of grasping that *s* expresses *p* contains and determines ("in a queer way") all future, potentially infinite, correct applications of *s*.

(MD-6) Metaphysical justification: The justification of our meaning sentences must come from ontological considerations.

Since classical realism is closely intertwined with the other assumptions of meaning determinism, there is no need for the sceptic to criticize it in any detail. If meaning determinism turns out be incoherent when applied to word meaning, concepts and rules, then it is of course also incoherent when applied to declarative sentences and propositions.

Having suggested how classical realism is best understood, it remains for me to explain why meaning scepticism in general, and assertability in particular, are compatible with a minimal form of factualism. Assertability is a revolutionary response to classical realism: it retains none of CR-1 to CR-7. Nevertheless, assertability neither asks us to stop using sentences such as "It is a fact that Jones means addition by '+'", nor proposes that "it is a fact that ..." really is an indicator of some performative or projective function.

Three ideas of meaning scepticism are particularly important in the present context. The first is the already familiar rejection of a truth-conditional conception of meaning:

> Wittgenstein replaces the question, "What must be the case for this sentence to be true?" by two others: first, "Under what conditions may this form of words be appropriately asserted (or denied)?"; second, given an answer to the first question, "What is the role, and the utility, in our lives of our practice of asserting (or denying) the form of words under these conditions?" (*WRPL*: 73)

In previous chapters we have already looked at some examples of assertability conditions. In the present context it seems natural to add the following remark. That Wittgenstein replaces truth-conditions with assertability conditions does not of course mean that the terms "truth" or "falsehood", or "true" or "false", can never appear and be used in assertability conditions. For instance, it surely is part of the assertability conditions of the registrar's statement "I hereby declare you husband and wife", that she has established that neither bride nor groom has given *false* information about their current marital status.

The second key idea is Kripke's claim that Wittgenstein, and hence the meaning sceptic, accept a deflationary account of truth and fact: "Wittgenstein accepts the 'redundancy' theory of truth: to affirm that a statement is true (or presumably, to precede it with 'It is a fact that …') is simply to affirm the statement itself, and to say it is not true is to deny it: ('*p*' is true = *p*)" (*WRPL*: 86). On this deflationary account of truth and facts, it is wrong to say that individual facts make individual propositions true. Facts are truth-makers of neither sentences nor propositions. Facts cannot play a role in explaining truth. This is not to say that we have to change everyday expressions such as the exhortation "you have to be true to the facts". The exhortation simply means that you have to say what you believe to be true.

The third central idea is a deflationist view of propositions: "We *call* something a proposition, and hence true or false, when in our language we apply the calculus of truth functions to it. That is, it is just a primitive part of our language game, not susceptible of deeper explanation, that truth functions are applied to certain sentences" (*WRPL*: 86). Propositions do not explain why certain sentences are true or false and hence are arguments in truth-functions. To say that a sentence is true or false *because* it expresses a proposition is, on the account offered by the meaning sceptic, to put forward a pseudo-explanation. The meaning-sceptical alternative is to treat the meaning-determinist *explanandum* as a primitive phenomenon. Given our language games, certain sentences simply are true or false.

Above I suggested that for all his revolutionary manoeuvres, the meaning sceptic can nevertheless accept at least the gist of Soames's MTC, although without treating it as a truth-conditional conception of meaning. At this point the reader might begin to wonder whether this can possibly be right. Have I not suggested that the meaning sceptic leaves no room for propositions? How then can the meaning sceptic accept MTC? After all MTC speaks of declarative sentences expressing propositions and speakers understanding sentences whenever they understand the propositions expressed.

The *prima facie* contradiction disappears once we recognize that the meaning sceptic is not barred from using the concept of proposition, provided only that he gives that concept a meaning that is compatible with the rough meaning-sceptical picture. In particular the meaning sceptic makes two crucial moves. The first move is to return talk of propositions (in the philosophical technical sense) to ordinary language: faced with an utterance of a sentence, the meaning sceptic has no problems with speaking of "what is said" or "what is stated" in the utterance. But the meaning sceptic does not accept that we need to go on from here and determine the metaphysical commitments allegedly incurred by using these phrases. Nor does the meaning sceptic approve of the picture according to which declarative sentences are paired with ideal Platonic entities. For the meaning sceptic this is just another instance where the Augustinian conception of "object and name" – here proposition and sentence – keeps us in its grip. And thus the meaning sceptic must insist that we do for propositions what Wittgenstein does for numbers:

> Many philosophers of mathematics – in agreement with the Augustinian conception of "object and name" – ask such questions as, "What entities ('numbers') are denoted by numerals? What relations among these entities ('facts') correspond to numerical statements?" … As against such a "Platonist" conception of the problem, Wittgenstein asks that we discard any *a priori* conceptions and *look* ("Don't think, look!") at the circumstances under which numerical assertions are actually uttered, and at what roles such assertions play in our lives. …
>
> (*WRPL*: 75–6)

The second crucial meaning-sceptical move with respect to propositions must surely be to relativize the underlying notion of cognitive or informational content.[61] "What is said" in an utterance is not determined by some real, natural and universal units of semantic information; "what is said" is relative to the speaker's and interpreter's assertability conditions (which will often be shared by many in their linguistic community).

Just as the inflationary factualism of classical realism must be understood in the context of meaning determinism as a whole, so deflationary factualism must be situated within the general picture of meaning scepticism.

(MS-1) Confidence: Subject to the correction by others, we are entitled to say what our utterances say.

(MS-2) Intersubjectivity: Attributions of *what is said* make sense only in a social setting. Assertability conditions for declarative sentences essentially involve communities.

(MS-3) Primitiveness: Our inclinations to use declarative sentences, and the fact that declarative sentences are true or false, are primitive phenomena. They cannot be explained by propositions.

(MS-4) Intersubjective normativity: There is no special form of normativity based on meaning-constituting mental states. We are guided by others; we justify our use of sentences on the basis of publicly available criteria.

(MS-5) Finiteness: We attribute infinitary concepts on the basis of finite, surveyable, evidence. What makes this possible is that "our eyes are shut" in similar ways.

(MS-6) Assertability: The meaning of declarative sentences is given by rough and ready assertability conditions.

(MS-7) Functional justification: Our practices of attributing "things said" to others are justified on the basis of social-functional considerations. There is no space for a metaphysical analysis of "things said".

In the light of the above, how then will the meaning sceptic gloss Soames's MTC, the minimal conception of truth and meaning? The following rendering seems most natural:

(i) A normal declarative sentence ("normal" judged by communal criteria) is meaningful for an interpreter if, and only if, he is able to make out, in his own terms, what the sentence says (here the interpreter will be guided by assertability conditions). If it is correct to say: "what the sentence says is true", then it is also correct to say "what the sentence says is a fact". A sentence is true if what it says is true.

(ii) A speaker understands a sentence *s* if he knows what that sentence says or states (in the present context). And hence he knows that *s* is true if he knows that what the sentence says or states is true.

The meaning sceptic happily embraces the minimal factualism captured in these definitions.

I have now distinguished in some detail the inflationary factualism of meaning determinism and the deflationary factualism of meaning scepticism. I conclude by addressing two obvious objections. According to the first objection, inflationary and deflationary factualism are two extremes on a scale of positions, where the most plausible views lie somewhere in the middle. I agree that there are many possible views *between* meaning-determinist inflationism and meaning-sceptical deflationism. Indeed, I have acknowledged as much ever since Chapter 1, where I distinguished revisionist, reformist and revolutionary responses to the original version of meaning determinism. In Chapters 2–4 I have tried to argue that revi-

174

sion and reform are unable to rescue meaning determinism. And this general failure of revision and reform is, of course, most likely to affect all forms of factualism that go beyond deflationism.

According to the second objection, I have lost track of an important strand of Kripke's interpretation; namely, the idea that by saying "Jones means addition by '+'" we recommend Jones as a reliable partner in certain language games, and thereby "take him into the community". Have I not, in my attempt to defend a factualist reading, lost sight of this important performative element? How can the alleged factualism of the sceptical solution be reconciled with it? It is true that the performative element of meaning attributions has not been central in my reconstruction of deflationary factualism. But the performative element poses no threat to factualism. One and the same utterance can *both* be a description *and* express an attitude or confer a social status. To claim otherwise is to commit the "speech act fallacy".[62] There thus is no difficulty about the idea that meaning attributions function both as descriptions and as performatives.[63] Note, however, that what makes meaning ascriptions *descriptions* is not just that we are willing to treat them as minimally truth-apt and fact-apt. Not every s that is minimally truth-apt is thereby necessarily a description. After all, many philosophers insist that, although "Stealing is bad" is minimally truth-apt, it is not a description. It would therefore seem to be more accurate to maintain that what constitutes meaning attributions as descriptions is that meaning attributions fit with our assertability conditions for "description". And in contemplating this question we need – as ever – to keep in mind the variety of uses of terms:[64]

> Think how many different kinds of things are called "description": description of a body's position by means of co-ordinates; description of a facial expression; description of a sensation of touch; of a mood. (*PI*: §24)

> What we call "*descriptions*" are instruments for particular uses. Think of a machine-drawing, a cross-section, an elevation with measurements, which an engineer has before him. Thinking of a description as a word-picture of the facts has something misleading about it: one tends to think only of such pictures as hang on our walls: which seem simply to portray how a thing looks, what it is like. (These pictures are as it were idle.) (*PI*: §291)

Conclusion

In this chapter I have discussed two radically different interpretations of the sceptical solution. According to the first, meaning scepticism proposes a non-factualist (projectivist or performative) reading of meaning attributions. According to the second interpretation, meaning scepticism advocates a minimal, deflationary form of factualism.

I began by outlining the case for the projectivist reading. There can be no doubt that *WRPL* contains a good number of passages that seem to point squarely in a projectivist direction. And this poses a problem for anyone who has set himself the goal of developing a defence of Kripke's Wittgenstein: if *WRPL* advances a radical (local or global) projectivism then it is in the gravest of difficulties. Although the existing refutations of local and global forms of projectivism themselves continue to be challenged, the prospects of finding a satisfactory version of projectivism are dim nevertheless.

Fortunately, in order to defend *WRPL* we do not need to develop a defence of local or global projectivism. A small but significant body of work has suggested that in rejecting meaning determinism and a truth-conditional conception of meaning, Kripke's Wittgenstein does not actually throw out all forms of factualism. This interpretation is not only supported by textual evidence in *WRPL*, it also places the "projectivist" passages in a new and harmless light. If this interpretational strategy is to succeed, it must be able to distinguish clearly between a form of meaning-determinist factualism refuted by the sceptical argument, and a form of meaning-sceptical factualism that functions as its revolutionary successor. I discussed Byrne's, Wilson's and Soames's attempts to draw the distinction between the two factualisms, but found all three proposals wanting.

In the last section I proposed my own suggestion. Its central idea is that meaning determinism and meaning scepticism put forward two different conceptions of terms such as truth, fact and proposition. The conception of the meaning determinist is realist; the conception of the meaning sceptic is deflationary. Both can accept the same general factual formula – which I adopted from Soames – but they fill it with very different ideas and commitments. I ended by insisting that the minimal factualism of the sceptical solution does not contradict the idea that meaning attributions are in part performative.

SIX

Intersubjectivity and assertability conditions

Introduction

According to traditional scholarship, §§243–315 of *PI* constitute Wittgenstein's "private language argument". Kripke challenges this view by insisting that "the real 'private language argument' is to be found in the sections *preceding* §243". These are the sections dedicated to rule-following (*PI*: §§138–242). Concerning §§243–315, Kripke holds that they are but an *application* of the general considerations concerning rule-following to the special problem of sensations (*WRPL*: 3). Kripke also proposes a reformulation of what the "real" private language argument establishes:

> What is really denied is what might be called the 'private model' of rule following, that the notion of a person following a given rule is to be analysed simply in terms of facts about the rule follower and the rule follower alone, without reference to his membership in a wider community. (*WRPL*: 109)

In this chapter I shall discuss various issues relating to the private language argument as *WRPL* presents it. I shall begin by distinguishing between two ways – the "official road" and the "improved road" – of arguing for intersubjectivity and against privacy. The official road seems to be favoured by Kripke himself. It defends a communal analysis of meaning and rule-following in three steps. The first step establishes that meaning determinism is unsatisfactory. The second step focuses on replacing classical realism with assertability (that is, on replacing explanatory truth-conditions with assertability conditions). And the third step shows that, properly understood, assertability conditions – indeed, the assertability conditions we actually have – rule out the private model of rule-following. I shall agree with the critics that the official road of arguing for intersubjectivity faces two insurmountable obstacles. On the one hand, it is difficult to see how an observation of our actually existing assertability conditions could generate an impossibility claim. On the other hand, it does not seem to be true that our existing assertability conditions involve communal commitments.

Fortunately, we do not need the official road to reach the sceptical solution's combination of intersubjectivity and assertability. The alternative "improved road" is to investigate the four different ways of combining privacy, intersubjectivity, classical realism and assertability (leaving the other changing ingredients of meaning determinism and meaning scepticism in the background):

(a) Privacy and classical realism
(b) Intersubjectivity and classical realism
(c) Privacy and assertability
(d) Intersubjectivity and assertability

Scrutinizing these combinations one by one for consistency leads to the result that only (d) can be maintained. Chapter 2 of *WRPL* is, of course, a long and sustained argument against (a). Kripke briefly rejects (b), and criticizes (c) at greater length in Chapter 3. This leaves only (d) in the running. If we argue for intersubjectivity & assertability in this manner then we can sidestep the problems besetting the official way. In doing so, we do not base our argument on assumptions about the form of actually existing assertability conditions. And our reasoning has no problems with modality.

Having established the "improved way" for defending intersubjectivity, I shall turn to debates over whether a social isolate can follow rules. Here I shall seek to respond to the many authors who have maintained – contrary to Kripke – that a Robinson Crusoe from birth could follow rules. I shall try to identify the precise reasons why Kripke rejects this possibility. I shall conclude by considering two general objections to intersubjectivity as advanced by *WRPL*. According to the first objection the sceptical solution goes wrong in trying to reduce normativity to regularities of behaviour, and in privileging communities over their members. According to the second objection the sceptical solution is committed to "communal interpretationalism": this is the view according to which "community assent" determines which interpretations of rules are correct. I shall show that both complaints are unfounded.

The official road to intersubjectivity

To repeat, according to the official road to intersubjectivity, we begin by refuting meaning determinism, continue by developing the idea of assertability, and conclude by observing that assertability conditions are communal. The textual evidence suggests that this is how Kripke conceives of the argument:

> Wittgenstein has invented a new form of scepticism. … Of course he
> does not wish to leave us with his problem, but to solve it: the scepti-
> cal conclusion is insane and intolerable. It is his solution, I will argue,
> that contains the argument against "private language"; for allegedly,
> the solution will not admit such a language. (*WRPL*: 60)

This passage does not claim that intersubjectivity is a direct result of the failure of
meaning determinism. It rather proposes that intersubjectivity turns out to be an
implication of the sceptical solution, as if the solution itself could be stated without
mentioning this implication. This take on the relationship between intersubjectivity
and the sceptical solution is even more pronounced in the following quotation:

> Wittgenstein also states a sceptical paradox. Like Hume, he accepts his
> own sceptical argument and offers a "sceptical solution" to overcome
> the appearance of paradox. His solution involves a sceptical interpre-
> tation of what is involved in such ordinary assertions as "Jones means
> addition by '+." The impossibility of private language *emerges as a cor-*
> *ollary* of his sceptical solution of his own paradox, as does the impos-
> sibility of "private causation" in Hume. *It turns out* that the sceptical
> solution does not allow us to speak of a single individual, considered
> by himself and in isolation, as ever meaning anything.
> (*WRPL*: 68–9; emphasis added)

If the impossibility of private language "emerges as a corollary of his [i.e. Wittgenstein's] sceptical solution", if "it turns out that the sceptical solution" rules out
private rule-following, then – at least in an initial formulation of the sceptical
solution – intersubjectivity obviously need not be prominent.

Kripke proceeds according to this plan. Having first explained the decisive shift
from classical realism to assertability (*WRPL*: 71–8), he then goes on to defend
a communal-intersubjective reading of assertability conditions against an individualistic reading (*WRPL*: 87–91). His defence begins with the exhortation to
develop his argument on the basis, not of *a priori* reasoning, but of careful observation of actual practice:

> We have to see under what circumstances attributions of meaning
> are made and what role these attributions play in our lives. Following
> Wittgenstein's exhortation not to think but to look, we will not reason
> *a priori* about the role such statements *ought* to play; rather we will
> find out what circumstances *actually* license such assertions and what
> role this license *actually* plays. (*WRPL*: 86–7)

And the argument against an individualistic rendering of assertability conditions
appeals directly to "our usual concept of following a rule":

All we can say, if we consider a single person in isolation, is that our ordinary practice licenses him to apply the rule in the way it strikes him.

But of course this is *not* our usual concept of following a rule: It is by no means the case that, just because someone thinks he is following a rule, there is no room for a judgement that he is not really doing so.
(*WRPL*: 88)

The only way to make sense of this gap – the gap between thinking one is following a rule and following a rule – is to introduce the community:

The situation is very different if we widen our gaze from consideration of the rule follower alone and allow ourselves to consider him as interacting with a wider community. Others will then have justification conditions for attributing correct or incorrect rule following to the subject, and these will *not* be simply that the subject's own authority is unconditionally to be accepted. (*WRPL*: 89)

These observations enable us correctly to "discern rough assertability conditions" for "I mean addition by 'plus'":

Jones is entitled, subject to correction by others, provisionally to say, "I mean addition by 'plus'," whenever he has the feeling of confidence – "now I can go on!" – that he can give "correct" responses in new cases; and *he* is entitled, again provisionally and subject to correction by others, to judge a new response to be "correct" simply because it is the response he is inclined to give. (*WRPL*: 90)

The official road to intersubjectivity suffers from two problems. The first problem concerns a tension between two modalities: observing our actually existing, *contingent* assertability conditions, and claiming on the basis of this observation that a private language is *impossible*. Boghossian develops this problem in the following way. He begins by pointing out that Kripke's emphasis on the advice "not to think but to look" is inevitable if Kripke wishes to avoid turning assertability conditions into truth-conditions. (Remember that Boghossian reads the sceptical solution as a form of projectivism.) Any *a priori* argument concerning assertability conditions, Boghossian insists, would fail by this standard. And thus "the sceptical solution can do no more than record the conditions under which speakers in fact consider the attribution of a certain concept warranted and the endorsement of a particular response appropriate".[1] But if this is all the sceptical solution can offer, then it is not clear how it can underwrite the impossibility claim with respect to private language:

[W]e ought to be puzzled about how the sceptical solution is going to deliver a conclusion against solitary language of the requisite modal force: namely, that there *could not* be such a language. For even if it were true that our *actual* assertibility conditions for meaning-attributing sentences advert to the dispositions of a community, the most that would license saying is that *our* language is not solitary. And this would be a lot less than the result we were promised: namely, that any *possible* language has to be communal.[2]

The second problem is the claim that our actual assertability conditions are communal. A number of critics have denied this claim.[3] The critics take Kripke to hold that our assertability condition for "Jones means addition by '+'" explicitly mentions a second person (who also means addition by "+"). For example:

I will judge that you (e.g.) mean addition by "+" if and only if I observe that your responses with "+" agree with mine sufficiently often (or with those of the community to which I belong).[4]

I will judge that Jones means addition by "plus" only if Jones uses "plus" enough times in the same way I am inclined to use it.[5]

The critics are happy to admit that *if* this interpretation of assertability conditions were correct, then it would indeed be impossible to make sense of private meaning or rule-following. A private meaning or rule would be such that attributing it to someone would not involve an agreement in responses. And if Kripke's interpretation of assertability conditions is correct, then there cannot be such meanings or rules.

The critics, however, deny that our assertability conditions of meaning attributions are communal. McGinn claims that the reference to my own responses is redundant: "for the correct condition is simply that I observe that you give the *sum* of pairs of numbers sufficiently often".[6] But if the assertability condition is changed in that way, then it no longer refers explicitly to agreement between speaker and meaning attributor: "This condition [you mean addition by "plus" if, and only if, you give sums] is, of course, entirely individualistic in that it refers only to the person to whom the rule is ascribed and to his behaviour – no mention here of me or my community".[7] And hence the argument against private language collapses:

it is clear that it is not *essential* to make reference to the community in giving the criteria for (e.g.) meaning addition by "+"; and it is the claim that it *is* essential that is supposed by Kripke to have the consequence that we cannot make *sense* of someone following a rule "considered in isolation".[8]

I believe that both problems are real. And it is not easy to deflect them from within the "official road" to intersubjectivity. Fortunately though, there is an alternative to the official road.

The improved road to intersubjectivity

The "improved road" differs from the official road in treating intersubjectivity not as a "corollary" of the sceptical solution but as a *well-nigh corollary* of the sceptical argument against meaning determinism. The argument against meaning determinism in Chapter 2 of *WRPL* fails to find any intrinsic mental state that could fulfil the meaning-determinist requirements for meaning something by a word. And this failure strongly suggests that private rule-following is impossible. I write "well-nigh corollary" and "strongly suggests" in order to emphasize that the argument for intersubjectivity is not *a priori* and that some further tidying-up remains to be done. The argument is not *a priori* and does not establish a strictly necessary claim since it is based on the study of a limited number of (existing) positions from within the "meaning-determinist spectrum". Kripke does not seek to provide an *a priori* proof to the effect that the options considered in Chapter 2 exhaust that spectrum. And he is right not to do so. New meaning-determinist options may be developed in the future; this is especially true if we include reformers within the range of meaning-determinist position. Any drawing of conclusions regarding the possibility or impossibility of private language must accept this openness of the argument. The strongest conclusion to be drawn is that given currently available versions of meaning determinism, private rule-following is impossible.

There also is a second reason for thinking that – at the end of Chapter 2 of *WRPL* –intersubjectivity is merely a "well-nigh conclusion". This second reason has to do with the tidying-up to which I referred in the previous paragraph. Leaving aside the other ingredients of meaning determinism, we might say that Chapter 2 establishes the insufficiency of a position that combines privacy and classical realism. But of course a conjunction is false not just if both conjuncts are false; it is false also if just one of the two conjuncts is false. The sceptical solution negates both conjuncts, and thereby endorses their opposites: intersubjectivity and assertability. Reformers of meaning determinism will demur. They will propose a more conservative modification: combine intersubjectivity with classical realism or privacy with assertability. The advocate of the sceptical solution therefore needs to block these two forms of escape. As I mentioned in earlier chapters, Kripke indicates his opposition to intersubjectivity cum classical realism late in his book:

> Wittgenstein's theory should not be confused with a theory that, for any *m* and *n*, the value of the function we mean by "plus", *is* (by definition) the value that (nearly) all the linguistic community would give

as the answer. Such a theory would be a theory of the *truth* conditions of such assertions as "By 'plus' we mean such-and-such a function," or "By 'plus' we mean a function, which, when applied to 68 and 57 as arguments, yields 125 as value." ... The theory would assert that 125 is the value of the function meant for given arguments, if and only if "125" is the response nearly everyone would give, given these arguments. Thus the theory would be a social, or community-wide, version of the dispositional theory, and would be open to at least some of the same criticisms as the original form.   (*WRPL*: 111)

This leaves privacy cum assertability. Kripke addresses this position, too; indeed, his criticism of it was cited above as part of the "official road". The question at this point is *by what means* Kripke is allowed to challenge it. The official road insists that Kripke may challenge privacy cum assertability only if, and only in so far as, it is ruled out by the contents of our existing assertability conditions. I cannot see why the improved road would have to stick to this demand. After all, the criticisms of privacy cum classical realism and intersubjectivity cum classical realism were not constrained in this way. So why should there be a problem with arguing that privacy cum assertability is unable to capture the distinction between "is right" and "seems right"? The argument may well be *a priori*, but in arguing in this way, Kripke is not committing himself to finding necessary and sufficient conditions for someone's meaning X by "*y*".

The improved road to intersubjectivity is not troubled by the two problems that caused difficulties for the official road. The improved road is not trying to derive an impossibility claim from a mere observation of contingent phenomena. It scrutinizes the coherence of the four possible ways of combining privacy, intersubjectivity, classical realism and assertability and concludes that only the combination of intersubjectivity and assertability does not fail the test. The specific form of our existing assertability conditions does not play an essential role in this investigation. Any assertability conditions – recognizable to us as such – will do. The improved road can thus grant that our assertability conditions need not always make explicit reference to interpersonal comparison in responses. The only thing that counts is how assertability conditions are used; and we know from the arguments over privacy that they must be used in an *intersubjective setting*.

The sceptical solution and Robinson Crusoe: criticism

The traditional tool for thinking about privacy and rule-following is a thought experiment involving Robinson Crusoe. Could Crusoe be said to follow rules? When asking this question, some philosophers think of the Crusoe as described in Defoe's novel: that is, a man who grows up in a human community but eventually ends up shipwrecked and socially isolated on an island (Friday's appearance is ignored here). Other philosophers modify the story and make Crusoe a social isolate from birth. If this second Crusoe is to be a rule-follower he must not just be able to follow rules in social isolation, he must also invent for himself the very notion of a rule. In what follows I shall always have the latter stronger form of Crusoe in mind.

Most readers of *WRPL* will naturally assume that Kripke's Wittgenstein must deny the possibility of a rule-following Crusoe. After all, is not the argument against privacy an argument against this very possibility? Thus it will come as something of a surprise to most first-time readers of *WRPL* that Kripke – late in Chapter 3 – writes as follows:

> Does this [i.e. the previous argument against privacy] mean that Robinson Crusoe, isolated on an island, cannot be said to follow any rules, no matter what he does? I do not see that this follows. What does follow is that *if* we think of Crusoe as following rules, we are taking him into our community and applying our criteria for rule-following to him. The falsity of the private model need not mean that a *physically isolated* individual cannot be said to follow rules; rather that an individual, *considered in isolation* (whether or not he is physically isolated), cannot be said to do so. Remember that Wittgenstein's theory is one of assertability conditions. Our community can assert of any individual that he follows a rule if he passes the tests for rule-following applied to any member of the community. (*WRPL*: 110)

And Kripke adds in a footnote to the third sentence: "If Wittgenstein would have any problem with Crusoe, perhaps the problem would be whether we have any 'right' to take him into our community in this way, and attribute our rules to him" (*WRPL*: 110, n.85).

Critics have raised a number of concerns regarding these passages. An initial problem, noted by Stuart Shanker, is that it remains unclear what tests Crusoe has to pass in order to be judged a rule-follower by our standards. Are there general tests for being a rule-follower, independently of being a follower of this or that of *our* rules? Or are all such tests meant to pick out the following of specific rules? The main text suggests the former, but the footnote suggests the latter. If the former were enough then Kripke's earlier remarks on accepting others into our community would seem to have been forgotten. These remarks suggested that we take individuals into our community if they follow our rules, and not if they fit some general criteria for following just any rule.[9] A further worry is that Kripke now makes it too easy for social isolates to follow rules. Noam Chomsky has even suspected that Kripke's treatment of Crusoe "defangs" the whole previous argument against private language. Chomsky's point is that even the social isolate might fulfil some of our criteria for being a rule-follower in general.[10] Moreover,

Kripke's most outspoken critics, G. P. Baker and P. M. S. Hacker, target the very idea that in thinking of Crusoe as a rule-follower we "are taking him into our community and applying our criteria for rule-following to him":

> This seems confused. … Does it mean that in saying that he is follow-ing a rule we are applying our criteria for rule-following to him? Well – are there other criteria? This, presumably, is what "rule-following" *means*. When we say of the cat that it is hunting the mouse, we are applying our criteria of hunting to it. Do we thereby take the cat into our community?[11]

At this point Baker and Hacker themselves propose a possible reply. Perhaps we should say that "taking Crusoe into our community" simply consists in our apply-ing our assertability conditions to him. His responses have to agree with ours for us to attribute any rule to him. Unfortunately, according to the critics, this reply will not do:

> Must we? Must Crusoe's rules be the same as ours? … Could he not invent new rules, play new games? To be sure, in order to *grasp* them, we must understand what counts, in Crusoe's *practice*, as following a rule. And that must be evident in Crusoe's *activities*. But that is not the same as checking to see whether his responses agree with ours, let alone a matter of "taking him into our community".[12]

As if this were not bad enough, a considerable number of writers have sought to defend the idea that Crusoe can follow rules even independently of our "tak-ing him into our community and applying our criteria for rule following to him". A number of different arguments can be distinguished here. I propose calling the first argument the "metaphysical argument". It appeals to our intuitions of what is conceivable and hence metaphysically possible. Allegedly we can easily imagine that God had created just one human being, and that God had created this human being as a rule-follower. And since this scenario is conceivable, so the thought continues, it is metaphysically possible as well.[13]

The second argument is the "internalist argument". It maintains that whether or not an individual is a rule-follower depends solely on facts about that individual's mental states. The point can be made forcefully by imagining catastrophes that have but a single survivor: "could not the rest of the human race be wiped out while you sleep and yet the next day you awake with your rule-following capaci-ties intact?"[14]

Thirdly, the idea of the "invention argument" is simple. If all rule-following had to be communal, then rules could not have a first follower. But rules must have first followers, or else rules could never be invented. The inventor of a rule is its first follower.[15]

A fourth line of reasoning is a parity argument. Since two different parity arguments have been advanced, I call the fourth line "parity argument A". It concerns the idea that we can speak of rule-following only where we find a distinction between *seems right* and *is right*, between "thinking one is following the rule (correctly)" and "following the rule correctly". Critics of individualism insist that this criterion makes it impossible for isolated individuals to follow rules. Parity argument A attacks this consideration by insisting on a parity between individual and community. Individual and community are on a par: if individuals cannot draw the distinction between *seems right* and *is right* then neither can communities as a whole. The individual cannot get access to an *is right* by referring to his community, for his community can at best offer him a "communal *seems right*". As John McDowell puts it:

> The trouble is that there is a precise parallel between the community's supposed grasp of the patterns that it has communally committed itself to and the individual's supposed grasp of his idiolectic commitments. Whatever applications of an expression secure communal approval, just those applications will seem to the community to conform with its understanding of the expression. ... One would like to say: whatever is going to seem right to *us* is right. And that only means that here we can't talk about "right".[16]

Fifthly, "parity argument B" insists on the parity of individual and group in a different way. The thought is that whatever social *intersubjective* structure the opponent of privacy insists on, the individualist can always point to a similar *intrasubjective* structure that can do the same work. For instance, granted that rule-following involves agreement and correction, why demand that such agreement and correction calls for groups of individuals? Why not accept that the time-slices of one and the same individuals can deliver the goods? Here is Blackburn's version of the objection:

> The members of a community stand to each other as the momentary time-slices of an individual do. ... And when the community says "well, we just see ourselves as agreeing (dignify, compliment ourselves as comprehending the same rule)" the individual just borrows the trick, and compliments himself on his rapport with his previous times.[17]

Sixthly, and finally, "similarity arguments" have the following form:

Premise One: When we follow rules we behave in ways *W*.
Premise Two: We can imagine social isolates behaving in ways similar to *W*.
Conclusion: We should allow that social isolates follow rules.

Here are three examples:

> [T]here is no reason why Crusoe should not follow a pattern or par-adigm, making occasional mistakes perhaps, and occasionally (but maybe not always) noticing and correcting his mistakes. That he is following a rule will show itself in the manner in which he uses the formulation of the rule as a canon or norm of correctness. Hence, to take a simple example, he might use the pattern ---...---... as a rule or pattern to follow in decorating the walls of his house; when he notices four dots in a sequence he manifests annoyance with himself. He carefully goes back and rubs one out, and perhaps checks carefully adjacent marks, comparing them with his "master-pattern". And so on. Of course, he is *not* merely following his "inclinations", but rather following the rule. And it is his behaviour, including his corrective behaviour, which shows both that he is following the rule, and *what he counts as following the rule.*[18]

> Consider the example (due to Michael Dummett) of a born Crusoe who finds a Rubik's cube washed onto his island, and learns to solve it. The fact is that he does it. He certainly doesn't solve it randomly, for he can do it on demand. It is natural to say that he follows prin-ciples (when there is a last corner left to do ...). Perhaps he has some rudimentary diagrams or other mnemonics which he consults. With these he can do it, and without them he cannot.[19]

> I find it perfectly possible to imagine that Romulus, upon reaching the age of reason, hits upon the idea of distributing sign-posts around his island as an *aide-memoire*. He wants to avoid the marshes, so he writes an arrow in the sand and undertakes to walk in the direction of its head when he comes across it in future; he follows his rule correctly in the future if he conforms his actions to his original intentions in respect of the arrow; and he may discover on occasion that he has fol-lowed his rule *in*correctly when, misremembering his original inten-tion, he finds himself wallowing in the marsh (he mistakenly thought that his original intention was to follow the *tail* of the arrow).[20]

The sceptical solution and Robinson Crusoe: reply to criticism

In the following I shall argue that the objections summarized above are not detrimental to Kripke's treatment of Crusoe. The natural starting-point of a re-evaluation is the passage from *WRPL* that sparked the criticism. Two points of clarification seem particularly important. The first concerns Kripke's contrast between "a *physically isolated* individual" and "an individual, *considered in isolation* (whether or not he is physically isolated)". This contrast could be put more clearly by distinguishing between *physical* and *social isolation*.[21] Social life is episodic; between our face-to-face encounters we are physically isolated from others. But even when we are physically isolated, we remain socially "embedded": we are related to others in our thinking, feeling and acting. We anticipate blame and reward, we make plans that involve others, and we harbour various feelings for them. To be physically but not socially isolated is a frequent experience for most of us. But we are never fully socially isolated. A wolf-child (before capture) would be a case of someone who was both physically and socially isolated from other human beings. And maybe a severely autistic child can be thought of as being socially but not physically isolated. The case of Defoe's Robinson Crusoe is not so clear. Crusoe grows up in human communities and washes up on the shores of his island only at a time when he is already an adult. Subsequently he spends twenty-six years on his own. Was Crusoe socially or just physically isolated? Intuitions diverge at this point. If we judge him to have been merely physically isolated, we are thinking of his twenty-six lonely years as a (very long) interval between face-to-face encounters. If we opt for social isolation we are guided by the idea that twenty-six years is too long a period to count as an interval between social interactions.

The second point of clarification pertains to Kripke's talk of "taking him [i.e. Crusoe] into our community and applying our criteria of rule-following to him". I have already proposed that to take someone into our community is to give them a *social status* within our community. One aspect of social status attributions is particularly important here. In order for someone – say Jones – to have a certain social status, a community (or its representatives) must have imposed this status on Jones. In deciding on this imposition of status, the community has some rough and ready criteria. But it is not enough for Jones to have the status that he fulfils these criteria. Unless the community (or its representatives) *actually confers* the status – perhaps by saying something like "we hereby declare you to be ..." – Jones does not have it. We might put this point by saying that one of the criteria of Jones having the status is that the community (or its representatives) has imposed the status on him. Applied to rule-following: if being a rule-follower is a social status, then Crusoe cannot be a rule-follower merely by fitting the rough and ready criteria on the basis of which a community decides who should be a rule-follower. Crusoe is a rule-follower – he has this social status – only if a community has actually conferred this status on him.

This way of interpreting talk of "taking into the community" helps immediately with one of Baker and Hacker's objections. They write: "When we say of the cat that it is hunting the mouse, we are applying our criteria of hunting to it. Do we thereby take the cat into our community?" The implied answer is of course "no". And by parity of reasoning, Baker and Hacker insist that the answer should be "no" also for the allegedly analogous case of deciding whether the isolated Crusoe could follow rules. At first sight, this seems plausible enough. Nevertheless, Baker and Hacker are wrong to see the two cases as analogous. "To be hunting" is not a social status. One can fit the criteria for hunting without being the member of any social community. But if the overall argument of meaning scepticism is correct then one cannot fit the criteria for being a rule-follower without having a social status (and thereby being a member of a community). In suggesting that rule-following is a natural property rather than social status, Baker and Hacker beg the question against the meaning-sceptical argument as a whole.

Baker and Hacker's criticism, of course, goes further. They also question the intelligibility of Kripke's reference to "our criteria" by wondering, "Well – are there other criteria?" Clearly they think that the answer is negative. In order to make progress here, and also to answer Shanker's and Chomsky's objections, one must attend carefully to two of Kripke's comments on *forms of life*:

> The set of responses in which we agree, and the way they interweave with our activities, is our *form of life*. Beings who agreed in consistently giving bizarre quus-like responses would share in another form of life. By definition, such another form of life would be bizarre and incomprehensible to us. ("If a lion could talk, we could not understand him" … [*PI*: 223].) However, if we can imagine the abstract possibility of another form of life (and no *a priori* argument would seem to exclude it), the members of a community sharing such a quus-like form of life could play the game of attributing rules and concepts to each other as we do. Someone would be said, in such a community, to follow a rule, as long as he agrees in his responses with the (*quus-like*) responses produced by the members of *that* community.   (*WRPL*: 96)

In this passage Kripke seems to allow that we can speak of rule-following in another form of life, and without taking members of this other form of life into our community. Note, however, that Kripke speaks of an "*abstract* possibility of another form of life" (emphasis added). I take this to mean that we might have difficulties once we try to imagine this possibility in more detail. This reading seems to be supported by a footnote two pages after the above quote:

> Can we imagine forms of life other than our own, that is, can we imagine creatures who follow rules in bizarre quus-like ways? It seems to me that there may be a certain tension in Wittgenstein's philosophy here. On the one hand, it would seem that Wittgenstein's paradox argues that there is no *a priori* reason why a creature could not follow a quus-like rule, and thus in this sense we ought to regard such creatures as conceivable. On the other hand, it is supposed to be part of our very form of life that we find it natural and, indeed, inevitable

that we follow the rule for addition in the particular way that we do. (See §231: "'But surely you can see …?' That is just the characteristic expression of someone who is under the compulsion of a rule.") But then it seems that we should be unable to understand "from the inside" (cf. the notion of "*Verstehen*" in various German writers) how any creature could follow a quus-like rule. We could describe such behaviour extensionally and behaviouristically, but we would be unable to find it intelligible how the creature finds it natural to behave in this way. This consequence does, indeed, seem to go with Wittgenstein's conception of the matter. (*WRPL*: 98, n.78)

Taking these two quotations together, it seems reasonable to say that there is a sense in which we can rightfully speak of "our criteria" for rule-following. We can – abstractly – make sense of the possibility of other forms of life. But there are limits to the sense we can make of this possibility. A radically different form of life – a form of life in which the quus-rule would be "natural" – cannot really be understood by us. And hence we also cannot make sense of attributing rules to the members of that form of life. We can only attribute rules where we can rely on a considerable degree of agreement in responses.

These considerations can also alleviate Shanker's and Chomsky's worries. The fact that *WRPL* discusses Crusoe from the perspective of assertability conditions does not make private rule-following too easy (as Chomsky alleges). On the contrary, Kripke's Wittgenstein's approach implies that we are able to attribute rules only where we find a broad agreement in responses. And we find an agreement in responses only among creatures who share the same form of life. Moreover, attributing rules to other human beings has a rationale: it has the point of recommending these human beings to others in our community, and the point of making them one of us (by imposing a social status on them). These features of rule-following radically limit the range of possible rule-followers. It makes it difficult – indeed, impossible – for social isolates to qualify.[22]

Shanker complains that Kripke's Wittgenstein seems to take two different positions. In some places Kripke's Wittgenstein insists that for someone to follow a rule (by our lights) he has to follow one of our rules. In the Crusoe passage the position is different; here Kripke seems to allow for general criteria for rule-following, criteria that do not involve criteria for following any particular rule of ours. I fail to see the problem. On the one hand, it is not claimed by Kripke's Wittgenstein that I can only attribute our (already shared) rules to others. (I have discussed such cases in Chapter 2.) On the other hand, it seems that Shanker reads too much into Kripke's sentence "What does follow is that *if* we think of Crusoe as following rules, we are taking him into our community and applying our criteria for rule-following to him". We need not read the expression "our criteria for rule-following" as referring to general criteria for rule-following over and above our criteria for deciding whether or not someone follows rules that we are able to make sense of. It seems much more intuitive to say that someone fits our criteria for being a rule-follower if we are able and willing to attribute a good number of specific rules to him.

Turning next to the metaphysical argument – surely it is conceivable, and thus logically possible, that God creates but a single rule-follower – I find the argument either question-begging or incomplete. It is question-begging if it is based on a certain view of what it means to be a rule-follower. This is the view of (low-brow) meaning determinism. If this conception is presupposed then it is simply wrong to say that we can conceive of God creating a single rule-following human being. The sceptical argument against meaning determinism shows that this conception is incoherent. Hence the metaphysical argument had better be based on an alternative view to meaning determinism.

The metaphysical argument – as well as many other arguments in favour of privacy – commits the mistake identified by Kripke when comparing Hume on causality with Wittgenstein on private language:

> Only when the particular events *a* and *b* are thought of as subsumed under two respective event types, *A* and *B*, which are related by a generalization that *all* events of type *A* are followed by events of type *B*, can *a* be said to "cause" *b*. ... Can one reasonably protest: surely there is nothing the event *a* can do with the *help* of other events of the same type that it cannot do by itself! Indeed, to say that *a*, by itself, is a sufficient cause of *b* is to say that, had the rest of the universe been removed, *a* still would have produced *b*! Intuitively this may well be so, but the intuitive objection ignores Hume's sceptical argument. ... Of course I am suggesting that Wittgenstein's argument against private language has a structure similar to Hume's argument against private causation. ... It turns out that the sceptical solution does not allow us to speak of a single individual, considered by himself and in isolation, as ever meaning anything. Once again an objection based on an intuitive feeling that no one else can affect what I mean by a given symbol ignores the sceptical argument that undermines any such naive intuition about meaning. (*WRPL*: 68–9)

The internalist argument – could not the rest of the human race be wiped out while you sleep and yet the next day you awake with your rule-following capacities intact? – is certainly guilty of this charge. It mirrors the objection to Hume that Kripke envisages but rightly rejects as missing the point: "Indeed, to say that *a*, by itself, is a sufficient cause of *b* is to say that, had the rest of the universe been removed, *a* still would have produced *b*!" (*WRPL*: 68). One cannot marshal an intuition against a position if that position has already shown the intuition to be indefensible. The problem in the present case is that all of Chapter 2 of *WRPL* is a refutation of the idea of an individual's intrinsic rule-following capacities. The internalist argument can seem plausible only against the background of a sudden amnesia.

The invention argument – if all rule-following had to be communal there could not be an inventor of rules – suffers from similar weaknesses. The first question for an advocate of this argument must be how he envisages the act of inventing a rule. This act must not be construed along familiar meaning-determinist lines or else the crucial issue is being begged. But if the advocate has another possibility in mind, we need to know what it is. What then would the sceptical solution have to say about the invention of rules? Can this phenomenon be accommodated? I do not see any difficulties here. Imagine that Jones contemplates a new form of chess (say, chess without castling). Under what circumstances would he be justified to say that he is following the rule "do not castle" in chess? The assertability conditions will be the familiar ones. He will be entitled to make this claim if he is confident of acting in accordance with his rule and if he is open to being corrected by others who have accepted his new variant of chess. Jones may even be looked on as the first follower of his rule. But that Jones can be so looked on by others does not show that social isolates can follow rules. It merely shows that there are rules and times in Jones's life when "mastery is simply presumed on the basis of his membership in the community" (*WRPL*: 104, n.83).

Parity argument A – the parity of group and individual as far as the *is-right/ seems-right* distinction is concerned – does not survive closer scrutiny either. It simply is not correct to say that individual and group are in the same boat here. The argument works only if one employs a simply dichotomy of "isolated individual" versus "isolated group as a whole". But these are not, of course, the only alternatives. Between the extremes of isolated individual and the group we can identify a third alternative: the individual within a community. And for such an individual there will be a distinction between actual and seeming correctness.[23] One may well suspect that Parity argument A is based on "treating the community as itself an individual, and supposing that there is one way of going on that seems to this superindividual as though it is correct".[24] Indeed, the history of theorizing about individual and group is full of misleading assimilations of one to the other: either the group is conceptualized as an individual writ large, or the individual is thought of as a community writ small.[25] It is easy to see how both metaphors can mislead. Take the former metaphor first. Once we routinely think of groups as akin to individuals, we will have few qualms about extending psychological vocabulary to groups in a direct and straightforward way: talk of group minds and collective wills will be hard to avoid. This will make it difficult for us to appreciate that all group phenomena are constituted in and through the *interaction* between individuals. Groups consist of interacting individuals. Parity argument A looks compelling only once we have lost sight of this obvious idea.

Assimilating individuals to groups is no less problematic. I submit that this assimilation underlies Parity argument B, that is, the claim that, as far as normativity is concerned, *intrasubjectivity* is not principally different from *intersubjectivity*.

This thought will seem natural and obvious if we think of the individual mind as a group of interacting voices or time-slices. Many philosophers will find this thought intuitive; after all, it has informed their theorizing as least since Plato's *Republic*. And yet, there are reasons for scepticism regarding this assimilation. The main problem is that *intrasubjectivity* can capture normativity only by either falling back on meaning-determinist concepts, or by distorting one's relationship to oneself. It just is not true that meaning-attributions to myself and for myself have the utility of informing me under what circumstances I can rely on myself.[26] As Kripke puts it:

> As members of the community correct each other, might a given individual correct himself? … it would appear that an individual remembers his own "intentions" and can use memory of these intentions to correct another mistaken memory. In the presence of the [sceptical] paradox, any such "naïve" ideas are meaningless. Ultimately, an individual may simply have conflicting brute inclinations, while the upshot of the matter depends on his will alone. The situation is not analogous to the case of the community, where distinct individuals have distinct and independent wills, and where, when an individual is accepted into the community, others judge that they can rely on his response … No corresponding relation between an individual and himself has the same utility. (*WRPL*: 112)

This leaves us with the similarity argument. It tries to convince us, by way of examples, that we must attribute rules to social isolates even when these share very little with us. A social isolate who successfully solves the Rubik's cube – occasionally consulting signs he has drawn in the sand – seems like an obvious case in point. However else we might differ, if he regularly manages to bring it about (without taking the cube apart) that each surface of the cube is of a single colour then surely he must be following rules. Or consider the Crusoe who draws himself arrows in the sand to get to the beach. Surely he can find out that he has followed his rule – if you want to get to the beach follow the arrows – incorrectly. It should be clear that these intuition pumps do not improve on the arguments already discussed. As ever the individualist begs the question against the sceptical argument. If the behaviour of Crusoe is to indicate rule-following how is that rule-following to be conceived? If the rule-following is to be conceived in terms of a mental state (perhaps reduced to dispositions) then we face all the familiar problems. If it is to be conceived in some other way then we need to know which way this is. Just appealing to the behaviour is not enough.

Other criticisms can be pressed as well. First, here is a forceful criticism by Norman Lillegard of the Rubik's cube example:

> Crusoe is sitting on the beach. The cube washes up. He picks it up, fools with it. For years perhaps. Then suddenly it pops into his mind:

"perhaps there is a solution to this". This is ludicrous. Or, nothing pops into his mind (in particular no English sentences) but he simply starts manipulating the cube, making little marks in the sand, looking back at them now and then, and eventually, he has it! What? The solution! I personally can neither imagine, conceive, nor make sense of this. In particular I do not see how anything that Crusoe did could be considered by him to be mistaken or incorrect, except in the sense of failing to get him from A to B in the way that some other "move" did. But there could not be anything "correct" about getting to B itself, (though doing so might be pleasing, satisfying, conducive to survival, etc.) We can imagine a born Crusoe finding the solution to the Rubik's Cube only by forgetting who a born Crusoe is, perhaps, by forgetting that he is a *born* Crusoe.[27]

The important point is that whatever a born Crusoe does, he is too different from us for us to be entitled to regard him as a rule-follower. We cannot regard him as a rule-follower simply on the grounds that he manipulates the cube while "consulting" his marks in the sand. The marks in the sand might cause him to produce a combination of colours on his cube such that we would count the cube as "correctly solved"; correctly solved, that is, if *we* had done the solving. Compare the current case with ants that leave odour marks in the forest to enable them to revisit a food source. We would not regard the ants as rule-followers possessing a sense of correct and incorrect, although they may well be guided by something external to themselves (i.e. the odour marks). We would not regard the ants as rule-followers, since we have no idea of how ants could acquire concepts such as "correct" and "incorrect". We know how we acquire these concepts and where they figure: in discursive practices of teaching and training and in justifications and negotiations with others. Put differently, in order for us to think of someone as a rule-follower, we must be able to think of "correctness" and "incorrectness" (or their analogues) as concepts that they possess (as actors' categories).[28] There is nothing in the Crusoe-cum-cube story that invites or allows for this hypothesis. In this story we find plenty of regularities and actions that accord with one of our rules, but we do not find rule-following.

Similar comments are appropriate concerning the pattern example introduced by Baker and Hacker: (---…---…). If Crusoe is not part of our community, then all hypotheses concerning his behaviour – that his behaviour constitutes a correction of earlier actions, an introduction or modification of a (new) rule – are fatally underdetermined.[29]

This brings us, finally, to McGinn's Romulus. His case has been discussed by Norman Malcolm:

McGinn imagines that Romulus "hits upon the idea" of employing directional signs to guide him. Now how are we to conceive of what went on when this "idea" occurred to Romulus? Did he *say* to himself, "In order to avoid the marsh I need signs to guide me"? But presumably Romulus has no language. So did he have that thought, without words? But whatever constellation of wordless images or feelings that Romulus had, by virtue of *what* would that constellation have the same meaning as the foregoing sentence? Why couldn't that constellation be translated into a sentence with a different meaning? Nothing could justify one translation rather than another. Nor could that thought be displayed in the *behaviour* of Romulus. ... nothing in his behaviour could display the thought "In order to avoid the marsh I need signs to guide me".[30]

David Pears is unconvinced. He grants that no meaning can be given to the idea of a wolf-child intentionally introducing a sign; to imagine this is to imagine that wolf-child having a language already. But Pears insist that the introduction of a sign might occur unintentionally:

An animal that always uses the same track on the journey out would be setting up signs which would guide it on the return journey, without any such plan, and perhaps without even the capacity to make plans. ... Is there anything to stop the development of a system of self-addressed signs out of this kind of pattern of behaviour, given the intelligence of a human child?[31]

Pears is right: there is nothing to stop the development of a system of self-addressed signs. And there is no reason why the argument against privacy would have to oppose its development. The crucial issue is not the existence of self-addressed signs of some sort; the crucial question is whether we can make sense of meaning and thought, intention and rule before the animal or child becomes part of our form of life.

I–we and I–thou

The sceptical solution has been attacked not only by defenders of private language but also by philosophers who advocate conceptions of intersubjectivity that differ from that put forward in the sceptical solution. I shall conclude by discussing the most important such criticism.

According to Brandom, Kripke's Wittgenstein is among those who "personify the community, [who] talk about it as though it were able to do the same sorts of things that individual community members can do – perform additions, apply rules, assess performances, and so on". Brandom cites the following evidence:

[T]o pick one page almost at random, Kripke talks about "the community's accepting" conditionals codifying relations between attributions of intentional states and commitments to act, what "the community regards as right", what "the community endorses", and so on.[32]

In such passages, Kripke allegedly emerges as a thinker who favours the "I–we" dyad over the "I–thou" dyad. That is to say, *WRPL* seems to neglect the one-to-one interaction between individuals, and focuses primarily on how individuals are evaluated and appraised by their community. Brandom takes the emphasis on "I–we" as a symptom of Kripke's Wittgenstein being a "communal assessment theorist". To explain this term, we need to attend to Brandom's broader concern.

Brandom is a normativist about meaning and mental content. And thus he sees the need for a philosophical elucidation of norms. Brandom rejects two traditional ways of aiming for such elucidation: "regulism" and "regularism". Regulism supposes that norms are explicitly formulated rules: "norms are likened to laws in the sense of statutes. For conduct is legally appropriate or inappropriate just insofar as it is governed by some explicit law that says it is".[33] Brandom believes that regulism has been refuted by Wittgenstein's regress arguments: no explicit norm can stand on its own feet; it can always be shown that in order to apply it (correctly) we need a further norm.

Regularism seeks to reduce norms to "regularities of performances": "The simple regularity approach is committed to identifying the distinction between *correct* and *incorrect* performance with that between *regular* and *irregular* performance".[34] A performance is correct, regularism alleges, if it is regularly performed (or endorsed). Regularism has also been discarded by Wittgenstein. However, in the case of regularism the damage is done by the possibility of gerrymandering not by regress considerations:

> The problem is that any particular set of performances exhibits many regularities. These will agree on the performances that have been produced and differ in their treatment of some possible performances that have not (yet) been produced. A performance can be denominated "irregular" only with respect to a specified regularity, not *tout court*.[35]

In order to answer this challenge, the regularist must privilege some regularities over others. Alas, at least a simple version of regularism lacks the tools for doing so.

Brandom grants that Kripke has "powerfully expounded" Wittgenstein's arguments against simple forms of regularism.[36] And Brandom maintains that the sceptical solution is nothing but a more sophisticated version of the same position. This more sophisticated version is the "communal assessment theory" mentioned above. A community assessment theory claims that the regularities relevant for, and constitutive of, normativity are not the regularities of individuals' performances or appraisals (of others' performances), but "regularities of appraisals by the community as a whole".[37] It is the "we", the community, that sets the standard for the "I", or the individual. Whatever the community regularly appraises as correct, is correct.

Brandom puts forward three objections against communal assessment theory, and thus three objections against the sceptical solution. The first says that communal assessment theory has a "mythological conception of communities": "the idea of communal performances, assessments, or verdicts on which it relies is a fiction".[38] Communities (as a whole) do not act, assess or pass verdicts. The second objection claims that communal assessment theory tends to cheat by smuggling normative notions into what claims to be a "reductive, non-normative regularity theory".[39] One important place where such smuggling occurs is the idea of community membership. To be a member of a community is to occupy a normative status: it comes with rights and duties.[40] Thirdly, communal assessment theory is defective also because it "*globally* privileges" the community. It assumes that the community sets the standard of objectivity, and in so doing "it cannot find room for the possibility of error regarding that privileged perspective; what the community *takes* to be correct *is* correct".[41]

Is Brandom right to accuse the sceptical solution of globally privileging the community, and is he right to direct his three objections against it? Let us start with the textual evidence. Brandom suggests that proof of Kripke's tendency to personify communities exists in abundance; after all, his three quotes from one page are prefaced by "to pick one page almost at random". Closer inspection reveals, however, that this is an exaggeration. Only four pages of the 113-page book (not counting the Appendix) contain the lamented expressions:

> Any individual who claims to have mastered the concept of addition *will be judged by the community* to have done so if his particular responses agree with those of the community in enough cases ...
> (*WRPL*: 92–3, emphasis added)

> A deviant individual whose responses do not accord with those of the community in enough cases will *not be judged, by the community*, to be following its rules; ... When *the community denies* of someone that he is following certain rules, it excludes him from various transactions ...
> (*WRPL*: 93, emphasis added)

> The rough conditional thus expresses a restriction on *the community's game of attributing* to one of its members the grasping of a certain concept: if the individual in question no longer conforms to *what the community would do* in these circumstances, *the community can no longer attribute* the concept to him.   (*WRPL*: 95 emphasis added)

On the other hand, if an individual passes enough tests, the *community (endorsing assertions* of the form (i)) *accepts him* as a rule follower, thus enabling him to engage in certain types of interactions with them that depend on their reliance on his responses…. the *community must be able to judge* whether an individual is indeed following a given rule in particular applications, i.e. whether his responses agree with their own. In the case of avowals of sensations, the way the *community makes this judgement* is by observing the individual's behaviour and surrounding circumstances.　　　(*WRPL*: 108–9 emphasis added)

Moreover, these passages using the I–we opposition stand side by side with passages that analyse the relationship between individuals: the I–thou. For example, Kripke asks under what conditions there is "justification for anyone to say of [another] person" that he has failed to follow a rule (*WRPL*: 88–9). The judgement is made here by one individual about another individual. Or think of the longish discussion of the one-to-one interaction between pupil and teacher, or Smith and Jones (*WRPL*: 89–92). The latter discussion contains a formulation of assertability conditions that refers to "others", not to a community as a whole:

From this we can discern rough assertability conditions for such a sentence as "Jones means addition by 'plus'." *Jones* is entitled, subject to correction by *others*, provisionally to say, "I mean addition by 'plus'," whenever he has the feeling of confidence – "now I can go on!" – that he can give "correct" responses in new cases; and *he* is entitled, again provisionally and subject to correction by *others*, to judge a new response to be "correct" simply because it is the response he is inclined to give.　　　(*WRPL*: 90, emphasis on "others" added)

Note also that for Kripke any interaction with the community is really an interaction "with others", that is, with individual community members:

The situation is very different if we widen our gaze from consideration of the rule follower alone and allow ourselves to consider him as interacting with a wider community. Others will then have justification conditions for attributing correct or incorrect rule following to the subject, and these will *not* be simply that the subject's own authority is unconditionally to be accepted.　　　(*WRPL*: 89)

The situation [where someone corrects himself] is not analogous to the case of the community, where distinct individuals have distinct and independent wills, and where, when an individual is accepted into the community, others judge that they can rely on his response
…　　　(*WRPL*: 112)

The second passage not only makes it clear that communities are not homogeneous, it also brings out that the accepting into the community is done by one or more individuals. In accepting Jones into the community individual group members provide information about Jones's reliability to "others", other individuals in the community. (It makes no sense here to make "the community" the subject of the accepting, for then there would be no "others" left to inform.)

I thus find it impossible to agree with Brandom when he says that *WRPL* – like other forms of the communal assessment theory – is committed to a "mythological conception of communities".[42] In my reading the occasional personification of the community in *WRPL* is rather innocent and must, and can, always be rendered in terms of what interacting individuals do. Brandom's first objection to communal assessment theories leaves the sceptical solution completely unaffected.

Brandom's second objection charges communal assessment theories with smuggling in normativity through the backdoor. Does this accusation apply to the sceptical solution, even if the evidence for a privileging of the I–we dyad seems weak? I do not think so. The sceptical solution is not a form of reductivism; it is not trying to reduce normativity to regularities, be they communal regularities of performances or communal regularities of sanctions. And since the sceptical solution is not attempting to get rid of normativity, it does not need to smuggle it in either. A reductive interpretation of the sceptical solution can seem natural only if one reads Kripke's comments on the importance of agreement in responses in a certain light:

> We respond unhesitatingly to such problems as "68 + 57", regarding our procedure as the only comprehensible one …, and we *agree* in the unhesitating responses we make. On Wittgenstein's conception, such agreement is essential for our game of ascribing rules and concepts to each other. (*WRPL*: 96)

> There is no objective fact – that we all mean addition by "+", or even that a given individual does – that explains our agreement in particular cases. Rather our license to say of each other that we mean addition by "+" is part of a "language game" that sustains itself only because of the brute fact that we generally agree. (*WRPL*: 97)

Someone who reads the sceptical solution as a form of regularism must be assuming that Kripke here proposes a reduction of our language game of attributing meaning – and the normativity that comes with it – to the brute fact that we generally agree in our non-intentional responses. But to say that one thing "sustains itself only because of" another thing, or to say that one thing is "essential" for another thing, is not to say that the first reduces to the second. Without our agreement in responses our language game of attributing meaning would not be possible; our agreement in our responses is a condition of the possibility of normativity – no less, no more. The sceptical solution does not try to reduce normativity, it relocates it: normativity is not a feature of a meaning-determining mental state, it is a feature of how we relate to one another. Remember that Kripke explicitly rejects all forms of communal dispositionalism: "Wittgenstein's theory should not be confused with a theory that, for any *m* and *n*, the value of the function we mean by 'plus' *is* (by definition) the value that (nearly) all the linguistic community would give as the answer" (*WRPL*: 111).

Finally, it is worth asking whether the sceptical solution leaves "room for the possibility of error regarding … what the community *takes* to be correct".[43] Here too *WRPL* provides an answer:

> [I]f the community all agrees on an answer and persists in its view, no one can correct it. There can be no corrector *in* the community, since by hypothesis, all the community agrees. If the corrector were outside the community, on Wittgenstein's view he has no "right" to make any correction. Does it make any sense to *doubt* whether a response we all agree upon is "correct"? Clearly in some cases an individual may doubt whether the community may correct, later, a response it had agreed upon at a given time. But may the individual doubt whether the community may not in fact *always* be wrong, even though it never corrects its error? It *is* hard to formulate such a doubt within Wittgenstein's framework, since it looks like a question, whether, as a matter of "fact", we might always be wrong; and there is no such fact. On the other hand, within Wittgenstein's framework it is still true that, for me, no assertions about community responses for all time need establish the result of an arithmetical problem; that *I* can legitimately calculate the result for myself, even given this information, is part of our "language game". (*WRPL*: 146)

We do not need to enter here into the complexities of evaluating other cultures; Kripke says too little on this problem for it to merit discussion here. The following sentences are more important. It would be a mistake to take the statement that in the framework of the sceptical solution a community cannot *always* be wrong as a commitment to the *infallibility* of the community. After all, Brandom himself adheres to the Davidsonian framework in which it makes no sense to say that *an individual* could always be wrong. And, clearly, regarding the impossibility of global error, individual and community are in the same position. Note also that according to the sceptical solution there is no onus on us to agree with our community: it is part of our very language game of arithmetic that I can reach – and legitimately deem correct – one result, even though everyone around me reaches another. The sceptical solution is descriptive about normativity: it tells us how we operate with normative concepts and what their proper location is. But it does not

tell us how we ought to respond when our own calculations – or meaning attributions – differ from those of others.

Interpretationalism and internal relations

Above we have already encountered Baker and Hacker as fierce critics of Kripke's
rendering of the private language argument (and in Chapter 8 I shall discuss their
attack on Kripke as an interpreter of Wittgenstein). But Baker and Hacker also
have a more general, systematic objection to *WRPL*. Although this objection goes
beyond the private language issue, it is nevertheless most naturally taken up in
the present context. It is an obvious bridge from the present topic to the issue of
semantic primitivism (to be addressed in Chapter 7).

Baker and Hacker's starting-point is the problem of how it is possible for a
rule to determine a specific set of correct future applications. As they see it, three
kinds of solutions have traditionally been offered: "Platonism", "psychologism"
and "interpretationalism". (Baker and Hacker do not use this last term, but it
naturally suggests itself.) Each of these three positions postulates different mediating or linking items between a rule and its applications: Platonism suggests
abstract entities, psychologism submits acts of meaning and interpretationalism
proposes interpretations. None of these theories work. Platonism is no more than
"a picture"; acts of meaning are "magical" and without explanatory value; and
interpretations are inevitably underdetermined. As far as these three positions
are concerned, Baker and Hacker thus explicitly side with Kripke's rule sceptic.[44]

In order to understand where Baker and Hacker nevertheless deviate from
Kripke, we need to recognize that they distinguish between two forms of interpretationalism: "individualistic interpretationalism" and the "community assent" thesis. Both forms of interpretationalism hold that the relationship between a rule and
its application is mediated by interpretations, but they differ over the source of the
interpretations. For individualistic interpretationalism, the source is the individual;
for the community assent thesis, the source is the community. Baker and Hacker
seem to hold that what Kripke calls "straight solutions" are all forms of Platonism,
psychologism and individualistic interpretationalism, and that what Kripke refers
to as "the sceptical solution" is a version of the community assent thesis.[45]

The key issue is Baker and Hacker's perspective on interpretationalism. They
agree with Kripke that individualistic interpretationalism is an untenable position. But they disagree with Kripke over why individualistic interpretationalism
is hopeless. Individualistic interpretationalism is – obviously – an individualistic
form of interpretationalism. As Baker and Hacker read him, Kripke rejects individualistic interpretationalism for its individualism, not for its interpretationalism. In the eyes of the two critics, this constitutes a decisive mistake and a fatal
deviation from Wittgenstein's own views. The correct criticism of individualistic

interpretationalism is that it is a form of interpretationalism, that is, that it takes the relation between a rule and its applications to be mediated by interpretations. Since Kripke misses this crucial Wittgensteinian insight, he falsely believes that the community assent thesis – a communal form of interpretationalism – avoids the shortcomings of individualistic interpretationalism. But it does not. Or so Baker and Hacker maintain.

What is wrong then with interpretationalism? To provide an answer to this question we need the distinction between *external* and *internal* relations. Traditionally, external and internal relations are distinguished by whether or not the relation constitutes the identity of the items related: if item *a* is externally related to item *b* then *a* and *b* would be what they are even if the relation between them had never obtained (think of the relation "heavier than" holding between two people on opposite sides of the earth). If item *a* is internally related to item *b* then *a* and *b* would not be what they are without the relation (think of the relation between a father and a son, or the relation between an intention and knowing what will fulfil this intention). Put differently, internal relations are conceptual and necessary, external relations are not. Causal relations are an important instance of external relations.

Baker and Hacker add a further twist to the traditional account. If *a* and *b* are externally related then it is possible to provide a further analysis of the relation; such further analysis might show that *a* and *b* are related to each other in virtue of each standing in a further relation to some third, mediating, entity. Such further analysis is not possible in the case of internal relations. An internal relation between *a* and *b* is not mediated by *a* and *b* each standing in some further relation to some mediating entity, say *c*. To see this, imagine we were to try to analyse the internal relation *a–b* further into the relations *a–c* and *c–b* (i.e. *a–c–b*). Then *a–c* and *c–b* would in turn be either external or internal relations. If at least one of the two, *a–c* or *c–b*, were an external relation then the relation between *a* and *b* could not be internal. If both *a–c* and *c–b* were internal, however, then – given the conceptual nature of internal relations – the analysis would be either redundant or lead into an infinite regress.[46]

Let us return to the alleged mistake of interpretationalism. Using the terminology of relations, Baker and Hacker insist that interpretationalism treats the relation between a rule and its application as an external relation. It does so since it takes this relation to be open to further analysis: after all, interpretationalism is the view that the relation between a rule and its applications is mediated by interpretations. And this, according to our two critics is false:

> [T]he concept of a rule and the concept of what accords with it (what is a correct application of it) are internally related. Understanding a rule and knowing what accords with it are, in this respect, akin to intending and knowing what will fulfil one's intention, or expecting something and knowing what will satisfy one's expectation. ... there is

no such thing as understanding a rule correctly, but being in general at a loss over how to apply it.[47]

Kripke's whole sceptical set-up is thus based on a false premise; the false premise that we can give an analysis of the relation between a rule and its applications. As our two critics have it, there is "nothing" (i.e. no third item) that determines me to answer "125" in reply to "68 + 57 = ?". The relationship between "125" and "68 + 57" is an internal relationship.

The idea that the relation between a rule and its applications is internal can also be expressed by saying that the presence of the one is a *criterion* for the presence of the other. We would not attribute the meaning "addition" to someone unless they generally gave answers that accord with the addition function. Baker and Hacker emphasize, however, that for Wittgenstein criteria are "defeasible": I can attribute to you the meaning "addition" even though you might make occasional mistakes in your calculations with the "+" sign.[48]

Finally, Baker and Hacker follow Wittgenstein in insisting that rules and applications exist only in "practices". This has to be taken in the right way: a practice is not a third item that links a given rule to its applications. The claim is rather that the internal relation between rule and application exists only as "a *Praxis*, a regular activity".[49] Practices are the mode of existence of both rules and applications.

I am not convinced by Baker and Hacker's analysis. First of all, they are wrong to read the sceptical solution as a form of communal interpretationalism. Kripke rejects both individual and communal forms of interpretationalism. The shift proposed by the sceptical solution is not a shift from individual to communal interpretations of rule formulations. The proposed shift is one from treating rules as certain determinants of actions to studying the conditions under which rules are attributed:

> [W]e must give up the attempt to find any fact about me in virtue of which I … must go on in a certain way. Instead we must consider how we actually use: [i] the categorical assertion that an individual is following a given rule … ; [ii] the conditional assertion that "if an individual follows such-and-such a rule, he must do so-and-so on a given occasion …" (*WRPL*: 108)

In the sceptical solution neither the community nor its interpretations are functioning as a mediating third item between rules and their applications. The shift to the community is rather motivated by the observations that to understand rules and meanings we must focus on how rules and meanings are attributed to others; and that the practice of rule attribution "depends on the brute empirical fact that we agree with each other in our responses" (*WRPL*: 109).

Secondly, it is simply wrong to accuse the sceptical solution of treating the relationship between rules and their applications as external. On the one hand,

Kripke insists that in a meaning conditional such as "If Jones means *addition* by '+' then he will (must) reply '125' to '68 + 57'" the relationship is criteriological: answering "125" to this plus-query functions as a (defeasible) criterion for the attribution of *addition* to Jones. If *a* is a criterion for *b* then their relationship cannot be external. On the other hand, Kripke comes close to saying himself that the relationship between rule and application is internal: "Wittgenstein's view that the relation between the desire (expectation, etc.) and its object must be 'internal', not 'external', parallels corresponding morals drawn about meaning in my text below (the relation of meaning and intention to future action is 'normative, not descriptive' …)" (*WRPL*: 25–6).

Thirdly, and finally, Baker and Hacker fail to appreciate that Kripke's Wittgenstein's meaning scepticism is *constitutive* (*ontological*) rather than *epistemological*. The question ultimately is not how I *know* what fact makes it so that in the past by "+" I meant *addition*; the question is whether there is, or can be, any such meaning-determining fact in the first place. Baker and Hacker never address the latter question. Their epistemological orientation is obvious not only from one of the previously quoted passages,[50] but also comes out clearly in the following quotation:

> The question "How do you know what you mean by '…'?" is as awry as "How do you know what you expect to happen?" … The question concerns one's certainty about one's possession of (the continuity of) an ability or skill. And inasmuch as one exercises the skill frequently, one is typically confident, and rightly so. There is no room here for a serious sceptical foothold.[51]

Baker and Hacker's misunderstanding of Kripke's Wittgenstein's scepticism matters. It matters because their invocation of internal relations between rules and their applications does work only against epistemological, not against constitutive, rule-scepticism. The epistemological rule-sceptic allows us possession of definite knowledge of rules but denies us definite knowledge of their correct applications. Clearly, this position is undermined if it turns out that the relation between rules and their applications is internal. If that relation is internal, then to know the rule is to know the applications. Compare this situation with the case of constitutive rule-scepticism. The constitutive rule-sceptic denies that there are meaning-determinist facts of a certain kind. This position is not undermined by the invocation of internal relations between rules and applications. The question of whether the relation between rules and applications is internal or external is simply orthogonal to the question of whether acts of rule-following are reducible or not.[52]

Conclusion

There are three main interpretational and substantive questions that a defence of the sceptical solution needs to address: whether the sceptical solution features a plausible successor for classical realism; whether the private language argument *as rendered by WRPL* is defensible; and how the sceptical solution relates to semantic primitivism. Chapter 5 tackled the first issue; Chapter 7 will address the third. This chapter concerned itself with the thorny problems surrounding privacy and intersubjectivity, that is, the private language argument.

My discussion had three parts. I began by distinguishing two ways – the "official road" and the "improved road" – of arguing for intersubjectivity and against privacy. Although the official road seems to be favoured by Kripke himself, the dialectic of the sceptical argument strongly suggests the improvement. The improved road is to investigate four different ways of combining privacy, intersubjectivity, classical realism and assertability and to show that only the dyad of intersubjectivity and assertability survives critical scrutiny. The suggested improvement avoids the forceful objections that have been levelled against the official version.

Having identified a satisfactory version of the private language argument in the context of rule-following, I turned to the traditional dispute over whether a Robinson Crusoe from birth could follow rules. I first provided a new interpretation for Kripke's somewhat cryptic comments on Crusoe. According to my interpretation, Kripke holds that Crusoe is a rule-follower if, and only if, a community *actually* confers that social status to him. It is not enough that Crusoe fit the community's criteria for rule-following in some abstract sense. Subsequently I discussed six arguments that have been put forward as establishing the possibility of a rule-following social isolate (the metaphysical argument, the internalist argument, the invention argument, two parity arguments, and the similarity argument). The common cause of their failing was that they were all based on intuitions already discredited by the sceptical argument.

In the final two sections I took up two further criticisms of Kripke's view of the community. Brandom interprets the sceptical solution as an attempt to reduce normativity to "regularities of appraisals by the community as a whole". Brandom laments both the reduction and the "global privileging" of the community. Of course Brandom's rendering fits neither my interpretation nor the actual text of *WRPL*. Baker and Hacker accuse Kripke of attributing to Wittgenstein a form of communal interpretationalism, that is, the view that the external relations between rules and their applications are established by the interpretations of the community. Against Baker and Hacker I showed that the sceptical solution construes the relations between rules and applications as internal.

Lest all these trees block our view of the wood, let me formulate the outcome of this chapter in five brief statements:

- *WRPL* contains a convincing and strong argument against the possibility of private rule-following (or private meaning, or private concept application).
- According to *WRPL*, "rule-follower" (and cognate terms) are social statuses. Someone occupies a social status when a community actually imposes the status on him.
- *WRPL* undermines the intuition according to which private rule-following *must* be possible. Hence one cannot appeal to the intuition without taking on the sceptical argument.
- The community of the sceptical solution is no mythical entity: we encounter the community in the form of other individuals.
- According to the sceptical solution, to apply a rule is not (generally) to act on an interpretation. The relation between rules and their applications is internal.

SEVEN

Semantic primitivism

Introduction

Four of the most influential commentators on *WRPL* – Boghossian, McDowell, Pettit and Wright – have argued that the sceptical challenge can best be met by primitivism about meaning and content. All four philosophers present their proposals as *non-sceptical, straight* responses to the sceptic, and two of them even ally their suggestions explicitly with the sixth of the seven responses discussed and dismissed in Chapter 2 of *WRPL*. At first sight, it might seem surprising for us to investigate these views only now, two chapters after we have left behind other straight responses to the sceptic. The reason for this transposition stems from my interpretation of the sceptical solution as a form of primitivism. This interpretation naturally leads one to ask how meaning-determinist and meaning-sceptical forms of primitivism differ. It will also enable us to see that – contrary to how they present their proposals – at least three of these four philosophers do not in fact defend meaning determinism at all. Once we relate their primitivist views with our reconstructions of meaning determinism and meaning scepticism, we shall realize that they are much closer to the latter than to the former.

Primitivism in meaning determinism

Kripke formulates meaning-determinist semantic primitivism as the following view: "[M]eaning addition by 'plus' is a state even more *sui generis* than we have argued before. Perhaps it is simply a primitive state, not to be assimilated to sensations or headaches or any 'qualitative' states, nor to be assimilated to dispositions, but a state of a unique kind of its own" (*WRPL*: 51). Kripke prefaces his criticism of this proposal with two noteworthy qualifications: that the proposal "may in a sense be irrefutable", and that "if it is taken in an appropriate way Wittgenstein may even accept it" (*WRPL*: 51). Nevertheless, Kripke goes on to brand the suggestion "desperate" and "mysterious". He gives two lines of argument to support this critical assessment. The first argument turns on our knowledge of such a state (*WRPL*: 51). The argument has three premises and a conclusion. Premise 1 is a definition of what makes a mental state primitive. Premises 2 and 3 Kripke simply takes for granted.

Premise 1: A primitive mental state of meaning addition by "+" is a mental state without a qualitative feel.

Premise 2: Only a mental state with a qualitative feel can be introspected by the subject who is in that state.

Premise 3: Knowledge of our mental states must be based on introspection.

Conclusion: A primitive mental state of meaning addition by "+" cannot be known by the subject who is in that state.

It follows further that primitive mental states cannot help against the sceptical challenge. According to the second line of criticism, there is a "logical difficulty" about the idea that there could be "a state of 'meaning addition by "plus"' at all". The problem is that such state would be a finite state of a finite mind. And yet, in order to be the state of meaning addition by "plus", the state would have to determine the results for an infinite number of plus-queries. The advocate of semantic primitivism thus owes us an explanation of how any finite mental state could possibly have this capacity. Put differently, the advocate of semantic primitivism must tell us why this finite mental state is not open to alternative quus-like interpretations. Kripke sums up this second line of criticism with a quotation from Wittgenstein: "Meaning is not a process which accompanies a word. For no process could have the consequences of meaning" (*PI*: 218). To link this quotation more tightly to Kripke's reasoning, we must read "mental process or state" for Wittgenstein's "process", and explain "the consequences of meaning" as "the determination of an infinite number of applications" (*WRPL*: 52–3).

Boghossian raises objections against both arguments.[1] Against the first he insists that it relies on too narrow a conception of introspection. We can have introspection of mental states that lack a qualitative feel.[2] This criticism is clearly on target. Concerning the argument from infinity Boghossian alleges that it violates the rules of engagement of the sceptical argument:

> [It] amounts merely to insisting that we find the idea of a contentful state problematic, without adducing any independent reason why we should. We know that mental states with general contents are states with infinitary normative characters; it is precisely with that observation that the entire discussion began.[3]

Boghossian also gives an indirect argument in favour of semantic primitivism. Allegedly there are four *prima facie* possible answers to the constitutive question concerning meaning: the non-factualism of the sceptical solution, Wright's proposal (to be discussed below), reductionism and semantic primitivism. Boghossian believes himself to have shown that the first three are all untenable. He therefore concludes that primitivism is the only remaining option:

> It is sometimes said that an antireductionist conception is too facile a response to the problem about meaning. It is hard not to sympathize with this sentiment. But if the considerations canvassed against the alternatives are correct, and if it is true that the "rule-following" considerations leave an antireductionist conception untouched, it is hard, ultimately, also to agree with it. Meaning properties appear to be neither eliminable, nor reducible. Perhaps it is time that we learned to live with that fact.[4]

My critical assessment of Boghossian's arguments naturally starts from this last idea. In previous chapters I have argued that the sceptical solution is neither non-factualist nor reductive. I have also sought to show that there are no good meaning-determinist replies to the sceptical challenge. If I am right about all this, then we do not have to swallow the bitter pill of semantic primitivism, at least not as long as it is presented as a way to reform meaning determinism.

It is important to distinguish between meaning-determinist and meaning-sceptical forms of primitivism. Meaning-determinist primitivism is non-reductive about a meaning-determining explanatory fact. Meaning-determinist primitivism assumes that there are facts that fit the intuitive ("low-brow") picture of meaning determinism, and that these very facts cannot be reduced. Put differently, meaning-determinist primitivism holds that there are irreducible mental states that constitute Jones's meaning addition by "+", that these facts are immediately known, private, originating in acts of grasping a meaning, normative, containing and determining future applications, fitting classical realism, and justifiable or analysable by metaphysical considerations. Meaning-sceptical primitivism is the recognition that since there cannot be meaning-determinist truth-conditions for meaning attributions in general, there also cannot be *non-intentional* meaning-determinist truth-conditions for meaning attributions in particular.

With this crucial distinction in mind, we can address the question of whether Kripke is right to dismiss primitivism on the grounds that "it remains mysterious exactly how the existence of *any* finite past state of my mind could entail that, if I wish to accord with it, and remember the state, and do not miscalculate, I must give a determinate answer to an arbitrary large addition problem" (*WRPL*: 53). As we saw above, Boghossian rejects this reply as question-begging. I disagree with this assessment. Of course, Boghossian is right to say that "the entire discussion began" with the assumption of "states with infinitary normative characters".

This view is indeed one of the key initial assumptions of meaning determinism in Chapter 2 of *WRPL* – called "objectivity" in Chapter 1 of this book. And it is true that this view is left untouched for much of the argument. In fact, it is used as a critical weapon against several high-brow forms of meaning determinism. For instance, reductive semantic dispositionalism is rejected precisely because it is unable to capture and preserve the meaning determinist's commitment to such states. Nevertheless, that the sceptic uses "states with infinitary normative characters" as an argument against certain forms of meaning determinism, does not mean that this ingredient of meaning determinism is beyond scrutiny or reproach. The sceptical argument has the structure of an immanent critique: it shows that the different ingredients of meaning determinism do not form a coherent whole, and that the lack of coherence is most visible in high-brow versions of the doctrine. If this picture of the sceptical attack is right, then it is obviously a mistake to think of any particular ingredient of meaning determinism as sacrosanct. Every ingredient is a potential target, and every ingredient can be attacked using the remaining ingredients as a backdrop.

On my reading then, Kripke's argument against meaning-determinist primitivism relies on the supposition that – at least on closer reflection – the meaning determinist himself should find a blanket assumption of objectivity problematic. The important thing to remember about meaning determinism is this. One becomes a meaning determinist by going "beyond or behind" our ordinary ways of speaking about meaning and content, that is, by trying to develop a "picture" (or later, a "theory") that analyses and explains how our meaning attributions can themselves be meaningful. Here meaning determinism is driven on by the sentiment that there is *something puzzling* about meaning and content, *something "queer"* that stands in need of metaphysical clarification and justification (hence metaphysical justification was earlier introduced as a key ingredient). The most important puzzlement of all concerns precisely the relationship between the finite and infinite: how a finite number of examples can represent an infinitary rule (*WRPL*: 7–8); how an infinitary rule can be represented in and by a finite mind (*WRPL*: 22, 54); how an infinitary meaning can be reduced to a finite number of dispositions (*WRPL*: 27); how a finite machine can embody an infinite function (*WRPL*: 34); and how a proof as a finite object can demonstrate something about the "infinitistic part of mathematics" (*WRPL*: 107). Since meaning determinism is puzzled by the relationship between the finite and the infinite in all these cases, how can it rest content with a semantic primitivism that treats objectivity as beyond the need for clarification and justification? Surely, to declare meaning facts irreducible must, from the meaning-determinist point of view, be a "desperate", "mysterious" and indeed "facile" manoeuvre. Note also that at this point we do not have the option of reform: we cannot just drop metaphysical justification from the definition of meaning determinism while leaving the rest unchanged. To take out metaphysical justification would be to take out the key motivation behind the whole position. Once we drop the demand for metaphysical clarifications and justifications of meaning sentences, we in fact abandon meaning determinism's very core. And to do that is to begin moving towards meaning scepticism.

Primitivism and the epistemology of intentions

Wright defends a highly sophisticated version of the "primitive state proposal" as a "straight response" to the sceptical challenge. As Wright sees it, there is nothing mysterious about a *sui generis* state of mind that yields decisions for an infinite number of circumstances: our common-sense concept of intention fits this specification perfectly. Our folk psychology assumes that intentions are irreducible to other mental states and events; that intentions do not have distinctive qualia; and that intentions can cover an infinity of situations.[5] And therefore our intuitive notion of intention can be used to answer the sceptic. Sceptical worries about knowledge of my past intentions can be blocked by insisting on the special way in which intentions can be known.[6]

Wright's starting-point is the observation that the ground rules for the debate between meaning determinist and meaning sceptic are unfair to the former. The meaning determinist is supposed to justify his belief that in the past he meant addition by "+". But the possible forms of justification are severely restricted. The ground rules stipulate that the meaning determinist must be able to point to some non-intentional facts about himself, and then infer from these facts that in the past he meant addition by "+". In other words, it is central to the debate that all content-bearing psychological states have been bracketed. The rationale for this requirement is to avoid circularity: since the very possibility of meaning and content are under dispute, they must not be invoked in an argument intended to demonstrate their possibility. Wright is unhappy with this restriction:

> If the sufficient and adequate ground of my knowledge that *P* is precisely my non-inferential apprehension of the very fact that *P*, then it is to be expected that I may fare badly if in discussion with someone who doubts that *P* I am allowed to proceed only by reference to considerations of a quite different kind, considerations which could in principle at best defeasibly warrant an *inference* that *P*.[7]

Assume I say "Yesterday, I saw it raining". And assume further that I am challenged by a sceptic to provide grounds for my belief. The sceptic insists that I must not invoke any fact that presupposes knowledge of my past perceptions; after all, it is the possibility of such knowledge that is under dispute. This reduces my arsenal of justifications to claims about what seems to me to have been the case, to the testimony of others and to physical traces such as puddles of water. Obviously, the sceptic will have no difficulty accommodating all these facts while still denying that I actually saw it raining. Thus I cannot deduce my past perception of the rain from these circumstances. However, we need not accept the sceptic's demand for inferences. I now know that I perceive the computer screen in front of me, and I do so directly and without inference. My knowledge of this perception is not inferred from knowledge of some other kind. Moreover, whenever a form of knowledge is non-inferential as regards the present, then it also is non-inferential as regards the past. My knowledge of a current perception of my computer screen is not inferred from knowledge of some other kind; and neither is my memory of the rain of yesterday. The sceptic can thus simply be answered by recalling what I formerly perceived.[8]

This line of reasoning can be applied directly to the sceptical argument in Kripke's *Wittgenstein on Rules and Private Language*:

> Kripke's sceptic persuades his victim to search for recalled facts from which the character of his former understanding of [expression] *E* may be *derived*. And that is fair play only if knowledge of a *present* meaning has to be inferential: otherwise the sceptic is satisfactorily answered simply by recalling what one formerly meant. The claim, then, is that the methodology of the Sceptical Argument is appropriate, if ever, only in cases where it is right to view the putative species of knowledge in question as essentially inferential. And no ground for the supposition in the present case has so far been produced.[9]

This is the point where intentions enter into Wright's considerations. Knowledge of my current intentions is not inferential and hence neither is my knowledge of my past intentions. And what is more, intentions and meanings are sufficiently similar for lessons about the former to carry over to the latter. Thus we have an answer to the sceptic: "Since I can know of my present intentions non-inferentially, it is not question-begging to respond to the sceptic's challenge to my knowledge of my past intentions … that I may simply remember them".[10]

Wright recognizes, of course, that specifications of intentions are open to various interpretations. But he insists that it is intentions that determine the specifications, rather than *vice versa*. If I have an intention to do something, then it is this intention that determines what can count as an appropriate specification of it:

> As far as the relation between intention and thought is concerned, it can come to be true of me that I have a certain intention without my engaging in any process of conscious deliberation or thinking any thought which specifies that intention's content. Rather I may simply find myself with my mind made up, as it were – able to give an account of my intentions if asked, but with no story to tell about the when or why of their onset. More important … it is a feature of the intuitive concept of intention that, even when there is an association with a

content-specifying train of thought, the subject does not know of his intention *via* that train of thought.[11]

Despite all that, Wright displays a certain ambivalence about using the intuitive concept of intention as a straight answer to the sceptical challenge. Although he insists that the sceptical argument has no force against this line of reply, he also grants that "it is not particularly *comfortable* to think of your former meaning of 'green' as consisting in your having had a certain general intention, construed along the lines of the intuitive conception".[12] To remove his discomfort, Wright sets out to develop a new theory of intentions.

Wright distinguishes between two ways of making sense of intentions and intention ascriptions. The most salient feature of intention ascriptions is that we grant *self*-ascriptions a special authority. Cases of self-deception aside, we generally assume that people's statements about their intentions are not to be questioned. Why is this? According to the traditional – broadly speaking, Cartesian – answer, the special authority of self-ascriptions of intentions is based on "a kind of cognitive advantage, expertise or achievement".[13] That is to say, the Cartesian assumes that my knowledge of my past and present intentions is based on inner observation of what goes on, or went on, in my mind when forming these intentions. Statements as to which intentions I have formed are therefore descriptive statements. Wright rejects this account. As he sees it, we do not know our intentions on the basis of inner observation or introspection. Our knowledge of our intentions is much more direct and immediate than the model of introspection allows for. Moreover, there is no link between specific phenomenological qualities ("qualia") and specific intentions:

> Whatever took place in *X*'s consciousness at the time he decided to play chess, for instance, that very same phenomenology could have accompanied a decision of a quite different sort. And … there is a case to be made that any actual phenomenology is also not necessary.[14]

Wright therefore introduces a new way of thinking about the special epistemic authority of avowals of intentions. On this account, the special authority is not based on any cognitive advantage. That you do not challenge my self-ascription of an intention is not based on your belief that I have better cognitive access to my inner mental life than you do. Instead it is based on your general conception of me as a rational person. Apart from special circumstances such as self-deception, lack of concepts or lying, we simply assume that a subject has the "right to declare what he intends, what he intended and what satisfies his intentions". And this right amounts to our giving such declarations "a *constitutive* rather than descriptive role".[15] In other words, in the absence of special circumstances, we take it for granted that the sincere avowal of an intention is constitutive of having this intention.

The difference between the Cartesian and the new reading can be made salient also in the following way. Consider the biconditional:

> X intends that P if and only if X is disposed to avow the intention that P, and would be sincere in so doing, and fully grasps the content of that intention, and is prey to no material self-deception, and ... and so on.[16]

The Cartesian gives priority to the left-hand side: that X intends that P is something that X can know and truthfully avow if, and only if, the various provisos are met. X has cognitive access to his intending that P provided only that he is not self-deceived, understands the content and so on. Wright reads the biconditional differently, that is from right to left: X intends that P is true provided X is disposed to avow as much in the absence of interfering factors. On this reading, X's avowal is not based on cognition of a fact, namely, that X has the intention. Instead, the avowal is part of what constitutes the fact in the first place.[17]

Wright regards the non-Cartesian – or, as he also says, "non-detectivist"– reading of the mentioned biconditional as fundamental to the human condition:

> It is part of regarding human beings as persons, rational reflective agents, that we are prepared to ascribe intentional states to them, to try to explain and anticipate their behaviour in terms of the concepts of desire, belief, decision and intention. And it is a fundamental anthropological fact about us that our initiation into the language in which these concepts feature results in the capacity to be moved, who knows exactly how, to self-ascribe states of the relevant sorts – and to do so in ways which not merely tend to accord with the appraisals which others, similarly trained, can make of what we do but which provide in general a far richer and more satisfying framework for the interpretation and anticipation of our behaviour than any at which they could arrive if all such self-ascriptions were discounted. The roots of first-personal authority for the self-ascription of these states reside not in cognitive achievement, based on cognitive privilege, but in the success of the practices informed by this cooperative interpretational scheme.[18]

We might say that this anthropological account explains why the (provisoed) biconditional is *de facto a priori*. But of course it does little to explain why the biconditional is constitutive. Wright therefore offers a second account that is meant to explain the *constitutive* reading of the biconditional. This second account veers towards the metaphysical, although Wright prefers not speak of necessity in this context. This second account tells us a fundamental truth about what intentions are.[19] Intentions are, in part, constituted by the dispositions to avow them under suitable conditions.[20] According to this explanation, the relationship between intention and avowal of intention is like the relationship between being red and looking red. In other words, intentions are like secondary qualities.

Take the following conditional [1]:

[1] Jones intends to φ, if, and only if, in cognitively ideal conditions Jones believes himself to intend to φ.

Restated in formal terms:

[2] (Jones intends to φ) ↔ (C(Jones) → (Jones believes he intends to φ))

What are the conditions under which we can read the biconditional right-to-left, that is, in a way such that Jones's belief about his intention determines what his intention is? According to Wright, four conditions have to be fulfilled. First, [1] (and thus [2]) has to be *a priori* true. Secondly, the cognitively ideal conditions must be *non-trivially specified*: it will not do to insert "whatever it takes" conditions. Thirdly, the cognitively ideal conditions must be *independent*; that is to say, what makes it so that the cognitively ideal conditions are satisfied must be independent from whatever it is that Jones intends. And fourthly, it must not be the case that we have a *better* explanation of why the first three points hold: the best explanation must be that Jones's best opinions about his intentions determine which intentions he has. Wright insists that, lacking evidence to the contrary, we are allowed to regard the cognitively ideal conditions as fulfilled. In other words, we are entitled to assume that such conditions obtain unless we have reason to believe the contrary. In particular, we are entitled to presume that a subject is not self-deceived as long as we have not encountered any evidence to the contrary.[21]

Wright's theory (in both its versions) is meant to be "broadly Communitarian". That is to say, he explicitly acknowledges that self-ascriptions of intentions can be defeated by discordant behaviour. Others are entitled to judge that my stated intention does not fit with my subsequent behaviour:

> [T]he constraint of having to have one's sincere self-ascriptions make sense in the light of one's outward performance in effect supplies the standard of correctness for one's impressions of self-knowledge of meaning ... The proposal reinstates both a standard of correctness for my opinions about what I mean and the authority of those opinions – but in order for it to do so, I need to be considered as an at least potential object of *interpretation*, with my claims about my own meanings essentially defeasible in the light of the shape assumed by my practice.[22]

Wright also tells us that a previously formed future-directed intention is not an independent measuring stick and determinant of subsequent decisions: "what, if any pattern of performance is imposed on a subject by the constraint of compliance with a former intention *is not settled independently of his judgement of the matter*".[23]

Wright thinks that his new theory of intentions provides us with an even better weapon against Kripke's sceptic than the "somewhat flat-footed response" according to which we know our intentions directly rather than on the basis of inferences. The new theory enables us to see why the flat-footed response "can *be* correct".[24] To answer the sceptic, I need not be able to "locate some meaning-constitutive fact in my former behaviour or mental life". It suffices that I currently believe that addition is what I meant in the past and that I can refer to the "a priori reasonableness of the supposition, failing evidence to the contrary, that this opinion is best". This move does not commit us to construing meaning as a species of intention. The argumentative strategy need rest only on the idea that the concepts of meaning and intention are relevantly similar: that "both sustain authoritative first-personal avowals".[25] Kripke's sceptical argument is successful only against theories of meaning and intention that construe these concepts detectively; indeed it provides a *reductio ad absurdum* of such theories.[26] But it is toothless against the new, non-detective, understanding of meaning and intention. The latter theory allows us to speak of facts of meaning and intention: "There are indeed facts about what I mean, contra Kripke's sceptic, and they are constitutively constrained by what I take them to be".[27]

Finally, acknowledging the existence of such facts does not, however, commit us to the view that meaning is "objective". In other words, meaning cannot:

> somehow be constituted, once and for all, either within a community or by a single subject, by finitely many events – explanations, uses, episodes in consciousness – so that thereafter there is only the objective question of *fit* between new uses of the relevant expression and the meanings thereby laid down.[28]

Once we give up a detective construal of intentions, we also lose the resources needed for maintaining and defending the objectivity of meaning.

Turning from a summary of Wright's proposal to its evaluation, my first comment concerns Wright's reasons for moving from the "somewhat flat-footed response" to his new theory of intentions. The move is not as optional as Wright makes it sound. This is because the flat-footed response on its own is inadequate as an answer the sceptical challenge. Once again it is important to remember that the sceptical challenge is not epistemological but constitutive: the ultimate question is not "How do you know that you mean addition by '+'?" but "What makes it so that you mean addition by '+'?" The flat-footed response – "I just know" – may be an adequate answer to an epistemological challenge, but it does not address the constitutive question. In order to address the latter we need to be told why it is that the avowal of an intention or meaning implies, and is implied by, the presence of that intention or meaning itself. The move beyond the flat-footed response is thus obligatory if Wright is to succeed in giving an answer to the meaning sceptic of *WRPL*.[29]

As concerns Wright's theory of intentions, my main quarrel is that I fail to see how it can possibly constitute a *straight* answer to the sceptical challenge and hence a defence of meaning determinism. First, note that Wright sees his account of meaning intentions as incompatible with the so-called "objectivity of meaning". But what is the objectivity of meaning? Is it not precisely one of the most central assumptions of meaning determinism (that is, objectivity)? In rejecting the objectivity of meaning, Wright is rejecting the view that the meaning of an expression can determine in advance (causally as well as normatively) how this expression is to be used. The meaning sceptic can only applaud this move.

Secondly, consider again Wright's two explanatory accounts. One account is pragmatic and anthropological, the other veers towards the metaphysical. Unfortunately, Wright does not tell us how the two accounts relate to one another. The problem is that the modality of the two accounts is rather different, and that the anthropological explanation undercuts a constitutive reading by giving a *naturalistic* explanation of why the biconditional is *de facto a priori*.[30] For present purposes the important point about all this is that the anthropological explanation is fully compatible with Kripke's sceptical solution. After all, it is central to the sceptical solution that philosophical–metaphysical proposals concerning facts of meaning are replaced by anthropological and biological observations concerning forms of life. There are no metaphysical foundations for our language games for attributing meanings and intentions to others and ourselves. We can dig no deeper than to the insight that it is our common biology and our common form of life that enables us to have language and understanding. We simply find ourselves with certain practices, such as the practice to grant each other a special authority in reporting our intentions. We will go astray if we try to ground this practice in some deep philosophical fact about ourselves. There is no deeper fact than that we happen to have this practice and that it fulfils a useful social function.

Thirdly, the parallel between Wright's anthropological account of intentions and the sceptical solution can be seen also in the details. There is, for instance, a strong similarity between Wright's insistence that we typically simply "find our minds made up" as far as our intentions are concerned and Kripke's claim that "ultimately we reach a level where we act without any reason in terms of which we can justify our action. We act unhesitatingly but *blindly*" (*WRPL*: 87). Or consider once more the assertability conditions for self-attributions of meaning:

> *Jones* is entitled, subject to correction by others, provisionally to say, "I mean addition by 'plus'", whenever he has the feeling of confidence – "now I can go on!" – that he can give "correct" responses in new cases; and he can give "correct" responses in new cases; and *he* is entitled, again provisionally and subject to correction by others, to judge

> a new response to be "correct" simply because it is the response he is inclined to give.
>
> (*WRPL*: 90)

Does this not state roughly what Wright insists on, namely, that we grant each other – subject to our corrections – the right to self-ascribe meanings and intentions? Read in this light it seems that Wright's answer to the sceptical challenge is not meaning-determinist at all; in so far as it is a response to the sceptical challenge, it is a meaning-sceptical response. Wright is answering the meaning sceptic on the basis of the meaning sceptic's own sceptical solution.

Fourthly, Wright has obscured this point for himself since he interprets the sceptical solution as a form of projectivism. This – mistaken – interpretation inclines him to think that a response to the sceptic qualifies as "straight" simply in virtue of identifying facts of meaning. Wright writes, "there are indeed facts about what I mean, contra Kripke's sceptic, and they are constitutively constrained by what I take them to be".[31] Alas, it can be shown that the meaning facts of Wright's theory are a far cry from what we need in order to defend the basic tenets of meaning determinism. Recall Wright's previously cited statement according to which "what, if any, pattern of performance is imposed on a subject by the constraint of compliance with a former intention *is not settled independently of his judgement of the matter*".[32] I read this as follows. Assume we have three times: t_{-1} is some point in the past; t_0 is the present moment; and t_{+1} is some point in the future. Assume further that at t_{-1} I formed the future-directed general intention to mean addition by "+". Wright's message concerning this intention is the following. What constraint this intention of time t_{-1} imposes on my manipulations with "+" at t_0 is not settled independently of my judgement of the matter at t_0. This is because my judgement at t_0 enters constitutively into determining what intention I formed at t_{-1}. The answer to the sceptic then would be that my judgements at t_0 – that is, my judgement that I meant addition by "+" in the past, and that I ought to answer "125" to "68 + 57 = ?" – are beyond the reach of sceptical doubts because they are part of what makes it so that I meant and mean addition by "+". (Needless to say, the "makes it so" is here to be taken in a constitutive and not in a causal sense.) This dependence of the content of the past intention on the present judgement conflicts, of course, with the view of intentions held by the meaning determinist.

Moreover, once we allow that later judgements – concerning the constraints on performance imposed by a former intention – enter constitutively into determining the content of that intention, we cannot stop at the present moment; we also have to consider the future. In other words, my judgements and intentions at t_{+1} are every bit as constitutive for what I intended at t_{-1} as are my judgements and intentions at t_0. And thus it becomes altogether unclear where the facts of meaning, or the facts of intention, are supposed to reside. They cannot have obtained at t_{-1} since at t_{-1} the intention and its constraints had not yet been fully constituted. It needs later judgements to constitute the intention as the intention it is. Unfortunately, the same is true for the present moment: although the present moment involves a judgement concerning the pattern demanded by the former intention, it is unlikely to be the last such judgement. Only all past, present and future judgements as a whole can give the past intention a fully determinate content. And perhaps when all such judgements are "in", we can speak of the fact that makes it so that someone has an intention with a given content. Alas, this is not much of a fact. It is a fact that is constantly being made (and perhaps remade) until it loses its role in the deliberations and actions of the agent: the fact is fully here only once the subject stops acting on this intention. It is certainly a far cry from the kind of meaning fact at issue in the sceptical argument. For the fact the meaning determinist is after is a fact that "must, in some sense, show I am justified in giving the answer '125' to '68 + 57 = ?'. The 'directions' … that determine what I should do in each instance, must somehow be 'contained' in any candidate for the fact as to what I meant" (*WRPL*: 11).

To conclude, contrary to Wright's own assessment, his new theory of intentions does not qualify as a straight answer to meaning scepticism, and thus as a defence of meaning determinism. This is – from Wright's point of view – the bad news. Fortunately, there is good news too from the point of view of meaning scepticism: Wright's proposal is best read as complementary to, or part of, the sceptical solution. Wright spells out some of the pragmatic–anthropological underpinnings of our language games of attributing meaning to others and ourselves.

Primitivism and the master thesis

John McDowell believes that the best arguments for primitivism can be found in Wittgenstein's *PI*.[33] At the same time, McDowell holds that *WRPL* is defective both as an interpretation of Wittgenstein and as a philosophical position in its own right.

The key concept in McDowell's discussion of Wittgensteinian primitivism is the "master thesis". This is the assumption that contents of the mind have a normative relationship to the world only under an interpretation; considered in themselves, contents of the mind are things that just "stand there like a sign-post" (*PI*: §85). A signpost considered in itself does not tell me what to do. It tells me what to do only if I first interpret it in some way. For instance, if the signpost contains an arrow, then I might interpret this as an invitation or demand to turn in the direction of the arrow. Other interpretations are, of course, possible.

Consider how the master thesis might affect our account of rule-following. Faced with the challenge to provide an account of how we are able to continue the number series "2, 4, 6, 8, 10, …" we are tempted to reason as follows. We look around for something that can function as a guide to our actions. This guide (or signpost) must be a content of the mind. Now one likely candidate for this role is the verbal formulation of an underlying rule, say "add 2". Unfortunately, at this point we easily fall prey to the sceptical consideration according to which (verbal) signs can always be interpreted in many different ways. On its own, the sign sequence "add 2" cannot tell us what we must do; on its own the sign sequence just "stands there like a sign-post". Put differently, until we impose an interpretation, the mental content remains "normatively inert". For a moment it might seem that our problem is solved: once we have the (correct) interpretation for "add 2", we can sort number sequences into those that follow the rule correctly and those that do not. Alas, the moment of satisfaction will last only as long as we fail to ask what it is to have a correct interpretation of something. But obviously this further question cannot be avoided. Under the influence of the master thesis, we will again start looking for a mental content; we will again be noting the need for its (correct) interpretation ... and so on. In other words, adherence to the master thesis pushes us into an infinite regress.[34]

According to McDowell, Kripke's *WRPL* is right to adopt and exploit Wittgenstein's attack on the master thesis: "Kripke gives a gripping exposition of this threatened regress of interpretations, and it is beyond question that the regress is one of the ingredients for a proper understanding of Wittgenstein's point".[35] As McDowell sees it, Kripke's crucial mistake lies not in the way he presents the regress argument, but in the conclusion he draws from it:

> Kripke's reading goes beyond identifying the threat and giving it vivid expression. On Kripke's account, Wittgenstein rescues the idea of understanding by abandoning the idea that someone's grasping a meaning is *a fact* about her. According to Kripke's Wittgenstein, as soon as we look for a fact about a person that is what her grasping a meaning consists in, we are doomed to have any appearance that what we pick might be the right sort of fact – specifically that it might have the right sort of normative links with her behaviour – crumble before our eyes under the impact of the regress of interpretations. So we should conclude that there can be no such fact.[36]

In other words, on McDowell's reconstruction, Kripke takes Wittgenstein to present us with the following binary choice. The first option is to defend, and give substance to, the master thesis. If we succeed in this endeavour then we have identified facts of meaning and understanding. We thereby earn the right to say that "Jones means addition by '+'" is made true and meaningful by a fact about Jones, namely, the fact that he has a specific mental content with the correct interpretation. The second option, and indeed the only alternative to the first, is a radical form of non-factualism: meaning attributions are ways "to record acceptance of individuals into the linguistic community".[37] Kripke shows that the first option is a chimera, that there is no way to make good on the master thesis. And thus follows the sceptical conclusion ("all language is meaningless"). Finally, since the first option fails, the second one has to be accepted. Projectivism remains as the only alternative. McDowell rejects the binary choice and the plausibility of non-factualism. To begin with the latter, he simply denies that projectivism can alleviate the sceptical conclusion ("that all language is meaningless"): "It is quite obscure how we could hope to claw ourselves back by manipulating the notion of accredited membership in a linguistic community".[38]

The binary choice offered by Kripke's Wittgenstein is equally mistaken, McDowell suggests. The real Wittgenstein offers a three-way rather than a two-way choice: "there are three positions in play: the two horns of the dilemma, and the community-oriented conception of meaning that enables us to decline the choice".[39] The first horn is indeed the regress of interpretations (as resulting from the master thesis). This horn is summed up in *PI*:

> This was our paradox: no course of action could be determined by a rule, because every course of action can be made out to accord with the rule. The answer was: if everything can be made out to accord with the rule, then it can also be made out to conflict with it. And so there would be neither accord nor conflict here.   (*PI*: §201)

The second horn is not – as (allegedly) Kripke would have it – a form of non-factualism but an unsatisfactory response to the difficulties of the master thesis. According to this response, the way to stop the regress of interpretations is to make meaning "the last interpretation": "Every sign is capable of interpretation; but the *meaning* mustn't be capable of interpretation. It is the last interpretation."[40] The problem with this proposal is that it allows for interpretations of signs but not for interpretations of meaning. It thereby pictures, McDowell suggests, "following a rule as the operation of a super-rigid yet (or perhaps we should say 'hence') ethereal machine".[41] This leaves as the only contender what McDowell calls "the community-oriented conception of meaning that enables us to decline the choice". McDowell finds this view in the second paragraph of *PI* §201: "there is a way of grasping a rule which is *not* an *interpretation*, but which is exhibited in what we call 'obeying the rule' and 'going against it' in actual cases". McDowell's main misgiving about *WRPL* is that the latter "makes nothing of Wittgenstein's concern to reject the assimilation of understanding to interpretation".[42] Once we recognize the third position we can see that there is a way of rejecting the master thesis *and* holding on to factualism, both at the same time.

In further elaborating on this third position, McDowell stresses the role of training, customs, practices and institutions in Wittgenstein. These concepts come together, for instance:

> "Then can whatever I do be brought into accord with the rule?" Let me ask this: what has the expression of a rule – say a sign-post – got to do with my actions? What sort of connexion is there here? – Well, perhaps this one: I have been trained to react to this sign in a particular way, and now I do so react to it.

> "But that is only to give a causal connexion: to tell how it has come about that we go by the sign-post; not what this going-by-the-sign really consists in." – On the contrary; I have further indicated that a person goes by a sign-post only in so far as there exists a regular use of sign-posts, a custom. (PI: §198)[43]

The alternative to the master thesis is centred around phenomena of training and acting blindly, in an unreflective manner. This alternative must be taken aright. Wittgenstein is not proposing a reduction of meaning and understanding to non-intentional and hence norm-free behaviour. If he did he would be involved in dismissing our ordinary conception of meaning, rules and understanding as an illusion.[44] This is where the reference to customs becomes crucial. We are creatures who understand what it is to act in accordance with meanings or signposts. Telling us that going-by-the-sign is a custom is meant to remind us of our natural ability to be sensitive to normative considerations.[45] In other places Wittgenstein refers to practices and institutions to make closely related points. For instancem we are told that obeying a rule is a "practice" (PI: §202); and elsewhere we learn that "A game, language or rule is an institution".[46] Practices and institutions function like customs: in each case we find responses and reactions that are not mediated by interpretations, and yet in each case we also find space for normativity. The idea that interpretation is not central to our ability to follow rules is also expressed in the formula "When I obey a rule, I do not choose. I obey rules *blindly*" (PI: §219) and in the passage about "bedrock":

> "How am I able to obey a rule?" – if this is not a question about causes, then it is about the justification for my following the rule in the way I do.
> If I have exhausted the justifications I have reached bedrock, and my spade is turned. Then I am inclined to say: "This is simply what I do."
> (PI: §217)

McDowell finds the same theme in Wittgenstein's "repeated insistence that the agreement that is necessary for the notion of following a rule to be applicable is not agreement in opinions":[47]

> "So you are saying that human agreement decides what is true and what is false?" – It is what human beings *say* that is true and false; and they agree in the *language* they use. That is not agreement in opinions but in form of life. (PI: §241)

McDowell writes that "it cannot be denied that the insistence on publicity in Kripke's reading corresponds broadly with a Wittgensteinian thought".[48] But

McDowell denies that Kripke has understood the role of such publicity in Wittgenstein: publicity is part and parcel of a non-sceptical factual understanding of meaning. It is not an element in a projectivist sceptical solution.

McDowell's Wittgenstein is then a factualist and a defender of our intuitive notion of objectivity ("idea of things being thus and so anyway, whether or not we choose to investigate the matter in question, and whatever the outcome of any such investigation"[49]). However, Wittgenstein does not grant our concepts the sort of "platonistic autonomy" according to which "possessing a concept is grasping a pattern of application that extends *of itself* to new cases".[50] It is this conception that is the main target of Wittgenstein's reflections on rules and meaning. McDowell warns of the dangers of taking Wittgenstein's criticism too far. First, the recoil from "platonistic autonomy" provides no licence for rejecting "the truth-conditional conception of meaning, properly understood". To properly understand this conception is to recognize that truth-conditions:

> are necessarily given by us, in a language that we understand. When we say "'Diamonds are hard' is true if and only if diamonds are hard", we are just as much involved on the right-hand side as the reflections on rule-following tell us we are. There is a standing temptation to miss this obvious truth, and to suppose that the right-hand side somehow presents us with a possible fact, pictured as an unconceptualised configuration of things in themselves.[51]

And, secondly, the recoil from platonistic autonomy must not reject "various ideas that are simply part of the idea of meaning's normative reach". Central among these ideas is the notion that "standards of correctness embodied in a grasped meaning are, as Crispin Wright puts it, ratification-independent". Given an instruction to extend a numerical series, ratification-independence is the thesis according to which the meaning of this instruction "determines what is correct at any point in the series in advance of anyone's working out the series to that point, so that the meaning yields a standard of correctness for what any calculator or group of calculators does or might do".[52]

Finally, McDowell urges us to take seriously Wittgenstein's "no theses thesis": "If one tried to advance *theses* in philosophy, it would never be possible to debate them, because everyone would agree to them" (*PI*: §128).[53] One does not take this "quietism"[54] seriously, if one attributes to Wittgenstein a reductive theory of meaning and intentionality. Any such attribution flies in the face of Wittgenstein's insistence that "[w]hat has to be accepted, the given, is – so one could say – forms of life" (*PI*: 192), or that "[c]ommanding, questioning, recounting, chatting, are as much part of our natural history as walking, eating, drinking, playing" (*PI*: §25). As McDowell reads the "no theses" view of philosophy, it amounts to a "diagnostic deconstruction" of reductivism. This is especially clear in a passage where McDowell contrasts two different ways of bringing the notion of custom to bear on the question of rule-following. "A constructive philosophical account" would accept customs as part of the explanation of rule-following only if customs were "characterisable in terms that do not presuppose meaning and understanding".[55] In contrast, Wittgenstein's "point is to remind us" that custom is a "natural phenomenon ... [and] already shaped by meaning and understanding".[56] Ultimately, Wittgenstein's goal is not to answer questions such as "How is meaning or intentionality possible?". Wittgenstein's interest is rather to free us of assumptions like the master thesis, assumptions that make these questions look pressing:

> Given a satisfying diagnosis, the inclination should evaporate, and the questions should simply fall away. There is no need to concoct substantial philosophical answers to them. The right response to "How is meaning possible?" or "How is intentionality possible?" is to uncover the way of thinking that makes it seem difficult to accommodate meaning and intentionality in our picture of how things are and to lay bare how uncompulsory it is to think in that way.[57]

McDowell's discussion, summarized above, is intriguing not least because he challenges *WRPL* both as an interpretation of Wittgenstein and as a plausible position in its own right. I shall begin with some comments on McDowell's interpretation of *WRPL* and then move on to investigate the possibility that McDowell's Wittgenstein offers us a novel and unassailable form of meaning determinism: meaning determinism without the master thesis.

There can be no doubt that something like the master thesis figures centrally in Kripke's book. After all, grasping as interpretation is a central ingredient of the intuitive picture of meaning determinism, and interpretation talk is prominent throughout Chapter 2 of *WRPL*. For instance:

> The sceptic claims (or feigns to claim) that I am now misinterpreting my own previous usage. (*WRPL*: 9)

> [I]f "plus" is explained in terms of "counting", a non-standard interpretation of the latter will yield a non-standard interpretation of the former. (*WRPL*: 16)

> It might be urged that the quus function is ruled out as an interpretation of "+" because it fails to satisfy some of the laws I accept for "+" (*WRPL*: 16)

> I am expounding Wittgenstein's well-known remarks about "a rule for interpreting a rule". (*WRPL*: 17)

How can I justify my present application of such a rule, when a sceptic could easily interpret it so as to yield any of an indefinite number of other results? (*WRPL*: 17)

Did I think explicitly of the Eiffel Tower when I first "grasped the concept of" a table, gave myself directions for what I meant by "table"? And even if I did think of the Tower, cannot any directions I gave myself mentioning it be reinterpreted compatibly with the sceptic's hypothesis? (*WRPL*: 19)

[T]he sceptic argues, in essence, that I am free to give any new answer to an addition problem, since I can always interpret my previous intentions appropriately. (*WRPL*: 32)

Can we conceive of a finite state which *could* not be interpreted in a quus-like way? (*WRPL*: 52)

Platonic objects may be self-interpreting, or rather, they may need no interpretation; but ultimately there must be some mental entity involved that raises the sceptical problem. (*WRPL*: 54)

The sceptical argument, then, remains unanswered. There can be no such thing as meaning anything by any word. Each new application we make is a leap in the dark; any present intention could be interpreted so as to accord with anything we may choose to do. So there can be neither accord, nor conflict. This is what Wittgenstein said in §202. (*WRPL*: 55)

[N]o matter what is in my mind at a given time, I am free in the future to interpret it in different ways. (*WRPL*: 107)

Except for the last two, these quotations are from sections where the meaning sceptic attacks the "use response", the "algorithm response", the "qualia response", "semantic primitivism" and "Platonism". In all these cases, the meaning sceptic counters the proposal with the observation that the proposed items (past behaviours, formulae, qualia, intentions and Fregean ideas) can be interpreted in many different ways. In all these cases Kripke does indeed work with the regress of interpretations. Note, however, that the same is not true in the case of reductive dispositionalism. It seems as though the dispositionalist is, in a way, doing precisely what McDowell's Wittgenstein urges us to do: get rid of any mental items that just "stand there like sign-posts". Moreover, the arguments that Kripke marshals against dispositionalism on Wittgenstein's behalf – the normativity considerations, the finitude objection, the mistake objection – do not make use of the regress of interpretations. Given the central place of dispositionalism in Chapter 2 of *WRPL* this should make us cautious about McDowell's reading of the book. Certainly McDowell's central claim according to which Kripke has us choose between the master thesis and non-factualism cannot be correct in the unqualified form in which McDowell presents it.

If my interpretation in the previous chapters is even roughly on target, then other elements of McDowell's rendering of the argument of *WRPL* must also be mistaken. The most important of such elements is the role of factualism in the sceptical solution. McDowell reads the sceptical solution as a form of projectivism (only); I have suggested that it is compatible with a minimal form of factualism. Furthermore, there is also reason to doubt McDowell's claim according to which Kripke fails to recognize Wittgenstein's crucial third option: a primitivism about meaning and rules that is centred around the ideas of training, acting blindly, agreement, custom, practice and institution. It is certainly true that Kripke does not make training a central issue; nevertheless he tells us that "almost all of us, after sufficient training, respond with roughly the same procedures to concrete addition problems" (*WRPL*: 96), and that "[w]hat it seems may be unintelligible to us is how an intelligent creature could get the very training we have for the addition function, and yet grasp the appropriate function in a quus-like way" (*WRPL*: 98, n.78). The importance of training for McDowell's Wittgenstein derives from the fact that training usually leads us to act blindly, without further reflection or interpretation. Now *this* idea is clearly very much present in the sceptical solution. Here are some telling passages:

> Even the very first section of the *Investigations* can be read, with hindsight, as anticipating the problem. ... See: "But how does he know where and how he is to look up the word 'red' and what he is to do with the word 'five'? – Well, I assume that he *acts* as I described. Explanations come to an end somewhere." (§1) In hindsight, this is a statement of the basic point that I follow rules "blindly", without any justification for the choice I make. The suggestion in the section that nothing is wrong with this situation, provided that my use of "five", "red", etc. fits into a proper system of activities in the community, anticipates Wittgenstein's sceptical solution ...   (*WRPL*: 81)

In this passage we find not only the idea of "acting blindly" but also the further insistence that blind action *qua* rule-following is part of a communal custom or practice. Kripke develops the same idea in greater detail six pages later. He first emphasizes the importance of acting blindly: "The entire point of the sceptical argument is that ultimately we reach a level where we act without any reason in terms of which we can justify our action. We act unhesitatingly but *blindly*" (*WRPL*: 87). Subsequently Kripke goes on to remind us that there must be more to rule-following than acting blindly; there must be more for there to be normativity, for there to be a distinction between "is right" and "seems right". And this distinction plays a role when we assess the performances of others who are engaged in more or less ordinary practices (such as going to the grocer). No regress threatens here, since our assessments of others are ultimately "unhesitating but blind" as well (*WRPL*: 90–91).

In light of this textual evidence I am puzzled by the fact that McDowell cites the second paragraph of *PI* §201 as telling against Kripke. McDowell suggests that Kripke overlooks Wittgenstein's insistence that "there is way of grasping a rule which is *not* an *interpretation*, but which is exhibited in what we call 'obeying the rule' and 'going against it' in actual cases" (*PI*: §201). Does not the sceptical solution try to elucidate precisely our normative practice of assessing instances of rule-following – and without making any assumptions about the interpretable mental states of either the rule-follower or the rule-attributor?

A final crucial issue on which Kripke's and McDowell's Wittgensteins are much closer than McDowell allows for is the "no theses" view of philosophy. McDowell's Wittgenstein's opposition to "constructive philosophical accounts" is really an opposition to, and "diagnostic deconstruction" of, all forms of reductivism. Kripke's Wittgenstein would obviously sympathize. His only proviso would be that reductivism is not the only candidate for "diagnostic deconstruction". Semantic and intentional reductivism is a natural upshot of meaning determinism, and unless we cure ourselves of the latter, we can never be sure that we are free of the inclination to be tempted by the former.

My comments above defended Kripke by showing that McDowell exaggerates the distance between them. One might almost say that I have assimilated the two positions to an extent that they almost become indistinguishable. This obviously sits badly with McDowell's claim that his Wittgenstein offers a "straight solution" to the paradox of *PI* §201.[58] Can we read McDowell differently? Can we perhaps read him as proposing an improved version of meaning determinism: meaning determinism without the master thesis?[59] I doubt that this reading can be squared with McDowell's commitments. McDowell's position questions or rejects almost all meaning-determinist assumptions. To begin with, McDowell is committed to downplaying or rejecting the idea that rule-following involves immediate knowledge of a mental state, and he applauds "the insistence on publicity in Kripke's reading". This rules out immediate knowledge, privacy, and an individualistic construal of semantic normativity. While some elements of grasping might survive, the crucial idea of grasping as interpreting must go. And McDowell's "quietism" is incompatible with metaphysical justification, that is, the idea that the justification of our meaning sentences must come from ontological considerations. This leaves objectivity and classical realism. Here the evidence is undeniably mixed. As far as objectivity goes, McDowell seeks to find a middle way between "platonistic autonomy" and "ratification-dependence": a concept is neither a pattern of application that "extends *of itself* to new cases", nor a pattern of application that we create step by step as we proceed. This is weaker than the meaning determinist's objectivity, which seems to be precisely a form of the autonomy thesis. Finally, McDowell does not advocate full-blown classical realism with its inflationary factualism. Note only McDowell's contention that "[w]hen we say '"Diamonds are hard" is true if and only if diamonds are hard', we are just as much involved on the right-hand side as the reflections on rule-following tell us we are".[60]

I am aware that the above comments on the relationship between McDowell and Kripke's Wittgenstein are somewhat inconclusive. To give more substance to my suggestions would involve us in a much more thorough discussion of McDowell's wide-ranging and intricate reflections on Wittgenstein and other matters. This is not the place for such an investigation. Here I will be satisfied if I have shown, first, that McDowell's reading of *WRPL* is deficient in several important respects, and, secondly, that McDowell's Wittgenstein is not obviously proposing a "straight" reply to the sceptical challenge.

Primitivism and the phenomenology of rule-following

Pettit's[61] form of primitivism regarding rule-following and meaning is not – like the other forms reviewed above – based on a direct and detailed critical discussion of *WRPL*. Pettit simply puts forward his proposal as a way of explaining how rule-following is possible.

Pettit's starting-point is what he calls "the phenomenology of rule-following".[62] This phenomenology has four "elements". First, rules are normative constraints on decisions. To follow a rule is to decide in one way – the way demanded by the rule – rather than another. A given normative constraint can become salient in an indefinitely large number of situations. That is to say, the rule-follower usually is not able to specify in advance all the situations in which some given rule will become relevant to his decisions. Some key aspects of the relationship between action and rule can be captured using the concept of a function. A rule can be looked on as a function that takes decision-types as inputs and produces options for action as outputs. Thus, for instance, the rule "Be polite!" takes as inputs types of social situations, and delivers forms of polite behaviour for each such situation as outputs. Thinking of rules in this way allows for a distinction between two notions of a rule: rule-in-extension and rule-in-intension. The rule-in-extension is a set of pairs of situations and behaviours. The rule-in-intension is the abstract object, universal or concept that we take to determine, for each situation, the appropriate behaviour. The second element of the phenomenology of rule-following is that a rule "should be determinable or identifiable by a finite subject independently of any particular application". The rule-follower must be able to identify the rule as something to which she can be faithful in her decisions on how to act. For this to be possible, the rule cannot simply coincide with its applications. Finally, elements three and four are that rules must be "directly" and "fallibly readable": rule-followers must be able to tell straightaway what the rules demand; and agents must be able to fail in their attempts to follow rules. Pettit calls the first element "objective" ("it tells us … what objectively, so to speak, a rule is"), and the other three elements "subjective" ("they tell us what an objective rule must be to engage subjectively with potential followers").[63]

Pettit interprets the meaning scepticism of *WRPL* as the challenge to explain how the objective and the subjective elements of the "phenomenology of rule-following" can be simultaneously satisfied. The meaning sceptic is doubtful that such synthesis is possible. To begin with, it is hard to see how any content of our mind could act as, or produce, an indefinite normative constraint. Contents of our mind are finite, whereas most rules-in-extension are infinitely large sets. Shifting from rules-in-extension to rules-in-intention does not improve the situation. Rules-in-intention are abstract objects, and we lack convincing accounts of how our mind can make contact with such objects. Moreover, the subjective conditions of rule-following cannot support the required objectivity. Qualia can be interpreted in multiple ways. Any given set of examples can always instantiate any number of rules. And semantic dispositionalism fails for familiar reasons: it cannot explain how rules can guide us.[64]

Pettit wishes to propose a "non-sceptical response to the challenge about rules". A response is non-sceptical, he tells us, if it "vindicate[s] the idea that we intentionally try to conform to entities that satisfy the objective condition: constraints that are normative over an indefinite variety of cases".[65] Pettit's starting-point is a new idea on the issue of how a rule can be represented to a learner. The natural answer is, of course, that rules are represented in and through examples of their correct applications. Unfortunately, this response is threatened by the phenomenon of underdetermination: any given set of examples instantiates many different rules. In order to overcome this underdetermination, Pettit distinguishes between "instantiation" and "exemplification". Instantiation is a one-to-many and two-place relation between one set of examples and many rules. Exemplification, however, is a three-place, one-to-one-to-one relation between one series of examples, one rule and one human subject. Given a human subject with her physiological and psychological limitations and abilities, a given series of examples may exemplify just one single rule.[66]

When a human subject is confronted with a set of examples she may well develop an inclination or disposition to extrapolate from this set to new cases. In such cases, the examples can be said to "generate" the inclination or disposition. For instance, on being shown, as examples of *red* things, a British fire-engine, a British post-box and a London bus, we develop the disposition to regard as red also the Communist flag, the torero's *muleta*, tomatoes and strawberries. The disposition to extrapolate from a given set of examples has a "dual function". On the one hand, it prompts the speaker or thinker to regard certain things in the world as red. On the other hand, the disposition "make[s] salient the rule she intends to follow: the rule which, given the inclination they engender, a certain set of examples can exemplify".[67] Once I have developed the mentioned disposition (to classify a British-fire engine, a post-box, a London bus and a tomato as sharing a colour property) I will take my further acts of classifying things as red as "doing the same thing" as my teacher did and "as following the same rule" that my teacher followed. Once I have the disposition in question, I am able to say which rule I am following in calling the newly encountered *muleta* "red": I am following *that* rule – the rule according to which the British fire-engine, the post-box and the London bus are all red. Four things are particularly important here. First, Pettit is not saying that the disposition or inclination is identical with the rule; to do so would be a form of reductivism. Instead he writes that the rule is "*associated ... with* the inclination generated by the examples".[68] Secondly, the rule as picked out by the inclination (in the examples) can now itself become an object of my thoughts: I can decide to follow it, I can follow it intentionally. Thirdly, all this is possible without it being the case that the inclination or disposition itself has to feature in consciousness.[69] And fourthly, Pettit believes that, "under idealisation", inclinations or dispositions can "stretch to an infinite number of instances".[70]

Pettit's final step introduces normativity and the distinction between "seems right" and "is right" into his account. He does so by adding an important proviso to his earlier way of associating inclination and rule: "The rule associated with the inclination will be ... the one that satisfies this inclination, *provided the inclination fires under [certain favourable] conditions ...*".[71] There is a *prima facie* problem with this suggestion. In the previous paragraph I mentioned that inclinations or dispositions need not feature in consciousness. But surely normativity *qua* favourable conditions has to enter consciousness in some way. How can both be true? Pettit's solution is based on the idea of a comparison between different "firings" of the same (type- or token-) inclination. Even when the inclination itself does not feature in my consciousness, I am still able to identify which rule I am intentionally following. And this in turn enables me to consciously pick out intertemporal or interpersonal differences in my following of one and the same rule. If I judge one and the same *muleta* as red and grey in one and the same afternoon, I must be able to say how this is possible: did the *muleta* get sandy, did I misjudge its colour when the torero moved from the sun into the shadow, or did my sunglasses "colour" my perception? These same considerations might also explain why you and I make different judgements about the *muleta*. Rules are normative phenomena since we are "committed to the principle that intertemporal or interpersonal differences in how the inclination ... goes are a sign that perturbing influences are at play".[72] This commitment includes the willingness to explain the differences and to correct some "firings" of our inclinations or manifestations of our dispositions. This analysis elegantly avoids the problem of having to store a fixed set of (un)favourable conditions into our minds. Which conditions are unfavourable is something that human subjects can learn as they compare their inclination-triggered actions over time, and with others.

The following passage nicely sums up Pettit's account and highlights its primitivist credentials:

Rule-following is possible ... under two conditions. The first is that on being presented with certain examples the rule-follower develops an inclination to carry on in a particular fashion, an inclination in virtue of which the examples exemplify a particular rule for the agent. The second condition is that the agent is able to explain any intertemporal or interpersonal discrepancies in spontaneous application by appeal to perturbing factors, so that the rule exemplified – though she will not think of it this way – is the rule which dictates those responses that the corrected or standardized inclination supports, not the inclination neat. This explanation of how rule-following is possible ... nowhere says what rule-following is, reductively characterized. It tells a story about how rule-following might get going; it offers a genealogy of rule-following on a par with Hume's genealogy of causal talk or, more notoriously, Nietzsche's genealogy of morals. But it does not analyse in reductive terms what it means to say that this or that is a rule, that this or that is what it means for a rule to require something, and so on.[73]

Pettit's proposal is meant to defend the common-sense phenomenology of rule-following. But he does so at the price of developing a position with, as he himself admits, *prima facie* "repugnant" corollaries. Pettit lists three. First, on the offered account rule-following is "precarious": my standardized inclination may at any time go awry. No perturbing factors may be in evidence and yet my inclination may leave me with an incoherent set of firings. Secondly, Pettit's proposal is explicitly "interactive". Although Pettit is impressed with Blackburn's and McGinn's arguments in favour of the logical possibility of Crusoe as a rule-follower, he emphasizes the need for others "in practice": "It may be that interaction with oneself across time is in principle enough to underpin the capacity to think [and thus to follow rules] but that interaction with other people is always part of the underpinning that is available in practice".[74] And thirdly, Pettit's account implies a "relativity [of rules] to our species, perhaps even to our culture". Exemplification is a three-place relationship between a set of examples, a rule and *a human subject*. Physiology, culture and history may all have a part in making that subject what it is. And someone who did not share my physiology, culture and history might not be able to hit on a counterpart inclination and thus "would have no capacity to tell what rule I was following or even that I was following a rule".[75]

Is Pettit's proposal a defence of a meaning-determinist form of primitivism? Is it a variant of the sceptical solution? Or is it some other form of revolutionary deviation from meaning determinism? A straightforward answer to these questions is not easy. The three "repugnant" corollaries seem a far cry from meaning determinism. And these revolutionary aspects contradict the way in which Pettit describes the dialectic of *WRPL*, and the position of his proposal within it. Pettit thinks that *WRPL* is an attack on "the phenomenology of rule-following". And he presents his own proposal as a "non-sceptical" answer. "Non-sceptical" presumably means "straight" (cf. *WRPL*: 66), and "straight" solutions fall within the meaning-determinist spectrum.

In order to get greater clarity here it will be useful to begin by challenging Pettit's reading of the target of *WRPL*. The target of Kripke's Wittgenstein is not the phenomenology of rule-following (as laid out by Pettit) but various versions of meaning determinism. And meaning determinism is not identical with this phenomenology. There is more to meaning determinism than the assumptions that rules (and meanings) are normative constraints, that they are identifiable independently of particular application, and that they are readable directly and fallibly. Indeed, the phenomenology of rule-following is such a weak set of assumptions that they are even compatible with, and acceptable by, the sceptical solution. It is not that meaning determinism accepts, and meaning scepticism rejects, the phenomenology of meaning and rules. Meaning determinism and meaning scepticism are two different proposals for clarifying and explaining this phenomenology. As the argument of *WRPL* unfolds, and as meaning determinism is put to the test, it turns out that meaning determinism is unable to deliver the goods: it is unable to offer a coherent explanation for the phenomenology. Enter the sceptical solution. It throws out meaning determinism alright, but just as it preserves our everyday use of meaning sentences, it also retains the phenomenology. (It is questionable anyway, to what degree talk and phenomenology are separable.)

In the same vein, Pettit's characterization of what is meant by a "non-sceptical response" also must be scrutinized. Such a response, he tells us, "has to vindicate the idea that we intentionally try to conform to entities that satisfy the objective condition".[76] It does not seem obvious to me that the sceptical solution denies the possibility of such vindication. Obviously, within the sceptical solution "intentional trying" and "conforming" receive descriptions that differ from those originally envisaged at the beginning of the book. To cut a longer (already told) story short, the meaning-sceptical account sees the prospective rule-follower as trying (at least sometimes) to fall into step with the established practice of his community, and as willing or obliged to justify her doings when challenged. This is what "intentional trying" and "conforming" *really* amounts to.

These issues of interpretation are not without systematic interest. If my comments are roughly right then there is good reason to suspect that Pettit's proposal may well be closer to the sceptical solution than he allows for. In order to give substance to this suspicion, it pays to compare his proposal with meaning determinism and the sceptical solution, respectively. The first thing to remember here is that Pettit's account is non-reductive. This already distinguishes it from most high-brow versions of meaning determinism. The distance increases yet further as we focus on the specific ingredients of the meaning-determinist picture. According to immediate knowledge, to be a rule-follower, Jones must have immediate and certain knowledge of his rule-constituting mental state. This is a much stronger demand than Pettit's constraint according to which a rule must be "directly readable". Immediate knowledge involves a form of introspective knowledge; Pettit's constraint does not. Pettit's proposal also denies privacy and semantic normativity. To be a rule-follower is, for Pettit, to stand in certain normative relations to others: previous or future selves, and other people. It is true that Pettit does not go so far as to say that a rule-following Crusoe is logically impossible. (Some of my criticisms of Blackburn and McGinn in Chapter 6 also apply to Pettit.) Nevertheless, Pettit goes far enough towards intersubjective normativity to leave a yawning gap between himself and the meaning determinist. At first sight it might seem as if there was more of a convergence in the case of grasping, especially the meaning-determinist idea that to grasp a rule is tantamount to forming intentions regarding a possibly infinite number of applications. Does not Pettit likewise insist that to grasp a rule is to follow it intentionally? The similarity in formulations belies, of course, a fundamental difference in outlook. The meaning determinist equates following a rule with having a system of intentions. That is to say, the meaning determinist reduces rule-following to intentions. Pettit does no such thing; he is a primitivist even within the circle of intentional concepts. Rules are the targets of intentions, but rules and intentions are different kinds of entities.

Things are slightly more complex regarding objectivity and classical realism. Pettit obviously does not accept the idea of a mental state that contains and determines "in a queer way" all future applications of a rule. Again, his invocation of rules as "normative constraints which are relevant in an indefinitely large number of decision-types"[77] is a weaker demand. In the same vein we need to register that two of Pettit's three "repugnant corollaries" weaken objectivity: if rule-following is precarious and relative (to culture and physiology) then rules cannot contain all of their future applications. All this is not to say that Pettit does not remain close to some elements of meaning determinism here. As we saw above, Pettit believes that, "under idealisation", inclinations or dispositions can "stretch to an infinite number of instances".[78] Here Pettit leans on Fodor's arguments in defence of semantic idealization. I have argued in Chapter 3 that Fodor's arguments are not convincing.

But does Pettit not offer at least a factualist account of rule-following? And does this not distinguish him from the sceptical solution? As we have seen in Chapter 5, when it comes to factualism we need to tread carefully: there are more forms of factualism than are dreamt of in standard interpretations and criticisms of *WRPL*. The sceptical solution is happy with a deflationary factualism, but opposed to the inflationary factualism of classical realism. Moreover, Pettit reformulates the issue of rule-following in such a way that the central debate over facts of meaning is, to some degree at least, suppressed: "He [Kripke] tends to ask after what fact about a person could constitute his following a rule whereas I shall ask after what sort of thing could constitute a rule that the person might follow".[79] Pettit also tells us that to explain "in familiar psychological terms how rule-following is possible" is not "to identify it reductively with any independent psychological fact".[80] Finally, we must not forget that even if there were more than minimal meaning or rule-following facts for Pettit, these are of a somewhat unusual kind: Jones meaning addition by "+" would be a fact that involves many of Jones's time-slices; a fact about Jones's willingness and commitment to compare his calculations with others; and a fact that is relative to one's nature and nurture. These are not the sorts of meaning and rule-following facts that would warm the heart of a meaning determinist.

In light of the above it cannot be maintained that Pettit's proposal is a defence of meaning-determinist primitivism. Unfortunately, Pettit's discussion of *WRPL* is too short for us to go further and decide between the two remaining options: a revolutionary alternative to the sceptical solution on the one hand, or a variant or complement of it on the other hand. Clearly Pettit's own genealogy for his proposal – "Hume's genealogy of causal talk or, more notoriously, Nietzsche's genealogy of morals"[81] – indicates that the distance to the sceptical solution may be short. It is equally obvious that further development of the details of the sceptical solution could only profit from trying to absorb the lessons of Pettit's ideas on exemplification, favourable conditions and intersubjective comparison.

Conclusion

I began the current chapter trying to explain how Kripke can make two different – *prima facie* even contradictory – claims about semantic primitivism. On the one hand, Kripke writes that if primitivism is "taken in an appropriate way Wittgenstein may even accept it" (*WRPL*: 51). On the other hand, Kripke suggests that Wittgenstein regards primitivism as "desperate" and "mysterious" (*ibid.*). I suggested that both statements make sense once we distinguish between two forms of semantic primitivism: a meaning-determinist form and a meaning-sceptical form. Meaning-determinist primitivism is non-reductive about the facts that fit the intuitive (lowbrow) picture of meaning determinism; that is, it is non-reductive about facts that satisfy the conditions of immediate knowledge, privacy, grasping, semantic normativity, objectivity, classical realism and metaphysical justification. Meaning-sceptical primitivism is the recognition that since there cannot be meaning-determinist truth-conditions for meaning attributions in general, there also cannot be *nonintentional* meaning-determinist truth-conditions for meaning attributions in particular. Kripke's Wittgenstein accepts meaning-sceptical primitivism, but he rejects meaning-determinist primitivism as desperate and mysterious.

Is Kripke's criticism of meaning-determinist primitivism justified? Boghossian offers a negative answer. He claims that Kripke's criticism is based on an illegitimate challenge to the idea that there are "states with infinitary normative characters". I suggested that Boghossian's argument fails to help the meaning determinist. The meaning determinist himself expresses his puzzlement about infinity in many places. And thus the meaning determinist cannot treat infinitary normative character as a primitive phenomenon.

The critical discussions by Boghossian, McDowell, Pettit and Wright are among the most influential commentaries on Kripke's text. They are impressive both as concerns their critical scrutiny of the text and as concerns the originality of their alternative suggestions. Interestingly enough, all four authors advocate versions of semantic primitivism *as direct or straight responses to the sceptical challenge*. As I have reconstructed *WRPL*, direct or straight responses to the sceptical challenge are – by definition – meaning-determinist responses. Do we have to conclude then that meaning determinism wins after all, albeit (only) in a primitivist guise?

In the main body of this chapter I have tried to justify a negative answer to this question. My strategy was twofold. On the one hand I have sought to show that all four authors misinterpret key elements of the sceptical solution. On the other hand I have undertaken to make it plausible that McDowell's, Pettit's and Wright's respective versions of semantic primitivism are in fact closer to meaning scepticism than to meaning determinism.

Wright's theory of meaning and intention rejects too many elements of the meaning-determinist picture for it to qualify as a mere revision or reform of that doctrine. Like Kripke's Wittgenstein, Wright replaces immediate knowledge with confidence, privacy with intersubjectivity, grasping with primitiveness, and objectivity with finiteness. And at least as far as Wright's anthropological explanation of the biconditional is concerned, he even opens the door to functional justifications. All this suggests to me that Wright's proposal is largely consistent with the sceptical solution.

McDowell's quietism meets a similar fate. McDowell misinterprets *WRPL* as offering us just two options: adopt the master thesis or side with non-factualism. This rendering of *WRPL* works only if one ignores the sorts of passages that I quoted above. Questions of misinterpretation aside, it is intriguing to note that – on my interpretation of both positions – McDowell's Wittgenstein and Kripke's Wittgenstein are friends. Both clearly and unequivocally reject immediate knowledge (in favour of confidence), privacy (in favour of intersubjectivity) and grasping (in favour of primitiveness). As regards semantic normativity, objectivity, classical realism and metaphysical justification it is not altogether clear whether McDowell's Wittgenstein accepts the meaning-sceptical successor ideas of intersubjective normativity, finiteness, assertability and functional justification. But there is no doubt that he throws out the meaning-determinist assumptions that the latter are meant to replace.

Finally, Pettit's allegedly non-sceptical response also turned out not to be less "non-sceptical" than Pettit thinks. His proposal neither defends nor presupposes any of the seven key ingredients of meaning determinism. What is more, Pettit's theory leaves no obvious space for them, at least as long as these ingredients are not heavily reformed. And thus it should come as no surprise that the sceptical solution can easily absorb and integrate Pettit's valuable insights into exemplification, favourable conditions and intersubjective comparison.

To conclude with a more minimalist summary, the sceptical solution is a form of semantic primitivism. Critics who have presented semantic primitivism as a straight solution to the sceptical challenge have misconstrued both the overall dialectic and the nature of their own alternatives. The sceptical argument rejects semantic primitivism only when it is presented as a form of meaning determinism. And hence the real merit of the four primitivist proposals discussed here is not that they rescue meaning determinism; their real value lies in the fact that they complement and confirm the sceptical solution.

EIGHT

Kripke's interpretation of Wittgenstein

Introduction

In previous chapters I have sought to interpret and defend the meaning-sceptical position that Kripke attributes to Wittgenstein. In doing so, I have, for the most part, left aside the question of whether Kripke's reading of Wittgenstein is correct. In this chapter, I shall finally address this issue. I shall argue that Kripke's interpretation of the sections on rule-following in *PI* and the *Remarks on the Foundations of Mathematics* is, by and large, on target. I shall make my case by taking on the most important of the opposite views: Baker and Hacker's 1984 book, *Scepticism, Rules and Language* (*SRL*). The detail and influence of Baker and Hacker's study should not come as a surprise: after all, who would be more qualified to assess the correctness of an interpretation of *PI* than the authors of a four-volume analytic commentary on that very work![1] Given the central position of Baker and Hacker's critique in the debate over *WRPL*, it seems defensible to confine the discussion of the interpretational issue mainly to a critical assessment of their objections.

Baker and Hacker's negative assessment of *WRPL* as an interpretation of Wittgenstein has become widely accepted. For instance, the leading Wittgenstein scholars Cora Diamond and Meredith Williams write that "the Baker–Hacker case against Kripke is entirely convincing",[2] and that Baker and Hacker have rightly "won the day".[3] Only rarely has "the Baker–Hacker case" been challenged. Jane Heal finds *SRL* "unpleasant and unrewarding",[4] and Edward Craig agrees: "Right or wrong, Kripke's book put the debate about rules on a high level of content and clarity. Regretfully, I can only conclude that Baker and Hacker have lowered it again".[5] My view falls somewhere between these two extremes: while the two critics have succeeded in pointing out some inaccuracies and mistakes in Kripke's text, the main core of Kripke's interpretation survives undamaged. What is more, in some cases Baker and Hacker's own work, especially their analytical commentary on *PI*, offers ideas and background information that can be used to strengthen Kripke's case. This too makes a careful study of Baker and Hacker's work imperative and rewarding.

Objection 1: Wittgenstein and scepticism

Baker and Hacker object to Kripke's characterization of Wittgenstein as a sceptic and as a common-sense philosopher (*SRL*: 4–5). As they see it, calling Wittgenstein a sceptic conflicts with the fact that Wittgenstein throughout his life regarded scepticism as nonsense.[6] The following two quotations come from the early and the late Wittgenstein, respectively:

> Scepticism is *not* irrefutable, but *obvious nonsense* if it tries to doubt where no question can be asked. For doubt can only exist where a question exists; a question can exist only where an answer exists, and this can only exist where something *can* be *said*.[7]

> The queer thing is that even though I find it quite correct for someone to say "Rubbish!" and so brush aside the attempt to confuse him with doubts at bedrock, – nevertheless, I hold it to be incorrect if he seeks to defend himself (using, e.g., the words "I know").[8]

Labelling Wittgenstein a "common-sense philosopher" makes things worse, Baker and Hacker maintain. In *WRPL* the two characterizations are connected: Wittgenstein-the-sceptic attacks philosophical doctrines in order to defend the beliefs of common sense. Baker and Hacker demur: Wittgenstein is not interested in the defence of any opinions, and thus, *a forteriori*, not occupied with an attempt to rehabilitate common-sense opinions. Wittgenstein writes: "On all questions we discuss I have no opinion; and if I had, and it disagreed with one of our opinions, I would at once give it up for the sake of argument, because it would be of no importance to our discussion".[9] Baker and Hacker insist that Wittgenstein tries to identify and remove the sources of philosophical puzzles. These puzzles arise from the misuse of ordinary concepts. Wittgenstein is not committed to the existence of an ordinary common-sense viewpoint on meaning, a viewpoint that allegedly will come to the fore once philosophical confusions have been removed.

In response to objection 1, we can note first of all that Kripke himself acknowledges that Wittgenstein would refuse the label "sceptic":

> Wittgenstein never avows, and almost surely would not avow, the label "sceptic" … Indeed, he has often appeared to be a "common-sense" philosopher, anxious to defend our ordinary conceptions and dissolve

traditional philosophical doubts. Is it not Wittgenstein who held that philosophy only states what everyone admits? (*WRPL*: 63)

As Kripke sees it, Wittgenstein would refuse the label "sceptic" in so far as it suggests a *general* attack on our beliefs about meaning and intention. But Wittgenstein's attack is not general but specific. The target of Wittgenstein's critical doubts are specific philosophical misconceptions of everyday expressions (*WRPL*: 66). At the same time, and as the above quotation makes clear enough, Kripke does move Wittgenstein into the proximity of common-sense philosophy. Objection 1 is right to find this move problematic. It seems to imply that Wittgenstein assumes the existence of a body of beliefs – namely common-sense beliefs – that give us the correct account of meaning. Scepticism about philosophical doctrines is then merely the way to unveil this correct view. At times Kripke comes close to presenting Wittgenstein in this light. For instance, in the context of a comparison between Berkeley and Wittgenstein, Kripke writes about the former:

> For him, the impression that the common man is committed to matter and to objects outside the mind derives from an erroneous metaphysical interpretation of common talk. When the common man speaks of an "external material object" he does not really mean (as we might say *sotto voce*) an *external material object* but rather he means something like "an idea produced in me independently of my will". (*WRPL*: 64)

As Kripke reads Berkeley, the common-sense view is the correct position, and it needs to be freed from philosophical misconceptions. Kripke attributes a similar stance to Wittgenstein:

> Wittgenstein makes a Berkeleyan claim of this kind. For … his solution to his own sceptical problem begins by agreeing with the sceptics that there is no "superlative fact" [*PI*: §192] … about my mind that constitutes my meaning addition by "plus" … But, he claims … [*PI*: §§183–93], the appearance that our ordinary concept of meaning demands such a fact is based on a philosophical misconstrual …
> (*WRPL*: 65)

Kripke backs up his interpretation with Wittgenstein's famous dictum that "we are, like savages, primitive people, who hear the expressions of civilised men, put a false interpretation on them, and then draw the queerest conclusions from it" (*PI*: §194; *WRPL*: 66).

Let us concede to objection 1 then that Kripke – in the above passages – errs in characterizing Wittgenstein as a common-sense philosopher. Kripke ought not to have presented Wittgenstein as seeking to uncover what the "common man" believes; Kripke should have confined Wittgenstein's aim to the unveiling of philosophical misconstruals of ordinary concepts.[10] How damaging is this concession to objection 1? In my view, it is not very damaging. Although Kripke lapses in the passages where he compares Berkeley and Wittgenstein, his overall presentation of the sceptical challenge and the sceptical solution is not premised on the idea of common-sense philosophy. For instance, nowhere does Kripke suggest that the sceptical solution, with its emphasis on assertability conditions and the community, is a common-sense idea. The sceptical solution is a description of things we always already do, not a description of things we always already mean or believe.

Turning from common sense back to the issue of scepticism, more can be said on the discrepancy between Kripke's "Wittgenstein-the-sceptic" and Baker and Hacker's "Wittgenstein-the-anti-sceptic". I believe that the discrepancy largely disappears once we recall that scepticism can be either epistemological or ontological. When philosophers talk of scepticism, it is invariably epistemological scepticism that they have in mind. This is certainly true of Wittgenstein. Consider for instance the two quotations that objection 1 presents as evidence of Wittgenstein's anti-sceptical stance. The first passage is from a notebook entry of 1 May 1915, and later became §6.51 of the *Tractatus*. The passage was a direct reply to Bertrand Russell's Humean view, according to which epistemological scepticism is "practically barren" although "logically irrefutable".[11] The second passage, entered into a notebook in 1951, is from *On Certainty*. *On Certainty* is an extended discussion of G. E. Moore's common-sense reply to the epistemological sceptic about the external world. In *On Certainty* Wittgenstein uses a form of epistemological contextualism in order to dismiss the sceptic. According to Wittgenstein's contextualism, radical epistemological scepticism invokes error possibilities that do not make sense within our existing language games. Whenever Wittgenstein denounces scepticism he is rejecting *epistemological* scepticism. The scepticism that Kripke attributes to Wittgenstein, however, is *constitutive* or *ontological*. Kripke's Wittgenstein is sceptical about the existence of meaning-determining facts, not about the idea of justification or knowledge regarding such facts. It is astonishing to note that Kripke's critics have exercised so little charity at this point; that is, that they have not noted the two senses of scepticism in play here. I am not alone in suspecting that at least in the case of Baker and Hacker the lack of charity is due to a misunderstanding of Kripke's position. Baker and Hacker simply fail to see the constitutive-ontological character of the scepticism invoked in *WRPL*.

Finally, recall that on the interpretation offered in this book the overall argument of *WRPL* is diagnostic. That is to say, rather than being a defence of blanket scepticism, *WRPL* tries to show that scepticism is unavoidable only *given a meaning-determinist understanding of rules and meaning*. The sceptical solution is sceptical in so far, and only in so far, as it preserves this negative point about meaning determinism. The sceptical solution is not sceptical about our ordinary talk of meaning in everyday life; in fact, it provides this talk with a new form of justification.

Objection 2: Wittgenstein's patient

Baker and Hacker believe that Kripke misconstrues the problem that occupies Wittgenstein in the rule-following considerations (*SRL*: 27).[12] Whereas Wittgenstein investigates how a rule determines its applications, Kripke asks how my past intentions regarding the use of "+" relate to my current intentions regarding that same use. Kripke's question is really rather foreign to Wittgenstein: "we just do not find Wittgenstein fretting over the question whether my present inclinations to apply a sign really conform with my past meaning".[13]

I am not convinced. I believe it can be shown that Wittgenstein's "patient" is pretty close to meaning determinism. Let me explain. Chapter 2 of *WRPL* is naturally treated as a dialogue between the meaning sceptic and the meaning determinist. *PI* can also be looked on as a dialogue. Picking up on a familiar Wittgensteinian idea, we might label the two characters "the patient" and "the therapist". The patient holds and defends certain general philosophical views. These views change under the argumentative pressure exerted by the therapist. Now, the best way to address the question of whether the key problem of *WRPL* is sufficiently similar to the central concerns of (parts of) *PI* is to ask how Wittgenstein's patient compares with Kripkenstein's meaning-determinist interlocutor. I believe that the two figures are fairly close to each other, close enough for Kripke's interpretation to be judged adequate. In order to see this, consider the following central pronouncements of the patient in the rule-following considerations:

> 139. What really comes before our mind when we *understand* a word ... [is] something like a picture ...
> 146. The understanding itself is a state which is the *source* of the correct use.
> 147. "... In my own case at all events I surely know that I mean such-and-such a series; it doesn't matter how far I have actually developed it."
> 152. ... "He understands" must have more in it than: the formula occurs to him. And equally, more than any of those more or less characteristic *accompaniments* or manifestations of understanding.
> 153. ... the mental process of understanding ... seems to be hidden behind those coarser and therefore more readily visible accompaniments.
> 154. ... I employ the sentence "Now I understand ..." or "Now I can go on" as a description of a process occurring behind or side by side with that of saying the formula ...
> 184. I want to remember a tune and it escapes me; suddenly I say "Now I know it" and I sing it. What was it like to suddenly know it? ... "It's a particular feeling, as if it were *there*" ...
> 186. ... "The right step is the one that accords with the order – as it was

meant." – … [When I gave him the order + 2 …] "… what I meant was, that he should write the next but one number after *every* number that he wrote; and from this all those propositions follow in turn."
188. [The] act of meaning the order had in its own way already traversed all those steps … And it seemed as if they were in some *unique* way predetermined, anticipated—as only the act of meaning can anticipate reality.
191. "It is as if we could grasp the whole use of the word in a flash."
…
194. … the possible movements of a machine are already there in it in some mysterious way …
195. "But I don't mean that what I do now (in grasping a sense) determines the future use *causally* and as a matter of experience, but that is a *queer* way, the use itself is in some sense present."
197. "It's as if we could grasp the whole use of a word in a flash." …
198. "But how can a rule shew me what I have to do at *this* point? Whatever I do is, on some interpretation, in accord with the rule." …
205. "But it is just the queer thing about *intention*, about the mental process, that the existence of a custom, of a technique, is not necessary to it." …
209. "But then doesn't our understanding reach beyond all the examples?"
210. "But do you really explain to the other person what you yourself understand? Don't you get him to *guess* the essential thing? You give him examples, – but he has to guess their drift, to guess your intention." …
213. "But this initial segment of a series obviously admitted of various interpretations (e.g. by means of algebraic expressions) and so you must first have chosen *one* such interpretation." – … it must have been intuition that removed this doubt …
218. … the beginning of a series is a visible section of rails invisibly laid to infinity …
219. … The rule, once stamped with a particular meaning, traces the lines along which it is to be followed through the whole of space. …
238. The rule … produce[s] all its consequences in advance …

These statements characterize a viewpoint that is very close to the position of the meaning determinist. First of all, the patient analyses meaning, rule-following and understanding in terms of intentions (§§186, 210), and mental states more generally (§§139, 146, 152, 153, 154, 205, 210). Secondly, the patient adheres to privacy in conceiving of understanding-constituting mental states as independent of social contexts, customs and techniques (§§147, 205). Thirdly, the patient holds immediate knowledge: mental states that constitute meaning and understanding are directly accessible and immediately known (§§147, 184). Grasping of a meaning or rule appears in a number of its expression: as cause (§146), as intending (§§205, 210), as extrapolating (§§191, 209, 210) and as interpreting (§§198, 213). Fourthly, the patient believes that acts of meaning and understanding a rule determine how the rule *ought* to be applied. In other words, the patient is committed to semantic normativity (§§146, 186, 238). Objectivity surfaces in many places, culminating in the idea that meaning determines application "in a *queer* way" (§§184, 186, 188, 191, 195, 209, 218, 219, 238). Classical realism and metaphysical justification are not mentioned in these passages most closely associated with the rule-following considerations, although the former is at least alluded to in §154. Classical realism and metaphysical justification are themes that – as Kripke documents (*WRPL*: 72-086) – surface throughout *PI*.

It is true, of course: Wittgenstein does not couch the problem in precisely the sceptical way Kripke does; we do not find the exact Kripkean sceptical challenge in *PI*. But this much deviation seems tolerable enough: after all, Kripke is offering us an *interpretation* of the original text, not a repetition or paraphrase. In any case, the adequacy of Kripke's interpretation should be judged on other grounds. The question should be whether the *targets* of Wittgenstein's therapist and Kripke's sceptic are sufficiently similar. And this question clearly demands a positive answer. The patient is a meaning determinist, and hence he must accept the sceptical challenge. To ask, as Kripke's Wittgenstein does, how my past intentions regarding the use of "+" relate to my current intentions is not to change the topic; it is to pick up on facets of the position of Wittgenstein's patient. Indeed it is to follow the patient's suggestions on how to approach the question of how a rule determines its application.

A similar reply can be given to the worry that "we just do not find Wittgenstein fretting over the question whether my present inclinations to apply a sign really conform with my past meaning".[14] The worry is misplaced. Wittgenstein's patient *is* fretting over the question of whether the learner's inclinations fit with the teacher's meaning (§186). And, from the perspective of the meaning-determinist patient, the teacher–learner relation is similar to the relation between past and present selves.

Objection 3: facts and superfacts

Kripke writes: "Wittgenstein holds, with the sceptic, that there is no fact as to whether I mean plus or quus" (*WRPL*: 70). Baker and Hacker claim that *PI* §187 disproves Kripke's claim:

> 187. "But I already knew, at the time when I gave the order, that he ought to write 1002 after 1000." – Certainly; and you can also say you

meant it then; only you should not let yourself be misled by the grammar of the words "know" and "mean".

Baker and Hacker interpret this exchange as follows. The voice in quotation marks (the "patient") insists that there is a fact of the matter as to whether he meant the student to write 1002 after 1000. Wittgenstein agrees. He agrees because he does not wish to deny what we all accept. Wittgenstein rejects philosophical theses, not the certainties of everyday life. And it is a certainty of everyday life that there is a fact that determines what I mean.

Baker and Hacker also summarize other of Wittgenstein's pronouncements concerning facts that they hold to be incompatible with Kripke's interpretation. First, for Wittgenstein facts are neither spatial nor temporal; hence facts are not part of the world. ("It is a fact that Oxford is in England, but that fact is not anywhere"). Secondly, Wittgenstein has no difficulties accepting that what makes a proposition *that p* true is the fact *that p*. For Wittgenstein this link between *p is true* and *it is a fact that p* is a grammatical convention. Thirdly, Wittgenstein opposes philosophical misunderstandings of such grammatical statements. The most important misunderstanding in the present case is to read the statement as a metaphysical profundity. Such a reading misinterprets facts as worldly items and then puzzles over the question how the structure of a fact fits with the structure of a thought or proposition (*SRL*: 9–10, 30–33).

Objection 3 reminds us of Wittgenstein's distinction between expressions as they are used in everyday life, and expressions as they are reinterpreted, or misinterpreted, by certain philosophical positions. (Recall once more: "When we do philosophy, we are like savages, primitive people, who hear the expressions of civilised men, put a false interpretation on them, and then draw the queerest conclusions from it" (*PI*: §194)) In this light, it is not surprising that Wittgenstein accepts the legitimacy of such statements as "But I already knew, at the time when I gave the order, that he ought to write 1002 after 1000". Nor does he question the propriety of adding a phrase such as "it is a fact that" to "I already knew …". What Wittgenstein objects to are certain philosophical renderings of the phrase "I already knew" and "it is a fact that I already knew". The phrase "I already knew" must not be interpreted as describing an act of knowing or understanding that has somehow traversed the whole sequence of numbers in advance. And the expression "it is a fact that I already know" must not be taken to add any metaphysical baggage to my knowing.

All this is fine as far as it goes; the question is whether Kripke's Wittgenstein sees things differently. And to this the answer must be "no". Kripke too refers to the distinction between the harmless everyday talk and the temptation to misinterpret this talk in the light of philosophical "superfacts":

> [Wittgenstein's] solution to his own sceptical problem begins by agreeing with the sceptics that there is no "superlative fact" (§192) about my mind that constitutes my meaning addition by "plus" and

determines in advance what I should do to accord with this meaning. But, he claims (in §§183–93), the appearance that our ordinary
concept of meaning demands such a fact is based on a philosophical
misconstrual – albeit a natural one – of such ordinary expressions as
"he meant such-and-such", "the steps are determined by the formula",
and the like.   (*WRPL*: 66)

We do not wish to doubt or deny that when people speak of themselves and others as meaning something by their words, as following
rules, they do so with perfect right. We do not even wish to deny the
propriety of an ordinary use of the phrase "the fact that Jones meant
addition by such-and-such a symbol", and indeed such expressions
do have perfectly ordinary uses. We merely wish to deny the existence of the "superlative fact" that philosophers misleadingly attach to
such ordinary forms of words, not the propriety of the forms of words
themselves.   (*WRPL*: 69)

At least in these passages Kripke takes considerable care to distinguish "superlative facts" (to be rejected) and ordinary "fact-talk" (to be accepted). At the same
time, it has to be conceded that Kripke is not always as clear and careful as he is
here, but then again a charitable interpretation of a text should be based on the
passages where the author expresses himself *modo stricto*, not the passages where
he is speaking loosely. In our case that means that statements such as "Wittgenstein holds, with the sceptic, that there is no fact as to whether I mean plus or
quus" (*WRPL*: 70) should be glossed by replacing the simple and unqualified
"fact" with the more specific "fact as construed by the meaning-determinist".

Finally, there is no reason to believe that Kripke would have any difficulties
with the ideas that for Wittgenstein facts are neither spatial nor temporal; that
for Wittgenstein a proposition *p* is made true by the fact *that p*; and that for Wittgenstein there is a grammatical link between *p is true* and *it is a fact that p*. As we
have seen in Chapter 5, Kripke's Wittgenstein has no quarrel with the notion of a
fact or with the minimal conception of truth-conditions.

Objection 4: the link between *PI* §198 and §201

Baker and Hacker have a number of objections regarding Kripke interpretation of
PI §§198–203. The first such objection concerns §201, especially its link to §198
(*SRL*: 16–21).[15] Here are the two key sections:

198. "But how can a rule shew me what I have to do at *this* point?
Whatever I do is, on some interpretation, in accord with the rule."

– That is not what we ought to say, but rather: any interpretation still hangs in the air along with what it interprets, and cannot give it any support. Interpretations by themselves do not determine meaning.

"Then can whatever I do be brought into accord with the rule?" – Let me ask this: what has the expression of a rule – say a sign-post – got to do with my actions? What sort of connexion is there here? – Well, perhaps this one: I have been trained to react to this sign in a particular way, and now I do so react to it.

But that is only to give a causal connexion; to tell how it has come about that we now go by the sign-post; not what this going-by-the-sign really consists in. On the contrary; I have further indicated that a person goes by a sign-post only in so far as there exists a regular use of sign-posts, a custom.

201. This was our paradox: no course of action could be determined by a rule, because any course of action can be made out to accord with the rule. The answer was: if *any* action can be made out to accord with the rule, then it can also be made out to conflict with it. And so there would be neither accord nor conflict here.

It can be seen that there is a misunderstanding here from the mere fact that in the course of our argument we give one interpretation after another; as if each one contented us at least for a moment, until we thought of yet another standing behind it. What this shews is that there is a way of grasping a rule which is *not* an *interpretation*, but which is exhibited in what we call "obeying the rule" and "going against it" in actual cases.

Hence there is an inclination to say: any action according to the rule is an interpretation. But we ought to restrict the term "interpretation" to the substitution of one expression of the rule for another.

Kripke reads §201 as presenting the sceptical paradox. As Baker and Hacker see it, this interpretation is wrong and in fact contradicted by the text. Wittgenstein has already presented the problem of multiple interpretations in §198 and without any reference to paradox. Even more importantly, Wittgenstein immediately offers a solution: to follow a rule is not to interpret a rule-formulation or instruction, it is to master a technique or custom. The same solution is also offered in §201. Thus, contrary to what Kripke alleges, Wittgenstein *does* offer an account of what understanding a rule consists in. To understand a rule is to master a technique and to participate in a custom.

It has to be admitted that Wittgenstein does not structure his therapeutic investigation in the precise way in which Kripke presents the dialectic between sceptic and meaning determinist. In *PI* the therapy for meaning determinism is not laid out on the model of a sceptical *reductio*: sceptical challenge; one-by-one criticism of attempts to give straight answers to the challenge; formulation of the sceptical paradox; and, finally, sceptical solution, or dissolution, of assumptions that made the sceptical challenge impossible to fend off. This discrepancy does not, however, tell decisively against Kripke. After all, Kripke's book is a "rational reconstruction" of Wittgenstein's text; it is an attempt to highlight one important strand in the complex web of ideas that make up *PI* (and the *Remarks on the Foundations of Mathematics*). The question to ask, therefore, is this: can we find in Wittgenstein the strand of ideas that Kripke chooses to emphasize?

There can be no doubt that Wittgenstein's patient himself recognizes that his position commits him to the sceptical possibility of a regress of interpretations. This much is clear from §198 and in §201. We also find similar scenarios elsewhere in Wittgenstein's discussion of rule-following. In *PI* §213 the therapist creates sceptical puzzles about intuition; and in §113 of Part I of the *Remarks on the Foundations of Mathematics* sceptical concerns are directed against logical inference:

> 213. "But this initial segment of a series obviously admitted of various interpretations (e.g. by means of algebraic expressions) and so you must first have chosen *one* such interpretation." – Not at all. A doubt was possible in certain circumstances. But this is not to say that I did doubt, or even could doubt. ...
>
> So it must have been intuition that removed this doubt? – If intuition is an inner voice – how do I know *how* I am to obey it? And how do I know that it doesn't mislead me? For if it can guide me right, it can also guide me wrong.
>
> ((Intuition an unnecessary shuffle.))   (*PI*)

> 113. "But am I not compelled, then, to go the way I do in a chain of inferences?" – Compelled? After all I can presumably go as I choose! – "But if you want to remain in accord with the rules you *must* go this way." – Not at all, I call *this* "accord". –"Then you have changed the meaning of the word 'accord', or the meaning of the rule." – No; – who says what "change" and "remaining the same" mean here?
>
> However many rules you give me – I give a rule which justifies *my* employment of our rules.
>
> (*Remarks on the Foundations of Mathematics*)

This much at least seems undeniable: Wittgenstein is willing to attack philosophical viewpoints by pointing out that they are unable to answer or deflect sceptical puzzles and paradoxes.

In challenging Kripke's interpretation, most objectors put their emphasis on a denial that Wittgenstein (or his therapeutic voice) accepts the sceptical paradox. It is true that in Wittgenstein's own text the sceptical paradox is put forward only by the patient: note the quotation marks around the relevant questions and assertions in §198. The sceptical paradox is a problem only for a certain mistaken view of rule-following, and it is not of interest outside the therapeutic sessions. But of course we must not forget that exactly the same is true in Kripke's rendering of Wittgenstein! Kripke says explicitly that the sceptical paradox is an issue only within a specific "framework":

> The sceptical paradox is the fundamental problem of *Philosophical Investigations*. If Wittgenstein is right, we cannot begin to solve it if we remain in the grip of the natural presupposition that meaningful declarative sentences must purport to correspond to facts; if this is our framework, we can only conclude that sentences attributing meaning and intention are themselves meaningless. ... (*WRPL*: 79)

Outside this specific framework, the sceptical paradox dissolves. And so does the claim of a fundamental difference between Wittgenstein and Kripkenstein concerning the question who accepts the sceptical paradox.

Finally, as I have already argued in Chapter 7 (against McDowell), Kripke does not overlook that custom and technique provide a solution to the sceptical paradox; indeed, custom and technique figure centrally in the sceptical solution itself.

Objection 5: *PI* §199, individualists versus communitarians

Wittgenstein writes, "To obey a rule, to make a report, to give an order, to play a game of chess, are *customs* (uses, institutions)" (*PI*: §199). Kripke reads this sentence as an endorsement of a communal account of rule-following. Baker and Hacker protest. For them Wittgenstein's "customs", "uses" and "institutions" can be the "customs", "uses" and "institutions" of a single and isolated individual (*SRL*: 16–21).[16] In other words, according to our two critics, §199 does not say that rule-following involves groups; §199 merely says that for something to be a rule it must be applicable more than once.

At this point we come face to face with one of the most important divides in Wittgenstein scholarship. One camp of interpreters, the "individualists", read §199 as presenting the "multiple application conception" of rule-following. The other camp, the "communitarians", take §199 to state a communal account of rule-following. Who is right? Individualists make much of the fact that "customs", "uses" and "institutions" can all be attributed to isolated individuals. This is true. But communitarians have a decisive response.[17] They can refer to the original German sentence – "*Einer Regel folgen, eine Mitteilung machen, einen Befehl geben, eine Schachpartie spielen sind* Gepflogenheiten (*Gebräuche, Institutionen*)" – and rest their case on the meaning of "*Gepflogenheiten*", "*Gebräuche*" and *"Institutionen"*. Let us take a closer look at these words. (I am here focusing on current usage. A cursory study of some older German literature suggests to me that this usage has not changed over the past hundred years.)

"Gepflogenheit" can be translated, depending on context, as "custom", "habit", "manner", "convention", "practice", "usage" or "tradition". The word is used more often in the plural than in the singular. In its – by far – most frequent use, the word refers to ways things are traditionally done in some group. The following news headlines represent this usage well:[18]

> *Europäische Gepflogenheiten in Prager Gaststätten?* [European customs in Prague restaurants?]
> *Rituale und Traditionen, oder: Klassische Gepflogenheiten* [Rituals and traditions, or: classical manners]
> *Besucher aus dem Ausland: Geschäftliche Gepflogenheiten beachten* [Visitors from abroad: paying attention to business customs]
> *Vor Urlaub: Gepflogenheiten des Landes studieren* [Before the vacation: studying the customs of the country]

It is possible to speak of the *"Gepflogenheiten"* of an individual, for example, *"Er hat so seine Gepflogenheiten* [he has his own customs]". However, the group-oriented use of the term is many times more frequent. (In over a thousand appearances of the term on internet web-pages, more than 99 per cent referred to the customs of a group.)

Turning from *"Gepflogenheit"* to *"Gebrauch"*, it seems almost a mistranslation to render Wittgenstein's *"Gebräuche"* as "uses". *"Gebrauch"* (in the singular) does indeed mean *use* or *usage*. But the plural form *"Gebräuche"* has become lexicalized in its own right and no longer does duty as the plural form of *"Gebrauch"*. Thus the hammer (singular) has its *"Gebrauch"*, but hammer and saw do not have their *"Gebräuche"*. *"Gebräuche"* are traditional ways and customs: typical expressions are *"einheimische Gebräuche* [local customs]", *"fremde Gebräuche* [foreign, unfamiliar customs]", or *"urtümliche Gebräuche* [native customs]". *"Gebräuche"* are always the customs of a group. Native speakers of German hear *"Er hat so seine Gebräuche"* as ungrammatical or metaphorical.

Finally, let us look at *"Institution"*. Here the situation is less complicated since the German word behaves just like the English. Institutions are always "of a group". It is possible to say "the institution is me", but this is clearly metaphorical (cf. Frederick the Great's *"L'état c'est moi"*). Institutions involve many people.

There is no reason to doubt that Wittgenstein used *"Gepflogenheiten"*, *"Gebräuche"* or *"Institutionen"* like other German native speakers do. For instance, in §337 of *PI* he speaks of the *"menschlichen Gepflogenheiten und Institutionen"* in which intentions are embedded. His example is the game of chess: surely a tradition and institution that involves many people and generations. Moreover, in a striking passage of the *Blue Book*, Wittgenstein brings the concept of institution into contact with "meaning". For present purposes we need only recognize that his understanding of institution is in step with ordinary language; institutions involve many people:

> "Meaning" is one of the words of which one may say that they have odd jobs in our language. It is these words which cause most philosophical troubles. Imagine some institution: most of its members have certain regular functions, functions which can easily be described, say, in the statutes of the institution. There are, on the other hand, some members who are employed for odd jobs, which nevertheless may be extremely important. – What causes most trouble in philosophy is that we are tempted to describe the use of important "odd-job" words as though they were words with regular functions.[19]

Two further striking uses of "institution" can be found in the *Remarks on the Foundations of Mathematics*. The first concerns the "*Urmeter*" in Paris and the comparison between the institutions of measuring and proving:

> III – §36 If I were to see the standard metre in Paris, but were not acquainted with the institution of measuring and its connexion with the standard metre – could I say, that I was acquainted with the concept of the standard metre?
> Is a proof not also part of an institution in this way?

And the second striking passage tells us that:

> VI – §32 A game, a language, a rule is an institution.

In light of the above, it seems wrong to read this last statement as anything else but the claim that rule-following is a social phenomenon.

Objection 6: *PI* §202 and practices

Objection 6 concerns §202: "And hence also 'obeying a rule' is a practice. And to *think* one is obeying a rule is not to obey a rule. Hence it is not possible to obey a rule 'privately': otherwise thinking one was obeying a rule would be the same thing as obeying it". Kripke claims that "Wittgenstein rejects 'private language' as early as §202" (*WRPL*: 79). Baker and Hacker contest this interpretation (*SRL*: 16–21). For them, the key idea of §202 is expressed in its first sentence: "And hence also 'obeying a rule' is a practice". Baker and Hacker insist that "practice" here contrasts with "interpretation" or "theory". In other words, Wittgenstein's claim in §202 is not that obeying a rule is matter of social rather than individual practice; his claim is that obeying a rule is a matter of *doing* rather than a matter of *interpreting*. For evidence of this understanding of "practice", Baker and Hacker point to §51 and §197. The two critics also have a way of dealing with the second and third sentence of §202: these sentences are merely an anticipation of the key idea of the private language argument, in particular of §258.

Baker and Hacker's evidence for reading "practice" as "practice-rather-than-interpretation" is unconvincing. Take §197:

> [W]hat kind of super-strong connexion exists between the act of intending and the thing intended? – Where is the connexion effected between the sense of the expression "Let's play a game of chess" and all the rules of the game? – Well, in the list of rules of the game, in the teaching of it, in the day-to-day practice of playing [*in der täglichen Praxis des Spielens*].

What is this practice? Two things are important here. On the one hand, the qualifying expression "day-to-day" (*täglich*) suggests a recurring phenomenon with a history; it invites a reading of "day-to-day practice" as "social custom" or "tradition".[20] On the other hand, note that Wittgenstein later returns to the very same idea in §337. Again he talks about the way in which intentions are embedded, and the example is chess. But now the social dimension is made totally explicit: "An intention is embedded in its situation, in human customs and institutions [*menschliche Gepflogenheiten und Institutionen*]". Setting §337 alongside §197 supports a social rendering of "practice" in §197.

Baker and Hacker's second example is §51. It builds on §48, in which the following sign system had been introduced: "R" corresponds to red squares, "B" to black squares, "G" to green squares and "W" to white squares. Complexes of squares can be captured by stringing these signs together in the obvious way:

> §51. In describing language game (48) I said that the words "R", "B", etc. corresponded to the colours of the squares. But what does this correspondence consist in; in what sense can one say that certain colours of squares correspond to these signs? For the account in (48) merely sets up a connexion between those signs and certain words of our language (the names of colours). – Well, it was presupposed that the use of the signs in the language-game would be taught in a different way, in particular by pointing to paradigms. Very well; what does it mean to say that in the *Praxis der Sprache* certain elements correspond to the signs? – Is it that the person who is describing the complexes of coloured squares always says "R" where there is a red square, "B" when there is a black one, and so on? But what if he goes wrong in the description and mistakenly says "R" where he sees a black square

– what is the criterion by which this is a *mistake*? – Or does "R'" s standing for a red square consist in this, that when the people whose language it is use the sign "R" a red square always comes before their minds?   (*PI*: §51)

Anscombe translates "*Praxis der Sprache*" as "technique of using the language" but for obvious reasons I have left the German original untranslated. Again, it is hard to see why "*Praxis der Sprache*" should be understood as "practice rather than theory of language". In the context of §51 no theory has been introduced that could be contrasted with the "*Praxis der Sprache*". The most obvious contrast for "*Praxis der Sprache*" is the teaching mentioned in the previous sentence. Wittgenstein asks us to consider not just how a language is taught but to move on and consider language in its everyday appearance where it is spoken by the "people whose language it is". This suggests not language *qua* doing but language as a social institution.

Objection 7: the history behind *PI* §§201–2

This objection builds on Baker and Hacker's detailed knowledge of the textual history of *PI* (*SRL*: 10–16). According to Kripke's interpretation, §§201–2 form the heart of the rule-following considerations, and thereby the core of the "real" private language argument. Indeed, according to *WRPL*, §§201–2 are the centre of *PI* as a whole. Section 201 states the sceptical paradox, and §202 presents the "community solution" (as *SRL* calls it). Baker and Hacker object that Kripke's claim is difficult to square with the history of *PI*. Between 1938 and 1946 the text went through several typescript stages, dated 1938, 1942–3, January 1945 and 1945–6 (the final version). Although the third version, the "intermediate version", contained both the rule-following considerations and the private language argument, it did not include what in the final version became §§201–2. If §§201–2 really were the centrepieces of *PI*, then one would expect them to have figured prominently throughout the different versions.

As if this was not bad enough, Baker and Hacker point out that §§201–2 appear in an earlier manuscript in an altogether different context. For instance, in manuscript 129 (written from August 1944 onwards), these sections are situated in a discussion of how I judge that something before me is red; this discussion later became *PI* §§377–81. According to the view under attack in these sections, my judgement that "this object before me is red" is based on the following process. I recognize that my visual impression of this object is of a certain kind, and I follow the rule of calling visual impressions of this kind "red". Wittgenstein attacks this view using previously established results: that rules can be interpreted in endless ways and that private definitions and rules are impossible. In manuscript 129 the sections that later become *PI* §§201–2 serve exactly this function. "Proto-section" 201 reminds the reader of proto-section 198 (on the importance of technique and custom), and proto-section 202 recalls the central lesson of what is traditionally called the private language argument (*PI*: §§243–315).

Baker and Hacker believe that the history of §§201–2 shows that these sections have little to do with scepticism or a community solution to rule-following. So far from pre-empting the real private language argument, these paragraphs presuppose it. Accordingly, we need to be careful in how we read §202 in particular. Rather than read it as a community solution, we must read it as an anticipation of what is to come:

> The remainder of §202 [i.e. what comes after the first sentence], is, in this context, incongruous. For Wittgenstein has not yet explained what following a rule "privately" means. The passage derives from MS 129, p. 121, where it occurs after the exposition of the private language argument ... There the allusion to ["following a rule 'privately'"] is perspicuously a *back-reference* to the private language argument. By transposition, this remark has become, perhaps inadvertently, an anticipation of §258 ... of the private language argument.   (*SRL*: 21)

Baker and Hacker's historical-textual remarks are undoubtedly interesting, but do they deal a decisive blow against *WRPL*? Baker and Hacker think not:

> Perhaps, after composing the Intermediate Version, Wittgenstein suddenly realized that these two manuscript remarks, embedded in a discussion of knowing that this is red, concerned with dissolving confusions about recognition, in fact contained in crystallized form the core of his book.   (*SRL*: 16)

Expanding on this admission, we might say that perhaps Wittgenstein came to realize – and perhaps not even quite so suddenly – that the two sections could be separated from the argument about recognition and in fact be given a more central role. After all, as Baker and Hacker themselves document beautifully and meticulously in their four-volume commentary on *PI*,[21] Wittgenstein frequently moved his sections from one context to another. And we know from the man himself why he did so: "I often copy my previously made philosophical remarks at the wrong place: where they do not *work*! They must be moved *there* where they do their full work!".[22] Wittgenstein eventually came to see that §§201–2 do their "full work" after §§198 and 199, and not in the context of knowing that something is red. Does not interpretational charity demand that we find a reading of the text that does justice to this idea of doing "full work"? Baker and Hacker fail by this criterion. Since they are unable to make sense of the bulk of §202 in the context of §§198–9, they are forced to declare that much of §202 is "incongruous" and "inadvertent". I am not alone in believing that an interpretation of an author fails if it ends up having to pass such verdicts on his text.[23]

There is an alternative to Baker and Hacker. We only need to accept that the German wording of §199 must be read as stating that rule-following is a social phenomenon. We then have the option of understanding §202 in the light of §199 and of making sense of the "privately" in §202. We would even then be in a position to comprehend why, in his previous versions of *PI*, Wittgenstein felt able to do without §§201 and 202. After all, whereas §198 clearly states both the sceptical paradox and the attack on interpretationalism, §199 introduces the idea of rule-following as a social institution. Sections 201 and 202 are not needed to present these ideas, although they do their "full work" in restating the problem and the solution.

Objection 8: the "real" private language argument

According to traditional Wittgenstein scholarship, §§243–315 of *PI* constitute Wittgenstein's private language argument. Kripke challenges this view by insisting that "the real 'private language argument' is to be found in the sections *preceding* §243" (*WRPL*: 3). These sections are the rule-following considerations (§§138–242). Sections 243–315 are an *application* of the rule-following considerations to the special problem of sensations:

> [T]hey [§§243–315] are much less likely to be understood if they are read in isolation. The "private language argument" as applied to *sensations* is only a special case of much more general considerations about language previously argued; sensations have a crucial role as an (apparently) convincing *counterexample* to the general considerations previously stated. Wittgenstein therefore goes over the ground again in this special case ... (*WRPL*: 3)

Baker and Hacker (*SRL*: 22–6) protest against this reconstruction. They believe that that there is no private language argument preceding §243; their reasons for this view have of course already been covered in discussing objections 4–7. At this point it is more important to register and address the further criticism according to which Kripke is wrong to present §§243–315 as an argument about sensation. Baker and Hacker insist that these sections deal with:

> the question of whether a "private" sample can be employed to give meaning to a word, whether a mental paradigm can be employed, in a stipulation or explanation to oneself, to constitute a norm of correct use. Do the foundations of language lie in mental ostensive definitions of simple "indefinable" perceptual predicates? (*SRL*: 23–4)

One central ingredient of objection 8 is definitely correct: §§243–315 are not confined to a discussion of sensations, and the relation between §§138–242 and §§243–315 is much more complex than Kripke's term "application" suggests. Sections 243–315 deal more generally with mental phenomena that, according to the position under attack, are "inalienable" ("everyone has their own") and "epistemically private" ("only I can know my pain"). For the "private linguist" such mental phenomena are sensations, experiences and thoughts.[24] Perhaps the most important strand of argument of §§243–315 is a refutation of the idea that a private language can be built up from private ostensive definitions of terms for inalienable and epistemically private items. The investigation of this idea of a private language makes use of some of the results from the rule-following considerations, in particular the idea of rules as objective standards of correctness (cf. §259). The upshot of this strand of the discussion is that a private linguist is unable to lay down rules of use. But this is not all. In these sections Wittgenstein is not just refuting a certain semantic picture of the working of language, he is also rejecting the view according to which sensations, experiences and thoughts are inalienable and epistemically private entities. And he offers an alternative sketch of how our talk of sensations, experiences and thoughts is to be understood. Central in this sketch are two ideas: that ascribing these mental states to others is based on characteristic behavioural manifestations, and that self-ascriptions of these mental states are typically "avowals", that is groundless expressions.[25]

Anyone who interprets Wittgenstein's rule-following considerations as propounding a social solution will of course find the two private language arguments very similar in spirit and outcome. After all, both are concerned to undermine conceptions of private rule-following: the first argument rejects the idea that rule-following can be made sense of outside a social setting; and the second argument demonstrates the unintelligibility of both private ostensive definitions and the concept of inalienable and epistemically private mental items. The friend of a social reading of the rule-following considerations must also conclude that there is a sense in which one strand of the second argument is but a special case of the first: to show that the private linguist is unable to lay down rules for himself is a special case of a more general argument to the effect that all rule-following is social. And yet, the critics are still right to insist that Kripke simplifies a bit too much in reducing §§243–315 to a mere application of the lessons of §§138–242.

Lest this reply sound too accommodating to the objection, I hasten to add that all these concessions can safely be made without doing much damage to the heart of Kripke's interpretation of the rule-following considerations. That he should have painted a more sophisticated and complex picture of the relationship between the two arguments does not change the fact that he is providing us with a largely correct interpretation of the first.

Objection 9: Robinson Crusoe

Baker and Hacker maintain that Wittgenstein was entirely comfortable with the idea of private rule-following. In support of their view they cite a number of passages from Wittgenstein's unpublished manuscripts:

> Is it not imaginable that each human being should think only for himself, speak only to himself? *(In this case each person could even have his own language).* ... The Private Language which I have described above is like the one Robinson had on his desert island in which he was able to talk to himself. Had somebody heard him and observed him, he could have learned this language of Robinson. For the meanings of the words are made manifest in Robinson's behaviour.
>
> (Quoted in *SRL*: 176)[26]

> One can of course imagine someone who lives by himself and draws pictures of the objects around him (say on the walls of his cave), and such a picture language could be readily understood.
>
> (Quoted in *SRL*: 175)

> We can indeed imagine a Robinson using a language for himself, but then he must *behave* in a certain way or we shouldn't say that he plays language-games with himself. (Quoted in *SRL*: 176)

The first passage is an early version of what later became *PI* §243:

> A human being can encourage himself, give himself orders, obey, blame and punish himself; he can ask himself a question and answer it. We could even imagine human beings who spoke only in monologue; who accompanied their activities by talking to themselves. – An explorer who watched them and listened to their talk might succeed in translating their language into ours.

Undoubtedly, these are striking passages. But it is difficult to assess the significance of individual sections in unpublished manuscripts. A proper interpretation must always look at the context in which these quotations appear. This is not the place to investigate in detail Wittgenstein's notebooks and various early versions of *PI*. Two comments will suffice here.

First, there is scope for scepticism regarding Baker and Hacker's use of the manuscript material in this context. Baker and Hacker suggest that Wittgenstein was eager to prevent a social reading of his comments on agreement; this is the function of the cited passages (*SRL*: 172). However, if Wittgenstein really did mean to "guard ... against [these] confusions" (*ibid.*), why then did he not use these passages in the final and carefully edited version of *PI*? At least one distinguished commentator, Eike von Savigny – the author of a paragraph-by-paragraph commentary on *PI*[27] – hints that Wittgenstein may have changed his mind on these matters.[28]

Secondly, as far as §243 is concerned, it must be remembered that Wittgenstein here introduces the idea of private "sensation language". The quoted passage continues:

> But could we also imagine a language in which a person could write down or give vocal expression to his inner experiences – his feelings, moods, and the rest – for his private use? – Well, can't we do so in our ordinary language? – But that is not what I mean. The individual words of this language are to refer to what can only be known to the person speaking; to his immediate private sensations. So another person cannot understand the language. (*PI*: §243)

Wittgenstein is making a contrast between something we can imagine and something we cannot even begin to imagine. We can imagine, and make a film of, a group of people who speak only in monologue. We can take the fantasy further and have an explorer arrive and figure out their language. What we cannot imagine, and cannot make a film of, is someone who gives himself a private ostensive definition. To be sure, we can represent his thoughts in the familiar cartoon convention: we can have text-bubbles rising from characters' heads. But as far as private ostensive definitions of sensation terms go, there is nothing we can write in the bubbles. This is what Wittgenstein wants us to see. As Diamond (whose discussion of §243 inspired this paragraph) puts it:

> There not being any movie that would satisfy us does not show that *something* is "logically impossible" or "conceptually impossible" (in contrast, as we might suppose, with those people taking in monologues in §243); it shows us that there was not anything at all that we were imagining.[29]

By contrast, in the case of the monologists there was something we were imagining. This does not imply, however, that Wittgenstein regards the case of lifelong monologists as a possibility that refutes a social account of rule-following.

Objection 10: agreement

There are, *prima facie*, two ways in which one might relate rule-following to agreement. Option 1 is to think of agreement as a *constitutive criterion* of rule-following. On this view, it is the agreement with others' responses that shows and makes it so that Jones is following a rule. Option 2 is to conceive of agreement as a *framework condition* for the possibility of rule-following. Unless there existed broad agreement in community responses, rule-following would be impossible. Baker and Hacker attribute the "constitutive" reading to Kripke's Wittgenstein, and the "framework" reading to the real Wittgenstein (*SRL*: 44–5). As far as Wittgenstein is concerned, their main evidence is the following quotation:

> It is no use, for example, to go back to the concept of agreement, because it is no more certain that one proceeding is in agreement with another, than that it has happened in accordance with a rule. Admittedly, going according to a rule is also founded on agreement.[30]

Baker and Hacker are wrong to lament the absence of the "framework" view in *WRPL*. Kripke is explicitly endorsing the framework account in the following passage:

> [I]f there was no general agreement in the community responses, the game of attributing concepts to individuals – as we have described it – could not exist. … we respond unhesitatingly to such problems as "68 + 57", regarding our procedure as the only comprehensible one (see, e.g. §§219, 231, 138), and we *agree* in the unhesitating responses we make. On Wittgenstein's conception, such agreement is essential for our game of ascribing rules and concepts to each other (see §240).
>
> The set of responses in which we agree, and the way they interweave with our activities, is our *form of life*. Beings who agreed in consistently giving bizarre quus-like responses would share in another form of life.   (*WRPL*: 96)

Baker and Hacker detect the "constitutive" conception of agreement in Kripke's claim according to which Jones is judged by the community to have mastered the concept of addition "if his particular responses agree with those of the community in enough cases" (*WRPL*: 92). Two things can be said in reply. First, one can find similar passages in Wittgenstein himself: "The only criterion for [a child's] multiplying 113 by 44 in a way analogous to the examples is his doing it in the way in which all of us, who have been trained in a certain way, would do it".[31]

Secondly, neither Kripke nor Wittgenstein (in this passage) commit themselves to a constitutive role of agreement. That is to say, neither holds that, say, agreement with community responses regarding plus-queries is the necessary and sufficient condition for someone meaning addition by "+". Here we only need to note that – following Wittgenstein – Kripke explicitly rejects the search for necessary and sufficient conditions: "It is important to realize that we are *not* looking for necessary and sufficient conditions (truth conditions) for following a rule" (*WRPL*: 87).

And yet, agreement is not only a framework condition; it also plays a role in figuring out what others mean. We can meaningfully ask whether someone else's – say, a child's – responses to plus-queries correspond to our own. That we can even ask this question concerning plus-queries is due to our fundamental agreement with the child over a wide range of responses. But the existence of this fundamental agreement does not preempt the question of whether there is agreement in our responses to specific plus-queries. In many cases we take our own responses as a *prima facie* yardstick for deciding on the correctness of incorrectness of the responses of others.

Objection 11: truth and assertability

Kripke claims that the shift from the early to the later Wittgenstein involves a change from thinking of meaning in terms of truth-conditions to thinking of meaning in terms of assertability conditions. In accordance with this view, Kripke claims that §§1–133 of *PI* contain a critique of the truth-conditional and fact-based approach to meaning that was championed in the *Tractatus*. Baker and Hacker disagree with these claims on three grounds (*SRL*: 32, 47–9). First, they deny that the early Wittgenstein advocated a truth-conditional conception of meaning. This is, allegedly, clear from the fact that the atomic propositions of the *Tractatus* do not have truth-conditions. Secondly, Baker and Hacker point out that *PI* §§1–133 does not contain any discussion of *Tractarian* facts:

> [I]f the repudiation of his earlier truth-conditional theory of meaning (understood as involving correspondence with facts-in-the-world) is *the* key issue in *Investigations* §§1–133 and is crucial to the solution of the sceptical paradox, it cannot but be surprising that Wittgenstein has *no* discussion of facts in the whole book. (*SRL*: 32)

Thirdly, Baker and Hacker are willing to grant that in the case of the meaning of *some* sentences – "in particular third-person sentences concerning psychological characteristics and sentences concerning abilities" – Wittgenstein focuses on the circumstances that justify their assertion. But our two critics deny that this occasional practice is based on a general theory: "The injunction to *look* at how sentences are used is not an implicit claim that all sentences have assertion-conditions" (*SRL*: 49).

A reply to objection 11 can follow this tripartite division. I begin with the question of whether the early Wittgenstein had a truth-conditional account of meaning. Here we can use Baker and Hacker's own words against them. In their analytical commentary on *PI*, they characterize the position of the *Tractatus* as follows: "Understanding a sentence consists in knowing what it describes, i.e.

what possible state of affairs would make it true. Its truth-conditions are what is understood in understanding it".[32] Assuming only the further truism that to understand a sentence is to understand its meaning, we get the result that the meaning of a sentence is given by its truth-conditions. Hans-Johann Glock's *Wittgenstein Dictionary*, a book strongly influenced by Baker and Hacker, agrees:

> Sense antecedes the facts: in order to decide whether a proposition is true, its sense must be determined; to understand its sense we need not know its truth-value, but only "what is the case if it is true" …. This idea goes back to Frege, and lies at the heart of modern truth-conditional semantics.[33]

Of course, Baker and Hacker are right to point out that Wittgenstein does not speak of the truth-conditions of atomic propositions. That is to say, an atomic, or elementary, proposition cannot have truth-conditions in the same way as do molecular propositions. In the case of the latter, the truth-conditions are determined by the truth-conditions of its constituent elementary propositions. And yet, it is wrong to say that we have here a fundamental difference between Wittgenstein and truth-conditional approaches to meaning. After all, Wittgenstein is clear in maintaining that an elementary proposition has "truth-grounds", and that to understand the truth-grounds of an elementary proposition is to know what is the case if it is true.[34]

Baker and Hacker maintain that Kripke's characterization of the early Wittgenstein is crude and does not do justice to the richness and detail of the *Tractatus* (*SRL*: 47–8); other critics hold similar views.[35] I am not convinced that this criticism is fair. Kripke does not claim to give a comprehensive and full account of the early Wittgenstein: he merely seeks to point to one important contrast between the views of the *Tractatus* and the *Philosophical Investigations*. And it is obvious that the *Tractatus* puts forward, and the *Philosophical Investigations* rejects, a certain truth-conditional account of meaning.

This brings us to the second point of contention: whether the initial 133 sections of *PI* can be regarded as an attack on the truth-conditional theory of the *Tractatus*. It might help to recall here what Kripke actually says. To begin with, Kripke explicitly speaks of the first 137 sections, not the first 133, as Baker and Hacker suggest (*WRPL*: 78). The difference is significant since §136 contains an endorsement of the redundancy theory of truth and thus a rejection of facts as truth-makers. Moreover, Kripke himself notes that the initial sections have a variety of functions. He writes for example that "the initial sections contain a refutation, not only of the most basic and apparently inevitable theories of the *Tractatus* (such as meaning as stating facts), but also of many of its more specific doctrines (such as that of a special realm of 'simples')" (*WRPL*: 78). And finally, Kripke notes that one aspect of these early sections has not previously been given full attention; it has not been sufficiently stressed that these sections are meant to break "the grip of the natural presupposition that meaningful declarative sentences must purport to correspond to facts" (*WRPL*: 78–9).

Are Baker and Hacker right to reject the last-mentioned point on the grounds that "Wittgenstein has *no* discussion of facts in the whole book" (*SRL*: 32)? I think not. For a start, Baker and Hacker's own analytical commentary on the initial sections contains a section entitled "Descriptions and Facts".[36] This section belongs to a discussion of Wittgenstein's attack on the idea that all sentences are descriptions. In "Descriptions and Facts" Baker and Hacker consider one possible defence of this idea. According to this defence, the variety of types of sentences corresponds to a variety of types of facts. Baker and Hacker tell their readers that "Wittgenstein makes many remarks that point to defects in this development of the Augustinian picture", and they refer the reader to seven sections of *PI* (§§13, 24, 136, 244, 304, 363, 586).

Furthermore, Kripke's claim that the initial sections attack the "natural presupposition that meaningful declarative sentences must purport to correspond to facts" may well be true even in the absence of an explicit discussion of facts in these sections. In the *Tractatus* the claim that all meaningful true propositions are descriptions of facts itself rests on the further assumption according to which (almost all) words are names of objects. It is this assumption that Wittgenstein subjects to relentless criticism in the early parts of *PI*. This assumption is the very centrepiece of the "Augustinian picture of language", as Baker and Hacker explain very convincingly in their wonderfully rich and detailed commentary.[37] Wittgenstein's assault on the "natural presupposition" in *PI* §§1–137 is thus mostly indirect: he undermines the sentence–fact correspondence by attacking the name–object correspondence.

Baker and Hacker's commentary also provides support for Kripke's interpretation in another respect. Their commentary emphasizes the significance of Wittgenstein's critical study of ostensive definitions in *PI*. In particular, Baker and Hacker stress that the idea of a name–object correspondence is inseparable from the view that "the fundamental form of explanation of words is ostensive definition".[38] Now, the *Tractatus* never said anything about ostensive definitions. But it seems that the later Wittgenstein assumed that the *Tractatus* theory makes sense only if ostensive definitions are the foundations of language. As Baker and Hacker quote from a later manuscript: "In the *Tractatus* I was confused about logical analysis and ostensive definition. I thought at the time that there is a 'connection between language and reality'".[39]

Several points are interesting here. One is that the early Wittgenstein was committed to the view that word–world relations are established by each speaker or thinker for himself via private mental acts of ostensive definition. The early Wittgenstein explicitly confined a study of these acts to empirical psychology. The early Wittgenstein thus believed that each one of us has their own private, or privately established, language.[40] A further point of interest is Baker and Hacker's comment that "an ostensive definition stands to the uses of the expression that it explains in the same relation as a rule stands to its applications".[41] It follows that an attack on a mistaken conception of the way a rule determines its applications is *eo ipso* an assault on a mistaken conception of the roles ostensive definitions can play in setting up word–world and sentence–fact correspondences. And finally, the *Tractarian* view of ostensive definitions is, of course, a variant of meaning determinism. I mean *cat* by "Katze" because this is how I have (privately and ostensively) defined the term. And once I have established the correspondence of name and object, it is fixed for good.[42] All this is, of course, grist to Kripke's mill: the early sections of *PI* turn out to attack not only the truth-conditional position in general, they even identify and criticize specific elements of meaning determinism in particular.

It remains for us to consider Baker and Hacker's claim according to which Kripke is wrong to ascribe to the later Wittgenstein an account of meaning in terms of assertability conditions. Here it is useful to remember that Kripke prefaces his discussion with two provisos. On the one hand he stresses that Wittgenstein offers no more than a "rough general picture": "Wittgenstein disclaims (§65) any intent of offering a general account of language to rival that of the *Tractatus*. Rather we have different activities related to each other in various ways" (*WRPL*: 73). On the other hand, Kripke finds the very term "assertability conditions" "oversimplified" since it privileges assertions over other forms of utterances. To speak more adequately, we are told, we should focus on "the conditions when a move (a form of linguistic expression) is to be made in the 'language game'" (*WRPL*: 74).

Assertability conditions, thus understood, are not a far cry from ideas that Baker and Hacker themselves attribute to the later Wittgenstein. Note in particular their claims regarding the role of "defeasible criteria" in the later work.[43] Concerning "criteria of understanding", Baker and Hacker write that "there are multiple kinds of criteria of understanding expressions, whether words or sentences, and many criteria of each kind":

> (a) Giving an explanation of an expression in accord with the practice of explaining it is a criterion of understanding it. ... (b) Using an expression in accord with the practice of using (and explaining) it is a criterion of understanding it. ... (c) Appropriately producing or reacting to a sentence is a criterion of understanding it. ... (d) The relations between different criteria for understanding an expression are contingent. What connects the practice of explaining an expression with the practice of using it correctly are patterns of behaviour normal for those who speak the language. ...[44]

Glock notes that Wittgenstein exempts avowals and ostensively defined concepts from being governed by criteria, and then goes on to give the following list of cases where Wittgenstein speaks of criteria:

> expressive behaviour is a criterion for third-person psychological utterances; performances are criteria for potentialities, powers and

abilities (notably applying and explaining a word correctly are criteria for understanding it); scientific concepts like angina are governed by criteria, although these often fluctuate ...; mathematical concepts are governed by "defining" criteria (having three sides is *the* criterion for a plane figure's being a triangle); mathematical proofs are criteria for mathematical truths, and the result of an arithmetical operation is a criterion for it having been carried out ...; and applying count-nouns requires "criteria of identity" ...[45]

We are also told that criteria *"determine"* – at least in part, and defeasibly – the meaning of the terms to which they relate. Although "screaming in circumstances of injury" does not *mean* "being in pain", the former in part, and defeasibly, determines when the latter is correctly used. Whether it does or not depends on the situation: in a play it does not, in a real-life situation it usually does.[46]

The account that Kripke gives of assertability conditions is, of course, very sketchy and vague, and he says little on how to handle the assertability conditions for various classes of utterances. But the same sketchiness and vagueness characterizes existing accounts of defeasible criteria. And thus the real puzzle arising from Baker and Hacker's critique is this: why is it wrong to speak – in Kripke's loose way – of the later Wittgenstein as suggesting a "picture" of meaning in terms of assertability conditions, when it is right to talk – in Baker and Hacker's manner – of the later Wittgenstein as proposing a "picture" of meaning in terms of criteria?

Conclusion

Baker and Hacker's criticism of Kripke's interpretation of Wittgenstein is detailed and wide-ranging. They challenge both Kripke's understanding of specific passages and his understanding of Wittgenstein's thought as a whole. Some of their criticisms are on target: they are right to lament Kripke's handling of the label "common-sense philosophy", and they are entirely correct to complain about his superficial handling of what is traditionally called the private language argument. The bulk of their critique, however, either misses its target, or does only slight damage to Kripke's overall interpretation. Kripke is entitled to call Wittgenstein a sceptic (of sorts); he does not misconstrue the problem that preoccupies Wittgenstein in the rule-following considerations; he is true to Wittgenstein in his comments on facts; he is correct in his "communitarian" interpretation of §§198–202; he is at least partially on target as far as the relationship between the two private language arguments is concerned; he does not distort Wittgenstein's views on agreement; and, finally, he is right to speak of a shift in Wittgenstein's understanding of meaning from truth-conditions to assertability conditions.

Notes

Acknowledgements

1. See, for example, D. Bloor, *Wittgenstein: A Social Theory of Knowledge* (New York: Columbia University Press, 1983), "Left and Right Wittgensteinians", in *Science as Practice and Culture*, A. Pickering (ed.), 266–82 (Chicago, IL: University of Chicago Press, 1992), *Wittgenstein: Rules and Institutions* (London: Routledge, 1997) and "Institutions and Rule-Scepticism", *Social Studies of Science* 34 (2004), 593–602; M. Kusch, "Rule-Scepticism and the Sociology of Scientific Knowledge", *Social Studies of Science* 34 (2004), 571–92, and "Reply to my Critics", *Social Studies of Science* 34 (2004), 615–20; M. Lynch, "Extending Wittgenstein: The Pivotal Move from Epistemology to the Sociology of Science", in *Science as Practice and Culture*, A. Pickering (ed.), 215–65 (Chicago, IL: University of Chicago Press, 1992) and *Scientific Practice and Ordinary Action: Ethnomethodology and Social Studies of Science* (Cambridge: Cambridge University Press, 1993).
2. L. Wittgenstein, *Remarks on the Foundations of Mathematics*, revised edn, G. H. von Wright, R. Rhees, G. E. M. Anscombe (eds), G. E. M. Anscombe (trans.) (Oxford: Blackwell, 1978), VII-57.

Preface

1. K. Marx, *Das Kapital: Kritik der politischen Ökonomie, Erster Band* (Berlin: Dietz, 1980), 27.
2. A. Miller & C. Wright (eds), *Rule-Following and Meaning* (Chesham: Acumen, 2002).
3. G. P. Baker & P. M. S. Hacker, *Scepticism, Rules and Language* (Oxford: Blackwell, 1984).

Chapter 1: Introduction

1. In other words, the semantic reductive dispositionalist wishes to reduce intentional phenomena to non-intentional phenomena. Roughly, a phenomenon is intentional if it has direction, propositional content and satisfaction conditions. For instance, my belief that I have two daughters is directed at my daughters, it has the content that I have two daughters, and it has satisfaction conditions: the belief is satisfied if I really do. Contrast this with the physical fact that I am 6'3" tall: this physical fact does not fulfil any of these three conditions.
2. P. A. Boghossian, "The Rule-Following Considerations" [1989], in *Rule-Following and Meaning*, Miller & Wright (eds), 141–87, esp. 150.
3. This claim is made by Boghossian (*ibid.*). Boghossian equates accepting the dialogic setting with taking the sceptical challenge to be epistemological. He gives no justification for this equation.
4. Here I agree with G. M. Wilson, "Kripke on Wittgenstein and Normativity" [1994], in *Rule-Following and Meaning*, Miller & Wright (eds), 234–59.
5. For example, Michael Williams, "Skepticism", in *The Blackwell Guide to Epistemology*, J. Greco & E. Sosa (eds), 35–69 (Oxford: Blackwell, 1999).

6. Although he does not use these terms, Wilson, "Kripke on Wittgenstein and Normativity", is the clearest case of this reading.

7. For instance, S. Cavell, *The Claim of Reason: Wittgenstein, Skepticism, Morality, and Tragedy* (Oxford: Oxford University Press, 1979). Cf. D. McManus (ed.), *Wittgenstein and Scepticism* (London: Routledge, 2004).

8. As Michael Esfeld has insisted (in conversation).

9. Here I follow Boghossian, "The Rule-Following Considerations", 143–4.

10. Here I am thinking of John McDowell, "Wittgenstein on Following a Rule" [1984], in *Rule-Following and Meaning*, Miller & Wright (eds), 45–80, and Rupert Read, "What 'There Can be no such Thing as Meaning Anything by any Word' Could Possibly Mean", in *The New Wittgenstein*, A. Crary & R. Read (eds), 74–82 (London: Routledge, 2000).

11. Bloor, *Wittgenstein*, and P. Horwich, "Meaning, Use and Truth: On Whether a Use-Theory of Meaning Is Precluded by the Requirement that Whatever Constitutes the Meaning of a Predicate Be Capable of Determining the Set of Things of Which the Predicate Is True and to Which It Ought to be Applied", *Mind* **104** (1995), 355–68, and *Meaning* (Oxford: Clarendon Press, 1998).

12. Boghossian, "The Rule-Following Considerations", 150.

13. I am assuming here that the combination of intersubjectivity and classical realism is no longer an option.

14. Cf. Boghossian, "The Rule-Following Considerations", 151.

15. Again ignoring the further conditions that have to be added to the antecedent to make it true.

16. A. J. Ayer, *Language, Truth, and Logic* (London: Gollancz, 1936); cf. A. Miller, *An Introduction to Contemporary Metaethics* (Cambridge: Polity, 2003), Ch. 2.

17. S. Blackburn, *Essays in Quasi-Realism* (Oxford: Oxford University Press, 1993); cf. Miller, *An Introduction to Contemporary Metaethics*, Ch. 4.

18. I here mimic Miller's formulation of quasi-realism for the moral realm: Miller, *An Introduction to Contemporary Metaethics*, 52.

19. See especially G. P. Baker & P. M. S. Hacker, *Wittgenstein: Rules, Grammar and Necessity* (An Analytical Commentary on the *Philosophical Investigations*, vol. 2) (Oxford: Blackwell, 1985), 40.

20. Cf. J. Heal, *Fact and Meaning: Quine and Wittgenstein on Philosophy of Language* (Oxford: Blackwell, 1989).

21. One advantage of my reconstruction of the dialectic of *WRPL* is that it allows us a simple and straightforward reply to the oft-heard objection according to which the sceptical solution begs the question against the sceptical challenge. (No objection to the sceptical solution has been raised as often as the objection that the sceptical solution fails to answer the sceptical challenge: Baker & Hacker, *Scepticism, Rules and Language*, 37; S. Blackburn, "Wittgenstein's Irrealism", in *Wittgenstein: Eine Neubewertung*, L. Brandl & R. Haller (eds), 13–26 (Vienna: Hoelder-Pickler Tempsky, 1990), 20; S. Cavell, *Conditions Handsome and Unhandsome: The Constitution of Emersonian Perfectionism* (Chicago, IL: University of Chicago Press, 1990), 75; A. Hattiangadi, "Oughts and Thoughts: Scepticism and the Normativity of Content", dissertation (Department of History and Philosophy of Science, University of Cambridge, 2001), 64–73; P. Hoffman, "Kripke on Private Language", *Philosophical Studies* **47** (1985), 23–8; B. Loar, "Review of Kripke, *Wittgenstein on Rules and Private Language*", *Noûs* **19**(2) (1985), 273–80, esp. 278; McDowell, "Wittgenstein on Following a Rule"; P. Seabright, "Explaining Cultural Divergence: A Wittgensteinian Paradox", *Journal of Philosophy* **84** (1987), 11–27, esp. 20–21; C. Wright, "Kripke's Account of the Argument Against Private Language", *Journal of Philosophy* **71** (1984), 759–78, esp. 770–71; J. Zalabardo, "Rules, Communities and Judgements", *Critica: Revista Hispanoamericana de Filosofia* **21** (1989), 33–58, esp. 37–41. Different authors press the point in slightly different versions.) Consider Crispin Wright's version of the charge. Imagine an advocate of the sceptical solution, say Smith, who has just decided that Jones means addition by "+". Let Smith's grounds be that Jones calculated "68 + 57 = 125". Enter a sceptic. His challenge to Smith is a second-order challenge: it does not concern whether by "+" Jones (or Smith) mean(s) addition or quaddition but whether Smith means to take "125" (in answer to "68 + 57 = ?") as the criterion for meaning addition or meaning quaddition. "How do you know, Smith, that the answer '125' to '68 + 57' is your criterion for attributing addition and not your criterion for

attributing some other function? Maybe in the past you really meant to use '125' (in response to '68 + 57 = ?') as a criterion for quaddition".

What makes "Smith follows assertability condition AS_1 rather than AS_2," true? Well, we will obviously not be able to give a satisfactory answer to this question as long as we remain tied to a meaning-determinist construction of truth-conditions. The latter would urge us to look for an answer to this question by investigating whether Smith has the appropriate mental state. By assumption, Smith is no longer tempted to go down this dead end. So what can he reply? He can certainly insist that "I mean AS_1," is true and a fact, provided only that his statement meets the assertability condition for self-ascribing the following of a rule. We have encountered the conditions for such self-ascriptions before: it suffices that Smith feels confident on how to go on, that he is willing to be corrected by others, and that currently no objections are there to be considered. At this point Wright might insist that Jones should have been allowed to reply in just this way to the initial sceptical challenge. Sure enough. But this is to misconstrue the dialectic of *WRPL*. *WRPL* starts with the intuitive picture of meaning determinism. Only by the end of Chapter 3 do we realize that and how this picture can be refused.

22. C. McGinn, *Wittgenstein on Meaning: An Interpretation and Evaluation* (Oxford: Blackwell, 1984), 146, 167; J. R. Searle, "Skepticism about Rules and Intentionalilty", in *Consciousness and Language*, 251–64 (Cambridge: Cambridge University Press, 2002).
23. Cf. P. A. Boghossian, Review of McGinn 1984, *Philosophical Review* **98** (1989), 83–92; "The Rule-Following Considerations"; J. Sartorelli, Review of Baker & Hacker, *Scepticism, Rules and Language*, *Philosophical Review* **100** (1991), 660–62.
24. See J. A. Fodor, *Psychosemantics: The Problem of Meaning in the Philosophy of Mind* (Cambridge, MA: MIT Press, 1987); M. Aydede, "The Language of Thought Hypothesis", *Stanford Encyclopedia of Philosophy*, http://plato.stanford.edu/entries/language-thought (2004, accessed May 2006).
25. Boghossian, "The Rule-Following Considerations", 151–2.
26. *Ibid.*
27. D. Hume, *An Enquiry Concerning Human Understanding* (Oxford: Oxford University Press, 1999), 119.
28. D. Hume, *A Treatise of Human Nature* (Oxford: Oxford University Press, 1990), 88.
29. Quoted from I. Tipton, "Berkeley, George", in *Routledge Encyclopedia of Philosophy*, E. Craig (ed.) (London: Routledge, 1998), retrieved from www.rep.routledge.com (subscribers only) (accessed April 2005), §13. I am greatly indebted to Tipton's discussion.
30. G. Berkeley, *Principles of Human Knowledge and Three Dialogues* (Oxford: Oxford University Press, 1999), §4.
31. *Ibid.*, §54.
32. *Ibid.*, §51.
33. Not all objections fit within this scheme. I am thinking in particular of objections that claim that the whole project of *WRPL* is somehow self-refuting. Here is the most important such objection. Simon Blackburn ("Theory, Observation and Drama", *Mind & Language* 7 (1992), 187–203, esp. 198–9) claims that the sceptical challenge is incoherent. If the sceptic is to convince us then we must be able to make sense of the following "master argument", Blackburn says:
    (1) For any given expression, say "+", we can formulate at least two rival hypotheses (*A* or *B*) as to what this expression means.
    (2) It is impossible to identify, or conceive of, a fact that would decide between *A* and *B*.
    (3) There is no fact of the matter as to whether *A* or *B* are true.
    Blackburn insists that this argument is self-undermining. In order to understand it, I must be able to understand *A* and *B* as presenting me with distinct possibilities. For instance, I must understand the difference between (*A*) "By '+' I mean addition" and (*B*) "By '+' I mean quaddition". If I were unable to understand that difference then I would not be able to follow the master argument. Alas, such understanding is precisely what the conclusion of the master argument denies me: according to the conclusion it is impossible for me to make any sense of the distinction between meaning addition and meaning quaddition.
    In light of the above reconstruction of *WRPL*, Blackburn's general charge of incoherence can be rejected. Using Blackburn's master argument, the dialectic of the sceptical argument can be

reconstructed as follows. The meaning-determinist is committed to two principles from the start: (1), and "if (1) & (2), then (3)". The sceptical argument demonstrates that – given the assumptions of meaning determinism – (2) follows from (1). Hence the meaning-determinist is forced to believe (3), and thereby finds himself in the quandary that Blackburn describes. But of course there is a way out: the way out is to give up meaning determinism and adopt meaning scepticism. The latter position is not caught in the quandary since it rejects the assumptions that force the meaning-determinist to accept (2). The meaning sceptic is committed to primitivism: in the present context this allows for a minimal fact that decides between addition and quaddition as the meaning of "+", namely, that we find the first hypothesis primitively obvious and the second not.

Chapter 2: Normativity

1. C. Wright, "Does *Philosophical Investigations* I.258–60 Suggest a Cogent Argument Against Private Language?", in *Subject, Thought, and Context*, J. McDowell & P. Pettit (eds), 210–66 (Oxford: Clarendon Press, 1986), 256.
2. A. Bilgrami, "Norms and Meaning", in *Reflecting Davidson*, R. Stoecker (ed.), 121–44 (Berlin: de Gruyter, 1993), 126.
3. McDowell, "Wittgenstein on Following a Rule", 45.
4. J. McDowell & P. Pettit, "Introduction", in *Subject, Thought, and Context*, 1–15, esp. 10.
5. Wright, "Does *Philosophical Investigations* I.258–60 Suggest a Cogent Argument", 256.
6. M. Dummett, *The Logical Basis of Metaphysics* (Cambridge, MA: Harvard University Press, 1991), 85.
7. R. Brandom, "Replies", *Philosophy and Phenomenological Research* 57 (1997), 189–204, esp. 193.
8. Horwich, *Meaning*, 186.
9. A. Wikforss, "Semantic Normativity", *Philosophical Studies* 102 (2001), 203–26, esp. 207. Of course, the semantic normativist might claim that there is a continuum of cases between the clearly semantic and the clearly pragmatic. But this will not give her all she needs. The cases that are clearly not pragmatic will fall outside the realm of the normative.
10. F. I. Dretske, *Perception, Knowledge and Belief: Selected Essays* (Cambridge: Cambridge University Press, 2000).
11. Ibid., 250–51.
12. This distinction is suggested in P. Engel, "Wherein Lies the Normative Dimension in Meaning and Mental Content?", *Philosophical Studies* 100 (2000), 305–21, esp. 308–9.
13. D. Davidson, "A Nice Derangement of Epitaphs" [1986], in *Truth, Language, and History*, 89–107 (Oxford: Clarendon Press, 2005); "James Joyce and Humpty Dumpty" [1989], in *Truth, Language, and History*, 143–58; "The Second Person" [1992], in *Subjective, Intersubjective, Objective*, 107–21 (Oxford: Clarendon Press, 2001); "The Social Aspect of Language" [1994], in *Truth, Language, and History*, 109–25; "Seeing Through Language" [1997], in *Truth, Language, and History*, 127–42.
14. Davidson, "The Social Aspect of Language", 117.
15. *Ibid.*
16. Davidson, "The Second Person", 113–14.
17. J. R. Searle, *Speech Acts: An Essay in the Philosophy of Language* (Cambridge: Cambridge University Press, 1969), 33. The same distinction was suggested earlier in J. Rawls, "Two Concepts of Rules", *Philosophical Review* 64 (1955), 3–32 and G. C. J. Midgley, "Linguistic Rules", *Proceedings of the Aristotelian Society* 59 (1959), 271–90.
18. K. Glüer, "Sense and Prescriptivity", *Acta Analytica* 14(23) (1999), 111–28; *Sprache und Regeln: Zur Normativität von Bedeutung* (Berlin: Akademie Verlag, 1999); "Bedeutung zwischen Norm und Naturgesetz", *Deutsche Zeitschrift für Philosophie* 48 (2000), 449–68; and K. Glüer & P. Pagin, "Rules of Meaning and Practical Reasoning", *Synthese* 117 (1999), 207–27.
19. Glüer, *Sprache und Regeln*, 165.
20. *Ibid.*, 166. For further discussion see C. Strub, "Zur Normativität konstitutiver Regeln", in *Institutionen und Regelfolgen*, U. Baltzer & G. Schönrich (eds), 207–23 (Paderborn: Mentis, 2002).
21. Glüer, *Sprache und Regeln*, 188.
22. Glüer, "Bedeutung zwischen Norm und Naturgesetz", 460. Glüer and Pagin also focus on the role of

rules in action explanations. If a rule is to have an action-guiding function for an agent, they point out, it must introduce a motivation for the agent. In performing action a, I am guided by rule R if I do a because R tells me that I must. Moreover, I not only have to know the rule, it must also be both "in force" for me and "accepted" by me. A canonical form of an action explanation in which rules play this guiding role is the following:

(Pro-attitude 1)	I want to do what R requires
(Belief 1)	R requires that I do A
(Pro-attitude 2)	So, I want to do A
(Belief 2)	(This action) a is a case of A:ing
(Intention)	So, I shall do a

(Glüer & Pagin, "Rules of Meaning and Practical Reasoning", 213)

Again, it is clear that constitutive rules could not be slotted into the second line, since there is nothing they require. One possible counter-suggestion might be the following. Let "Making an utterance of s count as saying that p" be a constitutive rule, and let "I want to say that p" be the initial pro-attitude. Does this not usher in the further pro-attitude "I want to make an utterance of s"? It certainly does, but this is no comfort for the normativist. Although here the constitutive rule plays a role in the reasoning of the actor, it does not play the right kind of role. The constitutive rule here is not in a *motivational* position but merely in a "*doxastic*" one. That is to say, it merely provides information on what one must do in order to do something else. But it does not itself require anything. It merely plays a role in the "theoretical" transition from one pro-attitude to another (*ibid.*: 219).

23. McGinn, *Wittgenstein on Meaning*, 174. See also Boghossian, "The Rule-Following Considerations", 146.
24. Boghossian, "The Rule-Following Considerations", 147.
25. *Ibid.*, 148.
26. *Ibid.*, 170.
27. *Ibid.*, 84.
28. I here follow J. Zalabardo, "Kripke's Normativity Argument" [1997], in *Rule-Following and Meaning*, Miller & Wright (eds), 274–93.
29. Boghossian, "The Rule-Following Considerations", 169.
30. *Ibid.*, 170.
31. *Ibid.*, 171.
32. *Ibid.*, 170.
33. *Ibid.*, 172.
34. *Ibid.*, 175, n.53.
35. *Ibid.*, 172.
36. J. A. Fodor, *A Theory of Content and Other Essays* (Cambridge, MA: MIT Press, 1990), 135–6.
37. Glüer "Sense and Prescriptivity"; *Sprache und Regeln*, 166–7; "Bedeutung zwischen Norm und Natur-gesetz", 460; Hattiangadi, "Oughts and Thoughts", 144–72.
38. Glüer *Sprache und Regeln*, 166–7. Glüer here follows the lead of Herbert Schnädelbach, who earlier argued a similar point with respect to the term "rational" (H. Schnädelbach, *Zur Rehabilitierung des animal rationale: Vorträge und Abhandlungen 2* (Frankfurt: Suhrkamp, 1992), 79–103).
39. J. Heal, "The Disinterested Search for Truth", *Proceedings of the Aristotelian Society NS* **88** (1988), 97–108; Horwich, *Meaning*, 192. Cf. D. Papineau, "Normativity and Judgement", *Proceedings of the Aristotelian Society*, Suppl. **73** (1999), 17–44, esp. 24–5; N. Zangwill, "Direction of Fit and Normative Functionalism", *Philosophical Studies* **91** (1998), 173–203.
40. Horwich, *Meaning*, 192. David Papineau agrees on the grounds that there are cases in which people choose to make themselves believe a falsehood. Think of the terminal cancer patient who believes he will live longer if he comes to believe that he will completely recover. As Papineau sees it, the patient is not in any way obliged to fit his belief to the evidence. No truth prescriptions are being violated here (Papineau, "Normativity and Judgement", 24–5).
41. Wikforss, "Semantic Normativity", 205.
42. T. Burge, "Individualism and the Mental", *Midwest Studies in Philosophy* **4** (1979), 73–121.
43. A. Millar, "The Normativity of Meaning", in *Logic, Thought and Language*, A. O'Hear (ed.), 57–73

(Cambridge: Cambridge University Press, 2002), 60–61.

44. Wikforss, "Semantic Normativity".
45. Zalabardo, "Kripke's Normativity Argument", offers a different form of "filtering out". His interpretation of the normativity considerations in *WRPL* is based on two passages in Kripke's text. The first is a response to the proposal according to which it is my disposition to add that justifies my present belief that I mean *addition* by "+":

> How does any of this indicate that – now *or* in the past – "125" was an answer *justified* in terms of instructions I gave myself, rather than a mere jack-in-the-box unjustified and arbitrary response? Am I supposed to justify my present belief that I … should answer "125" … in terms of a *hypothesis* about my *past* dispositions? (Do I record and investigate the past physiology of my brain?) (*WRPL*: 23)

The second passage is part of Kripke's criticism of a different view. According to this view, I can justify my belief that in the past I meant addition rather than quaddition by "+" by invoking considerations of simplicity. Allegedly, the hypothesis that I meant addition is simpler than the hypothesis that I meant quaddition. Kripke responds as follows: "I immediately and unhesitatingly calculate '68 + 57' as I do, and the meaning I assign to '+' is supposed to *justify* this procedure. I do not form tentative hypotheses, wondering what I should do if one hypothesis or another were true" (*WRPL*: 40).

As Zalabardo sees it, these passages show that Kripke's normativity argument is concerned with justification. Whatever the facts of meaning turn out to be, they must potentially justify my applications of terms, they must be able to tell me which applications of terms I should endorse. Moreover, Zalabardo suggests the following generalization of Kripke's addition example. Assume that we seek to answer questions of some given kind K and that we intend to do so systematically on the basis of procedures. Not all procedures will do, of course: given the nature of K, some procedures will be justified as procedures for answering questions of kind K, while other procedures will not be so justified. What makes one procedure, say P_i, justified and another procedure, say P_j, unjustified, is that P_i but not P_j, stands in the right relation to the facts that determine which answers are the correct answers to questions of kind K. For instance, assume that we are trying to determine answers to questions about the current weather conditions outside my office. Possible procedures include reading last week's weather report, guessing and looking out of the window. The facts that determine correct answers to these weather questions are the current meteorological facts: whether it rains, snows or shines, and so on. Obviously, given these facts, the only procedure that is fully justified is to look out of the window. In this example, it is the correctness-determining facts that act as a criterion of adequacy for the procedures. But the reverse case is possible too: once we know what our K-questions are and once we have formed a hypothesis about which procedures are justified, then we have a criterion of adequacy for accounts of possible correctness-determining facts (Zalabardo, "Kripke's Normativity Argument", 285). (Once we have decided to answer questions about the weather and have settled on looking out of the window as an appropriate procedure, only observable meteorological facts will be adequate as determinants of correct answers.)

Zalabardo proposes that Kripke's normativity argument concerns a special case of the relationship between K-questions, correctness-determining facts and procedures. The K-question is "How should I apply the sign '+'?" The correctness-determining facts are dispositions and their manifestation: either past dispositions and their manifestations, or manifestations of dispositions under ideal circumstances. The procedures are – and here we return to the two quoted passages – either the recording and investigating of the past physiology of my brain, or, more generally, the forming of tentative hypotheses.

As Zalabardo reads the cited passages in Kripke, they amount to formulating a demand on how – at least in this case – procedures and facts have to be related:

> Kripke seems to think that if the correct answers to "+"-questions were determined by the past physiology of my brain, the only justified procedure for answering these questions would be to "record and investigate" the relevant physiological facts. This suggests that, for Kripke, a procedure for answering K-questions would not be justified unless it involved *conscious engagement* with the facts that determine how these questions should be answered.
> (*Ibid.*: 286)

If conscious engagement with the facts is the decisive criterion, then not even sophisticated dispositionalism – built upon what I would do under ideal conditions – can pass muster. For obviously I cannot have conscious engagement with what I would do under ideal conditions.

Finally, Zalabardo thinks that his reconstruction of Kripke's normativity argument – referred to by him as the "justification argument" – succeeds where Boghossian's standard argument failed. He also recognizes, however, that the justification argument is tied to an epistemological assumption that no longer enjoys universal support among epistemologists. This is the assumption of "epistemological internalism", that is, the view that whatever justifies a knower's beliefs must be directly accessible to her.

I agree with Zalabardo to the extent that his justification argument plays a role in the sceptic's assault on dispositionalism (*qua* high-brow meaning determinism). What Zalabardo gives us is a more detailed development of the argument from justification of unhesitating application. Ignoring the problem of its limited scope (the ignoring of externalism), the argument seems successful as far as it goes. But I disagree with Zalabardo's contention that the view he outlines is "Kripke's normativity argument". Too much of the network of assumptions of meaning determinism is missing for this to be true. Zalabardo seems to think of his reconstruction as showing that Kripke wishes to give us a general normativity argument against dispositionalism, an argument that is (at least potentially) independent of the intuitive picture of low-brow meaning determinism. But if what I have said in this and the previous chapter is correct, then Zalabardo must be wrong. The justification argument will only cut ice against a dispositionalist who is committed to justification of unhesitating application. Reformist and revolutionary deviations from meaning determinism have the option of giving up this commitment.

46. Glüer, *Sprache und Regeln*, 136.
47. Of course there are also important differences between deliberation and justification, but for present purposes these do not matter. See J. Dancy, *Practical Reality* (Oxford: Oxford University Press, 2000).
48. Cf. K.-O. Apel, *Understanding and Explanation: A Transcendental-Pragmatic Perspective* (Cambridge, MA: MIT Press, 1984), 116; M. Black, "Some Remarks about 'Practical Reasoning'", in *The Philosophy of Georg Henrik von Wright* (The Library of Living Philosophers, Vol. XIX), P. A. Schilpp & L. E. Hahn (eds), 405–16 (La Salle, IL: Open Court, 1989); E. Itkonen, *Causality in Linguistic Theory* (London: Croom Helm, 1983), 101.
49. Glüer, *Sprache und Regeln*, 111–12.
50. Dretske, *Perception, Knowledge and Belief*, 250–51.
51. P. Coates, "Meaning, Mistake and Miscalculation", *Minds and Machines* 7 (1997), 171–97; see also "Kripke's Sceptical Paradox: Normativeness and Meaning", *Mind* 95 (1986), 77–80.
52. Coates, "Meaning, Mistake and Miscalculation", 183.
53. For further detailed criticism of Coates's objection, see J. Toribio, "Meaning, Dispositions and Normativity", *Minds and Machines* 9 (1999), 399–413.
54. P. Horwich, "Wittgenstein and Kripke on the Nature of Meaning", *Mind and Language* 5 (1990), 105–21, esp. 112.
55. *Ibid.*, 112–13.
56. *Ibid.*, 113.
57. Millar, "The Normativity of Meaning", 71.
58. Boghossian, Review of McGinn 1984, 84.
59. Fodor, *A Theory of Content and Other Essays*, 135–6.
60. R. G. Millikan, "Truth Rules, Hoverflies, and the Kripke-Wittgenstein Paradox", *Philosophical Review* 94 (1990), 323–52, esp. 329.
61. *Ibid.*, 344.
62. Bloor, *Wittgenstein*, 104–5.
63. See J. R. Searle, *The Construction of Social Reality* (London: Allen Lane, 1995), 15–17.
64. For a highly damaging further criticism of Millikan's position, see Fodor, *A Theory of Content and Other Essays*, 64–76.
65. Davidson, "A Nice Derangement of Epitaphs", 107.

66. My brief exposition follows M. Kölbel, *Truth Without Objectivity* (London: Routledge, 2002), ch. 5; A. Miller, *Philosophy of Language* (London: UCL Press, 1998), ch. 8; M. Platts, *Ways of Meaning: An Introduction to a Philosophy of Language* (London: Routledge & Kegan Paul, 1979), 49–58; and S. Soames, *Philosophical Analysis in the Twentieth Century, Vol. 2: The Age of Meaning* (Princeton, NJ: Princeton University Press, 2003), ch. 12.
67. D. Davidson, "Truth and Meaning" [1967], in *Inquiries into Truth and Interpretation*, 17–36 (Oxford: Clarendon Press, 1984), 22.
68. In A. Tarski, *Logic, Semantics, Metamathematics* (Oxford: Blackwell, 1956).
69. D. Davidson, "Reply to James Higginbotham", in *The Philosophy of Donald Davidson*, L. E. Hahn (ed.), 687–9 (Chicago, IL: Open Court, 1999), 688.
70. D. Lewis, "Languages and Language" [1975], in *The Philosophy of Language*, A. P. Martinich (ed.), 538–57 (Oxford: Oxford University Press, 1996).
71. Davidson, "The Second Person", 107.
72. *Ibid.*
73. D. Davidson, "Communication and Convention" [1982], in *Inquiries into Truth and Interpretation*, 265–80, esp. 277.
74. Davidson, "A Nice Derangement of Epitaphs".
75. D. Davidson, "Reply to Richard Rorty", in Hahn, *The Philosophy of Donald Davidson*, 595–600, esp. 598.
76. Davidson, "A Nice Derangement of Epitaphs", 100.
77. *Ibid.*, 103.
78. *Ibid.*, 101.
79. Davidson, "The Social Aspect of Language", 115–16.
80. Davidson, "A Nice Derangement of Epitaphs", 107.
81. *Ibid.*, 107.
82. Davidson, "The Social Aspect of Language", 110.
83. Davidson, "Communication and Convention", 277.
84. Davidson, "The Social Aspect of Language", 117.
85. Davidson, "The Second Person", 116.
86. *Ibid.*, 117–21; Davidson, "Seeing Through Language", 138–41. Cf. D. Føllesdal, "Triangulation", in Hahn, *The Philosophy of Donald Davidson*, 719–28.
87. Horwich, *Meaning*, 72–4; cf. G. Harman, "Meaning and Semantics" [1974], in *Reasoning, Mind and Meaning*, 192–205 (Oxford: Oxford University Press, 1999).
88. Davidson, "Reply to Richard Rorty", 598.
89. Davidson, "A Nice Derangement of Epitaphs", 95
90. D. Davidson, "Reply to Tyler Burge", in Hahn, *The Philosophy of Donald Davidson*, 251–4, esp. 252.
91. D. Davidson, *Truth and Predication* (Cambridge, MA: Harvard University Press, 2005), 126.
92. *Ibid.*, 122. On this point I found G. Kemp, "Reply to Heck on Meaning and Truth-Conditions", *Philosophical Quarterly* **52** (2002), 233–6, extremely helpful.
93. Davidson, *Truth and Predication*, 130.
94. Davidson, "Reply to Richard Rorty", 598.
95. Here I follow Kölbel, *Truth Without Objectivity*, ch. 5.
96. Davidson, "Truth and Meaning", 23.
97. *Ibid.*, 31.
98. D. Davidson, "The Structure and Content of Truth", *Journal of Philosophy* **87** (1990), 279–328, esp. 300.
99. J. McDowell, "Truth Conditions, Bivalence and Verificationism", in *Truth and Meaning*, G. Evans & J. McDowell (eds), 42–66 (Oxford: Clarendon Press, 1976).
100. M. Dummett, "A Nice Derangement of Epitaphs: Some Comments on Davidson and Hacking", in *Truth and Interpretation*, E. Lepore (ed.), 459–76 (Oxford: Blackwell, 1986).
101. Davidson, "Seeing Through Language", 111.
102. Føllesdal, "Triangulation", 725. I am grateful to Dagfinn Føllesdal for correspondence on this point.
103. Davidson, "The Second Person", 110–11.

104. *Ibid.*, 113.
105. *Ibid.*, 114–15
106. Davidson, "The Social Aspect of Language", 109.
107. Davidson, "The Second Person", 113–14.
108. *Ibid.*, 107.
109. Davidson, "Reply to Richard Rorty", 598.
110. P. F. Strawson, *Freedom and Resentment* (London: Methuen, 1974).

Chapter 3: Dispositions and extensions

1. Here I follow Boghossian, "The Rule-Following Considerations", 143–4.
2. Here are two other lines of argument that I can discuss here only in a footnote. The first is the "containment strategy" of agreeing with Kripke as far as mathematics is concerned, while denying that his arguments carry over to non-mathematical concepts and words. For example, McGinn insists that "most words, after all, do not have (like '+') infinite extensions" (*Wittgenstein on Meaning*, 162). This version of the containment strategy proves unconvincing the moment we allow that words have extensions also in possible worlds. A related line of thought is advanced by Tomoji Shogenji. What distinguishes an ordinary word such as "table" from mathematical concepts is that "there is a *finite set of features* that makes an object its reference. For example, a table is recognized as such by its hard flat top supported by legs. Some might point out that a table could still turn up in infinitely many possible situations, but the recognition of the finite set of table-features in any of these situations requires no infinite capacity" ("The Problem of Rule-Following in Compositional Semantics", *Southern Journal of Philosophy* 33 (1995), 97–108, esp. 99). This does not work either. What about possible tables that exceed our tables in size? What about the possible tables in the world of giants? What about possible tables so huge that even many lifetimes were not sufficient for us to recognize them as tables? Or what about tables so small that it would take brains the size of the universe for us to develop microscopes to see them?

   The second strategy seeks to exploit the idea that dispositions can be masked and altered (J. Hohwy, "A Reductio of Kripke-Wittgenstein's Objections to Dispositionalism about Meaning", *Minds and Machines* 13(2) (2003), 257–68). The objection to Kripke goes as follows. The core of Kripke's case against semantic dispositionalism is the "mistake problem": this is the problem of distinguishing between the adder and the skadder. (Skaddition is the function that results from adding without "carrying": the skaddition sum of 18 and 19 is 27, and that of 787 and 999 is 1676.) Kripke's mistake problem ignores an important distinction. Take an object to which we attribute some disposition. And assume that the object fails to behave in ways that would accord with our attribution. There may be three different kinds of explanations for why our expectation is disappointed. First, the object may simply not have the attributed disposition; for instance, a cup made of steel simply lacks fragility. Secondly, the favourable conditions needed for a manifestation of the disposition may not be present; for example, the porcelain cup may not be meeting a hard surface at sufficiently high speed. Thirdly, and finally, the disposition may be "masked" or "altered"; that is to say, something or someone may be interfering with the course of nature in order to prevent the manifestation of the disposition. Maybe an angel turns the porcelain cup into a steel cup the moment it touches the hard surface. Kripke overlooks the distinction between the second and the third category. The dispositionalist is not obliged to judge that Otto is a skadder, albeit that Otto's arithmetical behaviour, even in favourable conditions, is extensionally equivalent with skaddition. Instead, the dispositionalist has the option of saying that Otto's disposition to add is "masked" or "altered" by his inability to carry. And thus the dispositionalist can capture our intuitive judgement that meaning *addition* by "+" is compatible with responding to plus-queries in ways that are extensionally equivalent with skaddition.

   The objection is right to say that the dispositionalist can capture our intuitive judgement by talking about masked or altered dispositions. But there remains an unresolved underdetermination problem. Remember that the dispositionalist wants to determine – on the basis of Otto's dispositions to react in certain ways to plus-queries – which arithmetical function Otto means. Of course, the dispositionalist has no direct observational access to Otto's dispositions. He therefore needs to form hypotheses concerning Otto's dispositions on the basis of Otto's actual behaviour. This actual behaviour consists of a string of answers to plus-queries. Sadly, these answers can be interpreted as manifestations of more than one disposition. The answers can, *inter alia*, be interpreted as "full" manifestations of the disposition to skadd, or as "partial" manifestations of the disposition to add. (The expression "partial manifestation" seems appropriate for the hypothesis that the answers are due to a disposition to add that is masked by a further disposition to fail to carry.)

The talk of "masking" and "altering" dispositions is illuminating in many ways, but it does nothing to help the dispositionalist around the key underdetermination problem: what evidence could lead us to hypothesize that Otto is a masked adder rather than an unmasked skadder? Why assume that Otto's behaviour consists of manifestations of a masked disposition to add rather than manifestations of unmasked dispositions to skadd?

In the case of cups and their fragility we have rough criteria for deciding the analogous question. We distinguish between conditions that form part of the normal course of events, and conditions that constitute deviations from it. We regard the former as favourable conditions, and the latter as masking circumstances. Encountering hard surfaces at sufficiently high speed belongs in the first category; intentional interventions into the course of nature – by angels, for example – fall into the second. Accordingly we are happy to attribute fragility to the cup even though interventions of angels can prevent it from ever breaking.

Unfortunately, the case of Otto's meaning one function rather than another is different. We do not have clear intuitions regarding the disposition not to carry. Is the systematic failure to carry an indication that the disposition to add is absent? That is, is carrying part of the disposition to add? Or is carrying merely a favourable condition for adding? Or, again, is it correct to think of the disposition not to carry as a factor that – like our angel above – masks the disposition to add? I doubt that our intuitions yield clear verdicts regarding this question. Given this result, it is unclear how the distinction between (un)favourable and masking conditions can help the dispositionalist. It is obscure how the dispositionalist can earn the right to decide (in all circumstances) between the two hypotheses of Otto being a masked adder and Otto being an unmasked skadder. And since the dispositionalist cannot have dispositional data in *all* cases, dispositions cannot constitute the contents of the two hypotheses.

3. I take this expression from P. van Inwagen, "There Is No Such Thing As Addition", *The Wittgenstein Legacy: Midwest Studies in Philosophy* 17 (1992), 138–59.

4. Fodor, *A Theory of Content and Other Essays*, 94–5.

5. Cf. also S. Blackburn, "The Individual Strikes Back" [1984], in *Rule-Following and Meaning*, Miller & Wright (eds), 28–44, esp. 35; G. Forbes, "Scepticism and Semantic Knowledge", *Proceedings of the Aristotelian Society* 85 (1984), 223–37, esp. 233–4; and D. McManus, "Boghossian, Miller, and Lewis on Dispositional Theories of Meaning", *Mind and Language* 15 (2000), 393–9. Simon Blackburn's objection goes as follows. Imagine a planet – call it "Alpha Centauri" – so far away from earth that any object sent on the trip would decay before reaching its destination. Now take some earthbound glass and its brittleness. This disposition licenses both the claim "*ceteris paribus*, if the glass were dropped on earth it would break", and the statement "*ceteris paribus*, if the glass were dropped on Alpha Centauri it would shatter". If this is granted, then Kripke's argument collapses. For the idealization needed for reaching enormous numbers is analogous to the idealization involved in ignoring the travel from earth to Alpha Centauri. Even though the glass cannot reach Alpha Centauri, it can still be regarded as brittle on that planet. And even though I cannot reach the realm of enormous numbers, I can still think of myself as an adder in the realm of those numbers.

Here is a reply to Blackburn's worry. The analogy between the two cases does not go far enough to support the conclusion. Starting with the case of the glass, the appropriate analogy in the mathematical realm would be "Assuming that I have the disposition to answer '15' to '7 + 8', I would give this answer even on Alpha Centauri". And beginning with the case of the enormous numbers, the appropriate analogue in the world of glasses would be "Even if this glass were much bigger than it is, say, the size of the universe itself, it still would break if dropped". I propose that the first sentence is true and the second false. Go back to the original scenario of the glass. Why do we find it natural to imagine it breaking on Alpha Centauri regardless of its inability to reach that planet? I suppose the answer is that in extending the counterfactual from earth to Alpha Centauri we only need to change a single parameter, that is, the physical location of the glass on a planet. We are not, however, changing anything about the dispositional structure of the glass itself. And thus our knowledge of the physics of the situation is kept constant. The scenario of the idealized adder is radically different. In going from non-enormous to enormous numbers, the dispositionalist introduces a change of the very disposition at issue. The calculator is altered so fundamentally that it is hard to see how *any* parameter remains unchanged. How would I be different if I had a brain the size of the Milky Way? Surely, to answer this question we would need an altogether new psychology or biology; our received knowledge of human beings would, in all likelihood, be useless at this point. If this is true, then Kripke can grant the objector his point regarding the glass, but he can refuse any implication regarding the disposition to add.

6. For a different attempt to defend Kripke on this score, see M. N. Lance & J. O'Leary-Hawthorne, *The Grammar of Meaning: Normativity and Semantic Discourse* (Cambridge: Cambridge University Press, 1997), 311–29.
7. E. McMullin, "Galilean Idealization", *Studies in History and Philosophy of Science* 16 (1985), 247–73.
8. Fodor, *A Theory of Content and Other Essays*, 95.
9. For a similar accusation, see C. Wallis, "Representation and the Imperfect Ideal", *Philosophy of Science* 61 (1994), 407–28.
10. This objection was first put to be my Mark Sprevak. For general discussion regarding the "cognitive penetrability" of psychological processes, see especially Z. W. Pylyshyn, *Computation and Cognition: Toward a Foundation for Cognitive Science* (Cambridge, MA: MIT Press, 1984), 130–45, 173–4. Concerning the cognitive penetrability of the Müller–Lyer law, contrast the debate between Fodor ("Observation Reconsidered", *Philosophy of Science* 51 (1984), 23–43; "A Reply to Churchland's 'Perceptual Plasticity and Theoretical Neutrality'", *Philosophy of Science* 55 (1988), 188–98) and Churchland ("Perceptual Plasticity and Theoretical Neutrality: A Reply to Jerry Fodor", *Philosophy of Science* 55 (1988), 167–87).
11. J. A. Fodor, "You Can Fool Some of the People All of the Time, Everything Else Being Equal: Hedged Laws and Psychological Explanation", *Mind* 100 (1991), 19–34; S. Schiffer, "Ceteris Paribus Laws", *Mind* 100 (1991), 1–17; J. Earman & J. Roberts, "Ceteris Paribus, There is no Problem of Provisos", *Synthese* 118 (1999), 439–78.
12. P. Mott, "Fodor and Ceteris Paribus Laws", *Mind* 101 (1992), 335–46.
13. Boghossian, "The Rule-Following Considerations". For discussion, see the following section.
14. This response was suggested to me by Peter Lipton.
15. P. Lipton, "All Else Being Equal (Ceteris Paribus Laws in Nature)", *Philosophy* 74 (1999), 155–68.
16. A further important extension is the arguments advanced by Crispin Wright. See Wright ("Kripke's Account of the Argument", 771; *Realism, Meaning, and Truth* (Oxford: Blackwell, 1987), 392–4). Sympathetic towards Kripke's criticism of dispositionalism are, among others, G. E. M. Anscombe ("Review of Kripke, *Wittgenstein on Rules and Private Language*", *Ethics* 95 (1985), 342–52, esp. 351) and A. Bilgrami (*Belief and Meaning: The Unity and Locality of Mental Content* (Oxford: Blackwell, 1992), 94).
17. Boghossian, "The Rule-Following Considerations", 177.
18. *Ibid.*
19. P. A. Boghossian, "Naturalizing Content", in *Meaning in Mind: Fodor and his Critics*, B. Loewer & G. Rey (eds), 65–86 (Oxford: Blackwell, 1990), 80–81.
20. A. Miller, "Does 'Belief Holism' Show that Reductive Dispositionalism about Content Could not be True?", *Supplement to the Proceedings of the Aristotelian Society* 77 (2003), 73–90. Miller's earlier contributions are "Boghossian on Reductive Dispositionalism: the Case Strengthened", *Mind and Language* 12 (1997), 1–10, and *Philosophy of Language*.
21. Miller, *Philosophy of Language*, contains an introduction to this technique. See also "Does 'Belief Holism' Show", 82–4.
22. Boghossian, "The Rule-Following Considerations", 179–80.
23. Miller, "Does 'Belief Holism' Show", 87.
24. *Ibid.*, 87–8.
25. I owe this point to email conversation with Miller himself.
26. Again, I owe this point to Miller himself.

27. Miller, personal conversation.
28. S. Teghrarian, "Wittgenstein, Kripke and the 'Paradox' of Meaning", in *Wittgenstein and Contemporary Philosophy*, S. Teghrarian (ed.), 223–59 (Bristol: Thoemmes Press, 1994), 253, objects to any counting of a person's dispositions: "How many dispositions does a courageous man have to behave in courageous ways?"
29. Blackburn, "The Individual Strikes Back"; Forbes, "Scepticism and Semantic Knowledge"; C. Ginet, "The Dispositionalist Solution to Wittgenstein's Problem About Understanding a Rule: Answering Kripke's Objections", *The Wittgenstein Legacy: Midwest Studies in Philosophy* **17** (1992), 53–73; Hattiangadi, "Oughts and Thoughts".
30. Blackburn, "The Individual Strikes Back", 36.
31. Blackburn writes as follows:

    [A] calculator can have, in addition to dispositions to give answers, dispositions to withdraw them and substitute others. And it is possible that putting the errant disposition into a context of general dispositions of this sort supplies the criterion for which function is meant. The equation would be: By "+" I mean that function φ that accords with my extended dispositions. An answer $z = \varphi(x, y)$ accords with my extended dispositions if and only if (i) it is the answer I am disposed to give and retain after investigation, or (ii) it is the answer I would accept if I repeated a number of times procedures I am disposed to use, this being independent. (*Ibid.*: 36)

32. Coates suggests improving on Blackburn's objection by introducing the concept of a "complete cycle of behaviour". Consider the following behaviour of a cat: first it tracks a mouse with its eyes; then it jumps up and grabs the mouse; and, in the end, it "makes discriminatory beneficial use" of the mouse – it eats it. This sequence of feline behaviour is an example of a "complete cycle of behaviour". Coates believes that identifying such a cycle in the behaviour of an animal is important for the attribution of mental content. Our identification of the cat's cycle of behaviour entitles us to say that the cat's thoughts are *about* the mouse. Complete cycles of behaviour help in drawing a distinction between correct and incorrect actions. An incorrect action fails to result in discriminatory beneficial use. As Coates sees it, this idea works also for Kripke's arithmetical example:

    [T]he subject will have dispositions to use the word "plus" … sometimes mistakenly. But she may find out, for example, in doing some carpentry in isolation, that certain calculations which she wrote down have led her astray: two lengths of wood do not match as had been expected, giving her the motive to check and revise her earlier employment of "plus". In this manner a person's extended dispositions will tend, in many cases, to lead her own use of a term to coincide with the correct one. Notice, however … that … the subject will sometimes make mistakes that she is not aware of and does not correct. Because in these cases there is no complete cycle of behaviour terminating in a discriminating beneficial use, such cases do not contribute to determining the content of the subject's states and utterances.
    (Coates, "Meaning, Mistake and Miscalculation", 178–9)

    Unfortunately, it is hard to see why Coates's proposal should constitute an improvement on the previous objection. Coates's suggestion suffers from the twin problems of circularity and underdetermination. It is circular if we allow for complete cycles of mathematical behaviour only in cases in which the calculator gets the arithmetic right. For now we have again put the cart before the horse: we wanted the behaviour to lead us to the meaning, but now we are using the meaning to select the relevant behaviour. It does not help to suggest that we identify the meant function on the basis of our observations of successful actions. This boils down to saying that a calculator means a function F, if, and only if, F enables her to achieve her intentions. But how do we identify the calculator's intentions? Any given piece of behaviour can be seen as achieving – or failing to achieve any number of different intentions. For further detailed criticism of Coates's objection, see Toribio, "Meaning, Dispositions and Normativity".

33. Ginet, "The Dispositionalist Solution".
34. *Ibid.*, 62.
35. *Ibid.*, 70.
36. *Ibid.*, 62–7. Ginet writes:

I do know some past tense counterfactual conditionals about myself as directly, by memory, as I know what some of my categorical conscious states were. Suppose I said the words, "the ordering of letters"; and thereby meant the alphabetic ordering of all the letters of the alphabet (rather than, say, a misspelled word that I had earlier referred to with that same phrase). A few moments later I can (normally) simply *remember* not only that I said those words, but also that I meant by them the function <"a", "b">, <"b", "c">, … etc. And I can simply *remember* that if I had then considered the question, I would have thought that the function I meant includes the pair <"f", "g">. I can directly remember that a certain counterfactual conditional was true of me. That is, we allow a *memory* impression with that content to justify me in claiming to know the truth of such a counterfactual. Compare one's knowledge of the truth of a subjunctive conditional that expresses one's *conditional intention*: in normal circumstances when I assert, "If the telephone were to ring now, I would answer it," I am not making a hypothesis about myself. And when I *remember* having had such an intention, I am not making an hypothesis about my past self: I know simply on the basis of memory that the conditional was true.   (*Ibid.*: 62–3)

Ginet is right for the cases mentioned. Alas, his point does not generalize. The case of the alphabet is persuasive only because we have chanted the alphabet so many times in the past. The case belaboured by the sceptic is different because we are dealing with scenarios that I have never encountered before.

37. A. Miller, "Horwich, Meaning and Kripke's Wittgenstein", *Philosophical Quarterly* **50** (2000), 161–74, esp. 161; cf. Horwich, "Meaning, Use and Truth", 360. Here I follow Miller's rather than Horwich's formulation, since Horwich's text is concerned specifically with what he calls the "use theory of meaning". This is a communal disposition theory. I shall discuss it below.

38. Horwich, "Meaning, Use and Truth", 364.

39. *Ibid.*, 361–2.

40. Miller, "Horwich, Meaning and Kripke's Wittgenstein".

41. S. Soames, "Scepticism about Meaning: Indeterminacy, Normativity, and the Rule-Following Paradox", *Canadian Journal of Philosophy*, suppl. vol. **23** (1998), 211–49, esp. 223.

42. *Ibid.*, 231.

43. Again, "*m*" and "*n*" are numerals. The assumption of determinism is needed to make sure that I will give the same answers on different occasions for the same values for "*m*" and "*n*".

44. Soames, "Scepticism about Meaning", 226–8.

45. *Ibid.*, 229.

46. *Ibid.*

47. The best general introduction to supervenience is D. Chalmers, *The Conscious Mind: In Search of a Fundamental Theory* (Oxford: Oxford University Press, 1996), ch. 2.

48. Perhaps Soames will protest here that just because he has not been very precise about which physical properties provide the supervenience base, it is unfair to saddle him with global supervenience. If this is his position then Soames owes us an account of how to restrict the class of the relevant physical properties.

49. Here I am indebted to discussions with Tim Crane, Peter Lipton, Barry Smith and José Zalabardo.

50. Cf. M. Dummett, "Realism", *Synthese* **52** (1982), 55–112, esp. 111: "A disposition of any kind is not a quality of which we can be directly aware …".

51. C. B. Martin & J. Heil, "Rules and Powers", *Language, Mind, and Ontology, Philosophical Perspectives* **12** (1998), 283–312, esp. 289.

52. C. Wright, *Truth and Objectivity* (Cambridge, MA: Harvard University Press, 1992), 117–18; S. Mumford, *Dispositions* (Oxford: Clarendon Press, 1998), 56.

53. Martin & Heil, "Rules and Powers", 304.

54. C. B. Martin, "Final Replies to Place and Armstrong", in D. M. Armstrong, C. B. Martin, U. T. Place, *Dispositions: A Debate*, T. Crane (ed.), 163–92 (London: Routledge, 1996), 190; Martin & Heil, "Rules and Powers", 305.

55. Martin & Heil, "Rules and Powers", 291.

56. Note that I am not making the general claim that wherever actual and counterfactual behaviour is the same, dispositional structure must be the same, too. I accept that in simple force cases such discrimination seems possible. My point is rather that in the given scenario such a distinction cannot be made without bringing in information about the intention of the designer of the machines. And this point carries over to the analogous case of dispositions to add or skadd.

57. Martin & Heil, "Rules and Powers", 302.

58. *Ibid.*, 305.

59. McGinn's capacities are similar to dispositions realistically construed (*Wittgenstein on Meaning*, 168–75). They fall by the same criticism. Cf. C. Wright, "Critical Notice of Colin McGinn's *Wittgenstein on Meaning*" [1989] , in *Rule-Following and Meaning*, Miller & Wright (eds), 108–28.

60. Horwich, "Wittgenstein and Kripke on the Nature of Meaning", 111.

61. Boghossian, "The Rule-Following Considerations", 173.

62. Horwich, "Wittgenstein and Kripke on the Nature of Meaning", 112.

63. Neil Tennant (*The Taming of the True* (Oxford, Clarendon Press, 1997), 125–42) offers a version of communal dispositionalism combined with elements of other strategies. Tennant thinks of minds as machines. In the case of machines we can work out which inputs will produce which outputs. We can write "machine tables" that both specify such input–output pairings and describe how these pairings are produced by the internal mechanism of the machine. The same goes for minds:

> For a materialist, the difference between … machines and your mind is only a matter of degree. When you learn new words, some part of your mind/brain is being redesigned to compute communally approved outputs for a given range of inputs. … Given a mature speaker, one could in principle open his head … and discover his sub-programme for "+", or "green". Idealizing, we can say that he ought to respond to "58 + 67 = ?" with "125".
>
> (*Ibid.*: 131)

Tennant admits that we know too little about function localization in the brain to give this suggestion much substance. To circumvent this problem, he makes a further proposal. We can counter the sceptic by agreeing with him on a machine table for addition (at least up to 57). And we can then build a machine that instantiates this machine table. This is meant to solve the problem of how we should decide "what the sum of two numbers *is* – what anybody's answer *ought to be*": "Having written down the machine table for addition, let any question as to how one *ought* to respond to an addition sum be answered by reference to the machine table, and its physical realisation …" (*ibid.*: 131).

Tennant realizes that the machine table can be interpreted in different ways by the sceptic. But he dismisses this possibility by shifting the burden of proof: "Let them show now how such deviant interpretations of machine-table symbols can sit coherently with the deviant interpretations originally offered by the sceptic for the function symbol (such as '+') for which the machine table was agreed upon" (*ibid.*: 133). Tennant also offers a solution to the problem of our machines going wrong. The solution is to run several machines in parallel (*ibid.*: 134).

Tennant claims to "have met the sceptical challenge, and have offered a physicalist account, based on neurological and behavioural dispositions, of what it is for the world of a language to have the meanings that (or to mean what) they do" (*ibid.*: 137). To the finitude problem he replies that a dispositionalist account does not demand that the adder be able to add numbers of any length. It suffices if he passes more limited tests of his ability to add (*ibid.*: 137–30). And, finally, Tennant invokes the community in order to solve the mistake problem:

> Kripke … ignores the recourse that the dispositionalist would have to the wider consensus to be obtained within a *community* of understanders. … part of true understanding on the part of any speaker or subject is a principled willingness to defer to communal correction. Such correction is usually adjudicated by a minority of experts if need be; but still it involves *other understanders* and *their* dispositions to compute (for such, it is being maintained, is all that there is to ground the normativites in question). … The pig-headed maker of mistakes who refuses ever to be corrected can indeed be said (by the dispositionalist) to mean skaddition rather than addition. But the fallible adder who is willing to have his mistakes pointed out to him, and accept corrections as called for, may by virtue of those very dispositions be said to be a true understander of addition.
>
> (*Ibid.*: 140)

I remain unconvinced. First, Tennant's machine analogy fails to make contact with the arguments that Kripke explicitly directs against it. Secondly, Tennant does not address the crucial problem of idealization. Thirdly, Tennant's answer to the finitude problem is obviously unsatisfactory. My dispositions to give sums in reply to plus-queries with non-enormous numbers cannot show that I have dispositions to give sums in reply to plus-queries with enormous numbers. And fourthly, Tennant's communitarian-dispositionalist treatment of the mistake problem fails to circumvent the difficulties we have just analysed with reference to Horwich's proposal.

Chapter 4: Other responses

1. Wright, "Kripke's Account of the Argument", 773, n.5.
2. A. Miller, "Introduction", in *Rule-Following and Meaning*, Miller & Wright (eds), 10, n.16.
3. C. Peacocke, "Content and Norms in a Natural Word", in *Information, Semantics, and Epistemology*, E. Villanueva (ed.), 57–76 (Oxford: Blackwell, 1990), 66.
4. *Ibid.*, 68.
5. *Ibid.*, 74.
6. Tennant, *The Taming of the True*, 111. For every [number] n, there are exactly $(n + 1)$ distinct addition sums with result n [n is the numeral for n], including, for every $p < n$, the sum "$p + (n - p)$" and the sum "$(n - p) + p$".
7. *Ibid.*, 112.
8. There is an x and there is a y such that: x is F and y is F and y is not identical with x; and for all y: if a w is F, then it is identical either with x or with y.
9. *Ibid.*, 113.
10. *Ibid.*
11. *Ibid.*, 114.
12. M. Devitt & K. Sterelny, *Language and Reality: An Introduction to the Philosophy of Language*, 2nd ed (Oxford: Blackwell, 1999), chs 4 and 5.
13. *Ibid.*, 90–93.
14. McGinn, *Wittgenstein on Meaning*, 165–6.
15. P. Maddy, "How the Causal Theorist Follows a Rule", *Midwest Studies in Philosophy* **9** (1984), 457–77, esp. 469–70.
16. *Ibid.*, 470.
17. *Ibid.*, 471–2; cf. also P. Maddy, "Mathematical Alchemy", *British Journal for the Philosophy of Science* **37** (1986), 279–314.
18. Boghossian, "The Rule-Following Considerations", 158.
19. F. Feldman, Critical Notice of Kripke, *Wittgenstein on Rules and Private Language*, *Philosophy and Phenomenological Research* **46** (1986), 683–7; M. Gilbert, *On Social Facts* (Princeton, NJ: Princeton University Press, 1989), 114–24; J. J. Katz, *The Metaphysics of Meaning* (Cambridge, MA: MIT Press, 1990), 163–74; J. Zalabardo, "Wittgenstein on Accord", *Pacific Philosophical Quarterly* **84** (2003), 311–29.
20. J. J. Katz, *Language and Other Abstract Objects* (Oxford: Blackwell, 1981).
21. Katz, *The Metaphysics of Meaning*, 89–90.
22. *Ibid.*
23. This reply is given in Katz, *The Metaphysics of Meaning*, ch. 4.
24. *Ibid.*, 163–4.
25. *Ibid.*
26. *Ibid.*, 166.
27. *Ibid.*
28. *Ibid.*, 167.
29. *Ibid.*
30. *Ibid.*
31. *Ibid.*, 171.
32. *Ibid.*, 173.
33. P. A. Boghossian, "Sense, Reference and Rule-Following", *Philosophy and Phenomenological Research*

54 (1994), 139–45. For other criticism of Katz's Platonism, see R. G. Gibson, "Katz on Indeterminacy and the Proto-Theory", *Philosophy and Phenomenological Research* 54 (1994), 133–9; P. Horwich, "Meaning and Metaphilosophy", *Philosophy and Phenomenological Research* 54 (1994), 145–50; G. W. Levvis, "Wittgenstein's Grammatical Propositions as Linguistic Examplars: A Refutation of Katz's Semantic Platonism", *Philosophical Investigations* 19 (1996), 140–58; and E. M. Zemach, "Katz and Wittgenstein", *Philosophy and Phenomenological Research* 54 (1994), 151–5. Katz replies to some of his critics in "Replies to Commentators", *Philosophy and Phenomenological Research* 54 (1994), 157–83
34. Boghossian, "Sense, Reference and Rule-Following", 142.
35. *Ibid.*, 143.
36. Katz, "Replies to Commentators", 170.
37. It is surprising to note, for instance, that Bob Hale's fascinating defence of Platonism (*Abstract Objects* (Oxford: Oxford University Press, 1987)) does not address Wittgenstein's and Kripke's objections. For a criticism of Hale's version of Platonism with Kripkenstein-inspired permutation arguments, see P. Pagin, Review of Hale, *Abstract Objects, History and Philosophy of Logic* 10 (1989), 111–13.
38. Cf. Zemach, "Katz and Wittgenstein".
39. C. Wright, *Wittgenstein on the Foundations of Mathematics* (London: Duckworth, 1980); M. Wilson, "Predicate Meets Property", *Philosophical Review* 91 (1982), 549–89; Bloor, *Wittgenstein*.
40. Feldman, Critical Notice of Kripke. Cf. Zalabardo, "Wittgenstein on Accord".
41. Feldman, Critical Notice of Kripke, 686.
42. *Ibid.*, 687.
43. Of course, the Platonist might claim that the reason is the incoherence of meaning scepticism. This reason can only be undercut by the demonstration that the sceptical solution is adequate.

Chapter 5: Factualism and non-factualism

1. Boghossian, "Naturalizing Content", 164.
2. S. Blackburn, *Spreading the Word: Groundings in the Philosophy of Language* (Oxford: Clarendon, 1984), 170–71. For a general overview of different forms of projectivism in metaethics, see Miller, *An Introduction to Contemporary Metaethics*.
3. Ayer, *Language, Truth, and Logic*. Cf. Miller, *An Introduction to Contemporary Metaethics*, ch. 2.
4. Blackburn, *Spreading the Word*, ch. 5. Cf. Miller, *An Introduction to Contemporary Metaethics*, ch. 4.
5. I here mimic Miller's formulation of quasi-realism for the moral realm. Cf. Miller, *An Introduction to Contemporary Metaethics*, 52.
6. Blackburn, *Spreading the Word*; J. McDowell, "Meaning and Intentionality in Wittgenstein's Later Philosophy", *The Wittgenstein Legacy: Midwest Studies in Philosophy* 17 (1992), 40–52 and "Wittgenstein on Following a Rule"; McGinn, *Wittgenstein on Meaning*; Wright, "Kripke's Account of the Argument"; Boghossian, "The Rule-Following Considerations".
7. M. Dummett, "Wittgenstein's Philosophy of Mathematics", *Philosophical Review* 68 (1959), 324–48, esp. 348.
8. A non-factualist reading is defended in C. Travis, *The Uses of Sense: Wittgenstein's Philosophy of Language* (Oxford: Oxford University Press, 1989), 325–8.
9. Wright, "Kripke's Account of the Argument", 769.
10. S. Soames, "Facts, Truth Conditions, and the Skeptical Solution to the Rule-following Paradox", *Philosophical Perspectives* 12 (1998), 313–48, also contains important criticisms of local non-factualism. Soames does not equate non-factualism with projectivism; he prefers to say that if meaning attributions are non-factual then they are "performatives" (in the sense familiar from speech-act theory). The key point is that performatives (such as "I hereby declare you husband and wife") do not express propositions and thus are not candidates for truth and falsity. On this analysis, to utter "Jones means addition by '+'" in the right circumstances is to "take Jones into one's linguistic community, to certify him as a competent user of '+' and to license him to use '+' to do what we call 'adding'" (*ibid.*: 323).
    Soames's first argument against this view is that a performative rendering of meaning attributions brings with it a performative rendering of propositional attitude ascriptions. If ascriptions of meaning are non-factual, then surely ascriptions of beliefs, desires and so on must be too. But a nonfactual reading of propositional attitude ascriptions does not seem plausible. All such ascriptions "are

unproblematically embeddable in ordinary truth-conditional constructions, such as antecedents of conditionals, … and all may themselves appear as objects of propositional attitude verbs, like 'know' and 'believe', which are used to indicate our cognitive relations to facts, and to propositions generally". And what holds for these attitude ascriptions actually also holds for meaning attributions: "Since meaning and propositional attitude ascriptions satisfy these conditions, they qualify as fact-stating" (*ibid.*).

Soames's second complaint is that a performative rendering of meaning attributions would in some important respects be too tame a proposal. To demonstrate that meaning attributions are performatives would show merely that the domain of the truth-conditional view is somewhat more limited than previously thought. It would leave the truth-conditional view intact, however, for a vast domain of sentences that are philosophically significant even though they do not ascribe meanings or mental contents. And if this domain remains unchanged, then Kripke can no longer insist that the sceptical solution has radical implications for the philosophy of mathematics and the understanding of private language (*ibid.*: 325).

Soames's third point against non-factualism about meaning attributions is that it is "incoherent". Take the sentence (a):

(a)   No meaning attribution expresses a proposition.

In so far as (a) makes a claim about a class of sentences, (a) itself expresses a proposition and states a fact. Moreover, if (a) expresses a proposition then surely so does its negation:

(b)   Some meaning attribution expresses a proposition.

Now, (b) is an existential generalization. As its instances it has sentences of the form (c):

(c)   *S* is a meaning attribution and *S* expresses a proposition.

Now, if (b) expresses a proposition then so must at least some of its instantiations. Alas, according to (a), instances of (c) do not express propositions. And thus non-factualism is incoherent (*ibid.*: 325).

The first two arguments are clearly very strong. Things seem less straightforward with respect to the third; it seems to rely on the questionable claim that (c) is itself a meaning attribution. But, like (a), it is not.

11. Boghossian, "The Rule-Following Considerations", 161–2.
12. P. A. Boghossian, "The Status of Content", *Philosophical Review* **99** (1990), 157–84, esp. 165.
13. *Ibid.*, 164.
14. Wright, "Kripke's Account of the Argument", 769.
15. Boghossian, "The Status of Content", 174–5.
16. I here rely on M. Devitt, "Transcendentalism about Content", *Pacific Philosophical Quarterly* **71** (1990), 247–63; Wright, *Truth and Objectivity*, 231–6; R. Kraut, "Robust Deflationism", *Philosophical Review* **102** (1993), 247–63; F. Jackson, G. Oppy, M. Smith, "Minimalism and Truth Aptness", *Mind* **103** (1994), 287–302; B. Hale, "Rule-following, Objectivity and Meaning", in *A Companion to the Philosophy of Language*, B. Hale & C. Wright (eds), 369–97 (Oxford, Blackwell, 1997); Miller, *Philosophy of Language*, 165–70.
17. Wright, *Truth and Objectivity*, 234.
18. Jackson *et al.*, "Minimalism and Truth Aptness".
19. *Ibid.*, 296. For a criticism of Jackson *et al.*, "Minimalism and Truth Aptness", see J. O'Leary-Hawthorne & H. Price, "How to Stand Up for Non-cognitivists", *Australasian Journal of Philosophy* **74** (1996), 275–92.
20. Kraut, "Robust Deflationism", 252.
21. *Ibid.*, 248.
22. Wright, "Kripke's Account of the Argument", 769.
23. *Ibid*.
24. *Ibid.*, 770.
25. Boghossian, "The Rule-Following Considerations", 160–61.
26. Wright, *Truth and Objectivity*, 217–20.
27. Jim Edwards, Mark Sprevak and especially Elie Zahar have helped enormously with successive drafts of the argument. Of course, I alone am responsible for any remaining mistakes.
28. Here is a more rigorous characterization of the system used. Again thanks are due to Elie Zahar.

$p, q, r, s \ldots$ are sentential variables; φ is a propositional variable.

The two important predicates are: the monadic truth-predicate T; and the dyadic predicate Δ. $\Delta(s, \varphi)$ says that φ is the proposition (i.e. the truth-condition) expressed by s.

$\Delta(s, p)$ says that p expresses the proposition (i.e. the truth-condition) expressed by s.

The recursive formation rules for well-formed formulas (wffs) are:

(a) $p, q, r, s \ldots$ are wffs.

(b) $\Delta(s, \varphi)$ and $\Delta(s, p)$ are wffs.

(c) $T(x)$ is a wff.

(d) If $H(x)$ and B are wffs, and if B is free for x in $H(x)$, then $H(B)$ is a wff.

(e) If A and B are wffs, then so are $\sim$A, A & B, A $\vee$ B, A $\rightarrow$ B, A $\leftrightarrow$ B, (x)B, (φ)B, $(\exists x)$B, $(\exists\varphi)$B.

The rules of inference are *modus ponens* and *generalization*, for both sentential and propositional variables.

The axioms are the usual logical truths, together with the truth schema: for any sentence B, $T(B) \leftrightarrow B$.

Note that (d) is needed if $\Delta(\Delta(x, y), \varphi)$ is to be meaningful. This is, of course, a weakness of the system: we have variables such that part of their range are the wffs of the system itself. This throws the legitimacy of the proof into some doubt.

29. Here is an alternative way of showing why global and local projectivism are wrong:

$b = $"$(s)(p) \sim \Delta (s, p)$"

$(p) (\sim\Delta (b, p))$	(universal quantifier elimination)
$\sim\Delta (b, p)$	(universal quantifier elimination)
$\sim T(b)$	(no truth conditions, no truth)
$\sim b$	(negation equivalence)

$\sim$ "$(s)(p) \sim \Delta (s, p)$"

Hence global projectivism entails its own negation and is a contradiction. But then, since local projectivism entails global projectivism, local projectivism must be a contradiction as well. (Here I am indebted to Sungho Choi.)

30. A. Byrne, "On Misinterpreting Kripke's Wittgenstein", *Philosophy and Phenomenological Research* **56** (1996), 339–43; D. Davies, "How Sceptical is Kripke's 'Sceptical Solution'?", *Philosophia* **26** (1998), 119–40; Wilson, "Kripke on Wittgenstein and Normativity", "Semantic Realism and Kripke's Wittgenstein", *Philosophy and Phenomenological Research* **58** (1998), 99–122 and "The Skeptical Solution", in *The Legitimacy of Truth*, R. Dottori (ed.), 171–87 (Münster: Litt, 2003).

31. Byrne, "On Misinterpreting Kripke's Wittgenstein", 342.

32. *Ibid.*

33. Wilson, "Kripke on Wittgenstein and Normativity", 246.

34. *Ibid.*, 247.

35. *Ibid.*

36. Wilson, "Semantic Realism and Kripke's Wittgenstein", 102.

37. *Ibid.*, 104.

38. *Ibid.*, 105.

39. *Ibid.*, 106.

40. *Ibid.*, 107.

41. *Ibid.*

42. *Ibid.*, 108.

43. Wilson, "Kripke on Wittgenstein and Normativity", 243; "Semantic Realism and Kripke's Wittgenstein", 109.

44. Wilson, "Kripke on Wittgenstein and Normativity", 248.

45. Soames, "Facts, Truth Conditions".

46. *Ibid.*, 330.

47. *Ibid.*, 329–30.

48. *Ibid.*, 331.

49. *Ibid.*

50. *Ibid.*, 331–2.
51. *Ibid.*, 332.
52. *Ibid.*, 337.
53. *Ibid.*, 333–4.
54. *Ibid.*, 336–7.
55. *Ibid.*, 335–7.
56. *Ibid.*, 337.
57. *Ibid.*, 338.
58. Kripke here quotes Dummett, "Wittgenstein's Philosophy of Mathematics", 348.
59. See, for example, P. Engel, *The Norm of Truth: An Introduction to the Philosophy of Logic* (Toronto: University of Toronto Press, 1991), ch. 1; G. Kemp, "Meaning and Truth-Conditions", *Philosophical Quarterly* **48** (1998), 483–93; J. C. King, "Structured Propositions", *Stanford Encyclopedia of Philosophy* (2001), http://plato.stanford.edu/entries/propositions-structured/ (accessed May 2006); M. J. Loux, *Metaphysics: A Contemporary Introduction* (London: Routledge, 1998), ch. 4; W. G. Lycan, *Philosophy of Language: A Contemporary Introduction* (London: Routledge, 2000), 80–85; S. Soames, *Understanding Truth* (Oxford: Oxford University Press, 1999), ch. 1; D. C. Dennett, *The Intentional Stance* (Cambridge, MA: MIT Press, 1987), ch. 5.
60. Cf. Loux, *Metaphysics*, 153.
61. Here I am taking a leaf out of Dennett's book. Commenting on Churchland's one-time idea that propositions are "ways of 'measuring' semantic information", Dennett objects that the units of measurement are less like numbers (as Churchland would have it), and more like dollars: "*There are no real, natural, universal units of either economic value or semantic information*" (Dennett, *The Intentional Stance*, 208).
62. This notion of "speech act fallacy" is not quite Searle's (cf. Searle, *Speech Acts*, 136–41). My use of the term comes from Blackburn: "it would be wrong to infer that *no* description is given from the fact that an attitude is *also* expressed" (Blackburn, *Spreading the Word*, 169).
63. Something like this is also advocated in David Bloor's insightful discussion of the sceptical solution (see Bloor, *Wittgenstein*). For further discussion of Bloor's proposal, see M. Kusch, "Rule-Scepticism and the Sociology of Scientific Knowledge", and Bloor's reply, "Institutions and Rule-Scepticism".
64. Here I am indebted to Wilson, "The Skeptical Solution", 181.

Chapter 6: Intersubjectivity and assertability conditions
1. Boghossian, "The Rule-Following Considerations", 155.
2. *Ibid.*, 156.
3. McGinn, *Wittgenstein on Meaning*; W. Goldfarb, "Kripke on Wittgenstein on Rules" [1985], in *Rule-Following and Meaning*, Miller & Wright (eds), 92–107; and Boghossian, "The Rule-Following Considerations".
4. McGinn, *Wittgenstein on Meaning*, 185.
5. Boghossian, "The Rule-Following Considerations", 157.
6. McGinn, *Wittgenstein on Meaning*, 185.
7. *Ibid.*
8. *Ibid.*, 187.
9. S. Shanker, "Sceptical Confusions About Rule-Following", *Mind* **93** (1984), 423–9.
10. N. Chomsky, *Knowledge of Language: Its Nature, Origin, and Use* (Westport, CT: Praeger, 1986), 233.
11. Baker & Hacker, *Scepticism, Rules and Language*, 40.
12. *Ibid.*, 40–41.
13. McGinn, *Wittgenstein on Meaning*, 191.
14. *Ibid.*, 198.
15. *Ibid.*, 195.
16. McDowell, "Wittgenstein on Following a Rule", 49.
17. Blackburn, "The Individual Strikes Back", 39.
18. Baker & Hacker, *Scepticism, Rules and Language*, 39.

19. Blackburn, "The Individual Strikes Back", 42; cf. G. Gillett, "Humpty Dumpty and the Night of the Triffids: Individualism and Rule-following", *Synthese* **105** (1995), 191–206, esp. 194; Wright, "Does *Philosophical Investigations* I.258–60 Suggest a Cogent Argument", 214.
20. McGinn, *Wittgenstein on Meaning*, 196–7.
21. Bloor, *Wittgenstein*, 92.
22. These comments might also provide an answer to C. Diamond ("Rules: Looking in the Right Place", in *Wittgenstein: Attention to Particulars*, D. Z. Phillips & P. Winch (eds), 12–34 (Basingstoke: Macmillan, 1989), 29). Diamond overlooks that Kripke's Wittgenstein's criteria for rule-following are holistic.
23. D. Summerfield, "*Philosophical Investigations* 201: A Wittgensteinian Reply to Kripke", *Journal of the History of Philosophy* **28** (1990), 417–38, esp. 436.
24. *Ibid.*
25. M. Kusch, *Psychological Knowledge: A Social History and Philosophy* (London: Routledge, 1999), 250–51.
26. Cf. Davidson, "The Social Aspect of Language", 119, and M. Esfeld, *Holism in Philosophy of Mind and Philosophy of Physics* (Dordrecht: Kluwer, 2001), 91, for similar objections.
27. N. Lillegard, "How Private Must an Objectionably Private Language Be?", *Paideia – Philosophy of Language* (1998), www.bu.edu/wcp/Papers/Lang/LangLill.htm (accessed May 2006).
28. Cf. Bloor, *Wittgenstein*, 105.
29. Cf. Meredith Williams, "Blind Obedience: Rules, Community and the Individual", in *Meaning Scepticism*, K. Puhl (ed.), 93–125 (Berlin: de Gruyter, 1991), 111.
30. N. Malcolm, *Nothing is Hidden* (Oxford: Blackwell, 1986), 177.
31. D. F. Pears, *The False Prison*, vol. 2 (Oxford: Clarendon Press, 1988), 365.
32. R. Brandom, *Making It Explicit: Reasoning, Representing, & Discursive Commitment* (Cambridge, MA: Harvard University Press, 1994), 38. The page in question is *WRPL*: 108.
33. *Ibid.*, 19.
34. *Ibid.*, 27–8.
35. *Ibid.*, 28.
36. *Ibid.*
37. *Ibid.*, 38.
38. *Ibid.*, 594.
39. *Ibid.*, 38.
40. *Ibid.*, 39.
41. *Ibid.*, 599.
42. *Ibid.*, 594.
43. *Ibid.*, 599.
44. Baker & Hacker, *Scepticism, Rules and Language*, 94–5.
45. *Ibid.*
46. *Ibid.*, 107.
47. *Ibid.*, 72.
48. *Ibid.*, 110.
49. *Ibid.*, 88.
50. *Ibid.*, 72.
51. *Ibid.*, 78.
52. Similar criticism can be found in E. Craig, Review of Baker and Hacker (1984), *Philosophical Quarterly* **35** (1985), 212–14, and J. Heal, Review of Baker and Hacker (1984), *Mind* **94** (1985), 307–10.

Chapter 7: Semantic primitivism

1. See also C. McGinn, "Wittgenstein, Kripke and Non-Reductionism about Meaning" [1984], in *Rule-Following and Meaning*, Miller & Wright (eds), 81–90, and T. Nagel, *The Last Word* (Oxford: Oxford University Press, 1997), 46.
2. Boghossian, "The Rule-Following Considerations", 179; see also McGinn, "Wittgenstein, Kripke and Non-Reductionism", 87. Boghossian writes: "It is interesting to note, incidentally, that one of the more striking examples of the introspective discernment of a non-qualitative mental feature is provided

by, of all things, an experiential phenomenon. I have in mind the phenomenon, much discussed by Wittgenstein himself, of seeing-as. We see the duck-rabbit now as a duck, now as a rabbit; we see the Necker cube now with one face forward, now with another. And we know immediately precisely how we are seeing these objects as, when we see them now in one way, now in the other. But this change of 'aspect', although manifestly introspectible, is nevertheless not a change in something qualitative, for the qualitative character of the visual experience remains the same even as the aspect changes" ("The Rule-Following Considerations", 179).

3. *Ibid.*, 180.
4. *Ibid.*, 186.
5. C. Wright, *Rails to Infinity: Essays on Themes from Wittgenstein's* Philosophical Investigations (Cambridge, MA: Harvard University Press, 2001), 112–13.
6. Wright's work on intention has been widely discussed. I have particularly profited from studying J. Divers & A. Miller. "Platitudes and Attitudes: A Minimal Conception of Belief", *Analysis* **55** (1995), 37–44; J. Edwards, "Best Opinion and Intentional States", *Philosophical Quarterly* **42** (1992), 21–33; D. H. Finkelstein, "Wittgenstein on Rules and Platonism", in *The New Wittgenstein*, A. Crary & R. Read (eds), 53–73; R. Holton, "Intention Detection", *Philosophical Quarterly* **43** (1993), 298–318; J. McDowell, "Intentionality and Interiority in Wittgenstein: Comment on Crispin Wright", in *Meaning Scepticism*, Puhl (ed.), 148–69 and "Response to Crispin Wright", in *Knowing Our Own Minds*, C. Wright, B. C. Smith, C. Macdonald (eds), 47–62 (Oxford: Oxford University Press, 1998); A. Miller, "An Objection to Wright's Treatment of Intention", *Analysis* **49** (1989), 169–73; P. M. Sullivan, "Problems for a Construction of Meaning and Intention", *Mind* **103** (1994), 147–68; and T. Thornton, "Intention, Rule Following and the Strategic Role of Wright's Order of Determination Test", *Philosophical Investigations* **20** (1997), 136–47, and *Wittgenstein on Language and Thought: The Philosophy of Content* (Edinburgh: Edinburgh University Press, 1988), 80–87. Wright is not the only author who invokes direct knowledge of intentions as an argument against Kripke; see S. Mulhall, "No Smoke Without Fire: The Meaning of Grue", *Philosophical Quarterly* **39** (1989), 166–89.
7. Wright, *Rails to Infinity*, 84.
8. *Ibid.*, 110–11.
9. *Ibid.*, 111.
10. *Ibid.*, 126–7.
11. *Ibid.*, 126.
12. *Ibid.*, 113.
13. *Ibid.*, 138.
14. *Ibid.*, 132.
15. *Ibid.*, 138.
16. *Ibid.*, 139.
17. *Ibid.*, 140.
18. *Ibid*, 140–41.
19. Edwards ("Best Opinion and Intentional States") claims that the second account is meant to state a metaphysical necessity. Wright (*Truth and Objectivity*, 108–39) seems to insist that necessity should not be used in expressing the response-dependent position. Nevertheless, it seems clear that the second account is meant to express a stronger form of modality. It is for that reason that I am using the more cautious statement "veers towards the metaphysical".
20. Wright, *Rails to Infinity*, 139.
21. Wright, *Truth and Objectivity*, 117–24, and *Rails to Infinity*, 195–6.
22. Wright, *Rails to Infinity*, 88.
23. *Ibid.*, 142.
24. *Ibid.*, 177.
25. *Ibid.*, 206.
26. *Ibid.*, 42.
27. *Ibid.*, 87–8.
28. *Ibid.*, 142.
29. This point is overlooked by Finkelstein, "Wittgenstein on Rules and Platonism".

30. Cf. Edwards, "Best Opinion and Intentional States", 30–31.
31. Wright, *Rails to Infinity*, 87.
32. *Ibid.*, 142.
33. McDowell, "Wittgenstein on Following a Rule" and "Meaning and Intentionality".
34. McDowell, "Meaning and Intentionality", 41–2.
35. *Ibid.*, 42–3.
36. *Ibid.*, 43.
37. McDowell, "Wittgenstein on Following a Rule", 51.
38. *Ibid.*, 51.
39. *Ibid.*, 64.
40. L. Wittgenstein, *The Blue and Brown Books* (Oxford: Blackwell, 1958), 34; McDowell, "Wittgenstein on Following a Rule", 53.
41. McDowell, "Wittgenstein on Following a Rule", 53.
42. *Ibid.*, 64.
43. I follow McDowell's proposal for changing the punctuation in this section.
44. *Ibid.*, "Wittgenstein on Following a Rule", 66–9. McDowell claims that Wright, *Wittgenstein on the Foundations of Mathematics*, is guilty of this sin. For a convincing defence of Wright, see Hale, "Rule-following, Objectivity and Meaning".
45. McDowell, "Meaning and Intentionality", 50.
46. L. Wittgenstein, *Remarks on the Foundations of Mathematics*, VI 32; McDowell, "Wittgenstein on Following a Rule", 64.
47. McDowell, "Wittgenstein on Following a Rule", 61.
48. *Ibid.*, 64.
49. *Ibid.*, 46.
50. *Ibid.*, 75.
51. *Ibid.*, 74.
52. McDowell, "Meaning and Intentionality", 48.
53. McDowell, "Wittgenstein on Following a Rule", 46.
54. McDowell, "Meaning and Intentionality", 51; McDowell takes this term from Wright.
55. McDowell, "Meaning and Intentionality", 50.
56. *Ibid.*, 51.
57. *Ibid.*, 47.
58. *Ibid.*, 43.
59. This interpretation of McDowell was suggested to me by Alex Miller.
60. McDowell, "Meaning and Intentionality", 74.
61. P. Pettit, "The Reality of Rule-Following" [1990], in *Rule-Following and Meaning*, Miller & Wright (eds), 188–208, "Affirming the Reality of Rule-Following", *Mind* **99** (1990), 433–9, and P. Pettit, *The Common Mind: An Essay on Psychology, Society, and Politics*, 2nd ed. (Oxford: Oxford University Press, 1996). There has been relatively little discussion of Pettit's proposal in the literature. Followers of Pettit are J. Haukioja, "Rule-Following, Response-Dependence and Realism", Reports from the Department of Philosophy, University of Turku (2000); J. Bransen, "On Exploring Normative Constraints in New Situations", *Inquiry* **44** (2001), 43–62; and Esfeld, *Holism in Philosophy of Mind*. For an early critical discussion, see D. Summerfield, "On Taking the Rabbit of Rule-Following out of the Hat of Representation: A Response to Pettit's 'The Reality of Rule-Following'", *Mind* **99** (1990), 425–32. Pettit replies to Summerfield in "Affirming the Reality of Rule-Following".
62. Pettit, "The Reality of Rule-Following", 202.
63. *Ibid.*, 189–90.
64. *Ibid.*, 193–6.
65. *Ibid.*, 196.
66. *Ibid.*, 196–7.
67. *Ibid.*, 198.
68. *Ibid.*, emphasis added.
69. *Ibid.*

70. *Ibid.*, 201, n.24. Here Pettit sides explicitly with Fodor, *A Theory of Content and Other Essays*.
71. Pettit, "The Reality of Rule-Following", 199. Pettit calls an inclination firing under favourable conditions "standardised".
72. *Ibid.*, 200.
73. *Ibid.*, 203.
74. Pettit, *The Common Mind*, 179.
75. Pettit, "The Reality of Rule-Following", 205.
76. *Ibid.*, 196.
77. *Ibid.*, 189.
78. *Ibid.*, 201, n.24.
79. *Ibid.*, 193.
80. *Ibid.*, 202.
81. *Ibid.*, 203.

Chapter 8: Kripke's interpretation of Wittgenstein

1. G. P. Baker & P. M. S. Hacker, *Wittgenstein: Understanding and Meaning* (An Analytical Commentary on the *Philosophical Investigations*, vol. 1) (Oxford: Blackwell, 1980) and *Scepticism, Rules and Language*; P. M. S. Hacker, *Wittgenstein: Meaning and Mind* (An Analytical Commentary on the *Philosophical Investigations*, vol. 3) (Oxford: Blackwell, 1990) and *Wittgenstein: Mind and Will* (An Analytical Commentary on the *Philosophical Investigations*, vol. 4) (Oxford: Blackwell, 1996).
2. C. Diamond, Review of Baker and Hacker (1985), *Philosophical Books* **26** (1985), 26–9, esp. 27.
3. Meredith Williams, Review of P. M. S. Hacker, *Connections and Controversies* (Oxford: Oxford University Press, 2001), http://ndpr.nd.edu/review.cfm?id=1077 (accessed June 2006).
4. Heal, Review of Baker and Hacker, 310.
5. Craig, Review of Baker and Hacker, 214.
6. Cf. McGinn, *Wittgenstein on Meaning*, 72; A. Lewis, "Wittgenstein and Rule-Scepticism", *Philosophical Quarterly* **38** (1988), 280–304, esp. 280; B. Harrison, "Wittgenstein and Scepticism", in *Meaning Scepticism*, Puhl (ed.), 34–69, esp. 34; Teghrarian, "Wittgenstein, Kripke and the 'Paradox' of Meaning", 245.
7. L. Wittgenstein, *Notebooks 1914–16* (Oxford: Blackwell, 1961), 44.
8. L. Wittgenstein, *On Certainty* (Oxford: Blackwell, 1969), 65.
9. L. Wittgenstein, *Wittgenstein's Lectures, Cambridge 1932–35*, A. Ambrose (ed.) (Oxford: Blackwell, 1979), 97.
10. Cf.: "One can defend common sense against the attacks of philosophers only by solving their puzzles, i.e., by curing them of the temptation to attack common sense; not by restating the view of common sense" (Wittgenstein 1969: 58–9).
11. H.-J. Glock, *A Wittgenstein Dictionary* (Oxford: Blackwell, 1996), 337.
12. Cf. McGinn, *Wittgenstein on Meaning*, 84.
13. *Ibid.*
14. *Ibid.*
15. Cf. *ibid.*: 68–71; R. McDonough, "Wittgenstein's Refutation of Meaning-Scepticism", in *Meaning Scepticism*, Puhl (ed.), 170–92, esp. 173; A. Collins, "On the Paradox that Kripke Finds in Wittgenstein", *The Wittgenstein Legacy: Midwest Studies in Philosophy* **17** (1992), 74–88, esp. 75; McDowell, "Meaning and Intentionality", 43; Teghrarian, "Wittgenstein, Kripke and the 'Paradox' of Meaning", 237.
16. Cf. McGinn, *Wittgenstein on Meaning*, 78.
17. Cf. E. von Savigny, *Wittgenstein's "Philosophische Untersuchungen": Ein Kommentar für Leser* (Frankfurt: Klostermann, 1988), 239.
18. These titles were the first four hits when searching the internet with Google for "Gepflogenheiten" (21 September 2003).
19. Wittgenstein 1969: 44.
20. von Savigny, *Wittgenstein's "Philosophische Untersuchungen"*, 247.
21. Baker & Hacker, *Wittgenstein: Understanding and Meaning* and *Wittgenstein: Rules, Grammar and Necessity*; Hacker, *Wittgenstein: Meaning and Mind* and *Wittgenstein: Mind and Will*.

22. Diary entry, 6 March 1937, in L. Wittgenstein, *Denkbewegungen: Tagebücher 1930–1932, 1936–1937*, I. Somavilla (ed.) (Frankfurt: Fischer, 1999), 94.
23. Cf. P. Leonardi, Review of Baker and Hacker (1984), *Noûs* **22** (1988), 618–24, esp. 620–21.
24. Cf. e.g. Glock, *A Wittgenstein Dictionary*, 304–15.
25. For a reliable summary, see Glock, *A Wittgenstein Dictionary*, 304–15.
26. G. P. Baker & P. M. S. Hacker, "Malcolm on Language and Rules", *Philosophy* **65** (1990), 167–79, esp. 173–4.
27. von Savigny, *Wittgenstein's "Philosophische Untersuchungen"*.
28. *Ibid.*, 241.
29. Diamond, "Rules: Looking in the Right Place", 21.
30. Wittgenstein, *Remarks on the Foundations of Mathematics*, 392.
31. L. Wittgenstein, *Lectures on the Foundations of Mathematics, Cambridge 1939: From the Notes of R. G. Bosanquet, Norman Malcolm, Rush Rhees*, C. Diamond (ed.) (Chicago, IL: University of Chicago Press, 1989), 58; cf. Diamond, Review of Baker and Hacker (1985), 27–8.
32. Baker & Hacker, *Wittgenstein: Understanding and Meaning*, 44.
33. Glock, *A Wittgenstein Dictionary*, 238.
34. L. Wittgenstein, *Tractatus Logico-Philosophicus*, D. F. Pears & B. McGuinnes (trans.) (London: Routledge & Kegan Paul, 1961), 5.101–5.121; Glock, *A Wittgenstein Dictionary*, 238.
35. C. Diamond, Review of Kripke (1982), *Philosophical Books* **24** (1983), 96–8, esp. 98.
36. Baker & Hacker, *Wittgenstein: Understanding and Meaning*, 111–13.
37. *Ibid.*, 33.
38. *Ibid.*, 37.
39. *Ibid.*, 168.
40. A. Kenny, *Wittgenstein* (Harmondsworth: Penguin, 1973), 6–7, 16, 58; Glock, *A Wittgenstein Dictionary*, 249.
41. Baker & Hacker, *Wittgenstein: Understanding and Meaning*, 183.
42. Cf. Glock, *A Wittgenstein Dictionary*, 301.
43. Cf. Heal, Review of Baker and Hacker, 310.
44. Baker & Hacker, *Wittgenstein: Understanding and Meaning*, 678–9.
45. Glock, *A Wittgenstein Dictionary*, 94.
46. *Ibid.*

Bibliography

Anscombe, G. E. M. "Review of Kripke, *Wittgenstein on Rules and Private Language*". *Ethics* **95** (1985): 342–52.

Apel, K.-O. *Understanding and Explanation: A Transcendental-Pragmatic Perspective* (Cambridge, MA: MIT Press, 1984).

Armstrong, B. F. "Wittgenstein on Private Languages: It Takes Two to Talk". *Philosophical Investigations* **7** (1984): 46–62.

Aydede, M. "The Language of Thought Hypothesis". *Stanford Encyclopedia of Philosophy* (2004), http://plato.stanford.edu/entries/language-thought (accessed May 2006).

Ayer, A. J. *Language, Truth, and Logic* (London: Gollancz, 1936).

Baker, G. P. & P. M. S. Hacker. "Malcolm on Language and Rules". *Philosophy* **65** (1990): 167–79.

Baker, G. P. & P. M. S. Hacker. *Scepticism, Rules and Language* (Oxford: Blackwell, 1984).

Baker, G. P. & P. M. S. Hacker. *Wittgenstein: Rules, Grammar and Necessity* (An Analytical Commentary on the *Philosophical Investigations*, vol. 2) (Oxford: Blackwell, 1985).

Baker, G. P. & P. M. S. Hacker. *Wittgenstein: Understanding and Meaning* (An Analytical Commentary on the *Philosophical Investigations*, vol. 1) (Oxford: Blackwell, 1980).

Berkeley, G. *Principles of Human Knowledge and Three Dialogues* (Oxford: Oxford University Press, 1999).

Bilgrami, A. *Belief and Meaning: The Unity and Locality of Mental Content* (Oxford: Blackwell, 1992).

Bilgrami, A. "Norms and Meaning". In *Reflecting Davidson*, R. Stoecker (ed.), 121–44 (Berlin: de Gruyter, 1993).

Black, M. "Some Remarks about 'Practical Reasoning'". In *The Philosophy of Georg Henrik von Wright* (The Library of Living Philosophers, Vol. XIX), P. A. Schilpp & L. E. Hahn (eds), 405–16 (La Salle, IL: Open Court, 1989).

Blackburn, S. *Essays in Quasi-Realism* (Oxford: Oxford University Press, 1993).

Blackburn, S. "The Individual Strikes Back" [1984]. See Miller & Wright (eds), *Rule-Following and Meaning*, 28–44.

Blackburn, S. "Reply: Rule-Following and Moral Realism". In *Wittgenstein: To Follow a Rule*, S. Holtzman & S. Leich (eds), 163–87 (London: Routledge & Kegan Paul, 1981).

Blackburn, S. *Spreading the Word: Groundings in the Philosophy of Language* (Oxford: Clarendon Press, 1984).

Blackburn, S. "Theory, Observation and Drama". *Mind & Language* **7** (1992): 187–203.

Blackburn, S. "Wittgenstein's Irrealism". In *Wittgenstein: Eine Neubewertung*, L. Brandl & R. Haller (eds), 13–26 (Vienna: Hoelder-Pickler Tempsky, 1990).

Bloor, D. "Institutions and Rule-Scepticism". *Social Studies of Science* **34** (2004): 593–602.

289

Bloor, D. "Left and Right Wittgensteinians". In *Science as Practice and Culture*, A. Pickering (ed.), 266–82 (Chicago, IL: University of Chicago Press, 1992).

Bloor, D. *Wittgenstein: Rules and Institutions* (London: Routledge, 1997).

Bloor, D. *Wittgenstein: A Social Theory of Knowledge* (New York: Columbia University Press, 1983).

Boghossian, P. A. "Naturalizing Content". In *Meaning in Mind: Fodor and his Critics*, B. Loewer & G. Rey (eds), 65–86 (Oxford: Blackwell, 1990).

Boghossian, P. A. Review of McGinn 1984. *Philosophical Review* **98** (1989): 83–92.

Boghossian, P. A. "The Rule-Following Considerations" [1989]. See Miller & Wright (eds), *Rule-Following and Meaning*, 141–87.

Boghossian, P. A. "Sense, Reference and Rule-Following". *Philosophy and Phenomenological Research* **54** (1994): 139–45.

Boghossian, P. A. "The Status of Content". *Philosophical Review* **99** (1990): 157–84.

Brandom, R. *Making It Explicit: Reasoning, Representing, & Discursive Commitment* (Cambridge, MA: Harvard University Press, 1994).

Brandom, R. "Replies". *Philosophy and Phenomenological Research* **57** (1997): 189–204.

Bransen, J. "On Exploring Normative Constraints in New Situations". *Inquiry* **44** (2001): 43–62.

Budd, M. "Wittgenstein on Meaning, Interpretation and Rules". *Synthese* **58** (1984): 303–23.

Burge, T. "Individualism and the Mental". *Midwest Studies in Philosophy* **4** (1979): 73–121.

Byrne, A. "On Misinterpreting Kripke's Wittgenstein". *Philosophy and Phenomenological Research* **56** (1996): 339–43.

Cavell, S. *The Claim of Reason: Wittgenstein, Skepticism, Morality, and Tragedy* (Oxford: Oxford University Press, 1979).

Cavell, S. *Conditions Handsome and Unhandsome: The Constitution of Emersonian Perfectionism* (Chicago, IL: University of Chicago Press, 1990).

Chalmers, D. *The Conscious Mind: In Search of a Fundamental Theory* (Oxford: Oxford University Press, 1996).

Champlin, T. S. "Solitary Rule-Following". *Philosophy* **67** (1992): 285–306.

Chomsky, N. *Knowledge of Language: Its Nature, Origin, and Use* (Westport, CT: Praeger, 1986).

Churchland, P. "Perceptual Plasticity and Theoretical Neutrality: A Reply to Jerry Fodor". *Philosophy of Science* **55** (1988): 167–87.

Coates, P. "Kripke's Sceptical Paradox: Normativeness and Meaning". *Mind* **95** (1986): 77–80.

Coates, P. "Meaning, Mistake and Miscalculation". *Minds and Machines* **7** (1997): 171–97.

Collins, A. "On the Paradox that Kripke Finds in Wittgenstein". *The Wittgenstein Legacy: Midwest Studies in Philosophy* **17** (1992): 74–88.

Craig, E. "Meaning and Privacy". In *A Companion to the Philosophy of Language*, B. Hale & C. Wright (eds), 127–45 (Oxford: Blackwell, 1997).

Craig, E. "Meaning, Use and Privacy". *Mind* **91** (1982): 541–64.

Craig, E. Review of Baker and Hacker (1984). *Philosophical Quarterly* **35** (1985): 212–14.

Dancy, J. *Practical Reality* (Oxford: Oxford University Press, 2000).

Davidson, D. "Communication and Convention" [1982]. See Davidson, *Inquiries into Truth and Interpretation*, 265–80.

Davidson, D. *Inquiries into Truth and Interpretation* (Oxford: Clarendon Press, 1984).

Davidson, D. "James Joyce and Humpty Dumpty" [1989]. See Davidson, *Truth, Language, and History*, 143–58.

Davidson, D. "A Nice Derangement of Epitaphs" [1986]. See Davidson, *Truth, Language, and History*, 89–107.

Davidson, D. "Reply to Akeel Bilgrami". In *Reflecting Davidson*, R. Stoecker (ed.), 145–7 (Berlin: de Gruyter, 1993).

Davidson, D. "Reply to James Higginbotham". See Hahn, *The Philosophy of Donald Davidson*, 687–9.

Davidson, D. "Reply to Richard Rorty". See Hahn, *The Philosophy of Donald Davidson*, 595–600.

Davidson, D. "Reply to Tyler Burge". See Hahn, *The Philosophy of Donald Davidson*, 251–4.

Davidson, D. "The Second Person" [1992]. See Davidson, *Subjective, Intersubjective, Objective*, 107–21.

Davidson, D. "Seeing Through Language" [1997]. See Davidson, *Truth, Language, and History*, 127–42 .

Davidson, D. "The Social Aspect of Language" [1994]. See Davidson, *Truth, Language, and History*, 109–25.

Davidson, D. "The Structure and Content of Truth". *Journal of Philosophy* **87** (1990): 279–328.

Davidson, D. *Subjective, Intersubjective, Objective* (Oxford: Clarendon Press, 2001).

Davidson, D. *Truth, Language, and History* (Oxford: Clarendon Press, 2005).

Davidson, D. "Truth and Meaning" [1967]. See Davidson, *Inquiries into Truth and Interpretation*, 17–36.

Davidson, D. *Truth and Predication* (Cambridge, MA: Harvard University Press, 2005).

Davies, D. "How Sceptical is Kripke's 'Sceptical Solution'?". *Philosophia* **26** (1998): 119–40.

Davies, S. "Kripke, Crusoe and Wittgenstein". *Australasian Journal of Philosophy* **66** (1988): 52–66.

Dennett, D. C. *The Intentional Stance* (Cambridge, MA: MIT Press, 1987).

Devitt, M. "Transcendentalism about Content". *Pacific Philosophical Quarterly* **71** (1990): 247–63.

Devitt, M. & K. Sterelny. *Language and Reality: An Introduction to the Philosophy of Language*, 2nd ed. (Oxford: Blackwell, 1999).

Diamond, C. Review of Baker and Hacker (1985). *Philosophical Books* **26** (1985): 26–9.

Diamond, C. Review of Kripke (1982). *Philosophical Books* **24** (1983): 96–8.

Diamond, C. "Rules: Looking in the Right Place". In *Wittgenstein: Attention to Particulars*, D. Z. Phillips & P. Winch (eds), 12–34 (Basingstoke: Macmillan, 1989).

Divers, J. & A. Miller. "Platitudes and Attitudes: A Minimal Conception of Belief". *Analysis* **55** (1995): 37–44.

Dretske, F. I. *Perception, Knowledge and Belief: Selected Essays* (Cambridge: Cambridge University Press, 2000).

Dummett, M. *The Logical Basis of Metaphysics* (Cambridge, MA: Harvard University Press, 1991).

Dummett, M. "A Nice Derangement of Epitaphs: Some Comments on Davidson and Hacking". In *Truth and Interpretation*, E. Lepore (ed.), 459–76 (Oxford: Blackwell, 1986).

Dummett, M. "Realism". *Synthese* **52** (1982): 55–112.

Dummett, M. "The Social Character of Meaning" [1974]. In *Truth and Other Enigmas*, 420–30 (London: Duckworth, 1978).

Dummett, M. "Wittgenstein's Philosophy of Mathematics". *Philosophical Review* **68** (1959): 324–48.

Earman, J. & J. Roberts. "Ceteris Paribus, There is no Problem of Provisos". *Synthese* **118** (1999): 439–78.

Ebbs, G. *Rule-Following and Realism* (Cambridge, MA: Harvard University Press, 1997).

Edwards, J. "Best Opinion and Intentional States". *Philosophical Quarterly* **42** (1992): 21–33.

Engel, P. *The Norm of Truth: An Introduction to the Philosophy of Logic* (Toronto: University of Toronto Press, 1991).

Engel, P. "Wherein Lies the Normative Dimension in Meaning and Mental Content?". *Philosophical Studies* **100** (2000): 305–21.

Esfeld, M. *Holism in Philosophy of Mind and Philosophy of Physics* (Dordrecht: Kluwer, 2001).

Feldman, F. Critical Notice of Kripke, *Wittgenstein on Rules and Private Language*. *Philosophy and Phenomenological Research* **46** (1986): 683–7.

Finkelstein, D. H. "Wittgenstein on Rules and Platonism". In *The New Wittgenstein*, A. Crary & R. Read (eds), 53–73 (London: Routledge, 2000).

Fodor, J. A. "Observation Reconsidered". *Philosophy of Science* **51** (1984): 23–43.

Fodor, J. A. *Psychosemantics: The Problem of Meaning in the Philosophy of Mind* (Cambridge, MA: MIT Press, 1987).

Fodor, J. A. "A Reply to Churchland's 'Perceptual Plasticity and Theoretical Neutrality'". *Philosophy of Science* **55** (1988): 188–98.

Fodor, J. A. *A Theory of Content and Other Essays* (Cambridge, MA: MIT Press, 1990).

Fodor, J. A. "You Can Fool Some of the People All of the Time, Everything Else Being Equal: Hedged Laws and Psychological Explanation". *Mind* **100** (1991): 19–34.

Føllesdal, D. "Triangulation". See Hahn, *The Philosophy of Donald Davidson*, 719–28.

Forbes, G. "Scepticism and Semantic Knowledge". *Proceedings of the Aristotelian Society* **85** (1984): 223–37.

Gerrans, P. "How to be a Conformist, Part II: Simulation and Rule Following". *Australasian Journal of Philosophy* **76** (1998): 566–86.

Gibson, R. G. "Katz on Indeterminacy and the Proto-Theory". *Philosophy and Phenomenological Research* **54** (1994): 133–9.

Gilbert, M. *On Social Facts* (Princeton, NJ: Princeton University Press, 1989).

Gillett, G. "Humpty Dumpty and the Night of the Triffids: Individualism and Rule-following". *Synthese* **105** (1995): 191–206.

Ginet, C. "The Dispositionalist Solution to Wittgenstein's Problem About Understanding a Rule: Answering Kripke's Objections". *The Wittgenstein Legacy: Midwest Studies in Philosophy* **17** (1992): 53–73.

Glock, H.-J. *A Wittgenstein Dictionary* (Oxford: Blackwell, 1996).

Glüer, K. "Bedeutung zwischen Norm und Naturgesetz". *Deutsche Zeitschrift für Philosophie* **48** (2000): 449–68.

Glüer, K. "Sense and Prescriptivity". *Acta Analytica* **14**(23) (1999): 111–28.

Glüer, K. *Sprache und Regeln: Zur Normativität von Bedeutung* (Berlin: Akademie Verlag, 1999).

Glüer, K. & P. Pagin "Rules of Meaning and Practical Reasoning". *Synthese* **117** (1999): 207–27.

Goldfarb, W. "Kripke on Wittgenstein on Rules" [1985]. See Miller & Wright (eds), *Rule-Following and Meaning*, 92–107.

Hacker, P. M. S. *Wittgenstein: Meaning and Mind* (An Analytical Commentary on the *Philosophical Investigations*, vol. 3) (Oxford: Blackwell, 1990).

Hacker, P. M. S. *Wittgenstein: Mind and Will* (An Analytical Commentary on the *Philosophical Investigations*, vol. 4) (Oxford: Blackwell, 1996).

Hahn, L. E. (ed.) *The Philosophy of Donald Davidson* (Chicago, IL: Open Court, 1999).

Hale, B. *Abstract Objects* (Oxford: Oxford University Press, 1987).

Hale, B. "Rule-following, Objectivity and Meaning". In *A Companion to the Philosophy of Language*, B. Hale & C. Wright (eds), 369–97 (Oxford: Blackwell, 1997).

Harman, G. "Meaning and Semantics" [1974]. In *Reasoning, Mind and Meaning*, 192–205 (Oxford: Oxford University Press, 1999).

Harrison, B. "Wittgenstein and Scepticism". See Puhl, *Meaning Scepticism*, 34–69.

Hattiangadi, A. "Oughts and Thoughts: Scepticism and the Normativity of Content". Dissertation (Department of History and Philosophy of Science, University of Cambridge, 2001).

Haukioja, J. "Rule-Following, Response-Dependence and Realism". Reports from the Department of Philosophy (University of Turku, 2000).

Heal, J. "The Disinterested Search for Truth". *Proceedings of the Aristotelian Society NS* **88** (1988): 97–108.

Heal, J. *Fact and Meaning: Quine and Wittgenstein on Philosophy of Language* (Oxford: Blackwell, 1989).

Heal, J. Review of Baker and Hacker (1984). *Mind* **94** (1985): 307–10.

Hoffman, P. "Kripke on Private Language". *Philosophical Studies* **47** (1985): 23–8.

Hohwy, J. "A Reductio of Kripke-Wittgenstein's Objections to Dispositionalism about Meaning". *Minds and Machines* **13**(2) (2003): 257–68.

Hohwy, J. "Semantic Primitivism and Normativity". *Ratio* **14** (2001): 1–17.

Holton, R. "Intention Detection". *Philosophical Quarterly* **43** (1993): 298–318.

Horwich, P. *Meaning* (Oxford: Clarendon Press, 1998).

Horwich, P. "Meaning and Metaphilosophy". *Philosophy and Phenomenological Research* **54** (1994): 145–50.

Horwich, P. "Meaning, Use and Truth: On Whether a Use-Theory of Meaning Is Precluded by the Requirement that Whatever Constitutes the Meaning of a Predicate Be Capable of Determining the Set of Things of Which the Predicate is True and to Which It Ought to be Applied". *Mind* **104** (1995): 355–68.

Horwich, P. "Wittgenstein and Kripke on the Nature of Meaning". *Mind & Language* **5** (1990): 105–21.

Hume, D. *An Enquiry Concerning Human Understanding* (Oxford: Oxford University Press, 1999).

Hume, D. *A Treatise of Human Nature* (Oxford: Oxford University Press, 1990).

Itkonen, E. *Causality in Linguistic Theory* (London: Croom Helm, 1983).

Jackson, F., G. Oppy, M. Smith. "Minimalism and Truth Aptness". *Mind* **103** (1994): 287–302.

Katz, J. J. *Language and Other Abstract Objects* (Oxford: Blackwell, 1981).

Katz, J. J. *The Metaphysics of Meaning* (Cambridge, MA: MIT Press, 1990).

Katz, J. J. "Replies to Commentators". *Philosophy and Phenomenological Research* **54** (1994): 157–83.

Kemp, G. "Meaning and Truth-Conditions". *Philosophical Quarterly* **48** (1998): 483–93.

Kemp, G. "Reply to Heck on Meaning and Truth-Conditions". *The Philosophical Quarterly* **52** (2002): 233–6.

Kenny, A. *Wittgenstein* (Harmondsworth: Penguin, 1973).

King, J. C. "Structured Propositions". *Stanford Encyclopedia of Philosophy* (2001), http://plato.stanford.edu/entries/propositions-structured/ (accessed May 2006).

Kölbel, M. *Truth Without Objectivity* (London: Routledge, 2002).

Kraut, R. "Robust Deflationism". *Philosophical Review* **102** (1993): 247–63.

Kremer, M. "Wilson on Kripke's Wittgenstein". *Philosophy and Phenomenological Research* **60** (2000): 571–84.

Kripke, S. *Wittgenstein on Rules and Private Language* (Cambridge, MA: Harvard University Press, 1982).

Kusch, M. *Psychological Knowledge: A Social History and Philosophy* (London: Routledge, 1999).

Kusch, M. *Knowledge by Agreement: The Programme of Communitarian Epistemology* (Oxford: Clarendon Press, 2002).

Kusch, M. "Rule-Scepticism and the Sociology of Scientific Knowledge". *Social Studies of Science* **34** (2004): 571–92.

Kusch, M. "Reply to my Critics". *Social Studies of Science* **34** (2004): 615–20.

Lagerspetz, E. *The Opposite Mirrors: An Essay on the Conventionalist Theory of Institutions* (Dordrecht: Kluwer, 1995).

Lance, M. N. & J. O'Leary-Hawthorne. *The Grammar of Meaning: Normativity and Semantic Discourse* (Cambridge: Cambridge University Press, 1997).

Leonardi, P. Review of Baker and Hacker (1984). *Noûs* **22** (1988): 618–24.

Levvis, G. W. "Wittgenstein's Grammatical Propositions as Linguistic Exemplars: A Refutation of Katz's Semantic Platonism". *Philosophical Investigations* **19** (1996): 140–58.

Lewis, A. "Wittgenstein and Rule-Scepticism". *Philosophical Quarterly* **38** (1988): 280–304.

Lewis, D. "Languages and Language" [1975]. In *The Philosophy of Language*, A. P. Martinich (ed.), 538–57 (Oxford: Oxford University Press, 1996).

Lillegard, N. "How Private Must an Objectionably Private Language Be?". *Paideia - Philosophy of Language* (1998), www.bu.edu/wcp/Papers/Lang/LangLill.htm (accessed May 2006).

Lipton, P. "All Else Being Equal (Ceteris Paribus Laws in Nature)". *Philosophy* **74** (1999): 155–68.

Loar, B. "Review of Kripke, *Wittgenstein on Rules and Private Language*". *Noûs* **19**(2) (1985): 273–80.

Loux, M. J. *Metaphysics: A Contemporary Introduction* (London: Routledge, 1998).

Lycan, W. G. *Philosophy of Language: A Contemporary Introduction* (London: Routledge, 2000).

Lynch, M. "Extending Wittgenstein: The Pivotal Move from Epistemology to the Sociology of Science". In *Science as Practice and Culture*, A. Pickering (ed.), 215–65 (Chicago, IL: University of Chicago Press, 1992).

Lynch, M. *Scientific Practice and Ordinary Action: Ethnomethodology and Social Studies of Science* (Cambridge: Cambridge University Press, 1993).

Maddy, P. "How the Causal Theorist Follows a Rule". *Midwest Studies in Philosophy* **9** (1984): 457–77.

Maddy, P. "Mathematical Alchemy". *British Journal for the Philosophy of Science* **37** (1986): 279–314.

Malcolm, N. *Nothing is Hidden* (Oxford: Blackwell, 1986).

Malcolm, N. *Wittgensteinian Themes: Essays 1978–1989*, G. H. von Wright (ed.) (Ithaca, NY: Cornell University Press, 1995).

Martin, C. B. "Final Replies to Place and Armstrong". In D. M. Armstrong, C. B. Martin, U. T. Place, *Dispositions: A Debate*, T. Crane (ed.), 163–92 (London: Routledge, 1996).

Martin, C. B. & J. Heil. "Rules and Powers". *Language, Mind, and Ontology, Philosophical Perspectives* **12** (1998): 283–312.

Marx, K. *Das Kapital: Kritik der politischen Ökonomie, Erster Band* (Berlin: Dietz, 1980).

McDonough, R. "Wittgenstein's Refutation of Meaning-Scepticism". See Puhl, *Meaning Scepticism*, 170–92.

McDowell, J. "Truth Conditions, Bivalence and Verificationism". In *Truth and Meaning*, G. Evans & J. McDowell (eds), 42–66 (Oxford: Clarendon Press, 1976).

McDowell, J. "One Strand in the Private Language Argument". *Grazer Philosophische Studien* **33/34** (1989): 285–303.

McDowell, J. "Intentionality and Interiority in Wittgenstein: Comment on Crispin Wright". See Puhl, *Meaning Scepticism*, 148–69.

McDowell, J. "Meaning and Intentionality in Wittgenstein's Later Philosophy". *The Wittgenstein Legacy: Midwest Studies in Philosophy* **17** (1992): 40–52.

McDowell, J. "Response to Crispin Wright". In *Knowing Our Own Minds*, C. Wright, B. C. Smith, C. Macdonald (eds), 47–62 (Oxford: Oxford University Press, 1998).

McDowell, J. "Wittgenstein on Following a Rule" [1984]. See Miller & Wright (eds), *Rule-Following and Meaning*, 45–80.

McDowell, J. & P. Pettit. "Introduction". See McDowell & Pettit (1986), 1–15.

McDowell, J. & P. Pettit (eds). *Subject, Thought, and Context* (Oxford: Clarendon Press, 1986).

McGinn, C. "Wittgenstein, Kripke and Non-Reductionism about Meaning" [1984]. See Miller & Wright (eds), *Rule-Following and Meaning*, 81–90.

McGinn, C. *Wittgenstein on Meaning: An Interpretation and Evaluation* (Oxford: Blackwell, 1984).

McManus, D. "Boghossian, Miller, and Lewis on Dispositional Theories of Meaning". *Mind & Language* **15** (2000): 393–9.

McManus, D. (ed.). *Wittgenstein and Scepticism* (London: Routledge, 2004).

McMullin, E. "Galilean Idealization". *Studies in History and Philosophy of Science* **16** (1985): 247–73.

Midgley, G. C. J. "Linguistic Rules". *Proceedings of the Aristotelian Society* **59** (1959): 271–90.

Millar, A. "The Normativity of Meaning". In *Logic, Thought and Language*, A. O'Hear (ed.), 57–73 (Cambridge: Cambridge University Press, 2002).

Miller, A. "Boghossian on Reductive Dispositionalism: the Case Strengthened". *Mind & Language* **12** (1997): 1–10.

Miller, A. "Does 'Belief Holism' Show that Reductive Dispositionalism about Content Could not be True?". *Supplement to the Proceedings of the Aristotelian Society* **77** (2003): 73–90.

Miller, A. "Horwich, Meaning and Kripke's Wittgenstein". *Philosophical Quarterly* **50** (2000): 161–74.

Miller, A. *An Introduction to Contemporary Metaethics* (Cambridge: Polity, 2003).

Miller, A. "An Objection to Wright's Treatment of Intention". *Analysis* **49** (1989): 169–73.

Miller, A. *Philosophy of Language* (London: UCL Press, 1998).

Miller, A. & C. Wright (eds). *Rule-Following and Meaning* (Chesham: Acumen, 2002).

Millikan, R. G. "Truth Rules, Hoverflies, and the Kripke-Wittgenstein Paradox". *Philosophical Review* **94** (1990): 323–52.

Mott, P. "Fodor and Ceteris Paribus Laws". *Mind* **101** (1992): 335–46.

Mulhall, S. "No Smoke Without Fire: The Meaning of Grue". *Philosophical Quarterly* **39** (1989): 166–89.

Mumford, S. *Dispositions* (Oxford: Clarendon Press, 1998).

Nagel, T. *The Last Word* (Oxford: Oxford University Press, 1997).

O'Leary-Hawthorne, J. & H. Price. "How to Stand Up for Non-cognitivists". *Australasian Journal of Philosophy* **74** (1996): 275–92.

Pagin, P. Review of Hale, *Abstract Objects. History and Philosophy of Logic* **10** (1989): 111–13.

Papineau, D. "Normativity and Judgement". *Proceedings of the Aristotelian Society*, Suppl. **73** (1999): 17–44.

Peacocke, C. "Content and Norms in a Natural Word". In *Information, Semantics, and Epistemology*, E. Villanueva (ed.), 57–76 (Oxford: Blackwell, 1990).

Peacocke, C. "Reply: Rule-following: The Nature of Wittgenstein's Arguments". In *Wittgenstein: to Follow a Rule*, S. Holtzmann & C. M. Leich (eds), 72–95 (London: Routledge & Kegan Paul, 1981).

Pears, D. F. *The False Prison*, vol. 2 (Oxford: Clarendon Press, 1988).

Pettit, P. "Affirming the Reality of Rule-Following". *Mind* **99** (1990): 433–9.

Pettit, P. *The Common Mind: An Essay on Psychology, Society, and Politics*, 2nd ed. (Oxford: Oxford University Press, 1996).

Pettit, P. "The Reality of Rule-Following" [1990]. See Miller & Wright (eds), *Rule-Following and Meaning*, 188–208.

Platts, M. *Ways of Meaning: An Introduction to a Philosophy of Language* (London: Routledge & Kegan Paul, 1979).

Price, H. "Semantic Minimalism and the Frege Point". In *Foundations of Speech Act Theory: Philosophical and Linguistic Perspectives*, S. L. Tsohatzidis (ed.), 132–55 (London: Routledge, 1994).

Puhl, K. (ed.). *Meaning Scepticism* (Berlin: de Gruyter, 1991).

Pylyshyn, Z. W. *Computation and Cognition: Toward a Foundation for Cognitive Science* (Cambridge, MA: MIT Press, 1984).

Rawls, J. "Two Concepts of Rules". *Philosophical Review* **64** (1955): 3–32.

Read, R. "What 'There Can be no Such Thing as Meaning Anything by any Word' Could Possibly Mean". In *The New Wittgenstein*, A. Crary & R. Read (eds), 74–82 (London: Routledge, 2000).

Robinson, G. "Language and the Society of Others". *Philosophy* **67** (1992): 329–41.

Sartorelli, J. Review of Baker & Hacker, *Scepticism, Rules and Language*, *Philosophical Review* **100** (1991): 660–62.

Schiffer, S. "Ceteris Paribus Laws". *Mind* **100** (1991): 1–17.

Schnädelbach, H. *Zur Rehabilitierung des animal rationale: Vorträge und Abhandlungen 2* (Frankfurt: Suhrkamp, 1992).

Seabright, P. "Explaining Cultural Divergence: A Wittgensteinian Paradox". *Journal of Philosophy* **84** (1987): 11–27.

Searle, J. R. *The Construction of Social Reality* (London: Allen Lane, 1995).

Searle, J. R. "Skepticism about Rules and Intentionalilty". In *Consciousness and Language*, 251–64 (Cambridge: Cambridge University Press, 2002).

Searle, J. R. *Speech Acts: An Essay in the Philosophy of Language*. (Cambridge: Cambridge University Press, 1969).

Shanker, S. "Sceptical Confusions About Rule-Following". *Mind* **93** (1984): 423–9.

Shogenji, T. "Modest Scepticism About Rule-Following". *Australasian Journal of Philosophy* **71** (1993): 486–500.

Shogenji, T. "The Problem of Rule-Following in Compositional Semantics". *Southern Journal of Philosophy* **33** (1995): 97–108.

Soames, S. "Facts, Truth Conditions, and the Skeptical Solution to the Rule-following Paradox". *Philosophical Perspectives* **12** (1998): 313–48.

Soames, S. *Philosophical Analysis in the Twentieth Century, Vol. 2: The Age of Meaning* (Princeton, NJ: Princeton University Press, 2003).

Soames, S. "Scepticism about Meaning: Indeterminacy, Normativity, and the Rule-Following Paradox". *Canadian Journal of Philosophy*, suppl. vol. **23** (1998): 211–49.

Soames, S. *Understanding Truth* (Oxford: Oxford University Press, 1999).

Strawson, P. F. *Freedom and Resentment* (London: Methuen, 1974).

Strub, C. "Zur Normativität konstitutiver Regeln". In *Institutionen und Regelfolgen*, U. Baltzer & G. Schönrich (eds), 207–23 (Paderborn: Mentis, 2002).

Sullivan, P. M. "Problems for a Construction of Meaning and Intention". *Mind* **103** (1994): 147–68.

Summerfield, D. "*Philosophical Investigations* 201: A Wittgensteinian Reply to Kripke". *Journal of the History of Philosophy* **28** (1990): 417–38.

Summerfield, D. "On Taking the Rabbit of Rule-Following out of the Hat of Representation: A Response to Pettit's 'The Reality of Rule-Following'". *Mind* **99** (1990): 425–32.

Tarski, A. *Logic, Semantics, Metamathematics* (Oxford: Blackwell, 1956).

Teghrarian, S. "Wittgenstein, Kripke and the 'Paradox' of Meaning". In *Wittgenstein and Contemporary Philosophy*, S. Teghrarian (ed.), 223–59 (Bristol: Thoemmes Press, 1994).

Tennant, N. *The Taming of the True* (Oxford, Clarendon Press, 1997).

Thornton, T. "Intention, Rule Following and the Strategic Role of Wright's Order of Determination Test". *Philosophical Investigations* **20** (1997): 136–47.

Thornton, T. *Wittgenstein on Language and Thought: The Philosophy of Content* (Edinburgh: Edinburgh University Press, 1998).

Tipton, I. "Berkeley, George". In *Routledge Encyclopedia of Philosophy*, E. Craig (ed.) (London: Routledge, 1998). Retrieved from www.rep.routledge.com (subscribers) (accessed April 2005).

Toribio, J. "Meaning, Dispositions and Normativity". *Minds and Machines* **9** (1999): 399–413.

Travis, C. *The Uses of Sense: Wittgenstein's Philosophy of Language* (Oxford: Oxford University Press, 1989).

van Inwagen, P. "There Is No Such Thing As Addition". *The Wittgenstein Legacy: Midwest Studies in Philosophy* **17** (1992): 138–59.

von Savigny, E. *Wittgenstein's "Philosophische Untersuchungen": Ein Kommentar für Leser* (Frankfurt: Klostermann, 1988).

Wallis, C. "Representation and the Imperfect Ideal". *Philosophy of Science* **61** (1994): 407–28.

Wikforss, A. "Semantic Normativity". *Philosophical Studies* **102** (2001): 203–26.

Williams, Meredith. "Blind Obedience: Rules, Community and the Individual". See Puhl, *Meaning Scepticism*, 93–125.

Williams, Meredith. Review of P. M. S. Hacker, *Connections and Controversies* (Oxford: Oxford University Press, 2001), http://ndpr.nd.edu/review.cfm?id=1077 (2002) (accessed June 2006).

Williams, Michael. "Skepticism". In *The Blackwell Guide to Epistemology*, J. Greco & E. Sosa (eds), 35–69 (Oxford: Blackwell, 1999).

Wilson, G. M. "Kripke on Wittgenstein and Normativity" [1994]. See Miller & Wright (eds), *Rule-Following and Meaning*, 234–59.

Wilson, G. M. "Semantic Realism and Kripke's Wittgenstein". *Philosophy and Phenomenological Research* **58** (1998): 99–122.

Wilson, G. M. 2003. "The Skeptical Solution". In *The Legitimacy of Truth*, R. Dottori (ed.), 171–87 (Münster: Litt, 2003).

Wilson, M. "Predicate Meets Property". *Philosophical Review* **91** (1982): 549–89.

Winch, P. "Facts and Superfacts". *Philosophical Quarterly* **33** (1983): 398–404.

Wittgenstein, L. *The Blue and Brown Books* (Oxford: Blackwell, 1958).

Wittgenstein, L. *Denkbewegungen: Tagebücher 1930–1932, 1936–1937*, I. Somavilla (ed.) (Frankfurt: Fischer, 1999).

Wittgenstein, L. *Lectures on the Foundations of Mathematics, Cambridge 1939: From the Notes of R. G. Bosanquet, Norman Malcolm, Rush Rhees*, C. Diamond (ed.) (Chicago, IL: University of Chicago Press, 1989).

Wittgenstein, L. *Notebooks 1914–16* (Oxford: Blackwell, 1961).

Wittgenstein, L. *On Certainty* (Oxford: Blackwell, 1969).

Wittgenstein, L. *Philosophical Investigations*, 3rd ed., G. E. Anscombe (trans.) (Oxford: Blackwell, 2001).

Wittgenstein, L. *Remarks on the Foundations of Mathematics*, revised edn, G. H. von Wright, R. Rhees, G. E. M. Anscombe (eds), G. E. M. Anscombe (trans.) (Oxford: Blackwell, 1978).

Wittgenstein, L. *Tractatus Logico-Philosophicus*, D. F. Pears & B. McGuinnes (trans.) (London: Routledge & Kegan Paul, 1961).

Wittgenstein, L. *Wittgenstein's Lectures, Cambridge 1932–35*, A. Ambrose (ed.) (Oxford: Blackwell, 1979).

Wright, C. "Critical Notice of Colin McGinn's *Wittgenstein on Meaning*" [1989]. See Miller & Wright (eds), *Rule-Following and Meaning*, 108–28.

Wright, C. "Does *Philosophical Investigations* I.258–60 Suggest a Cogent Argument Against Private Language?". In *Subject, Thought, and Context*, J. McDowell & P. Pettit (eds), 210–66 (Oxford: Clarendon Press, 1986).

Wright, C. "Human Nature?". *European Journal of Philosophy* **4** (1996): 235–53.

Wright, C. "Kripke's Account of the Argument Against Private Language". *Journal of Philosophy* **71** (1984): 759–78.

Wright, C. *Rails to Infinity: Essays on Themes from Wittgenstein's* Philosophical Investigations (Cambridge, MA: Harvard University Press, 2001).

Wright, C. *Realism, Meaning, and Truth* (Oxford: Blackwell, 1987).

Wright, C. "Self-Knowledge: The Wittgensteinian Legacy". In *Knowing Our Own Minds*, C. Wright, B. C. Smith, C. Macdonald (eds), 13–46 (Oxford: Oxford University Press, 1998).

Wright, C. *Truth and Objectivity* (Cambridge, MA: Harvard University Press, 1992).

Wright, C. *Wittgenstein on the Foundations of Mathematics* (London: Duckworth, 1980).

Wright, C. "Wittgenstein's Later Philosophy of Mind: Sensation, Privacy and Intention". See Puhl, *Meaning Scepticism*, 126–47.

Zalabardo, J. "Rules, Communities and Judgements", *Critica: Revista Hispanoamericana de Filosofia* **21** (1989): 33–58.

Zalabardo, J. "Kripke's Normativity Argument" [1997]. See Miller & Wright (eds), *Rule-Following and Meaning*, 274–93.

Zalabardo, J. "Wittgenstein on Accord". *Pacific Philosophical Quarterly* **84** (2003): 311–29.

Zangwill, N. "Direction of Fit and Normative Functionalism". *Philosophical Studies* **91** (1998): 173–203.

Zemach, E. M. "Katz and Wittgenstein". *Philosophy and Phenomenological Research* **54** (1994): 151–5.

Index

Davies, D.   xii, 158, 282
Defoe, D.   183, 188
Dennett, D.   283
Descartes, R.   4, 214
Devitt, M.   279, 281
diagnostic vs. direct anti-scepticism   16, 163, 240
dialogical setting   x, 15, 241
Diamond, C.   237, 257, 284, 287–8
dispositionalism   xi, 17–19, 22, 26, 49, 56–7, 66, 72, 92, 96–127
  communal   24, 69, 70, 98, 123–4, 200
  simple vs. sophisticated 18, 91, 95, 124
Divers, J.   285
Dottori, R.   282
Dretske, F. I.   268, 271
Dummett, M.   xii, 52–3, 85, 147, 187, 272, 277, 280, 283

Earman, J.   275
Edwards, J.   281, 285–6
emotivism   36, 149
Engel, P.   268, 283
enormous numbers   96, 105, 122–5
epistemology of intentions   211–19
Esfeld, M.   266, 284, 286
extensional requirement   xi, 18–22, 58, 94, 125

factualism   ix, 37, 49, 148–76, 223, 226, 233
  deflationary vs. inflationary xii, 148, 163–4, 168, 173–6, 226, 228, 233
Feldman, F.   xii, 146, 279–80
finiteness   39, 41, 174, 235
finitude problem   95–7, 99, 116, 120–24, 142–3, 225
Finkelstein, D. H.   285
Fodor, J. A.   x–xi, 59, 71, 95, 100–105, 125, 233, 267, 269, 271, 274–5, 287
Forbes, G.   274, 276
form of life   39, 46, 189
Føllesdal, D.   85, 272
Frege, G.   136, 138, 143, 147
functional justification   34–5, 41, 174, 235

Gibson, R. G.   280
Gilbert, M.   279
Gillett, G.   284
Ginet, C.   xii, 95, 113–15, 125, 276–7
Glock, H.-J.   260, 262, 287–8
Glüer, K.   xi, 268–9, 271
Goldfarb, W.   xii, 283
Goodman, N.   146
Gödel, K.   143
grasping   5–7, 10–11, 38, 41, 45, 62, 80, 87, 142–

3, 157, 170, 209, 227, 233–5, 243
Greco, J.   265

Hacker, P. M. S.   xii–xiii, 185, 188–9, 194, 201–5, 237–63, 265–6, 283–4, 287–8
Hacking, I.   272
Hahn, L. E.   271–2
Hale, B.   280–81, 286
Harman, G.   272
Harrison, B.   287
Hattiangadi, A.   xi, 266, 269, 276
Haukioja, J.   286
Heal, J.   237, 266, 269, 284, 288
Hegel, G. W. F.   x
Heil, J.   xii, 95, 120–23, 126, 277–8, 287
Higginbotham, J.   272
Hoffman, P.   266
Hohwy, J.   273
Holton, R.   285
Horwich, P.   x–xi, 70, 95, 115–16, 123–4, 126, 266, 268–9, 271, 277–8, 280
Hume, D.   ix, 1, 15, 43–7, 151, 179, 191, 234, 267

idealization   xi, 90, 95–7, 100–105, 112–13, 136, 147, 230, 233, see also ceteris paribus clauses
idiolect vs. sociolect   88, 90, 144
immanent critique   64, 92, 210
immediate knowledge   4, 11, 14, 20, 22, 29, 41, 62–3, 73, 170, 209, 227, 232, 235, 242–3
institutions   221–2, 249–54
intensional requirement   18–20, 58, 59, 94, 125
intentional vs. non-intentional phenomena   265
internal vs. external relations   64, 202–3
internalist argument (for private language)   185, 191
interpretationalism   178, 201–2, 254
intersubjectivity   29–32, 37–8, 41, 49, 63, 173, 177–206
intrasubjectivity   30, 192–3
invention argument (for private language)   185, 192
Inwagen, P. van   274
isolation, physical vs. social   188
Itkonen, E.   271

Jackson, F.   281
Johnstone, M.   120
Joyce, J.   53, 89, 91, 268

Kant, I.   4
Katz, J. J.   xii, 136–47, 279–80
Kraut, R.   281
Kemp, G.   283